Essays

Discipleship, Missions, Spiritual Warfare

Second Edition

Wilbur N. Pickering, Th.M., Ph.D.

Copyright, 2017

Typesetting by:
Dwayne Green

These essays deal with Christian discipleship and transcultural mission, as well as biblical spiritual warfare. There is also a detailed chronology of the life of Christ that takes account of every verse of the four Gospels. www.prunch.org.

First Printing 2016

ISBN Print: 978-0-9974686-0-1

Wilbur N. Pickering

TABLE OF CONTENTS

CONTENTS

APPENDIX

MISSIONARY STRATEGIES OF CHRIST

It has been almost two thousand years since our Savior and Sovereign, Jesus Christ, shortly before His return to Heaven, left certain marching orders for His subjects: "Make disciples in all ethnic nations", "Preach the Gospel to every person", "You will be my witnesses to the ends of the earth". However, even at this stage of the game the followers of Jesus have scarcely managed to get halfway. Probably a third of the ethnic nations in the world have yet to meet their apostle, and I doubt that much more than a third of them will have a true disciple of Jesus among their members. Half of the individual people in the world, apart from ethnic membership, have yet to hear the Gospel for the first time. To **hear**, let alone understand.

What should we think when faced with such a situation?! Did not the Lord Jesus expect to be obeyed? He just liked to talk, enjoyed the sound of His own voice? No. He was serious, obviously. So much so that the first generation, that of the Apostles, practically reached its world. They did wonders—and that without cars, planes, radio, TV, computers, etc. Even so, they reached their world, beginning with a handful of people. They achieved all that precisely because they took Christ's commands seriously, apparently understanding their strategic effect. Alas, as the years went by the Church lost the perspective that the Apostles had received from Jesus, with the tragic consequence that from then till now Christ's commands have generally been ignored or misunderstood. Yes, misunderstood, because there are many today who think they are obeying one or another of the commands but without understanding its true meaning, to say nothing of its strategic content.

Now then, if the Apostles managed to reach their world in one generation, why can we not do the same? Why should we not repeat that achievement? I sincerely believe that all we would have to do is recover Christ's missionary strategies, contained in His commands, and order our lives and ministries on that basis. I believe we could finish reaching the world within our generation. Actually, everything leads me to believe that Jesus is coming soon, our time is getting short. Perhaps we need go no further than Luke 21:24—I take it that Jerusalem stopped being "trodden down by the Gentiles", in the prophetic sense of the word, in 1967 when the city of Jerusalem returned to the control of the nation of Israel for the first time since the Lord spoke those words. And, "when you see these things happening, know that the kingdom of God is near. I tell you assuredly, this generation will by no means pass away till all be fulfilled" (Luke 21:31-32). The interrelationship between the return of Christ and transcultural missions will be discussed presently.

Again I insist: if the mass of evangelical believers, starting right now, will wake up to and start implementing Christ's missionary strategies, we can finish reaching the world in this generation.

You think that is preposterous? Please evaluate what follows with care.

Pray to the Lord for Laborers

Let us begin with the words of the Lord Jesus Christ that we find in Matthew 9:37-38. "The harvest is great but the laborers are few; therefore pray the Lord of the harvest to send out laborers into his harvest."

The Great Harvest

This word, addressed to His disciples, begins with the harvest that lies before us—it is great. If it was great two millennia ago, imagine today! In Matthew 28:19 the Lord Jesus commands us to make disciples in all "nations". That word 'nation' is a translation of the Greek word from which we get such words as 'ethnic' and 'ethnology'. We find the same word in Revelation 5:9, listed with the words 'tribe', 'language' and 'people' (see also Revelation 7:9, 11:9 and 14:6). It refers to a people defined ethnically. Any people that is distinct from all other peoples in the world in terms of language and culture is a 'nation' as far as the Great Commission given in Matthew 28:19 is concerned.

So then, since Jesus commands us to make disciples in **all** of them, how many are there in today's world? It depends. Different sources use differing criteria, with different results. The U. S. Center for World Mission, that has done so much to challenge God's people with the unreached peoples of the world, informs us that there are around 12,000 such peoples. That is the unreached ones—the peoples that have been 'reached' also number some 12,000 (evidently there is a great disparity in the size of these peoples, some very large, some very small; in general the populous peoples are among the reached and the small groups among the unreached). It happens that the Center defines 'people' mainly in cultural terms, so that a number of such peoples may speak the same language.

On the other hand, the Wycliffe Bible Translators preferred to define peoples in terms of language. The twelfth edition of their *Ethnologue* (1992) lists over 6,500 languages spoken in the world today. The declared policy of the editors is to err on the careful side, using information that is considered to be reasonably valid. Since there are areas of the world about which we lack such information and since the advent of better information usually adds languages to the list I personally have no doubt that there are over 6,000 distinct, viable languages in today's world. I conclude that to really fulfill Matthew 28:19 we will have to translate God's Word into all those languages, because of the terms of the Commission. So then, I prefer to define 'nation' in terms of **language** and culture. I gather that there are at least 6,000 such ethnic nations in the world today.

In Mark 16:15 the Lord Jesus commanded us to preach the Gospel to every person. In July, 1986 the newspapers declared that sometime during the month the population of the world would break the five billion mark. Today the total population is well over six billion. Six billion—it is hard to imagine so many people! But there they are. That is our harvest, and is it ever great! Six thousand ethnic nations and six billion individual people.

The Few Laborers

Returning to Matthew 9:37, the Lord Jesus then declares that the laborers are few. Well, faced with such a harvest one might conclude that the workers will always be too few. In fact, it seems to me that many believers have already given up—they are resigned to the idea that the Church will never reach the world.

The fact is that at this point in history the laborers are not just 'few'. For many places and peoples they are nonexistent—there simply are not any! I believe it is true to say that **half** of the ethnic nations in today's world, 3,000 of the 6,000 therefore, do not yet have their apostle of Jesus Christ.

And what about the individual people? It is the same tragic picture. Those who are researching this question tell us that half of the persons in the world, that is 3 billion, have yet to hear the Gospel of Jesus Christ (at least with some understanding). There you have a world-class calamity. Whether we measure by individual or by nation, that is the picture: half the world waiting to hear, half the ethnic nations without an apostle. This in spite of the fact that Christ's Church has been around for almost 2,000 years.

It is true that the picture has been improving. The statistics 200 years ago were a whole lot worse. The missionary effort of the last 200 years has made a tremendous difference. In Africa and in Asia the Church is growing at an impressive rate. Just the Wycliffe Bible Translators have worked with over 1,000 languages (one sixth of the total), and that during the last fifty years. If work were begun with another ethnic group about every ten days, on the average, at that rate it would still take 100 years to reach the last 'nation'. We must improve, because it is unlikely that God will give us that much time.

The Missionary Strategy

The command, or strategy, that we find in Matthew 9:38 is to the point: pray to the Lord of the harvest for laborers. It is absolutely necessary that there be a laborer for each people, for each place, and the remedy that Jesus pre-scribes is to pray for laborers. Note that we are confronted with an order, not a suggestion. Jesus **commands** us to pray for laborers, but are we doing it, do you suppose? Should we not be obeying at least this command, since it is apparently something that any believer could do? How about your church, are you obeying this command—say, every Sunday? If not, why not? Why not start now! And how about in your personal life? Could we not spend one minute each day—say, as you get dressed or comb your hair—crying out to God to raise up and send out workers to the lost world, to the unreached ethnic nations? Please note that nobody may say he is too poor to pray, or too unedu-cated to pray. Any believer can pray, no matter how lowly. Right? So here we have at least one of Christ's commands that is within everyone's reach. However, there seems to be some difficulty since apparently not many people are really obeying this command. Let us consider the strategy more closely.

What might the strategic content of this command be? Well, if I am going to pray to God for laborers I should be sincere, don't you think? I should be consistent—no? So then, if I, being sincere and consistent, cry to God for laborers I my-self must be ready to hear God's answer. Surely, because some fine day God may say to me: "That's good, my child, I hear you, loud and clear; now then, one of those I want to send is **you**!" Any problem? Or else He may say: "I won't send you to another nation but you must contribute more than you have been to support those that I do send." And certainly God will require more intercession from all of us. There you have the strategic effect of this command: if each evangelical believer would obey at least this order in a sin-cere and consistent way, there would be no lack of laborers, no lack of money to support them and no lack of interces-sion, spiritual backing to ensure the work. We would take the world by storm! Only it is not happening, right? That is the problem—to obey this command requires **commitment**. We need consider the point only a little to see clearly that we cannot obey even this command without being truly committed to Christ and His kingdom.

I believe that at every step we will verify that the essential problem is this: there is a lack of commitment to Jesus and His cause. The tragic consequence of this fact is that half the world continues to perish without having heard the Gospel of Jesus Christ. So, let us commit ourselves without reserve to Sovereign Jesus and His cause, really and truly. What a tremendous harvest it is that awaits us—3 billion people who have not heard, 3,000 ethnic nations without an apostle. And Jesus is coming!

Simultaneously Reach Jerusalem . . . and the Ends of the Earth

Now let us consider the words of the Lord Jesus that we find in Acts 1:8. "You will receive power when the Holy Spirit has come upon you, and you will be witnesses to me both in Jerusalem, and in all Judea and Samaria, and to the end of the earth." They are the last words that He spoke here on earth before returning to Heaven, His body about to lift off the ground. Would He not have chosen those words with care? Without doubt, and doubtless He expects us to pay close attention to them. Even on a superficial reading it is clear that Christ is concerned for the whole world. But beyond this obvious meaning His words contain a strategy, a tremendous strategy, a strategy capable of reaching the world in one generation!

The Strategy

As often happens in the Bible, the secret is in the small words, in this case "both . . . and . . . and". Please note that Jesus did <u>not</u> say: "You will be witnesses to me **first** in Jerusalem, **then** in all Judea and Samaria, and **finally, if there is ever any people, time and money left over**, to the ends of the earth." (Is that not the attitude of many Christians, judging by their actions?) No, the statement reads "both . . . and . . . and", which is to say, simultaneously. We must work to reach our "Jerusalem, Judea and Samaria" and the ends of the earth **simultaneously**. If our evangelical churches, across the board, will really commit themselves to this strategy we will finish reaching the world in this generation. If the Apostles did it, why cannot we?

The Apostles, and presumably the generation that they discipled, evidently understood and obeyed this strategy. So much so that in that generation, beginning with a handful of people (and without modern technology), they managed to practically reach their world. The Apostle Paul made plans to visit the Iberian Peninsula. If we can trust the tradition of the Church, the Apostle Thomas actually managed to get to the south of India! But after the apostolic age the Church, in the main, lost that vision, and that is how things stood throughout the centuries until the age of modern missions.

The deplorable consequence of the loss of that vision is that down through the centuries and to this day the majority of people are born, live and die without ever hearing of Jesus Christ. That is the greatest tragedy of all time!

On the other hand, if down through the ages the Church had always followed this strategy then without much delay the Word of God would have been carried to every people in the world and from then on each new generation would have had the option of accepting or rejecting the Gospel. Would that not have been marvelous? Down through the centuries each people would have had ready access to God's Word, to the Gospel of Christ.

An Appeal

We can still do it, even if rather late (better late than never!). Consider. If beginning today the mass of Christ's followers would really take this strategy seriously then the following should occur: the many young people that God is calling will receive spiritual and financial backing from their churches. They should get adequate preparation, including the tools for dealing with other languages and cultures (recall that many of them have never been studied). Once prepared, they will be scattered all over the world, in the areas and with the peoples that do not have effective access to the Gospel. They will spend some two years acquiring a command of the local language and culture such that they can explain about Jesus without too much danger of inventing heresy. From then on there should be conversions and the springing up of new churches, where there had not been any. Now then, those churches should also embrace this missionary strategy of Christ and thus they will not only begin to evangelize their own 'Jerusalem' but also their 'Judea and Samaria'. In this way, within one generation, there would not remain a single place or people without ready access to the Gospel of Christ. For example, there are indigenous peoples in Brazil that received God's Word in their languages (for the first time) only a few years ago, yet the believers are not only concerned to reach the rest of their ethnic nation, their 'Judea', they also want to send missionaries to other peoples. (I am well aware that there are serious religious and political barriers out there to get in our way; I will take them up in another essay, but our Master holds the Key of David—Revelation 3:7.)

Let us cooperate with the Holy Spirit! Let us take Christ's commands seriously. Let us get behind those that God is calling to transcultural work. Let us motivate them to get adequate preparation and then move out to the fields of the world. Let us help them find an appropriate infrastructure with which to work so as to be more efficient. It may be necessary to help in the support of such infrastructures (missions). In short, let us do whatever may be necessary to reach the ends of the earth in our generation!

But, just a minute. The hard facts of life oblige us to speak a word of caution. Emotional appeals are not the answer. No one should think of taking on a transcultural challenge without preparing adequately. That preparation should include the technical tools for dealing with new languages and cultures. Even more important, absolutely necessary, the person needs to be a true disciple of Jesus Christ (total commitment) and must know how to conduct spiritual warfare. These two subjects occupy the following essays: "Make Disciples, not just Converts" and "Liberate People from the Power of Satan".

The Second Coming of Christ

I have lectured on the subject of transcultural missions many times. I have found that the most frequent question that is asked, in connection with Christ's return, has to do with Matthew 24:14. It is as good a place to start as any. "This Gospel of the Kingdom will be preached in all the world as a witness to all the nations, and then the end will come."

The question most frequently posed is whether Christ can return before we reach the last ethnic nation. The temporal adverb "then" indicates that something has to happen first, in this case the preaching of the Gospel to each ethnic nation. That part of it seems clear enough. The interpretation of the verse depends on the meaning or reference of "the end". The end of what? I suppose all will agree that this day has an end, this week has an end, this month has an end, this year, this decade, etc., but they are distinct 'ends' that occur on different dates (usually). Similarly, in eschatology there are several 'ends'. This world has an end; the millennium has an end; the great tribulation has an end; this age of grace has an end—in my understanding of God's Word these ends are different and distinct, and will not coincide. So to which of these ends was Jesus referring in Matthew 24:14?

If He was referring to the end of the world or the end of the millennium then the passage has no bearing on Christ's return, for He will have already come. And it will not be our problem because during the millennium God Himself will see to it that all hear. "No more shall every man teach his neighbor, and every man his brother, saying 'Know the LORD,' for they all shall know me, from the least of them to the greatest of them, says the LORD" (Jeremiah 31:34). "They shall not hurt nor destroy in all my holy mountain, for the earth shall be full of the knowledge of the LORD as the waters cover the sea" (Isaiah 11:9). If there is any part of the ocean without water then someone might get by without knowing the Lord. See also Revelation 21:24.

But if Jesus was referring to the end of the great tribulation, what then? Does Christ's return depend upon our missionary activity? I think not. Consider Revelation 14:6. "Then I saw another angel flying in the midst of heaven, having the everlasting Gospel to preach to those who dwell on the earth—to every ethnic nation, tribe, tongue and people." Since this angelic activity takes place during the great tribulation, before its end each ethnic group will have been "evangelized", the speakers of each language will know the truth about God and His Kingdom. So Christ will be free to come and set up His Messianic (millennial) Kingdom.

Only if Jesus was referring to the end of this age of grace, the Church age, **and** if the pre-tribulation, or pre-wrath, rapture position is the correct one, do we have a problem— only in that event does Christ's return depend upon our missionary efforts. If the rapture of the Church precedes the great tribulation **and** if the last ethnic nation must hear the Gospel before the rapture can occur, then we are in a bad way! Since perhaps some 2,000 ethnic nations have yet to hear the Gospel, the time has come for all true believers to roll up their sleeves and do what can be done to reach those nations! Many of the transcultural missionaries at work around the world have precisely that understanding, and that is why they are missionaries—they are committing their lives to the effort of seeing the last ethnic nation reached so that Jesus can come again! I wish that everyone would feel that way and invest their lives to see Christ's great commission fulfilled. Would that it were so!

There is one interpretation of Acts 1:8 that should be mentioned here. This word of our Lord is usually taken to be a declaration with the practical effect of an order. However, there are those who say that Jesus' statement is a prophecy. The phrase "to the end of the earth" is indeed singular and can be understood to refer to the last place, or perhaps even the last ethnic group, on the earth. They argue that Jesus was addressing His disciples, so if His words were prophetic then it is His disciples who must reach the "last place". If their position is correct then it would appear that it is the **Church** that must finish reaching the world—we cannot 'pass the buck' to the angel of Revelation 14:6.

However, I myself do not understand the Sacred Text in the aforementioned ways. My theological training was strongly pre-tribulationist, but I have migrated to meso-tribulation position—I take it that the interpretation that does the best job of accommodating **all** the relevant passages (to build a position on just one or two of them is illicit) is the one that sees the rapture of the Church preceding the outpouring of God's wrath.[1] **However**, the Text does present us with

---

[1] **Before or after? 2 Thessalonians 2:2 X 2:7-8**—In Matthew 24:44 we read, "Therefore you also be ready, because the Son of the Man is coming at an hour that you do not suppose." I take it that for there to be the element of surprise the Rapture of the Church must occur before the "abomination of desolation". When the Antichrist takes his place in the Holy of Holies and declares himself to be god there will be precisely 1,290 days until the return of Christ to the earth. "An hour that you do not suppose" presumably requires a pre-'abomination' rapture—if the rapture is pre-wrath but post-abomination, only a fool will be taken by surprise, unless the Rapture happens immediately after the 'abomination' (2 Thessalonians 2:3-4).

Let us begin with 2 Thessalonians 2:2. Some 15% of the Greek manuscripts have 'day of the Lord' (as in NIV, NASB, LB, TEV, etc.); the 85% that have 'day of Christ' (including the best line of transmission) are doubtless correct. I remember one day in a Greek exegesis class, the professor stated that one reason he preferred the 'critical' text (that reads 'Lord' here) is that it fit better with his view of eschatology—the 'Day of Christ' is usually associated with the Rapture and blessing of the saints, while the 'Day of the Lord' is usually associated with heavy judgment upon the world and unrepentant Israel, including the outpouring of wrath just before and after the Second Coming of Christ, when He returns in glory to establish His Millennial Reign. The perceived difficulty here would appear to be that while verses 1, 6 and 7 evidently relate to the Rapture, verses 3-4 and 8-10 evidently relate to the Great Tribulation and the Second Coming. What to do? Look carefully at the Text. In verse 2, why would the Thessalonian believers be "disturbed"? Someone was teaching that the Rapture had already happened and they had been left behind—I would be disturbed too! So 'day of Christ' is precisely correct with reference to the content of verses 1 and 2. The trouble comes in verse 3 because a clause is elided; as an aid to the reader translations usually supply a clause, preferably in italics, to show that it is an addition, as in NKJV—"*that Day will not come*". But that would put the Rapture <u>after</u> the revelation of the man of sin and the 'abomination of desolation'— definitely not congenial to certain eschatological systems. An easy 'solution' would be to change 'Christ' to 'Lord' in verse 2, but that would put the Rapture within the 'day of the Lord'—also not congenial. I submit that

some ambiguity; yes it does, which is why no one should attempt to declare the issue closed, much less to excommunicate anyone who disagrees.

Returning to Matthew 24:14, I understand that "the end" Jesus refers to is that of the great tribulation because immediately, in the next verse, He speaks of the "abomination of desolation", which will happen during that period. In that event, that angel in Revelation 14:6 will get us out of our predicament. Whatever is left undone by the Church that dear angel will complete. Ah blessed angel! But wait just a minute! Let no one cross his arms and say: "Well, since that angel is going to solve our problem we can stop worrying about it and do our own thing; those unreached peoples have already waited for all this time and they won't know the difference if they have to wait some more; it's their problem." Whoever thinks and acts in such a fashion will be severely punished at the judgment seat of Christ! We need to develop more respect for the final accounting—it is not going to be a soft touch!

Let us just suppose we are watching when a negligent believer has his turn; he is standing before the Judgment Seat. So Jesus asks him in what ways he exerted himself with a view to seeing His commands carried out. Then the self-centered believer begins to stammer: "Well, er, um, you know Lord; that angel, somewhere in Revelation

---

fine-tuning our view of eschatology is preferable to tampering with the Text.

If the 'Restrainer' in verses 6-8 is the Holy Spirit, then the Rapture happens before the 'abomination', and may be viewed as its 'trigger'. I translate verse 7 as follows: "For the mystery of the lawlessness is already at work; only He who now restrains *will do so* until He removes Himself." Perhaps more literally, 'gets Himself out of the middle' (the verb γινομαι is inherently middle in voice). I would say that the Holy Spirit is the only one who satisfies the description. But if the 'Day of Christ' includes the Rapture, then verse 3 would appear to place the Rapture after the 'abomination'. So where does that leave us? Although my own training was strongly 'pre-trib', I have moved to a 'meso-trib' position. If the Rapture follows immediately upon the 'abomination', then the 'surprise' factor remains untouched. If the 'abomination' and the Rapture happen within minutes of each other, then from God's point of view they form a single 'package', and the actual sequence is not important—for all practical purposes they happen at the same time.

doesn't it say something about an angel . . . ?" Does anyone actually imagine that Jesus will accept such a monstrously stupid argument? Be not deceived! Jesus will demand to know what we did about His **orders!**

Really, people, I very much doubt that He will insist that we be precisely correct about every detail in the end time chronology. Whatever for? If I am effectively living as a disciple, as His slave, if I am doing my best to please Him, if I am expending all my energies on behalf of His Kingdom, what difference does it make if I am mistaken about the time of the rapture? **But**, if my view of things leads me to be careless, to be negligent, then it is different. Unfortunately, many who defend the pre-tribulationist view, rather than spending themselves to 'bring back the King', are sitting around waiting for the rapture. If the news media report ever greater tragedies, they are pleased, because it means the rapture must be getting close—such an attitude is an aberration that does not derive from the doctrine itself. Strange to relate, many who criticize such pre-tribulationists are themselves doing little or nothing to fulfill the Great Commission. What is our problem?

Dear people, let us cut our losses. Let us give it all we have. If Christ returns before we reach the last ethnic nation, amen! If He comes upon our reaching that last one, hallelujah! If we finish the job and He still does not come, at least we can hope to hear His "Well done, good and faithful servant!" (Matthew 25:21). I trust no one wants to hear Him say, "You wicked and lazy servant!" (Matthew 25:26). Anything but that!

I wish to finish by insisting again upon the absolute necessity of our taking Christ's commands seriously. We may be completely certain; among all the things that will be required of us when we stand before Christ's Tribunal, none will be more weighty than **His commands**. So whatever your eschatological position may be, let us get on with obeying those **commands**. Shall we go for it? May God help us!

Conclusion

I have discussed seven missionary strategies of Christ. There may be others, of course, but these are the ones God moved me to present. The seven are:

1) Pray to the Lord of the harvest for laborers—being consistent.
2) Simultaneously reach our Jerusalem, our Judea and Samaria, and the ends of the earth.
3) Preach the Gospel to every person—for no one is innocent.
4) Make **disciples**, not just converts.
5) Live for the Kingdom of God, not yourself.
6) Liberate people from the power of Satan.
7) Follow Jesus' example.[1]

I recognize that my focus is transcultural, but then the commands of Christ and the heart of God encompass the world. If everything was progressing nicely, if we were hitting the bull's-eye of God's plan, there would be no need for this book; we could just keep on keeping on. But since our greatest omission involves the ends of the earth, the lost ethnic nations of the world, since it is this aspect of Christ's commands that has generally been most ignored, this is the side I have emphasized. However, do these strategies not have direct implications and applications for our churches, for our daily lives, for local evangelism and ministry? I think it obvious that they do. Again I say, these truths have the potential and the ability to transform our lives, our homes, our churches, our society, maybe even our world!

Frankly, if across the board we got serious about just one, any one, it would take only one, of these strategies nothing could stop the Church. But if we get serious about two, three or all (why not all?) of them, then we can certainly finish reaching the world within this generation.

It will be worth it to set aside our egotism, our meanness, our provincialism, our ethnocentricity, our merely personal

---

[1] Strategies 3-7 are treated in separate essays in this book.

ambitions, our denominationalism, in short our smallness of spirit—all things that Satan exploits to neutralize our potential—it will be worth it to set such things aside and join forces to reach our common objective. Let us learn from each other. The time is short; we can no longer afford the 'luxury' of learning everything on our own, forever repeating the same mistakes. A certain analysis of missionary history in Central America, which I consider to be highly significant, distinguished three phases in the relationship between the foreign missionaries and the national leadership that emerged as a result of the missionary activity. The first phase is characterized by paternalism: the missionaries tend to belittle the opinion of the local believers, imposing their own ideas and the religious culture of their home country. The second phase is characterized by a nationalistic reaction: the local leadership repays in kind, rejecting the ideas (and sometimes the participation) of the missionaries. In the third phase a level of spiritual and emotional maturity is reached such that all concerned can work together in an atmosphere of mutual respect, each one contributing what he can do best. It is natural for a victim of paternalism to want to get even, and in fact some intransigent paternalists may require rough treatment, but we really must do all we can to get to phase three as soon as possible. The challenge we face demands a united effort, it demands the best that each one can give.

I propose the following. We must humble ourselves before God and His Word, doing our best to distinguish between the true values of the Kingdom and the values of our own religious and national culture. Dear friends, we must reach the point of giving priority to the values of God's Kingdom— whenever there is a clash between some value of the Kingdom and some value of our culture (be it national or religious), **the value of the Kingdom must prevail**. Please, people, to elevate our values above God's values is a form of idolatry! May God help us to quit it! Consider: if we proceed in that fashion we will have a common ground where no human culture is considered to be better than any other and thus it should be possible to work together in harmony. What do you think, will it not be worth it?

There are other things that divide us; polarizations exist that just might go beyond what the Sacred Text teaches. When we impose our ideas on the Text and take radical positions on the basis of those ideas, we give lots of room to Satan to work in our midst and we become unwilling to respect each other or to work together. That said, however, we should insist upon the objective authority of the Biblical Text. We need to close ranks around the fundamental truths that define our Faith.

To conclude, I invite the reader's attention to an interesting detail. It is this: in each version of the Great Commission that we find in the Gospels and Acts there is a declaration of **power**. "All power (authority) has been given to me in heaven and on earth" (Matthew 28:18). "These signs will follow those who believe:" (Mark 16:17). ". . . until you are endued with power from on high" (Luke 24:49). "Receive the Holy Spirit!" (John 20:22). "You shall receive power" (Acts 1:8). The mainspring is the power that the Holy Spirit gives us. Without His power we will not make it. So then, my fellow-servants, let us consciously submit ourselves to the Holy Spirit so as to walk full of His power, because in this way we will be able to fulfill the commands of our Master—even to the point of finishing to reach the world in this generation.

PREACH TO EVERY PERSON

Moving on, let us consider the words of the Lord Jesus that we find in Mark 16:15. "Go into all the world and preach the gospel to each person." (Or, "As you go throughout the world preach . . . .") Once again the words are directed to His disciples. The strategic effect is transparent—if we really do preach to each person then each one will have had his opportunity to know Jesus as Savior and Lord of life. The problem does not lie in understanding this command, it lies in **believing** it.

A Growing Neo-universalism

God has allowed me to minister in many churches around Brazil, churches from more than twenty denominations. I have verified something alarming. Many believers, and even pastors and leaders, simply do not think that it is necessary to preach the Gospel to every person in the world. There is a growing 'neo-universalism' in that country. A certain pastor expressed the idea very well, some years ago now: "A God who is loving, just and good could never condemn an innocent Indian." (In those days the Brazilian government had placed severe limitations upon the activity of foreign missionaries with reference to indigenous peoples and I was traveling around the country challenging the Brazilian believers to get involved in that type of ministry.) That pastor could not have cared less; there was no need to worry about the salvation of the 'Indian'—God would work something out.

We are face to face with a hypothesis that carries with it very serious consequences. You do not need to be a prophet to see that such a hypothesis simply destroys any sense of urgency, any real concern about the spiritual destiny of the persons and peoples that have never heard of Jesus. Surely—if God is going to work something out then He is going to take care of the problem and we can forget about it. Obviously any solution that God provides must be adequate. If the 'Indian' is innocent and therefore may not be condemned then God will have to save him (because the human spirit is immortal and only has two possible destinies: to be with God, which is life eternal, or to be separated from Him, which is eternal condemnation). If there exists an 'innocence' which results in salvation we must revise our soteriology, for in that event there would be more than one way to achieve eternal life.

But really, our **Lord**, Christ Jesus, commanded us to make disciples in **all** ethnic nations. Are we going to obey or not? He commanded us to preach the Gospel to **each** person, going throughout the whole world. Are we going to obey or not? If someone decides that there is no need to obey, and even rejects the very terms of the commands, he should be consistent and stop presenting himself as a servant of Christ! Any doubts? Well, I know we are not going to dispose of the problem in this way; people are not always consistent. So, let us take a closer look at the neo-universalist hypothesis.

No One Is 'Innocent'

It seems to me that the debate hinges on the question of innocence. It is because the 'Indian' (for example) is 'innocent' that God should not condemn him. But how shall we define that 'innocence'? I will use an indigenous people as an example because I have personal experience with them. I lived in a village of the Apurinã people, in the middle of the Amazon jungle, for a total of 24 months. I believe my observations will be valid for any unreached ethnic group around the world. So what is 'innocence'?

There are many who doubt the mental, and even moral, capacity of so-called 'primitive' peoples. I have heard the opinion expressed that 'the language of the Indian' is a very rudimentary something with about 300 vocabulary items. They are completely mistaken. People who belong to 'primitive' societies are just as intelligent as anyone else. There is no lack of evidence to that end—for instance, language. An English verb may have up to five different inflections, variations in the internal structure of the word. Certain irregular

Portuguese verbs may have up to 66 such inflections. An Apurinã verb, with its three relative orders of prefixes and fourteen relative orders of suffixes (I have isolated some 60 affixes that occur in those orders, but there are others), if every mathematically possible combination did actually occur (there are a few co-occurrence restrictions), may have upwards of twenty million different inflections. Yes, that is what I said, twenty million; and those are the possible variations within **one word**!

I wish you could have been in our little palm leaf house in the village and listen to the men discussing the pros and cons of the Gospel, evaluating the implications in terms of their own belief system—it was a convincing demonstration of their ability to reason. Be not deceived, the members of 'primitive' societies are just as much human beings as we are, created in the image and likeness of God. In short, we may not define 'innocence' in terms of lack of intelligence, reasoning ability or moral capacity. Or at least, if we did, none of the indigenous peoples of the world would fit the definition.

Most of the indigenous groups of South America, and the world (so far as I know), practice some form of animism or spiritism. Their religion revolves around the effort to pacify the demons, the evil spirits that they hold responsible for the assorted ills that overtake them. (I understand that the numerous ethnic groups in Africa and Asia that have converted to Islam are still dealing with the demons—of necessity.) They know that good spirit beings also exist, but they deliberately worship the bad. What they do is not brainless superstition. Their attitude is both reasonable and intelligent, given the reality that they have to live with. They most certainly are bothered by the spirits, which do indeed exist and attack human beings. Since they do not know of any benevolent power that is greater than the demons to which they can appeal for help or, in the case of those who do believe in a Creator who is good but lost contact with Him in the distant past and despair of getting His ear, they take the only viable option that seems to be left. They try for a dialog with the spirits to see if things will improve, at least a little.

Now then, someone who is consciously, deliberately worshipping evil spirits, and by extension Satan (they know the demons have a boss), leaving the good spirits and the Creator Himself to one side, is not 'innocent'. No way.

Then there is the conscience that the Creator places in each human being (Romans 2:14-16). Don Richardson, in his book *Eternity in their Hearts*, makes an important contribution on this subject. He argues that not only individuals but whole cultures have features, like memories of the distant past, that prepare the people for the coming of the Gospel and sort of predispose them to receive it. He gives a good number of interesting examples.

And there is the light furnished by the creation, which should move every rational being to bow before the Creator (Romans 1:18-20), because the whole cognitive process of the human being is based on the principle of cause and effect. We observe an effect and try to isolate the cause that produced it; logic requires that the cause must be equal to or greater than the effect that it produced, or else it could not have produced it. I must confess that I do not understand the scientists who profess to be materialists; all scientific experimentation is also based on this principle—it seems to me that they are inconsistent.

I conclude that there is only one definition of 'innocence' that could possibly stand the light of day: ignorance, the lack of information. That is to say, a just God could not condemn a person who never heard of Jesus Christ. But there is a slight problem—God does not accept it. Romans 1:18-20 makes clear that every rational being has the light of the creation, and God will demand an accounting of that light: "so that they are without excuse" (see also Psalm 19:1-4). Romans 3:10-12 is more than clear: before God no one is 'innocent'!! According to Isaiah 64:6 even our "righteousnesses" look like "filthy rags" to God.

God Is Just

However, God is just. He recognizes the difference between a little light and lots of light. "There is no partiality with God: whoever has sinned without law will also perish without law, and whoever has sinned under the law will be judged by the law" (Romans 2:11-12). Although everyone has the light of the creation it cannot compare with the light of God's written revelation. Luke 12:47-48 refers to the judgment seat of Christ, not to the judgment of the lost, but it also shows clearly that God recognizes degrees of responsibility. However, please note that those without the law will "perish" and the servants who did not know "will be beaten", albeit less.

Now let us go to the final judgment of the unbelievers, the great white throne that is described in Revelation 20:11-15.

> "I saw a great white throne and the one who was sitting on it, from whose face the earth and the sky fled away; and no place was found for them. And I saw the dead, the great and the small, standing before the throne; and books were opened (another book also was opened, the Book of Life). And the dead were judged by what was written in the books, according to their deeds. The sea gave up the dead who were in it, and Death and Hades gave up the dead who were in them, and each one was judged according to his deeds. Then Death and Hades were thrown into the lake of fire. This is the second death—the lake of fire; and whoever was not found written in the Book of Life was thrown into the lake of fire."

I would like to note in passing that I do not expect to appear before the white throne, but if I were to do so and be judged on the basis of my deeds I would certainly wind up in the Lake. That is because no one can be saved by his deeds (see Isaiah 64:6, Jeremiah 17:9, Romans 3:20 and 23, among other passages—I am referring to salvation, not rewards). I will not wind up in the Lake because by the grace of God my name is written in the Book of Life. Thank you, Lord Jesus! But I would like to imagine that we will be able to watch that judgment. Let us suppose that someone from an unreached people has his turn as we look on.

As he gets the drift he protests: "But God, how could you!? No one ever came to our village, or to our people to tell about Jesus. All of us were born, lived and died without ever hearing the Gospel of Christ, even once. How can you judge me?" Obviously what follows is mere speculation, but I imagine that God's response might go something like this: "Yes, I know. You never heard and it is a disgrace. Down through the centuries I kept telling my professed servants to go, but no one ever did and you never heard. I am more sorry than I can say! But I want you to know that I will not judge you on the basis of a Gospel that you never heard. I will indeed judge you, but **on the basis of your deeds**." Twice our text repeats the phrase, "according to his deeds".

Now then, how can we arrive at a fair evaluation of someone's deeds? We must take account of the context in which he lived. We should know what he was thinking, what pressures he was feeling. Every people has law, moral code, norms of conduct. Their moral code will presumably be inferior to the Biblical standard, but they have one. They understand that some things are good while others are bad. So, God will judge the person within the context of his own culture, of the law and moral code that he knew, recognized and embraced. And He will prove that even within his own context the person did not measure up (and do not forget that the light of creation and conscience will also be required). Before the great white throne no defendant will be able to say that God is unjust.

No, my friends, let no one be deceived! The 'Indian' who never heard the Gospel is condemned. Before God no one is 'innocent'.

The Neo-universalist Hypothesis

However, the influence of that 'neo-universalist' idea upon many people is so strong that prudence calls for a little further analysis. I will start with the only definition of 'innocence' that is possibly valid, ignorance. That is, a just God could not condemn someone who never heard. Well then, on that basis the neo-universalist 'Christian' has a Jesus that is a monster and a god that is a fool. (I am well aware that such language may shock the reader's sensibilities, but I use it on purpose as a pale reflection of how God Himself must feel about that hypothesis.)

Of course. If God cannot condemn someone who never heard (according to the hypothesis) then such a person will have to be saved (recall that there are only two possible destinies for the human spirit). But in that case the Gospel of Christ becomes a message of condemnation rather than salvation, a message of death rather than life. That is because as long as someone has not heard, he is saved (according to the hypothesis), but as soon as he hears, if he does not receive it, he is condemned. Then to be a preacher of the Gospel becomes a terrible thing, because you will be destroying people's 'innocence'! And Jesus would have to be some type of ogre, because He **commands** us to preach to every person, thereby condemning multitudes that would otherwise be saved (according to the hypothesis). Can you imagine it?

And God would have to be a 'fool', because to send the Son to take on human form and suffer all that He did would be simply unnecessary (according to the hypothesis). God should have stayed up in Heaven, not said or done anything, because then everyone down here would remain in perfect ignorance, of necessity, and therefore would have to be saved. Obviously neither is God a 'fool' nor is Jesus a 'monster'. The neo-universalist hypothesis is false.

(Isn't it strange how people consider themselves to be more wise and just than the Creator? The Bible says that God created man in His own image and likeness, but from then till now it seems that man has done his best to return the favor. For example, the neo-universalist: not liking the Bible's God, he dreams up a god more to his taste, a god without unpleasant surprises, a god of his sort and size. It should be obvious that any god that we create will of necessity be less than we are, and therefore completely worthless.)

Conclusion

To conclude, we must take Mark 16:15 seriously. The Gospel of Christ is the only solution for all people. Since God accepts no one as 'innocent' it is altogether necessary to preach to each one. But someone is sure to raise the question: what happens if someone responds adequately to the light of the creation? Theoretically it is possible, but in practice it is extremely difficult because of the pressure that his culture exerts upon a person. As it says in 1 John 5:19, the whole world "is under the control of the evil one"—the cultures of the world are under heavy satanic influence. As already explained, in general it is precisely the cultures of the unreached ethnic groups that revolve around the demons. In other words, a person born within such a culture is 'programmed' with that world view from his earliest days, and so it becomes almost impossible for him to reflect freely upon the creation and reach an appropriate conclusion, submitting to the Creator.

Once again we face a question about God's justice. How could He create a race that He knew very well would fall under Satan's domination with the result that people would be programmed by their cultures in a way that would leave them virtually incapable of reacting correctly to the creation, the price for this being to spend eternity in the Lake of Fire? How could He?! I do not know. God does not explain. When God does not explain something like this, we have two options: accept or reject, rebel against Him or bow before Him. Certain matters pertain to the Sovereignty of God, and whoever among us is wise will leave them there! Is that not what Deuteronomy 29:29 declares? "The secret things belong to the LORD our God." We have neither the right to understand everything nor the responsibility to explain everything. That seems to me to be the central message of the book of Job: all said and done God did not explain, He did not resolve Job's perplexity. What He said in essence was: "I am big and you are small; I am the Creator and you are not competent to argue with me" (chapters 38 to 41). And that was the end of the discussion. Job came out well because he humbled himself and shut his mouth (Job 40:3-5, 42:1-6).

Whenever we intrude our humanistic ideas into a question like this, it is to demonstrate yet again the idolatrous bent of our hearts. Consider the case of a baby that dies: does it go to heaven or to hell? The Bible does not say; it remains silent about this question. The point of Matthew 19:14, Mark 10:14-15 and Luke 18:16-17 is not that all and only children will be saved, but that we must receive the kingdom in the way that a child would or does. A child is unaffected, a child is a literalist, a child trusts implicitly (until hard experience teaches him otherwise). But we cannot stand the idea that a baby should be condemned, so we declare that it will go to heaven. Really? Have you ever stopped to think through the implications?

If a baby is born 'saved' but later on does not submit to Christ, does he 'lose his salvation'? The fact is that most people never trust in the Lord Jesus for the forgiveness of sins, and so will go to hell. Would it not be better to kill a baby while he was still 'saved' rather than let him grow up and become condemned? To allow someone to go to hell when we could certainly prevent it (by killing him while still a baby) would seem to be terribly perverse! What kind of sadist would do something like that?! What do you think? Should we kill all babies? Obviously that suggestion is absurd! It is equally clear that God Himself would not tolerate such a 'solution', because He forbids murder. It is more likely that killing a baby will not guarantee his salvation because it is doubtful that anyone is born 'saved'. In fact, Romans 5:12 and Psalms 51:5 may be understood to mean that we are born sinners. If death is "the wage for sin" (Romans 6:23), what is a baby that dies being paid for? Be that as it may, my whole purpose here has been to demonstrate that our humanism does not solve the problem. All said and done we must turn the question over to the **sovereignty of God**.

However, I am fully convinced that we can trust our God— He knows what He is doing and one day, when we are glorified, we will understand. Just look at what is placed right in the middle of the ten commandments, that which was engraved on the tablets of stone: "visiting the iniquity of the fathers upon the children to the third and fourth generation of those who hate me, and showing mercy to the thousandth generation of those who love me and keep my commandments" (Exodus 20:5-6, compare Deuteronomy. 7:9)! Have you ever thought about that? It means that God's mercy is at least 250 times greater than His punishing! There have scarcely been 300 generations since Adam—God's mercy is virtually inexhaustible. We can trust the justice of our God, my friend.

Two or three cases in the history of modern missions have come to my attention where God worked a miracle to ensure that someone who was responding appropriately to the light of creation should hear the Gospel of Christ. The case of Cornelius (Acts 10) could almost be a Biblical example, but he was surrounded by Jews and presumably had added light. (Personally, I suppose it is precisely in this way that God takes care of the occasional instance where someone reacts correctly to the creation. He moves heaven and earth, if necessary, to furnish the added light of the Gospel.) Even so, we should never base our missionary strategy on occasional exceptions. Certainly Jesus, God the Son, would know that such instances could occur, but as He gave His commands He did not even mention the possibility. As He elaborated His missionary strategies the Lord Jesus ordered us to preach the Gospel **to every person**. Are we going to obey?

FOLLOW CHRIST'S EXAMPLE

Let us look at the words of the Lord Jesus that we find in John 20:21; once again words addressed to His disciples. "Jesus said to them again: Peace be with you! Just as the Father sent me, so I send you." As often happens, the key lies in the small words, in this case "just as". "Just as" the Father sent me—and how was that, what did the Father do? Rather, what did the Son do upon being sent? Did He stay at home, so to speak? No, He left His 'home', He left His 'country', He came down here. And what did He do once He was here? He took on flesh and blood, He identified Himself with us. "And the Word became flesh and dwelt among us" (John 1:14). Even more than the Apostle Paul, Jesus is the supreme example of what a transcultural missionary is to be and do. He covered the greatest 'distance'; He humbled Himself the most.

As we have seen, Christ's missionary commands and strategies have to do with **transcultural** work, of necessity. The 2,000 ethnic nations without a witness and the 3 billion people who have never heard represent precisely a transcultural challenge; if they are to be reached someone must face and overcome a barrier of language and culture. Whoever undertakes such a ministry should follow Christ's example, which reflects certain basic attitudes. All the other strategies, already discussed, are relevant to all of God's people, and some may even be more important for those who stay at home than for those who go to the foreign field, but this seventh strategy[1] is primarily for the missionary. Although, with a little more thought we may find some very

---

[1] The seven strategies are:
1) Pray to the Lord of the harvest for laborers—being consistent.
2) **Simultaneously** reach our Jerusalem, our Judea and Samaria, and the ends of the earth.
3) Preach the Gospel to every person—for no one is innocent.
4) Make **disciples**, not just converts.
5) Live for the Kingdom of God, not yourself.
6) Liberate people from the power of Satan.
7) Follow Jesus' Example

practical applications for those who never leave their home town, as well. We turn now to the basic attitudes.

Identify Yourself

The Word "became flesh and dwelt among us". God the Son accepted the body that had been prepared for Him (Hebrews 10:5); He really identified Himself with us. Thinking of that time and place, Jesus ate what they did, spoke their language, lived as a poor man among a poor people; in short, He put on their 'skin', as it were. We also have Paul's example. He declares his procedure in 1 Corinthians 9:20-22.

> *20 I became as Jew among the Jews, to win the Jews; as under the law among those under the law, to win those under the law;*
> *21 as without law among those without law (. . .), to win those without law.*
> *22 I became as weak among the weak, to win the weak. I became all things to all men so that I might by all means win some.*

Then in verses 24 and 25 he gives the example of athletes who subject themselves to certain disciplines so as to attain the goal.

It is clear that Paul worked at identifying himself with the people, or the individuals, that he was trying to win to Christ. In the history of modern transcultural missions there has been a good deal of failure in this area. There is no lack of cases where a missionary has not been sensitive to the culture, and even the language, of the people he was trying to reach. At times there are features of a culture that are objectively sinful, practices that the Bible plainly forbids, and a messenger of Christ may not participate in such, but any unnecessary failure to identify will diminish the worker's efficiency. It will delay their acceptance of him as a person, which will delay their acceptance of the Gospel. If a people rejects a messenger they will also reject his message. The strategic effect of this attitude is such that it merits further consideration.

Try for a 're-birth'

The easiest way to learn the language and culture of a people is as a child, being born in their midst. It happens that we no longer have that option; we begin our missionary careers as adults. Still, I believe we should set ourselves the goal of working for a re-birth, as it were, in the target language and culture. That is to say, we should consciously work toward learning the language and culture to the point where we feel 'at home' in them, work toward the day when the group no longer looks on us as outsiders. To this end we need to 'die' to our own culture, while living among them. It is not a question of rejecting our own culture in any absolute sense, because when we return to our home country we must return to our home culture as well. We become bilingual and bicultural, or trilingual and tricultural, etc. But while living among another people we need to do all we can to understand and take on their culture—it is an important tactic for winning them to Christ.

Very well, let us suppose that God gives us the assignment of making disciples among a people that has never heard of Christ. Now what, how should we proceed? When dealing with a culture that has not been formally studied and a language that has never been written there will be no course anywhere in the world to teach us that language and culture. The only solution is to go to where they are and ask permission to live among them. There will almost always be some sort of trade language and some avenue of peaceful contact to provide a non-threatening context in which to present the request—it would be unreasonable to expect them to welcome a stranger with enthusiasm; it is enough that they tolerate our presence, for a start. To attempt contact with a 'wild' group demands wisdom and prudence, and specific direction from God.

To live in a 'primitive' village, for example, is like being in another world—different food (sometimes very different), a 'house' made of thatch or mud, strange customs that can even be revolting, no hygiene (at least as we see it), and a language that is so complex that it is easy to despair of ever being able to communicate the Gospel freely in that place. It is a daunting challenge, no doubt, but the apostle must accept it. The people themselves will most probably test your willingness to identify with them. In our own case my wife and I had to eat palm grubs (they eat them raw but allowed us to fry them!). They probably would not have harmed us if we refused, but what would the consequences have been if we had? We would have failed the test. It would have been a defeat for us; they would have said something like: "If that's the way you want to be, you can just paddle your own canoe!" Try as we may, in the beginning we will be strange and different, but we need to work hard to diminish the cultural barrier that separates us from the people, to **diminish** it rather than enlarge it.

The key to a people's heart is their mother tongue. A self-respecting apostle will not rest until he controls the language of the group he wants to disciple. Until he does he will continue to be an outsider. Worse still, a missionary who does not control the language of the people is condemning the Gospel to be always foreign, something on the outside. How could you?! A people's language is the key to their heart; woe to the messenger of Christ who does not give due respect to this factor!

I would say that the most usual failing in missionary practice is lack of identification (with the people): due to faulty orientation, preparation or even personal disposition the worker falls shy of the mark. However, it is possible to identify very selectively, which can also be damaging—the damage would result from a lack of appreciation for the whole picture precisely because the person could not be bothered to try for a comprehensive understanding of the language and culture. It is easy to become taken up with social, political and economic problems, but you cannot be too careful.

Watch Out for Political and Economic Interests

To achieve a reasonable control of a language and culture (in a pioneer situation) can easily take at least two years. Faced with the frustration of not being able to transmit God's Word during that time one can easily turn to political and economic problems as an 'escape valve', as a way to 'help' the people. But one's ignorance of the people's worldview can set up a booby-trap. You can easily wind up trying to impose 'solutions' that derive their 'validity' from your own worldview but which are not sensitive to theirs—a form of imperialism or paternalism. There is also the danger of creating dependencies. At times one falls into the trap 'innocently', because of not thinking through the implications. But, in our day there are those who vigorously propagate a social interpretation of the Gospel, a marxist hermeneutic that is imposed on the Bible (when it isn't marxist ideology, pure and simple), and they teach that the missionary should concentrate his efforts precisely in the social arena, whether or not he speaks the language or understands the culture.

You cannot be too careful! Our viewpoint should be God centered and not man centered. Do not stumble into the stupidity of serving selfish interests, and do not create false hope. Any activity based on humanistic or materialistic presuppositions will likely yield bitter fruit. Selfish interest is selfish interest, whosoever it may be. The Gospel of Jesus Christ does not exist to satisfy our selfish interests; rather it exists to satisfy **the glory of God**. Consider the Lord's own teaching on the subject.

First, let us look at His words as recorded in Matthew 5:38-41.

> 38 You have heard that it was said, "an eye for an eye" and "a tooth for a tooth".
> 39 But I tell you not to resist the evil doer; if someone hits you on your right cheek offer the left one as well;
> 40 and if someone sues you for your cape give him your coat also;
> 41 and if someone obliges you to go with him one mile, go two.

Well, have you really thought about that? Just a little difficult to put into practice, wouldn't you say? But there it is. The 'second mile' invites further comment. In the Roman Empire, in any conquered country, a Roman soldier could force a local citizen to carry his pack for one mile. Now that is a humiliating and unjust situation for you! Talk about conquest and exploitation! So why did Jesus not say to spit in the soldier's face and fight to free the land from the imperialistic oppression?

In Matthew 22:17-21 Jesus said to pay tribute to Caesar, Caesar the conqueror, Caesar the exploiter, Caesar the unjust. In Luke 12:14-15 someone asked Jesus to take sides in a matter of selfish interest, but He responded with general principles that have the power to transform lives and societies; however, these principles must be embraced freely, they may not be imposed by force.

Now let us look at Luke 7:18-22. John the Baptizer sent some men to ask Jesus directly if He was the Messiah. After they had watched Him cure a variety of people He said: "Go and tell John what you have seen and heard: the blind see, the lame walk, the lepers are cleansed, the deaf hear, the dead are raised and to the poor the Gospel is preached." **To the poor the Gospel is preached**. There is nothing about passing out weapons, about organized revolt, about demanding a more 'just' distribution of material goods. To the poor the Gospel is preached. Now then, in this same passage Jesus responded to physical suffering with compassion—He healed all the sick that came to Him. To heal, yes; to involve oneself in political or economic controversy, no.

It is not the case that Jesus lacked courage or conviction; He even used violence on occasion. In John 2:14-17 He used physical violence to cleanse the temple. In Acts 13:6-11 Paul might be said to have been 'violent' with Elimas. The same could be said about Peter with Ananias and Sapphira (Acts 5:1-10) and with Simon (Acts 8:18-24). Such energetic reactions on the part of the Lord Jesus or the Apostles were always in defense of spiritual principles, not questions of politics or economics.

Romans 13:1-2 and 1 Peter 2:13-18 give us a relevant Biblical principle—civil authorities are from God (strange though that seems at times). Whoever preaches hate and violence is not of God. Indeed, it is impossible to be a Christian and a Marxist at the same time—they are inimical ideologies.

I wish to make clear that what has been said above about involvement in matters political and economic is to be applied only to a missionary who is among a people where he is not a native. Within our own culture we can and should have an influence upon the political and economic reality, acting in a responsible manner.

Humble Yourself

Another basic attitude that the Lord Jesus exemplified is stated in Philippians 2:5-8.

> 05 Let this mind be in you which was also in Christ Jesus,
> 06 who, although subsisting in the form of God, determined not to clutch His being equal with God,
> 07 but emptied Himself, taking on the form of a slave by becoming the image of a man;
> 08 and being found in human shape He humbled Himself, becoming obedient to death, even death on a cross!

He humbled Himself! Anyone who is not willing to be humbled will be no good as a missionary. Actually, a proud, arrogant person is of little use anywhere in God's kingdom. The Bible is clear: "God resists the proud" (James 4:6 and 1 Peter 5:5). To become proud is a sure way to turn God against you, and no servant of Jesus Christ can afford to let that happen. But when it comes to transcultural work we do not really have a choice—the missionary will be humiliated whether he likes it or not, and several times a day.

When we first went to the Apurinã people both my wife and I had done graduate work. Someone might suppose that we went to the jungle to teach the 'Indian'. Well, perhaps one day, but in the beginning we had to learn from them—when it comes to living in the jungle they are the masters, our college degrees make little difference. In a small close-knit society each person has a role or function, so it is predictable that they will try to fit us into a niche also. If you try to help them medically you may be viewed as a shaman, if you try to make basic trade goods more affordable you may be viewed as a merchant, etc. But the first role we fill is that of a learner, learner of language and culture.

So what is wrong with that? Well, in such cultures learner of language and culture is the role of a child! I remember it well—after only two months or so in the village someone said to me: "Wilbur, what is your problem? Our children speak the language well by the time they are five years old, but here you are, a grown man, and can't manage it. What's wrong with you?!" I must admit that it hurt a little, and it happened more than once. My wife also suffered— one of the women liked to make fun of her efforts to speak; she would ridicule her without mercy. At times my wife would become distressed, to the point that the other women would feel sorry for her and tell the first one to lay off. It is not easy.

Folks often think of a jungle Indian (for example) as being an exotic figure, but I want to say that when we first arrive in their village **we** are the strange and different ones. It is as good as a circus! There is a constant audience observing all that we do and have—observing and commenting! Their comments are sprinkled with titters (and occasional bursts of laughter), and we cannot understand a thing—well, we know they are laughing at **us**, we just cannot understand what they are saying. If space permitted I could give further examples at great length, but I think enough has been said to make the point. You may be sure that ignorance of the language and culture will serve up humiliating experiences to the missionary every day. On top of them there will be no lack of other things to test our humility. We really need to have "the same mind that was also in Christ Jesus".

Limit Yourself

In Matthew 15:21-28 we find a moving account. A certain Canaanite woman cried out to Jesus asking deliverance for her daughter. He paid no attention. But since she would not stop crying out the disciples finally asked Him to do some-thing. Whereupon Jesus said: "I was only sent to the lost sheep of the house of Israel" (verse 24). There follows a conversation between Jesus and the woman where she gives an example of humility almost without equal in the Scriptures, and she received her "crumb".

But our concern at the moment is with the Lord's declaration in verse 24—during His earthly ministry He limited Himself. He concentrated His efforts on reaching just one people. He gave an occasional 'crumb' to others, but did not allow such to distract Him from His ministry to the people of Israel. It was on the cross that He would "draw all" to Himself (John 12:32), but just before saying that He apparently refused to receive some Greeks (John 12:20-23), even though He was only a few days from that cross.

A transcultural missionary needs to know how to limit himself, and especially in a pioneer situation. It will be hard and long even if he concentrates his efforts on reaching just one people. If he splinters or dilutes his effort it is unlikely that he will succeed in winning the people to Christ. For this reason, in my opinion, the 'tent-maker' strategy will not be viable for pioneer work among unreached peoples. The apostolic function requires one's total effort.

It is a question of purpose and responsibility, in the sense of commission or task. If Jesus sends me to make disciples among a certain ethnic group then that is my task. Unfortunately, to work with a minority people is like entering a war zone. Minority peoples are always exploited by the dominant culture. There is always prejudice, of race, religion, culture or whatever—always! There are always conflicting interests, be they economic, political, personal or whatever—always! To work with a minority people is like entering a war zone.

The village where we went to live was about an hour's walk into the jungle from a town on the banks of the Purus River. The townspeople were insulted by our choice (to live with the 'Indians' rather than with them), they did not like it one little bit. Our presence would proportion some advantage and protection to a group they despised and exploited. But our task was to reach the village, not the town (in fact, there already was an evangelical church in the town, with which we maintained good relations). If we had chosen to live in the town the villagers would have understood that we were identifying with their exploiters, which would have created a psychological barrier that would have hindered us for quite a while. Even against our preference, we are sometimes obliged to take sides, obliged by the social tensions that exist and by the very people we are trying to reach. It is a question of purpose and responsibility.

One other point should be made here. When it comes to working with a minority group, a foreigner will often fare better than a citizen of the country, because of the conflicts that exist and because he has not been a party to those conflicts. In many parts of the world neighboring peoples have been at odds for centuries, and there is hate and bitterness that only God can heal. In such a context, someone who is obviously a foreigner may be received with less reserve than someone who could be an 'enemy'. On the other hand, the political climate at the national level is often just the opposite. I have no solution to offer, unless it be the use of our spiritual weapons (2 Corinthians 10:4-5), I am just recording the problem. We need to be forewarned, and prepared to face limitations.

Be Respectful

Although I have no text in support of this attitude, it would seem to be obvious and implicit in the need to identify. Culture is a necessity. In essence it is the sum of the behavioral norms that a given community adopts or recognizes. Only a hermit can do without it. No culture is all good, nor all bad. The expression 'pagan culture' should not be understood to mean something useless. Whether one eats with a fork, a spoon, chopsticks or fingers is not a question of morals; whether one sleeps in a bed, a hammock or on the ground, ditto. Many practices are morally neutral; they are merely a matter of custom. Anytime two or more people wish to co-exist peacefully in the same area, culture must exist.

A transcultural missionary needs to know how to respect the culture of his target people. He should not arrive with the idea of imposing changes upon them. The Gospel may not be imposed. God Himself is not interested in pretended worship, in forced 'obedience' (at least in this age of grace). He wants sincere worship, obedience that comes from the heart (John 4:23-24). When we impose some change upon a group, but they do not understand or have conviction about it, we not only create hypocrites but we run the risk of creating a vacuum. When a people abandons some practice because of outside pressure, the reason why they did it is no longer covered and the consequences are frequently negative.

In any event, if you feel that you just have to do something about some practice, please, try to understand the purpose first. It is almost inevitable that a pioneer missionary will encounter practices that strike him as being absurd, immoral, horrifying and even criminal. What to do? **Try to learn the purpose**! Consider just one example. In many indigenous cultures, when a woman gives birth the father of the child takes to his hammock and stays there for a week, or more—the woman has to get up and work as usual. I can imagine that some would feel quite put out upon witnessing such a scene. So let us suppose that you decide to 'rectify' the situation; you begin to berate the man, you really tell him off, you carry on to such an extent that he finally gets up and goes to work. Well, it would have been good to understand the reasons for that procedure. It is like this: they believe that in some mysterious way, during the first days of a child's life, whatever energy the father is able to conserve is transferred to that child, thereby ensuring its health and well-being. Your own opinion about that idea is beside the point—that is what **they** believe and that is why the man acted as he did. Now let us consider the consequences of your interference: if the baby gets sick the father will be held responsible (he deprived his child of the necessary strength), and if the baby should die, . . . One more thing, when a man takes to his hammock like that he is recognizing the legitimacy of the child; if he does not do it he is declaring to the community that the baby is not his! The social implications are serious and far-reaching.

Friends, it is better not to interfere; it is better to leave such initiatives to the Holy Spirit. Let us work toward furnishing the Word of God as soon as possible so they can be converted and become true disciples of Jesus Christ. Then they too will have the indwelling Holy Spirit and He will bring about the necessary changes in their culture. When we let Him do it we see the following: He changes some things that we had not considered and leaves intact others that we would change. In this way each culture reflects the grace of God a little differently, like the different facets of a diamond.

It is true, unfortunately, that there have been cases where a missionary has caused some damage to a culture (it is also true that some who make a business out of criticizing missionaries cause much more damage themselves when they deal with indigenous peoples). A missionary may cause some damage, it has happened, but he does not 'destroy' the culture, as is sometimes alleged. It is important to distinguish between a missionary and the Gospel. The Gospel does not destroy cultures, nor does it damage them—the Gospel **perfects** cultures, any and all, including our own. We urgently need to create an awareness and enhance our ability to distinguish between the Word of God and our own religious culture. Much of what we preach and teach has little or no Biblical basis. By all means let us preach the **Gospel**, and not our own religious culture!

One more thing requires comment here. We need to respect the people's culture, but at the same time we must confront the kingdom of darkness. We should identify with the people, except for practices that the Bible condemns. Since the missionary is there precisely to offer an alternate worldview, he should not compromise it. Dealing with evil spirits is a central ingredient in many cultures. We need spiritual discernment to separate neutral things from those that are directly related to the demons. Such discerning is not always easy. I have referred to Hebrews 2:14 several times, but the whole sentence includes verse 15 as well, which gives us a sad but important truth. In all human cultures the fear of death enslaves people. Many practices are intended to avert death, but it is impressive to observe how often they actually contribute to it (recall that one of Satan's pastimes is to get people killed). For example, a lot of bloodshed results from the suspicion of witchcraft; the person deemed responsible is killed before he can kill. We could fill the page with further examples. I have no magic formula to offer for clearing up all doubts. Again I must content myself with calling attention to the problem. May we look to the Lord for respect and discernment!

Prepare Yourself

The Lord Jesus prepared Himself during 30 years for three years of public ministry. Pioneer trans-cultural work is at least ten times more difficult and time consuming as ordinary evangelism (i.e. in one's own language and culture). That is right, at least ten times, and I am being cautious. Further-more, even with the best available training and orientation, a worker who takes on a transcultural situation will certainly suffer culture shock. Culture shock is a psychological and emotional malady that results when you immerse yourself in a strange language and culture. Our psychological equilibrium is quite dependent upon routine, upon recognized procedures, upon the predictable—when we find ourselves in a situation where everything is different, where we cannot understand anything, where we do not know how to act, we become disoriented and start to feel ill. I would recommend that a new missionary not attempt more than three months without a break the first time he is isolated in a different culture. In any case, he needs to be forewarned so he will understand what is happening to him and not go into a panic supposing he is losing his mind. Each time he returns to the culture he will feel less shock.

I would declare and insist that before facing a transcultural situation a worker needs special training. To send a missionary to another land without such training is irresponsible, even criminal—the poor soul will suffer needlessly and will be less efficient and productive than he could be; and the risk of failure is greater. Biblical or theological training is necessary, but not enough. One needs the technical tools to face language and culture, and most especially when it is necessary to start from scratch.[1]

Some will be thinking of the second coming of Christ, the possible, if not probable, scarcity of time. If Jesus is about to return, to what extent should we 'waste' time on preparation? Well, on the basis of what I have heard and experienced I would almost say that no matter how much training you have you will still wish you had more, but obviously if no time is left to do the work the training loses its purpose and justification; we must find a middle ground.

Let us imagine that in some way God gives us a sure revelation to the effect that Jesus will return five years from today. In this way we would know that we only had five years to finish doing what remains to be done. Let us suppose we have two young men of comparable age, Biblical training (say three years of Bible School), commitment and native ability. Each one feels he should try to evangelize an unreached culture. One says: "Wow, Jesus is coming; we only have five years; I cannot afford to spend another minute on training; off I go!" And he does. The other says: "Wow, Jesus is coming; but I am not ready to face a pioneer work; I will secure the technical tools first." So he spends two years in special training. In the three remaining years the second worker will achieve more than the first did in five—the first one was there, but did not know how to proceed. The longer the remaining period of time the greater will be the disparity in the achievement of the two. Without at least a minimum of specific training there is hardly any point in going to a pioneer field.

Implications

In some evangelical circles it may be necessary to work at creating a new mentality, one that recognizes the realities

---

[1] Some people are born with the limitation that they can only learn the language into which they are born. As adults they are simply incapable of learning another language. Such people should be encouraged to stay at home.

of transcultural work. This will be especially so where they are used to fairly quick and easy results.

I believe a surgeon can readily understand the situation. To remove an appendix is simple (if it did not rupture) and is relatively inexpensive. But heart surgery is far more complex, delicate and expensive—it demands much more training and ability on the part of the surgeon. A construction engineer can also understand it. To build a house is one thing; to build a twenty-story building is another—the time, materials and knowhow cannot be compared. I wish to suggest that pioneer transcultural work is like the twenty-story building, or the heart surgery—it is much more expensive in both time and money than local evangelism, and demands more training. If we are going to take the commands of Christ seriously we must face up to this reality.

As was said at the beginning of the chapter, this strategy applies primarily to transcultural work, but not exclusively so. Someone from the middle class who tries to work in a slum area will face the sort of difficulties that have been discussed, but to a lesser extent. There are sub-cultures that require different approaches. And there are diverse ethnic communities—German descendants will think differently than Japanese descendants, or Mexican descendants, even in a third generation—that need distinct treatment. Furthermore, everyone needs to understand this strategy, for this reason: those who are not personally involved in transcultural work need to understand what the others are facing, so they can intercede intelligently, be encouraging, sympathetic and supportive, spread the vision, etc. Everyone needs to be actively involved, in some way, in the effort to fulfill the Great Commission.

MAKE DISCIPLES, NOT JUST CONVERTS

Now let us look at the words of the Lord Jesus that we find in Matthew 28:18-20, Christ's Great Commission. The first thing that catches our attention is the declaration in verse 18: "All authority has been given to me, in heaven and on earth." In other words, Jesus declares Himself to be the Sovereign of the Universe, the Greatest. This declaration embodies at least two consequences for Christ's followers.

First, it is a basic condition for success that we know that our Commander is the Greatest. It is this unshakable certainty that will enable us to face the enemy and adverse circumstances without fear or vacillation.

Next, any order given by the Highest Authority of the universe demands total attention and absolute respect. To begin, such respect should translate into close attention to the precise meaning of the order. We must define the semantic content as completely and exactly as possible. When our Master gives an order He obviously expects to be obeyed, correctly and completely. So then, let us consider the semantic content of the command.

What Does the Command Mean?

A strict translation could go something like this: "As you go, disciple all ethnic nations, baptizing them in the name of the Father and of the Son and of the Holy Spirit, teaching them to keep everything that I have commanded you." (We could also translate, "make disciples in all ethnic nations".) We observe that only one verb is imperative, namely 'to disciple'. It follows that the essence of the order will be found in this verb. I am aware that we are used to reading the verb 'to go' as if it were imperative also, but it is not—it is a past participle. Therefore it may not carry the main action, it is circumstantial. If we just think about it a bit I believe it will become clear. One 'goes' so as to arrive where he intends to work. One could spend his whole life 'going' and never do anything, a professional tourist. The Lord Jesus assumes that we will be going, or have already gone (strictly speaking the translation would be "having gone"). In other words, wherever each one may be, in line with God's will for each, the command is to make disciples.

The command is to make **disciples**. Unfortunately the Authorized Version misleads us with the rendering "teach"—the verb 'to teach' does indeed come at the beginning of verse 20, but is not in verse 19. (In passing we may note that almost all the Greek MSS that have this passage [95%] do not have the word 'therefore', which is why I did not include it in my rendering.) Given that the command is to make disciples, the first thing we need to do is understand the precise meaning that Jesus gave to the word 'disciple', because therein lies the essence of the order.

So then, what did **Jesus** understand by 'disciple'? The immediate context gives us a good idea, because verse 20 says: "teaching them to keep everything that I have commanded you." That means that making disciples involves **teaching** (not just preaching). But, teaching what? Teaching to keep (that is, obey) everything that Jesus commanded. But since one does not obey something he does not know about, we must begin by teaching the commands themselves, all of them. Now, is that really what we are doing in our churches, by and large?

I invite the reader's attention to Luke 14:25-33, the only passage that preserves in Christ's own words His definition of 'disciple', where He uses the word so there can be no doubt what He is describing (the concept of discipleship is doubtless present in other passages too, but since the word 'disciple' does not occur the point could be disputed). Three times we encounter the expression "cannot be my disciple", an expression that is emphatic in the original Text. The effect is to present us with three absolute conditions—if you do not meet them there is no way you can be Jesus' **disciple**. So, let us consider these conditions.

"Hate"

We find the first condition in verse 26. "If anyone comes to me but does not hate his father and mother, wife and children, brothers and sisters, yes, and even his own life, he cannot be my disciple." What a difficult statement! Are we really supposed to "hate", and particularly those who are nearest and dearest to us? Does not God command us to love? This is really a hard word; what can Jesus mean by it? It should be understood in comparative terms, as in the parallel passage in Matthew 10:37: "whoever loves father or mother more than me is not worthy of me."

In other words, if I propose to follow Jesus as His disciple He demands that I place my relationship with Him above every relationship in this life, be it with father, mother, wife, children or myself (which is the bottom line). Jesus demands first place, without competition. Now then, whoever maintains such a relationship with Sovereign Jesus will now and again be obliged (by Jesus Himself) to act in ways that those who do not have such a relationship with Him will not understand. They will not know how to interpret his attitude correctly. They will mistake it for carelessness, belittling, disdain, even hate. Consider the following.

On more than one occasion I have had someone tell me to my face that I must disdain my wife and children in that I took them to live in an 'Indian' village in the middle of the Amazon jungle. They just could not understand my course of action. How could a husband and father with my training and abilities possibly expose his family to such a difficult, primitive and even dangerous life, depriving them of the comfort and advantages of the city? They could only interpret my attitude as irresponsible, at best.

And how many missionaries, whose parents did not share the ideals of their children, when it came to the leave-taking, that difficult hour when they were about to embark for a foreign shore, have not heard from the lips of their own parents words to this effect: "My son, you must hate us, you are abandoning us, you are throwing your life away; how can you do this?!" In their distress the parents use just such language—they interpret their child's action as irresponsibility, disdain, even hate. So we see that Jesus was not exaggerating, He was not being ridiculous when He said "hate".

However, I wish to pursue the question of acting responsibly. Did I act irresponsibly by taking my family to live in the jungle? Which is better, the jungle with Jesus or the city without Him? If I take my family to the jungle in obedience to Jesus' command then He must accept responsibility for the consequences. If I remain in the city against His will then I am the one who must answer for it. The question is both serious and practical—I know a man who understood clearly that he had a missionary call, but he did not obey; he "could not" subject his wife to such a life.

Actually, the Old Testament gives us the account of certain men that took a similar position. I am thinking of the 'warriors' of Israel at Kadesh Barnea (Numbers 13 and 14). On God's calendar it was time to invade the promised land, but ten of the twelve spies discouraged the crowd and they rebelled against God's order, an order that had already been given. To justify their attitude the men used their families— if they obeyed they would be killed, and then what would happen to the women and children? As if that were not enough, they made a counter proposal to God: it would be better to die right there. (It is dangerous to offer God a counter proposal, because He is likely to accept it, as in this case.) As a result they spent 38 more years wandering in the desert (see Deuteronomy 2:14) until each one of the men who voted against God in Kadesh Barnea died. Not a single one crossed the Jordan. As for the women and children, the supposed excuse for the disobedience, God caused them to enter the promised land!

My brethren, better by far to face any danger than to disobey the known will of God. Do not even think of making a counter proposal! Our Master takes full responsibility for the consequences of His orders, when they are obeyed. The way to be really irresponsible is to deprive your family of God's protection, exposing them to the consequences of your disobedience. A true disciple of Christ will choose to 'hate' his family, and his own life, rather than disobey. That is the way it is supposed to be.

We find the second condition in verse 27 (Luke 14). "Whoever does not bear his cross and follow me cannot be my disciple." What do you suppose the Lord means by "cross"? Would it be the ornament some people wear, some problem in your life or that neighbor you cannot stand? No. Two thousand years ago 'cross' represented just one thing—death. It represented a form of execution, in fact the most shameful one at the time (with prolonged suffering). Luke 9:23 sheds more light on this matter: "If anyone wishes to come after me, let him deny himself, take up his cross each day, and follow me." The semantic content of the verb "bear" (Luke 14:27) gives the idea of continuous action. Here in Luke 9:23 we must take up our cross "each day"—evidently it is a daily dying that is called for.

Indeed, the Apostle Paul uses just such an expression in 1 Corinthians 15:31, saying that he died daily. But how are we to understand that statement? Clearly it does not refer to physical death. What then? I believe the "let him deny himself" of Luke 9:23 gives us the necessary clue. It is death to self, to one's own ideas, ambitions and desires; it is to give up my supposed right to run my own life. And this disposition must be renewed each day, and maybe every hour. Romans 12:1 says it a different way when it speaks of presenting our bodies as a "living sacrifice".

But does not that phrase seem a little strange to you? In the Old Testament, among all those sacrificed animals, was there ever a "living" sacrifice? When and how did an animal become a sacrifice? Was it not when its throat was cut and its blood shed? So there were only dead sacrifices. But Paul speaks of a "living" sacrifice. I believe it refers to the same thing as "bear your cross"—it is to live dying, to die constantly. It is to deny yourself at every step. And Jesus affirms that without this attitude it is impossible to be His disciple.

The third condition is in verse 33 (Luke 14). "So also, who-ever among you does not renounce all that he has cannot be my disciple." The "so also" links this verse to the two illustrations given in verses 28-32. I would say that those illustrations relate to the act of entering the relationship of disciple, which will be treated presently, but it is worth not-ing that we are looking at a deliberate, considered decision, an act of the will. And nothing else will do, because Jesus demands complete renunciation, unconditional surrender—in short, "all that we have".

Taking the three conditions together, they can be taken as three different ways of saying the same thing. Although one condition deals with relationships, another with ambitions and the third with possessions, they are all expressions of one basic reality. Our Lord Jesus Christ requires total com-mitment! Now we can affirm the definition that the Lord gave to 'disciple'. To Jesus, a disciple is someone who is totally committed to **HIM**.

Returning to Matthew 28:19, we can give a clear meaning to the command. We are ordered to make disciples—**disciples**, not merely believers or converts—**disciples**, in the sense that the Lord Jesus gives to the term—**disciples**, people whose lives really and truly revolve around Christ's Cause and Will, people who are living with a view to the Kingdom, in very truth!

The Strategic Effect

So, how are our churches doing it, by and large? In general the focus is on evangelism, is it not? We are concerned to 'win souls', to see people 'get saved'. (That is in the church-es that still believe the Bible; there are others that are little better than social clubs and are already in the enemy's hand.) In 'traditional' or 'historical' churches the new be-liever is urged to attend the services and participate in the life of the church; if he wants to be really good he should be a tither. In 'pentecostal' or 'charismatic' churches the new believer should also seek the 'second blessing'; once he has been 'baptized in the Spirit' then he has really arrived. But who is making disciples of the sort that Jesus commanded?

What might the practical consequence of our emphasis be? It is precisely the tragic picture that has already been presented: half the people in the world have yet to hear the Gospel; a third of the ethnic nations still lack a spokesman of Christ. Of necessity. The emphasis on merely winning souls fills the churches with children, children spiritually (regardless of physical age). So, what is wrong with that? Well, do children work? Children don't work, they **make work** (and how!). My dear friends, we are face to face with a problem as big as the world, literally. Even though it may hurt, we need to study this matter objectively and with courage—the eternal destiny of the world is at stake.

Abandoned Children Are Bad News!

What should we think of a man who goes around fathering children without giving a thought to food, shelter, education, in short the necessary care for those children? We will be perfectly justified in calling him irresponsible, an enemy of our society. Yes, because he will be contributing abandoned children to our society, and in all probability many, if not most, of them will become delinquent and criminal elements. Abandoned children are bad news! I would like to suggest for the reader's careful consideration that there is an almost perfect analogy between the physical and spiritual realms in this matter.

When we give birth to spiritual children (so to speak), but do not disciple them, do not lead them to a total commitment to Jesus, do not help them to become spiritual adults, we reap a variety of negative consequences. What makes a pastor age prematurely? Is it the unbelievers out in the world, or is it the childishness in the church? Obviously it is the spiritual childishness in the church. (One might observe in passing that justice may be served, because when a pastor only preaches evangelistic sermons he himself is mainly responsible—he does not feed the sheep. Goat food is no good for sheep.)

In doing personal evangelism what is the most frequent objection one hears? Is it not the way believers live? It is spiritual childishness in the church. And then there are the 'scalded cats'—those who say, "I used to be a believer". What do you suppose happened? Presumably he listened to the preaching, responded to the invitation, followed the instructions and gave signs of life, participating in the activities of the church. But then Satan landed on him, the Christian life was not the 'bed of roses' it was supposed to be, there were more problems than blessings. And since nobody explained what was happening, nobody discipled him, he began to be discouraged, to become perplexed, to feel disillusioned and abandoned. So he begins to withdraw, and before you know it has fallen away. Now he is a 'scalded cat', he has been 'vaccinated'. To win him back is hard work, not to mention the negative ripples that have gone out to his family and neighborhood.

When we think of the unreached peoples of the world the problem of the spiritual childishness in the churches becomes critical. We need soldiers, and children are not very good at that. Fortunately few of them offer themselves. But it does happen that not everyone who volunteers, and who winds up being sent to the mission field, is a disciple—some are little better than children. And if a child tries to do a man's work, will the job be done properly? Not likely. The child, poor thing, is doing the best that he can, but he does not have the strength, knowledge, experience or ability of a man. He is a child. A lost and dying world needs adults, it needs disciples.

Dear people, let us be responsible parents! It is terribly, tragically irresponsible to give birth to children (in the spiritual realm too) without accepting the natural and necessary consequences—to feed them, protect them and train them until they become adults. **Abandoned children are bad news**. I believe that our Master's example is very much to the point.

The Example of Christ, and of Paul

What procedure did the Lord Jesus use during His three years of ministry here in this world? With whom did He spend most of His time? Was it not with twelve men? They walked together, ate together, slept in the same place, heard and observed all that the Master did, during two years. And Jesus staked everything on those men. When He returned to Heaven the future of the Church was in their hands. If they had failed altogether the Church would have been finished before it got properly started.

And when Jesus was dealing with the crowds, what did He do? Did He promote evangelistic campaigns? It is not in the record. What the Sacred Text does record is that in the main He **taught** the people, sometimes the whole day. That is because Jesus wanted disciples. At any given time the well-being of the Church depends on the disciples that are in existence.

It would appear that the Apostle Paul, at least, understood Christ's example and strategy, because he too was concerned to make disciples. As he said goodbye to the church in Ephesus he affirmed: "I kept back nothing that was helpful, but proclaimed it to you, and taught you publicly and from house to house" (Acts 20:20), and again: "I did not avoid declaring to you the whole counsel of God" (verse 27). Paul did not limit himself to an evangelistic message—he wanted disciples. I gather that his main purpose in writing his epistles was to help the believers become disciples. Colossians 1:28 says it well: "whom [Christ] we preach, warning every man and teaching every man in all wisdom, that we may present every man perfect in Christ Jesus."

Ephesians 4:11-13 is even more to the point, because Paul ascribes this purpose to Christ Himself. He it was who gave apostles, prophets, evangelists, pastors and teachers to the Church, "for the equipping of the saints for the work of the ministry, for the edifying of the body of Christ, till we all come to the unity of the faith and the knowledge of the Son of God, to a perfect man, to the measure of the stature of the fullness of Christ." In other words, Christ wants **disci-**

ples, in the sense that was explained above. In 2 Timothy 2:2 Paul makes clear that there are to be successive generations of disciples, presumably until the return of Christ.

So what was the result when the Apostles followed this strategy? They reached their world in their generation. And if we regain the same emphasis, should not we also be able to reach our world in this generation? I believe so. Let us see how it can work.

How it Works

To make disciples takes time and may be uncomfortable, but it is the fastest and surest way to effectively reach the world. At first glance this may seem unreasonable. In fact, the idea that seems to prevail in today's evangelical world is mass evangelism—we must win as many souls as possible. The more souls and the less time, the better. The only trouble is that it does not work. It may yield an apparent rapid growth, but the work will collapse for lack of an adequate foundation and infrastructure. Children don't work, they make work.

To make a disciple one must spend time with him, like Jesus did. And we need to be open and honest; we must not pretend to be 'super-saints' that have no problems, never sin, are never attacked by Satan, etc. We must explain the reason for things, give 'hands on' orientation, really ground them in the faith. (It is possible to attain the category of 'disciple' on your own, but it tends to be a long and painful process, precisely for lack of orientation.)

It may appear to be too slow, but it winds up being the fastest. Let us just suppose that I am the only true disciple of Christ in the world today (obviously that is not true, and thank God it is not!), just for the sake of the argument. Let us say that this year I manage to make one disciple—I not only win a soul but I teach and establish him, I lead him to really commit himself to Jesus. So then there will be two of us, right?

(Perhaps someone is questioning the possibility of making a disciple in a year. The main secret is in a total commitment to Jesus. Until someone yields in this way his spiritual growth will be slow, if there is any—we have all seen how it goes, three steps forward and two (or three) steps back. When we acknowledge Christ's right to rule us we give the Holy Spirit free rein to work in our lives and may grow rapidly, reaching levels of spirituality that most Christians do not even dream of.)

Returning to our 'argument', during the next year each of us makes another disciple—we not only win two souls but we teach and establish them, we lead them to really commit themselves to Jesus. And then there will be four of us, right? The third year we four each win and disciple one more, which makes eight. (You do not have to be a renowned evangelist; you do not have to win 300 souls a year; just win one, provided you also disciple him.) The fourth year we double again, which brings us to sixteen. If we repeat this procedure year by year at the end of ten years we will have 1,024 disciples! Can you imagine it? What pastor would not be pleased if he planted a church and after ten years' work had 1,000 members? But let us move on and look at the second decade.

If we continue at the same rate, we will finish the eleventh year with 2,048 disciples. Doubling each year we will finish the second decade with all of 1,048,576 disciples! Then the 21st year we would have 2,097,152, and so on until the end of the third decade when we would have 1,073,741,824 disciples. That is right, more than one **billion** as the result of only thirty years of disciple making, each one making one more per year. If we kept on for just four additional years we would reach the figure of over 17 billion. Of course, there are less than seven billion people in the world today, so we could lose over half of our total on the way and still reach the world within 34 years! What do you say, shall we go for it?

But, wait just a minute. That was if we started with only one, but of course there are many more. Do you suppose there might be one million true disciples (not just believers) in the world today? I believe so, and there are doubtless many more. Well then, that being the case we can subtract twenty years from the 34 that would be needed to reach the world. Surely, because according to the suggested plan it would take twenty years to get from one to a million. So if we already have over a million disciples we could finish reaching the world **within fourteen years**. Fair enough?

I know that you have already thought of several objections. That plan is too ideal; it does not allow for the numerous barriers that exist: barriers ideological, political and religious, barriers of geography, language and culture, the barrier of human weakness with its many manifestations, and above all the barrier of satanic and demonic activity in the world. So where does all that leave us? Well, I recognize the existence of all those barriers, and they are indeed imposing, but our Commander is greater. The barriers of ideology, politics and religion we may circumvent using the weapons mentioned in 2 Corinthians 10:4-5, while the activity of Satan and his angels (the demons) we can defeat using the full range of spiritual weapons that Sovereign Jesus has placed at our disposal (see the essays on spiritual warfare). Nor should we forget the "key of David" (Revelation 3:7). As for the barriers of geography, language and culture, we can overcome them with modern technology—the tools and techniques we have are already good and are getting better. And human weakness? The solution is precisely a life of discipleship, with the power and enabling of the Spirit of God.

(A word of caution is called for here: by 'discipleship' I mean the process of being and making disciples of **Jesus**, not of ourselves. Many times the obsessions of a discipler or the founder of a movement become 'doctrine' for his followers and sooner or later they wind up in the ditch. Let us make disciples of **Jesus**; let us lead others to depend directly on the Holy Spirit and the Word of God, not on us. In this way the ones whom we disciple may free themselves from our errors, since we all err.)

There are a few other things that may be said in relief of possible objections. The plan speaks of making only one disciple per year, but in fact we can make more—one thinks immediately of the multiplied millions of believers and nominal Christians that could be discipled in shorter periods of time. The strategy presented in chapter II deals with the problem of the poor geographic distribution of disciples at the moment. It is well to remember also that we will never win everybody—there will always be those who knowingly and deliberately reject the Gospel of Jesus Christ. Jesus never told us to **win** everybody (that would violate their will); rather we are to make sure that each person hears and has an intelligent choice. The plan presented above gave the theoretical possibility of discipling the world within fourteen years, but that will not happen (not everyone will become a disciple). According to Matthew 28:19 and Mark 16:15 our objective is to see some true disciples within each ethnic nation and to give each person an informed chance to embrace the Gospel. So then, with all those explanations and allowances don't you think we can accept the challenge of fulfilling our Master's orders within a few years? Let us give it a good try!

Implementing the Strategy

Now let us look at how to implement this strategy. There are at least three questions that must be considered, but first I want to return to the command in Matthew 28:19: "Make disciples in all ethnic nations." Considering the precise meaning we have established for this command I understand two things. First, the order is to make **disciples**, nothing more and nothing less.

Second, it seems to me to be obvious that before one can make disciples he must first **be** a disciple (no?). How could I lead someone else to surrender unconditionally to Jesus when I myself refuse to do so? Or how can I guide someone else along the path of discipleship if I have never been there? That being the case, until I am a disciple I remain out of the real action—I can scarcely do much toward fulfilling Christ's Great Commission. And that goes for you, too. It follows that the first thing we need to verify is whether we are genuine disciples. Which leads us to the first question: how to be a disciple.

How to Be a Disciple

The question divides naturally into two parts: how to enter the relationship of disciple and then how to maintain it, in practice. So, how do we enter the relationship? If we may compare the life of a disciple to a path that must be traveled (daily), then entering is like passing through the gate that gives access to the path.

I understand that entering the relationship of disciple involves a deliberate submission, an act of the will. I imagine it is possible for someone to be converted almost on an impulse, like a leap in the dark. He is in despair; someone comes up and gives a superficial presentation of the plan of salvation; he accepts it, albeit with little understanding. But becoming a disciple is different. I believe the two illustrations in Luke 14:28-32 are to the point.

Recall that in verse 33, as He gave the third condition, Jesus said, "so also". He was referring to the two examples He had just given. A man wanted to build a tower. A king heard that a neighboring king was already marching against him with 20,000 men, and he only had 10,000. What to do? In each case the man studies the situation, checks his own resources, considers the cost, tries to foresee the probable consequences. Then he makes his decision; to build or refrain, to fight or surrender. Whatever he decides to do, he must accept the consequences of his choice. That is the way it is with discipleship—you begin with a studied choice, by taking a deliberate position. I believe that is what Paul wrote about in Romans 12:1 when he spoke of presenting our bodies as living sacrifices. The word 'bodies' is presumably a case of synecdoche, where the body represents the life (can I separate the soul from the body and still function in this world?). The verb 'present' refers to the act of the will, without reservations. My friend, have you surrendered unconditionally to Jesus? If not, you are not His disciple and are not qualified to make disciples.

I am well aware that this presentation may be somewhat troubling to the reader—it may appear that I am being a bit too radical or demanding, a little too 'open and shut'. I know. That is because I start with a radical definition of 'disciple', precisely the definition given by the Lord Jesus in Luke 14:25-33. A 'disciple' is someone totally committed to Him.

I wish to emphasize again that absolute surrender is the key to spiritual growth. Without such a surrender the believer remains a spiritual child and grows slowly (if at all). The surrender, which needs to be renewed each day, allows the Holy Spirit to work freely in his life and then his growth can be rapid. Surrender is the key because God respects our volition. This absolute surrender is also the basic condition for the filling and enabling of the Holy Spirit, which we must have if we are really going to reach the lost world.

To enter the relationship of disciple is one thing, to maintain it in practice is another. It is not at all automatic. Not even the 'baptism in the Spirit' guarantees it. We have already talked about taking up the cross daily and the living sacrifice. It is completely necessary to renew **each day** our determination to embrace the will of God in everything. It is an attitude that needs renewing every hour, as often as necessary. Now then, to write these words is easy, but to do it is something else again! The daily struggle of the disciple lies just there, to maintain the relationship. The fact is that we need help. One of the main benefits of sharing discipleship with others is the example and stimulus that the participants receive mutually. The sharing contains an element of accountability that helps. When we 'tell it like it is' the others can intercede for us in a specific way—another crucial help. To be a disciple all by yourself is possible, but it is difficult. However, aside from the benefits of sharing there is an indispensable ingredient to discipleship.

In John 8:31 Jesus said to those who had believed in Him: "If you continue in my word you are really my disciples." And if you do not "continue"? (And how can you "continue" in the Word if it does not exist, in your language?) 2 Timothy 3:16-17 reads like this: "All Scripture is God-breathed and is profitable for instruction, for reproof, for correction, for training in righteousness, so that the man of God may be perfect, thoroughly equipped for every good work." A man of God who is "perfect and thoroughly equipped" is presumably a disciple who is taking the relationship seriously. The phrase "so that" indicates that it is the use of the Scriptures that leads us to the stated result. 1 Peter 2:2 teaches us that the Word is our food; we need it like a baby needs milk. Psalm 1:2-3 is clear to the effect that our spiritual health depends on the "Law of the Lord"; it is our spiritual water, which we need every day. In fact, we need to meditate upon it. In Joshua 1:8 it is God Himself who tells Joshua to meditate upon the book of the Law, and promises the following result: "then you will make your way prosperous and then you will have good success." In short, **it is impossible to be a disciple of Christ without effective access to God's Word**.

Once again I am being radical; by 'be a disciple' I mean the maintaining of the relationship. But, can it really be necessary to meditate upon the Word every day? Well, there we have several relevant texts, among others. If we are to exhort one another **daily** because of "the deceitfulness of sin" (Hebrews 3:13), how much more should we not look in our "mirror" (James 1:22-25) and expose ourselves to the "Sword of the Spirit" (Hebrews 4:12, Ephesians 6:17) each day?

But how then could the Apostle Paul make disciples, and what about the righteous in the Old Testament? We should remember that Psalm 1:2-3 and Joshua 1:8 (and Deuteronomy 32:47) are from the Old Testament, but I believe that the 'ground rules' change somewhat with the progress of Revelation. We have more than the righteous of the Old Testament, and certainly God will require more of us. For example, the standard of grace is higher than the standard of law. The law required the tithe, grace requires 100% (Luke 14:33). The law required us to love our neighbor as ourselves, grace requires us to love our brother as the Father loves the Son (John 13:34 and 15:9)! And we have the Holy Spirit who dwells in us. I also believe that the age of the Apostles was in some sense transitional. However all that may be, Paul applied himself to write what was 'lacking', complementing the New Testament materials that already existed and that others were producing. As he said good-bye to the Ephesians he stated his philosophy clearly: "I commend you to God and to **the Word of his grace**, which is able to build you up and give you an inheritance among all those who are sanctified" (Acts 20:32). I know that although the Biblical standards are presented in absolute terms our practice is not absolute. But there the goal is, and I do not dare to diminish it. Now let us consider the second question.

Make Disciples of Whom?

To begin, any and every person comes within the realm of Christ's orders and therefore is a legitimate candidate for discipling. Of course. That being granted, however, I would like to return to the command in Matthew 28:19, "make disciples **in all ethnic nations**". Across the centuries and millennia God has demonstrated His concern for the well-being of all the ethnic groups in the world.

The first overt statement of this concern is in the Abrahamic Covenant: "in you all the families of the earth will be blessed" (Genesis 12:3). We can gain some idea of the importance that God attaches to this matter from the unparalleled circumstance that He repeats it four more times, in Genesis 18:18, 22:18, 26:4 and 28:14! Hebrews 6:13-18 explains that when He swore by Himself (see Genesis 22:16-18) God gave the greatest possible guarantee to the declared purpose. **All** the families of the earth **must** be blessed. Both Peter (see Acts 3:25) and Paul (see Galatians 3:8) link the Gospel of Christ to God's promise that He will bless all the families of the earth. In the New Testament several passages reaffirm this divine purpose: Matthew 12:21 and 24:14, Mark 13:10, Luke 2:32 and 24:47; much of Acts and of Paul's ministry in general has to do with the nations. Revelation 5:9 (where every extant Greek manuscript except one reads: "have bought **us** for God with your blood out of every tribe and language and people and ethnic nation"), 7:9 and 14:6 are emphatic, not to mention Revelation 22:2.

So then, the Lord Jesus wants disciples in each ethnic nation or 'family'. In the first chapter we saw that there are at least 6,000 such nations in the world. And many of them still do not have an ambassador of Christ. Worse yet, two thirds of the languages of the world still do not have so much as a verse of Scripture. As we have already argued, without the Word it is impossible to maintain the relationship of disciple. That means that at this writing we are unable to make disciples in 4,000 ethnic nations! How can we tolerate such a situation?

When we speak of 2,000 ethnic nations without ambassador, or 4,000 ethnic nations without Scripture, we need to clarify something. The unreached peoples are minority groups. Although most of those groups number in the thousands and tens of thousands (and even hundreds of thousands), there are ethnic nations with less than a thousand people. In Australia and Brazil there are numerous groups that are quite small, sometimes less than a hundred people. At this point a logical query comes to mind. Is it worth the bother to try to reach such a group? Can we justify the expense in time, money and personnel? (Keep in mind that pioneer transcultural work is at least ten times more difficult then doing evangelism in your own language and culture—it usually takes years to achieve a disciple.)

Does size matter? Did Jesus command us to make disciples only in groups of over a thousand people, or ten thousand? Did Jesus not tell us to preach to each person? (An ethnic nation reduced to a sole survivor still falls within the scope of that order.) Here I wish to ask some apparently silly questions. Did anyone choose who would be his father or mother, where he would be born, to what culture he would belong? I did not choose to be born to parents who were followers of Jesus Christ, to a language that has had the Bible for centuries, within a culture that permitted me to choose whatever occupation the present world offered. I did not choose it, nor did I deserve it; God just gave it to me. By the same token, not a single Catauixi Indian (there are less than 100) chose to be born in the middle of the Amazon jungle, to a people decimated, despised, exploited and almost finished, to a language that has yet to be written, within a culture that condemns him to die in the jungle without any knowledge of the Gospel and after a life of struggle with evil spirits and the 'green hell' (whoever called the jungle a green hell must have been there once). He did not choose either.

Now, I would like you to consider all that Jesus means in your life, both here and hereafter. Ready? Now I am going to ask you to exercise your imagination. Try to imagine that you do not have any of that, that all of a sudden you changed places with a Catauixi and it is you who are in that jungle without Christ, without hope and without escape, and he is the one who is here. In such an event would you not wish that someone would think it worth the bother to go to you with the light of the Gospel?

Having said that, I wish to make it very clear that I am not here to make a merely emotional appeal. I do not want everyone to take off for the jungle in search of an unreached 'Indian'. In fact, I would even say, "Don't go!", unless you are sure that is God's will for your life. Transcultural work is very hard and should not be attempted on the basis of an emotional appeal, nor because of a romantic idea—rather it should be based on an unshakable certainty as to God's specific will for your life. There is no emotion or romantic idea that can stand up to the rude reality.

People, we must take seriously the challenge of the unreached ethnic nations. But as soon as we do we will be confronted by several implications. Before considering them let us take up the third question.

How does one Make Disciples?

The first step is to be a disciple. Bear in mind what has already been offered on this subject. The rest is summed up in Matthew 28:20, "teaching them to keep everything that I have commanded you". To disciple involves **teaching**. Teaching what? Teaching to "keep", that is **obey**. Obey what? Obey **everything** that Jesus commanded. Since we cannot obey rules that we do not know about, it is necessary to start by teaching the commands—like Paul did, teaching "the whole counsel of God" (Acts 20:27).

Do you suppose that is what happens in most of our churches? Is it not mainly evangelistic messages that one hears? But evangelistic preaching is virtually useless for a believer. What is he supposed to do, get saved all over again every Sunday? Here is a believer who has gone to church every Sunday for twenty years; next week he goes again and what does he hear? For the thousandth time he hears how to be saved. But he is already saved. That message is of no use to him; he came in hungry and goes out the same way. What a tragedy! Goat food is no good for sheep! (I am using the metaphors we find in Matthew 25:33.) In spite of that, if there are 300 sheep and three goats in a church service, you guessed it! The preaching is aimed at the three goats. If there are 300 sheep and no goats—the preaching is for the goats that are not there! Is that not the way it is? My dear friends, **goat food is no good for sheep**. However, sheep food is also good for goats. If the preacher serves up a delicious three course dinner any goats present just may decide that they would like to eat too! Don't you think? But the main thing is that the sheep be well fed. After all, the objective is to make disciples, and that is the emphasis that should predominate in our church services.

Up to here I have presupposed that the Bible is available in the language of the people. In order to teach the Scriptures they must exist. When Jesus said in John 8:31, "if you continue in my word you are really my disciples", of necessity He was presupposing the existence of that Word. How can you remain in something that does not exist? The point is, it must exist **for the person**; the individual must have effective access to the Word. So, if God sends you to one of the 4,000 ethnic nations that are completely without Scripture, how are you going to proceed?

Even if you think that all you need to do is evangelize, how can you speak with authority if there is no Scripture in their language? Would you not be forgetting the truth expressed in Romans 10:17? "Faith comes by hearing and hearing by the **Word of God**." But if you win a few converts even so, where is the food for those newborn babies? How are they going to become disciples? If someone does not furnish God's Word in that language those new believers will be condemned to perpetual babyhood. Is that what you want, to condemn a people to perpetual babyhood? God forbid!

Among Christ's commands there is not any that tells us to translate the Bible. But there is the Great Commission that tells us to make disciples, and if we understand that it is impossible to be a disciple of His without effective access to His Word then furnishing that Word becomes a logical necessity. We cannot fulfill the Great Commission with reference to the 4,000 Bibleless tribes until someone translates the necessary Scripture into their languages.

Where the Bible exists but there are illiterate believers, we need to set up literacy courses in our churches so that each one will be able to meditate upon the Word at home. I believe there is a close analogy between the physical and spiritual realms in the area of nutrition. Can you imagine eating only on Sundays? Who could survive physically on that basis? Can they be healthy and strong? A believer who can read and has a Bible goes hungry because he chooses to—he could read and meditate upon the Word at home. An illiterate believer is stuck, unless someone reads to him out loud, personally or via a recording. But in that event how can he **study** the Word and meditate upon it at his own convenience? It seems clear to me that the best option is to help people to learn how to read for themselves, whenever possible. I know that some missiologists will disagree with the emphasis I am giving to literacy and reading, especially with reference to peoples whose languages were unwritten until recently and who are used to doing all communication orally. I respect their right to disagree but for all the reasons already given I maintain the position herein presented. Let us work at enabling and encouraging everyone to meditate upon the Word at home, daily.

When it comes to transcultural work, I believe that we will succeed in making disciples only if we respect the language and culture of the people—like Jesus did. He incarnated

Himself in the language and culture of the Jews of that time (John 1:14). On the day of Pentecost the Holy Spirit respected the mother tongue of each person present to the extent that He worked a miracle to guarantee that each one heard the message in his own language (Acts 2:4-11). As long as a missionary does not embrace the language and culture of the people, and (more important still) as long as the Word of God does not exist in that language, the Gospel is condemned to remain something foreign, something on the outside. Should not every ambassador of Christ be concerned to make his ministry as efficient as possible?

It is not difficult to encounter those who do a lot of their ministering by means of interpreters. But I ask you to reflect on the following question: is it possible to make disciples through an interpreter? Whoever uses an interpreter has no way of verifying or rectifying the alterations that he will **invariably** introduce. Invariably. When the interpreter is a servant of Christ, is familiar with the content of the message and is completely bilingual then the communication has a reasonable chance of being adequate (although seldom as good as if the speaker controlled the language of his audience). But even with such an interpreter, if the missionary tries to disciple someone will it not actually be the interpreter who does the work? Now then, when the interpreter is not even converted the message will most certainly be distorted, often to the point of being unrecognizable. The interpreter will filter the message through his own worldview, inescapably, maybe even unconsciously. If the missionary could understand what the interpreter was really saying he would be horrified and consternated. I doubt that you can make disciples through an interpreter.

And be careful with bilingualism. Many missionaries content themselves with using a trade language even when dealing with people whose mother tongue is different. I suspect that only infrequently will one succeed in making a **disciple** through a second language (not the candidate's mother tongue), no matter how bilingual the person seems to be (to buy and sell and talk about the weather he may be fluent in the trade language), because the spiritual life of a person is almost always mediated through the mother tongue. Here I could cite various examples from my own experience. When someone is so bilingual that he virtually has two mother tongues (so to speak), or if he has reached the university level in the second language, then that second language may be adequate—in that event he will have reached the point of being able to handle abstract and philosophical ideas in that language. But such individuals are comparatively few among the 350 million people who make up the 4,000 ethnic nations that lack God's Word. Surely we should elaborate our plans and strategies so as to handle the main challenge, not the exceptions. Watch out for bilingualism!

In short, whoever takes on a transcultural work should exert himself to really learn the language and culture of the people to which he has been sent. If there is no Scripture in the language he should make sure that it becomes available. Where the Bible exists we should encourage its use, by all means. In other words, we must teach them to obey everything that Jesus commanded. And we must give the example, because in order to make disciples we ourselves must **be** disciples. A variety of ministries have prepared detailed material and instructions on discipleship. These may be obtained from any evangelical bookstore.

Implications

In closing this chapter I would like to comment on some of its implications. First, your understanding of this command and strategy of Christ will determine your procedure, the way you go about your work, of necessity. If someone wishes to build a shanty, he will use appropriate materials and procedure. If someone else wishes to build a twenty-story building, the procedure and materials must be quite different. It is evident that not everyone is competent to build a skyscraper—it requires adequate training. Likewise, not everyone is competent to feed the sheep. When a pastor works eight hours a day in a secular activity will he have the time and energy to fix good meals? It seems to me that this question needs to be studied. If we are going to take the discipleship strategy seriously we may well find it necessary to modify our lifestyle. To make disciples is one thing; to merely win souls is another.

Please, do not misunderstand me! I am not against winning souls; I am not against evangelism. Obviously we must win souls—you cannot grow up until you are born! We run into difficulties when that is all we do, when we do not rear our children. Nor am I belittling the gift of an evangelist. If you have this gift, thanks be to God! I would only like to suggest that as you exercise your gift you take care not to leave a trail of abandoned children. You should team up with those who have the gift of teaching so that together you may do a better job.

When I emphasize the 2,000 unreached ethnic nations, or the 4,000 languages without a verse of Scripture, it is not to suggest that everyone should try to go to another people, absolutely not. I imagine that if every believer were equally available to God He would not send more than 10% to other nations. In the first place, transcultural work is very difficult and not everyone has the capacity to do it. In the second place, someone has to stay and make disciples around here. In the third place, pioneer transcultural work is a full time job and the laborers who take it on will need full financial support—someone has to work to produce that support. Not everyone should 'go', but everyone is obligated by Christ's Great Commission. We all must intercede, give, inform and encourage. All that we do should be on behalf of Christ's Kingdom here on earth.

Again I say, not everyone should do transcultural work, but **everyone should be a disciple and make disciples**, each in the place and capacity that God may determine. I understand that Jesus wants His disciples operating in all honest areas and professions of our society—being and making. Anyone can put on the mask of a 'saint' at church, on Sundays, but to reflect God's character in the market place during the week, that is another story. The home-maker disciples her own children, and then the women and children in her neighborhood. Teachers and students make disciples at school. Carpenters, truckers, lawyers, bankers, merchants, politicians, etc., etc., each one being a disciple and making disciples in his own sphere. I suppose that is the best way to do our evangelizing. Instead of taking a 'goat' to church to be evangelized we should win him first and then take the new 'lamb' to church to be fed and discipled (as a supplement to our own efforts). I believe that the ministry of the Word in our churches should be for the benefit of the sheep!

To conclude, Christ's command and strategy is to make disciples, not just win souls. <u>Children don't work; they make work</u>! On the basis of all we have seen, I say again that it is indispensable that the missionary candidate be a genuine disciple of Jesus Christ. Otherwise he is sure to fail. But even more important, if possible, is the following area: he must know how to conduct spiritual warfare, so to that we now turn ("Liberate people from the power of Satan").

LIVE FOR THE KINGDOM, NOT YOURSELF

Moving on, let us look at the words of Sovereign Jesus that we find in Luke 12:31. "Rather, seek the kingdom of God, and all these things will be added unto you." Once again Jesus is addressing His disciples. Before considering the strategic effect of this command, let us review the immediate context. This verse is part of a larger passage that goes from verse 13 to verse 48. Jesus was presenting certain basic truths when a man interrupted Him with a question of selfish interest. The Lord used it to give some sound advice to the multitude, a word for everybody. "Take heed and beware of covetous-ness, for one's life does not consist in the abundance of the things he possesses." Then He told the parable of the rich fool, who reacted to material abundance like this: "My soul, you have many goods stored up for many years; relax, eat, drink, have fun!" But God said to him, "Fool! this very night your soul will be required of you; so who will get what you have prepared?" Then Jesus concluded, "So is he who lays up treasure for himself, and is not rich toward God."

In our society there is a general lack of understanding with reference to the basic values, the fundamental principles that apply to life on this planet—everyone's life, be he a Christian or not, whether he believes or understands it or not. Here Jesus states two of those principles: first, one's life does not consist in things (verse 15—a warning against materialism); second, he who stores up treasure for himself is a fool (verse 21—by the end of the chapter we will see why). At verse 22 the Lord restricts the audience and addresses His disciples.

The Kingdom Mentality

The command that furnishes the strategy under discussion is really a summary of verses 22-34. These verses contain no less than ten commands, whether positive or negative, commands that distill a mentality, a mentality that revolves around the Kingdom of God. Please pause here and read Luke 12:22-34.

There are ten commands—"do not worry", "consider the ravens", "consider the lilies", "do not seek what you will eat or drink", "do not be anxious", "seek the Kingdom", "do not fear", "sell what you have", "give alms", "provide a treasure in heaven"—ten commands. These are **orders**, not optional points. They require a mentality that frees itself from the things and values of the world that surrounds us, a mentality that revolves around God's kingdom, that lives for it. If each evangelical believer had this mentality there would be no lack of workers to reach the world, nor would there be any lack of **money** to support them and underwrite the enterprise in general.

In verse 22 Jesus starts His comments with "therefore". He is building on the basic principles set out in verses 15-21. In verse 34 our passage ends with these words: "where your treasure is there your heart will be also." That is the big question! Where is your heart? Your heart, my friend, where is it? If it is in this world, you are to be pitied. Yes, because that means your treasure is here and this world is no place to have your treasure. "Because we brought nothing into the world and it is certain we can take nothing out" (1 Timothy 6:7). (Verse 8 continues, "having food and clothes let us be content with that".) We can send it on ahead, investing in the Kingdom, but we cannot take it with us. From the perspective of eternity, whoever thinks only in terms of the few years we spend on this earth is truly a fool.

Focusing on verse 31, we note that Jesus made a promise. He declares that "all these things" **will** be added to those who live for the Kingdom. And what are "these things"? The immediate context makes clear that they are precisely what to eat, what to drink and what to wear. That is all! Is that not strange? Jesus does not promise luxury, only the basics. I see at least two reasons for that. First, it is in accord with His own example (see Philippians 2:5-8). Beginning with the circumstances of His birth He lived among the poor; He did manual labor; He traveled the dusty roads of Palestine on foot; during the three years of His public ministry He was financially dependent on others. (All of which would seem to be the sufficient answer to the 'children of the King' philosophy. It goes like this: we are sons of God; God is King; a son of a king is a prince; a prince may reasonably expect to live in a palace and go first class, etc. Isn't that an attractive idea? Only it does not follow—Jesus is not merely **a** son of God, He is **the** Son of God, and He did not go first class in this world.)

Second, those who research such things inform us that some 50% of the people in today's world are undernourished, they have less than the basics. Another 40% have the basics, but no more. Only 10% of those who now inhabit out planet have more—they are the privileged few, in terms of material things. The logic of the situation seems to me to be obvious: of any ten workers available in God's hand, nine should be allocated among the needy. And any spokesman for Christ who sets up shop as an island of plenty in a sea of poverty is self-contradictory—Jesus did not do that. He identified with the people. He is our example. When we lived in the village in the Amazon jungle our shanty was of palm leaves, much like those of the indigenous tribe; we ate what they did, paddled a canoe, etc. We tried to identify with their situation. When in the city (Brasília) we had a modest apartment (the zoning and building codes do not allow palm leaf shanties) and we drove a car (also modest)—to work in Brasília without a car is inefficient. God may give us a comfortable situation, but He does not promise it. It is a question of context.

I imagine you are thinking of the promises made to the tither in the Old Testament. To be sure, material prosperity was promised to those who were faithful in tithing. In fact, I understand that God still blesses the tither, even though many of them seem to feel that the 90% belongs to them and how it is used is none of God's business. However, the tithe is no longer the standard. What Jesus expects of us is no longer 10%; He now expects 100%, everything! Is that not what He said in Luke 14:33? "Whoever among you does not renounce all that he has cannot be my disciple." Is not "all" 100%? Is not 100% all? I know, you are objecting. The idea seems absurd! So how about us? What are we going to eat? In short, how can we possibly give 100%? Simple, just be a slave of Jesus!

Be a Slave of Christ!

When someone asks me how I view my relationship with Jesus Christ, and if there is time to explain, I say that I am His slave. I am in good company since Paul (Romans 1:1), James (James 1:1), Peter (2 Peter 1:1) and Jude (Jude 1) said the same thing. It is a slavery that you choose because of love (see Exodus 21:1-6), love of Jesus, as a free and spontaneous act of the will. Presumably some will not like the idea of being a slave, but do not forget one little detail: everyone is a slave! It is an inherent aspect of the human condition. We are born as slaves, we live as slaves, we die as slaves. In John 8:34 the Lord Jesus declared: "Most as-suredly I say to you, whoever commits sin is a slave of sin." Apart from God the human being has no option; he is born a sinner and remains a slave of sin until he dies. "Slave of sin" is another way of saying 'slave of self'—this is what destroys us; we are self-centered (it leads us to rebel against God)—and to be a slave of 'self' is to be a slave of Satan, because the unaided, self-centered person cannot withstand him. But Jesus offers a choice. Hallelujah! The choice is not to stop being a slave, oh no! The choice is to change masters.

I became a slave of Christ on the 13th of April, 1956, when I was almost twenty-two years old. I have been a 'believer' virtually from birth—I cannot remember a time when I did not believe in the Lord Jesus. I was a believer, but I was not a disciple; I had not yet surrendered my will. Before 4/13/56 I was still ruled by my own ideas and ambitions, my own wishes and desires. I was still trying to choose my own way, to guide my own steps. I had a bad time of it! It seemed like I was always 'falling on my face'. Of course. Wherever would a twenty-year-old gain the wisdom, the knowledge, the capacity to run his own life? When and from whom could he have learned it? (Or a forty-year-old, or a sixty-year-old—do you suppose the situation improves sufficiently?) The Bible states plainly that the human being is not competent to direct his own steps (here please read Jeremiah 10:23, Proverbs 28:26, Jeremiah 17:9 and Proverbs 20:24). Before I became a slave of Jesus I was under the control of a master that lacked understanding, lacked power and lacked competence—I was really in a bad way. Now I have a Master who has all knowledge, has all power, and loves me so much He died for me. What could be better than that?

Let us see how it works. Consider the situation of a slave in Jesus' time. Did he have any rights? No. Why did a slave exist? To serve, his owner. A slave owned nothing, not even himself. It follows that the owner must meet the slave's physical needs—the slave has nothing. For over fifty years I have lived on the basis of Luke 12:22-34. For over fifty years I have not known from month to month just how much God would give me; rarely has it been the same two months in a row. Yet neither I nor my wife and children ever went hungry. I have seen a time when there were at least four knots in my shoelaces, but I have never been without shoes. In short, we have never lacked.

If the owner gives an order that involves expense (e.g. to build a house), then he must furnish the materials, etc. In other words, what the owner orders he himself has to pay for. When Jesus orders something He pays for it. In my case He ordered two master's degrees and a doctorate. They cost plenty—Jesus paid everything; I have nothing. The distance I have traveled by air would girdle the globe more than once—Jesus paid it all; I have nothing. **What Jesus orders He pays for**.

In fact, I have just one major concern in life: to understand just what my Owner wants me to do. Once I am sure, I move forward, without looking back. It is a sure thing. Can I imagine that my Master will go back on His word? Can I doubt His ability or willingness to supply my needs (Psalm 24:1)? Are there any other relevant doubts? I must confess that I find it hard to understand why so many believers refuse to be slaves (or true disciples) of Jesus, why they won't turn their lives over to Him. Can it be that they are asking the wrong question? I suppose many ask themselves, "What is it going to cost me to be a slave/disciple of Christ?" That is not the right question.

The correct question to ask is, "What will it cost me if I am **not** His slave/disciple?" Instead of thinking about what Jesus may demand, about giving up our ambitions and desires, about maybe being sent to the jungle to work with 'Indians', we should really think about the consequences of refusing to surrender our lives to Jesus. The price you pay for not living for Christ's kingdom is to lose your life. That's all it costs, just your life! Consider the words of the Lord Jesus recorded in Luke 9:24-25. Let us begin with verse 23. "If anyone desires to come after me let him deny himself, take up his cross each day and follow me. For whoever wants to save his life will lose it, but whoever loses his life for my sake, he will save it. For what will it profit a man to gain the whole world but waste or forfeit himself?" What does the Lord mean when He speaks of losing one's "life"? One does not lose one's soul for love of Christ. Nor is the reference to being killed. Rather, Jesus has in mind the life we live, the accumulated results of our living. All that I have done up to this moment plus all that I will yet do until overtaken by death or the rapture of the Church, whichever happens first—that is the "life" that is at risk (in my own case).

Let us look at our Lord's words a little more closely. There seems to be a contradiction here—if you lose, you save; if you want to save, you lose. How can it work? The following context helps us out. In verse 26 Jesus explains verses 24-25 in terms of His second coming. The parallel passage, Matthew 16:27, is clearer. "For the Son of Man is going to come in the glory of his Father, with his angels, and then he will repay each according to his deeds." Christ was thinking of the day of reckoning. In other words, "we will all stand before the judgment seat of Christ" (Romans 14:10) and "each of us will give account of himself to God" (Romans 14:12). "For we must all appear before the judgment seat of Christ, so that each one may receive his due according to what he has done while in the body, whether good or bad" (2 Corinthians 5:10). I understand that 1 Corinthians 3:11-15 is referring to the same occasion, the day of reckoning. After declaring that Jesus Christ is the only foundation, Paul speaks of different materials that one might use in building on it: "gold, silver, precious stones" or "wood, hay, straw". (Although the primary interpretation of this passage presumably has to do with the performance of teachers and leaders in the church, I believe it clearly applies to the daily life of each believer as well.) The point is, our deeds will be tested by fire. If fire has any effect upon gold or silver it is only to purify them, but its effect on hay and straw is devastating! Okay, so what?

Let us go back to the beginning. God created the human being for His glory; to reflect it and contribute to it. I suppose we may understand Psalm 19:1 and Isaiah 43:7 in this way, at least by extension. But Adam lost this capacity when he rebelled against God. For this reason the sentence that weighs against our race is that we "fall short of the glory of God" (Romans 3:23). But the Son came into the world to restore our lost potential. Ephesians 1:12 and 14 tell us that the object of the plan of salvation is "the praise of His glory" (see also 2 Corinthians 1:20). And 1 Corinthians 10:31 puts it into a **command**: "Whether you eat or drink, or whatever you do, do all to the glory of God." Now then, the point of all this is not to 'ruin' our lives, to take all the 'fun' out of them (as many seem to think). God is not being arrogant, unreasonable, too demanding. Quite the contrary—He is just trying to save us from throwing away our lives. Surely, because the glory of God is eternal (Psalm 104:31), and when I do something for His glory that something is transformed and acquires eternal value—it becomes "gold, silver, precious stones". Works done for the glory of God will go through the fire without harm. On the other hand, what is done with a view to our own ambitions and ideas is "straw". We all know what fire does to straw!

So there it is. To be a slave of Christ means to live with reference to the Kingdom; it means to do everything for the glory of God. In this way the slave "saves" his life because he will be building it with "gold and silver", which will pass through the fire at the judgment seat of Christ without loss. In contrast, the believer who refuses to be a slave of Jesus builds his life with "hay and straw", which will be consumed by the fire—and so he "loses" his life; he lived in vain; the potential that his life represented was wasted, thrown away. What a tragedy!

(I suppose there might be someone who will say: "Okay, okay! I get the point. I'm throwing away my life. So what? What business is it of yours? If I want to lose my life that's my problem!" Well, sure, that is right, it is your problem. But I wish you would consider one detail: the problem is not exclusively yours; it is not just **yours**! It also concerns the individuals who should have been reached through your life but were not. And it concerns Christ Himself who was cheated out of His right in your life.)

I conclude that every believer should live in terms of the Kingdom, should be a true disciple of Christ, should be a slave of Jesus. But I do not want to leave the impression that everyone should live just like I have (also, I have not been a perfect example of a slave or disciple; I regret to say that now and again I still rebel against my Master—I am a sinner). I imagine that God's will for many, if not most, will involve a regular salary or wage. The basic issue is our mentality. Around what does our life revolve? What are we living for? Deep down inside are we depending on God, or on the salary? And that salary, who is in charge of it?

It does not follow that everyone is supposed to be poor. Not necessarily. In fact, I would say that some people have the 'ministry' of making money. I say 'ministry' because God gives the money to be invested in the Kingdom. The names of several men come to mind who had this ministry. They were multi-millionaires. God blessed them to a remarkable extent, presumably because they had the mentality of the Kingdom. They understood that all they received was not to be wasted on themselves. They invested 90% of their profit in the cause of Christ—that was their function in the kingdom of God. The basic issue is our mentality.

To sum it up, being a slave of Jesus involves unconditional surrender, a total commitment to Him. However, I can imagine that someone may be thinking: "Well, that whole song and dance may work all right in areas where everyone has plenty, but here in Brazil [or wherever] it is different. Here we are in the middle of a serious economic crisis, and furthermore most of the evangelical believers in this country are really poor." This question deserves careful evaluation.

Are We Too Poor?

Can we say that we are too poor? Is obeying the commands of Christ the exclusive privilege of the rich? How about the first believers, there in Jerusalem, were they rich or poor? It would appear that the vast majority were poor; so much so that the few well-to-do were selling their property to feed the rest. (That is what gave rise to the case of Ananias and Sapphira [Acts 4:32-5:11].) They evidently did not want to leave Jerusalem, in spite of the Lord's words recorded in Luke 24:49 and Acts 1:8. So God Himself sent the persecutions to disperse them. And they scattered, preaching as they went, poor though they were.

In 2 Corinthians 8:1-5 we find an account that is very much to the point. Those Macedonian believers were very poor ("extreme poverty"). Furthermore, they were experiencing a "severe test of affliction". Even so, they insisted on giving. From verse 4 it almost seems that Paul felt a bit embarrassed about asking them to give—they needed help themselves! But they insisted; they wanted to give. And they gave more than they properly could ("beyond their ability"). But how was that possible? They had the mentality of the Kingdom—in verse 5 we read that "**first** they gave themselves to the Lord". And they must have understood the secret of God's economy, as described in 2 Corinthians 9:8. Before looking at that secret I would like to take up the question of **our** poverty as we contemplate a world perishing without Christ.

One thinks of the feeding of the five thousand (Mark 6:31-44, Matthew 14:13-21, Luke 9:10-17, John 6:1-13). Jesus tried to get away from the crowds, going by boat to an isolated spot. But someone figured it out and the crowd ran along the shore and got there first. As always, He was moved with compassion, because they were like sheep without a shepherd. So He went to teaching them, the whole day. Finally the disciples stepped up and urged Him to dismiss the crowd; it was getting late, and there was no source of food nearby. Do you remember the Lord's response to their initiative? "**You** give them something to eat!" Have you ever thought about that? Really? Then please tell me, what with? Just how could the disciples obey that command?

Let us pause and recall the scene. The Sacred Text affirms that there were about five thousand men, **without counting the women and children**. Now then, whenever you see a crowd of people, what is there usually the most of—is it not women and children? In other words, I suppose that crowd was made up of at least 15,000 people. Okay, now try to imagine that you are one of those twelve disciples and you have just heard the Master say: "**You** feed them!" Now what? Did the disciples have anything? As a matter of fact, no. They had neither money (which would not have helped much since they were a long way from town) nor food. Even the five loaves and two fish belonged to somebody else.

Can it be that Jesus was playing a joke on them, or was He serious? I don't know, but I prefer to think that He would not make a joke out of such a situation. But if He was serious, how could the disciples obey? Only with a miracle. In fact, they could not see a solution and gave the problem back to Jesus to solve; which He did. But did Jesus Himself hand the bread and fish to the crowd? No. Let us think about that scene a little more and we will see that the disciples still had to exercise faith.

The Record affirms that they all ate until they were "full" or "satisfied". It was not just a little something to tide them over. Have you ever considered how much bread and fish it would take to fill 15,000 people (who had gone without lunch)? It seems to me certain that when Jesus blessed and broke those loaves and fish there was not an instant multiplication such that there was enough for everybody; the tremendous pile would have buried Jesus, the disciples and the closest of the people! Really. Just stop and think about it. It must not have been instantaneous. When Jesus placed some bread and fish in the hands of each disciple that is all there was, up to that moment.

Now then, try to imagine that you are one of those disciples with a handful of bread and fish, and you have to feed at least a thousand people (12 disciples and 15,000 people). Can you picture it? Wouldn't you feel just a little ridiculous taking that first step toward the crowd? Somehow the disciples find the courage and approach the people. The first one helps himself and, wonder of wonders, the supply is undiminished! The second one helps himself and the supply is unchanged. It was never used up—as they went around distributing the food kept multiplying. If they had tired and stopped in the middle, half the people would have stayed hungry. If the disciples had decided to eat first, I rather imagine that the miracle would have been frustrated and the crowd would have gone hungry. The disciples ate last but they ate very well, thank you very much! (Have you ever tried eating a bushel of bread?)

I tend to chuckle as I imagine that scene, until I remember that the Lord Jesus is still saying to us: "**You** give them something to eat!"—only this time we face some 2,000 ethnic nations and 3 billion people that are perishing for lack of the Bread of Life. And we, like the disciples of old, tend to say, "What with, Lord?" As long as we look at our empty hands we will not find the courage to accept the challenge of reaching the lost world. But it does not depend on our empty hands, it depends on **Jesus'** full hands! It does not depend on our weakness and smallness, it depends on Jesus, on His power and wealth. We must learn how to cooperate with God, and really do it. In short, we need to understand how God's economy operates.

God's Economy

All of chapters 8 and 9 of 2 Corinthians deal with money, in one way or another. But the description of how God's economy operates begins at 9:6. This verse enunciates a fundamental principle that has global application. "Whoever sows sparingly will also reap sparingly, and whoever sows bountifully will also reap bountifully."

Any farmer understands that. If he only plants a few beans that is all he will get. If he wants more he has to plant more. Any businessman will also understand it. If he wants money he has to invest it. But there is one detail that can be quite bothersome—we must plant first, and reap later. It is better to tighten your belt than to eat the seed, no matter how hungry you are. Is it not obvious? If you eat the seed you will not have anything to plant, and if you plant nothing you reap nothing!

In the Creator's goodness nature is often quite generous. I suppose corn is the champion. We usually plant three or four kernels in a hill, but suppose we just plant one. If that grain germinates we get one stalk. That stalk should produce two good ears (a third ear will likely be a nubbin). Now then, have you ever counted the number of kernels on an ear of corn? I have. A poor ear may have 300 kernels. A good ear will have around 500. A **super** ear can have up to 800! Let us suppose our stalk gives us two good ears—we planted one kernel and got back 1,000! Is that not a deal? Even beans that only give us several dozen to one are a deal. That is God's way.

As already noted the context is financial, and verse 7 makes clear that when the author speaks of planting and harvesting he wants us to apply the principle to giving. "God loves a cheerful giver." I believe the following conclusion is beyond reasonable doubt: whoever gives nothing receives nothing. Maybe that is why many believers, including those in 'full-time Christian service', often seem to be in a financial bind. They do not give; they never contribute. Luke 6:38 shows the reaction of men, and Proverbs 3:9-10 that of God when someone gives.

And now for the 'secret'; it is in verse 8. "Further, God is powerful to make all grace abound to you so that, always having all sufficiency in everything, you may abound to every good work" (2 Corinthians 9:8). Let us consider the meaning with care. It is **God** who is powerful, not us. He it is who will cause to abound, not we ourselves. And what He causes to abound to us is "all grace". The grace in view here is the grace of giving (as in 2 Corinthians 8:1, "the grace of God given to the churches of Macedonia", which was precisely the grace to give, even beyond their means). Now the Text piles up emphatic words: "always, all, sufficiency, everything, abound, every." All that emphasis serves to guarantee two results: we ourselves should always have enough (at least), and we should be a significant channel of blessing to others. Let us see how it works.

I understand that it is as follows. God wants us to be channels, conduits through which He can send a flow of blessings, both material and spiritual, to others. Much of what we receive may not be intended for our own use—it has another address and we are supposed to pass the blessing along (the precise address must be discerned through the Spirit). When we get the point and cooperate with God, He sends more. The more sensitive and faithful we are, the more God sends, an ever increasing flow of blessings. But if God sends a blessing, suppose a sum of money, that has another destination and we choose not to understand, decide not to cooperate, if we retain it for ourselves we become like a water pipe that corrodes shut. (Now a plugged pipe is a sad thing; it has lost its reason for being.) With that the flow of God's grace through our lives is staunched, because He stops sending it. Sure. Why should God keep on sending if we will not let it pass? Can it be that our churches are full of 'plugged pipes'?

When we cooperate with God, He gains, the others gain, and we gain. But whoever holds back or abstains will be cheating himself, others and even God. Consider verses 9-14. Verse 9 is a quote from Psalm 112:9, bearing on the last clause of verse 8. Now verses 10 and 11: "He who supplies seed to the sower and bread for food will supply and multiply your seed and increase the fruits of your righteousness, you being enriched in everything for all generosity, which produces thanksgiving to God through us." This is marvelous! God even gives the seed to be planted, and lest we eat the seed He also gives us bread to eat. He wants us to plant, He wants to see fruit! When we are faithful and cooperate, then God not only meets our needs but augments our planting; in other words, He increases our generosity, or at least He will do so to the extent that we cooperate with His purpose. As a reasonable and proper consequence of this process God receives what He deserves: the beneficiaries give praise and thanks to Him.

Verse 12 and 13 elaborate on this aspect. When we line ourselves up with God's economy He receives the glory due Him, the needs of the saints are supplied, and we are blessed. First, the people who receive the benefits from our ministry will pray for us, and certainly God will listen to those prayers. Next, even if they do not pray, our obedience will receive the effects of God's faithfulness. This we know, not only from the promises and affirmations in this passage, but as an inference from God's own interests—a faithful and useful 'water pipe' must not die of hunger.

So there it is, my friends. God is no man's debtor. That is worth repeating: **God will not be anybody's debtor**! We are too small; He will not allow Himself to be in debt to the likes of us. We may rest assured: whoever gives much, receives much; whoever gives little, receives little; whoever gives nothing, . . . It seems to me that this principle, much like the tithe, works even when one's motivation is selfish or self-serving. However, I trust that the reader will agree that my whole appeal has been against selfishness. It is because of the "mercies of God" that we should present our lives as a "living sacrifice" (Romans 12:1). It is the privilege and pleasure of participating in God's grace that should motivate us to give. I believe it is fair to say that our prosperity is in our own hands, at least in part (unfortunately it is also true that we may suffer because of others' disobedience, just as they may suffer because of ours). What is more, the financial condition of the missionary enterprise is also in our hands. If we cooperate with God there will be no lack of money to support the missionaries that He is calling, as well as underwrite every other aspect of the work.

The 'Faith Promise Offering'

There is a procedure that is widely used in our day to raise money for missions called 'faith promise giving'. I understand it to be a specific application of the truth given in 2 Corinthians 9:8. I will use the example of a local church, though it will work for an individual (or a whole denomination, for that matter) as well. (Some years ago I expounded this procedure in a church and only one man took up the challenge—soon he, all by himself, was giving more to missions than the rest of the church put together.) The principle applies irrespective of the size of the group. Here is how it works.

The church organizes a missions conference—once a year, presumably (the procedure would work without the conference, but it is good for informing, challenging and generating interest). Each person is urged to seek God's face and ask, "Lord, how much do You want to send to missions through me during this year?" Let us go slowly to make sure we understand the idea. Notice first that we are asking what **God** is going to send. It is not a question of trying to squeeze a spare dime out of an inadequate income. Nor are we to take away from our tithe or other commitments that exist with our church or other agencies of God's Kingdom. I would go further—it is not even a matter of modifying our domestic budget or lifestyle, necessarily (though we need to ask ourselves if we are wasting God's resources). No, the idea is to see what **God** is going to do. He will supply in surprising, even miraculous ways. But when He does, that money is sacred, it is for missions! (Please do not eat the 'seed'.)

Okay. So each one makes his agreement with God. Then all are asked to put the amount (in monthly or yearly terms) on a slip of paper and these are collected. These slips of paper are not legally binding —they are a 'faith promise'. They are a statement of what we believe God will do during the year. The statements are collected and added up so the church can have a general idea of how much should come in for missions that year. In this way existing commitments to missionaries and ministries can be renewed, added to, or whatever. Evidently such commitments will also be by faith and all concerned should understand what is involved.

I have suggested that the 'faith promise offering' is a specific application of the truth in 2 Corinthians 9:8, but I see one difference. In God's economy as described above, the initiative lies with the Holy Spirit and it is up to us to be alert and sensitive to discern when to pass on a blessing. With the 'faith promise offering' we deliberately seek God's face with a view to a specific proposal in advance, which may also include the beneficiary. It so happens that it works, and with tremendous results. By now there must be thousands of churches that use this procedure.

At times, when a church first hears about this, the leaders are quite dubious. They figure it must be some kind of 'con' game and that any money given to missions will in fact be subtracted from the regular giving to the church. However, as it is reiterated that the idea is not to re-route normal church giving but to see God bring in extra money from other sources, sometimes they agree to put the idea to the test. When a church does decide to give it a try the result is usually as follows. All the money promised by faith for missions does indeed come in during the twelve-month period. The regular budget of the church actually improves. If they are in a building program it moves faster than expected. The attendance increases. In short, God blesses that church. Examples abound.

I wish to emphasize that this principle works even if a people is poor. In 1975 I was at the missions conference of the Peoples Church, Toronto, Canada (that was the year they broke the million dollar barrier). One of the speakers was an evangelical leader from Liberia and he recounted what happened when his people decided to put into practice the faith promise offering for missions. His people live in the interior in a semi-desert region where life is difficult. They are very poor. With tears coursing down his face he told us that they had just given the equivalent of $8,000 to missions in one year. Can you imagine it? A people who live in poverty, but whose God is **GREAT**.

Just consider what we could do if each believer gave only 1% of his income for missions; but there are churches that do much more. Some years ago I heard of a church in the Philippines (recall that the economic situation there is not good). At that time they had 500 members and supported 50 missionaries. On average each ten members supported one missionary. It can be done!

What do you say, folks? We have the necessary resources, both human and financial. What is lacking is commitment to the Cause; what is lacking is the mentality of the Kingdom. If all evangelical believers would really start living for Christ we would take the world by storm. Shall we go for it?

The Accounting

Before bringing this chapter to a close I wish to return to Luke 12. Our discussion of the 'Kingdom mentality' stopped at verse 34, but the Lord's discourse continues and we need to consider verses 35-48. They relate to our subject. Without stopping, apparently, Jesus started to speak of His return, the second coming—note especially verses 35-36 and 40. Then Peter asks if that word (verse 40) was just for them, or for everybody. For reply the Lord says that whoever receives a stewardship is a steward, and must give an accounting for what was entrusted to him. Then in verse 46 He proffers this dire warning—the irresponsible steward will be assigned a place among the **unbelievers**!

Now consider verses 47 and 48: "The servant who knew his master's will yet neither got ready nor acted according to that will shall be beaten with many blows, but one who did not know, albeit doing something deserving of blows, will be beaten with few. From everyone who has been given much, much will be demanded; . . ." We are looking at the accounting, the judgment seat of Christ. It is important to notice that this word is addressed to His disciples, and even more specifically to Peter, being an answer to his question. It is the **servant** who knew and did not obey that will be punished with many blows. (I do not know what form those "blows" will take, but it may be related to the pain and loss of seeing one's life burned up—recall what has already been said about the cost of not being a slave of Jesus.)

The servant who knew and did not do, . . . And what about us, my friends, what about us? Do we not know the will of our Master? Does our Bible not contain Matthew 28:19, Mark 16:15 or Acts 1:8? Have we never heard of Christ's commands? Is 'the Great Commission' a strange expression to our ears? Whatever are we going to do when we face the accounting, when Jesus queries us about the unreached ethnic nations, when He asks us why half the people in the world continue to die without having heard the Gospel? How will we explain our omission, our terrible irresponsibility? What can we say?

We need to consider that our 'stewardship' is very great. The Word of God has existed in English for centuries. More evangelical literature and tools for Bible study exist in English than any other language. We have more people with theological training than any other culture, etc. 2 Peter 3:12 speaks of "hastening the coming" of the day of God. The point is, we have choice, we have will. Our choices have value; they make a difference. We actually can speed up the return of Christ—it follows, of necessity, that we can also slow it down (within the limits imposed by God's sovereignty). That is why there is an accounting. That is why Jesus is going to require the investment/stewardship that our life represents, namely all that we are and have.

One more thing. God has placed in our hands an unprecedented technology. Is this without purpose? I doubt it. God is not in the habit of engaging in random activity. I gather that it is this generation that has the privilege, and responsibility, of fulfilling the Great Commission, of finishing what remains to do before Christ comes again. If the generation of the Apostles, being few in number and with limited resources, managed to reach its world, why can't we reach **our** world in this generation? We are so many! We have so much!

My father traveled by horseback in the Bolivian hinterland searching out the settlers scattered in the jungle. On one of those trips he got sick—he barely made it to the humble dwelling of a young couple 'lost' in the forest. He fell into his hammock and was delirious for two weeks, with a high fever. The couple kept him alive with tea and broth. Finally word reached the town where we lived and an army truck went out to pick him up—he arrived home a month late. Thirty years later his son also traveled about the Amazon jungle, looking for indigenous peoples—only I used an airplane and carried a two-way radio (I have also traveled by canoe and on foot, but that is another story). I also got sick on one of those trips. I turned on the radio transmitter and informed my colleagues in the city, asking for prayer (just that was a real comfort that my father did not have—I was no longer alone). When it did not please the Lord to heal me I called for the plane and a few hours later was on my way to the city and medical resources. What a difference thirty years made! Today missionaries are taking laptop computers and cell phones to the jungle. We have satellites, television, etc., etc.

Considering the Kingdom mentality one more time, I would like to make an appeal. My dear people, let us exorcise the spirit of denominationalism that is endemic among us. I understand that differing denominations can be useful, and even necessary, for practical reasons. If I want to give a new convert a complete bath while someone else only wants to wet his head, it can be awkward for both of us to minister under the same roof. We might well choose different roofs precisely to preserve the peace and not be quarreling over a detail that is not a condition for salvation. But that should not keep us from cooperating in the basic task, the fulfilling of Christ's commands. Rather than acting as if we have a corner on the truth and fighting among ourselves, let us concentrate our fire against the enemy of our souls. In the face of a lost world we need to join forces—no denomination has what it takes to finish the job alone. When we think of the ethnic nations that have never been reached and the difficulties inherent in transcultural work, a common effort is imposed upon us. Such a common effort will include the specialized entities that God has raised up to make available to the churches the requisite experience, know-how and infrastructures that they lack (and would take many years to acquire). Such entities should be considered as an extension of the churches, not as 'competition'. We can respect each other, recognize a variety of convictions about secondary points and still join hands to take on a world without Christ. May God help us.

In order for us to finish reaching the whole world and fulfill Christ's Great Commission we are basically lacking but one thing, **the mentality of the Kingdom**!

LIBERATE PEOPLE FROM THE POWER OF SATAN[1]

Now let us consider the words of the Lord Jesus that we find in Acts 26:18. Words of Jesus in Acts 26? Yes, for Paul is recounting, years afterward, the encounter he had with Him on the road to Damascus. Here is his story:

> 13 At midday, O king, as I was on the road, I saw a light from heaven brighter than the sun, blazing around me and those traveling with me.
> 14 Well we all fell to the ground and I heard a voice speaking to me and saying in the Hebrew language: "Saul, Saul, why are you persecuting me? It is hard for you to kick against the goads."
> 15 So I said, "Who are you, Lord?" And he said, "I am Jesus, whom you are persecuting.
> 16 Now get up and stand on your feet; because I have appeared to you for this purpose, to appoint you a servant and a witness both of the things you have seen and of the things I will reveal to you,
> 17 delivering you from 'the people' and from the ethnic nations, to which I am sending you:
> 18 to open their eyes, so as to bring them back from darkness into light and from the authority of Satan to God, so that they may receive forgiveness of sins and an inheritance among those who are sanctified, by the faith into me."

Of specific interest to us here is the missionary commission that Paul (he was still Saul) received. I think it is worth mentioning that this commission was given somewhat after the others that have already been discussed. Matthew 28:19, Mark 16:15 and Acts 1:8 took place between the resurrection and the ascension, but to commission Paul Jesus returned from Heaven! One other detail deserves special notice—the responsibility that Paul received was pri-

---

[1] This is a chapter taken from a book on the missionary strategies of Christ. It was first written and published in Portuguese; the translation into English is only now being published.

marily concerned with the nations ("Gentiles" is a translation of the same word that in Matthew 28:19 is rendered "nations", and should be understood as 'ethnic nations'). For these reasons it seems to me that this missionary commission takes on a special importance for us, and the more so for whoever is going to do transcultural work. So let us consider this commission in more detail.

Paul's Missionary Commission

Paul is sent to the nations (defined ethnically), "to open their eyes, so as to bring them back from darkness into light and from the authority of Satan to God, so that they may receive forgiveness of sins and an inheritance among those who are sanctified by the faith into Me." Let us visualize the structure of the verse so as to understand more clearly the effect of this command:

I rendered the second verb as 'bring back' rather than 'turn' or 'convert' because I take that to be the correct nuance of the Text. It gives the impression that someone is in the wrong place or situation and needs to be returned to the correct one. And now for the main point: the purpose clause introduced by the conjunction 'so that' is subordinated to the verbal phrase dominated by the verb 'bring back'. In other words, before someone can receive forgiveness of sins, even, he must be freed from the power of Satan! Were you aware of that? Well, there it is. Before a person can be saved someone must do something about Satan's influence upon him.

But I am getting ahead of myself; we need to start at the beginning, "to open their eyes". If their eyes are shut, they are blind. What good is light to a blind person? It should be obvious that the glorified Jesus was not saying that all Gentiles were physically blind; He was referring to spiritual blindness. In Matthew 15:14 He referred to blind guides leading blind people, and He was not speaking of physical blindness, except as an illustration of the spiritual. In Romans 2:19 Paul refers to the spiritually blind. In 2 Corinthians 3:14 he refers to that blindness as a 'veil'. In 2 Corinthians 4:4 Paul spells it out.

In verse 3 he refers to the Gospel being hidden from those who are perishing, or wasting themselves, and then proceeds: "among whom the god of this age has blinded the minds of the unbelieving, so that the light of the Gospel of the glory of Christ, who is the image of God, should not dawn on them." The Text clearly states that Satan, 'the god of this world', is in the business of blinding the minds of unbelievers when they hear the Gospel, so they will not understand, so they will not be convicted, so they will not repent and convert. This is a terrible truth. The enemy has access to our minds, access in the sense that he has the power or ability to invade them, whether by introducing thoughts or by jamming our reasoning. The Lord Jesus had already declared this truth previously, when He explained the parable of the sower. "These are the ones by the wayside where the word is sown; but, as soon as they hear it Satan comes and takes away the word that was planted in their hearts" (Mark 4:15). In the parallel passage in Luke 8:12 Jesus adds the following words: "lest they believe and be saved". Note that the Word is already in the mind or heart of the person, but then Satan comes, invades the mind and 'takes away' that word. I am not sure just how this intrusion by the enemy works, perhaps he causes a mental block of some sort, but the practical effect is that the Word becomes ineffective, as if the person had not even heard it.

It seems obvious to me that whoever does not take this truth into account will be condemning himself to produce little effect in the spiritual realm, to work hard and achieve little. So how can we open people's eyes? We must deal with the cause of the blindness, we must free them from the power of Satan, we must do something about Satan's influence upon them.

The Lord Jesus had already said the same thing in different words during His earthly ministry. We find it in Mark 3:27. "No one can plunder the strong man's goods, invading his house, unless he first binds the strong man; then he may plunder his house." I have used the definite article with the first occurrence of 'strong man' because the Greek text has it, the point being that this particular strong man has already been introduced in the immediate context. "The strong man" here is Satan. (The Jewish leaders tried to explain Jesus' authority over the demons by saying that He expelled them by the power of Beelzebub, prince of the demons. In His retort Jesus doesn't waste time with that name but uses the enemy's proper name, Satan.)

So then, the Lord Jesus declares that it is impossible to steal Satan's goods unless we bind him first. (From His use of "no one" it seems clear that the Lord is enunciating a general principle or truth.) And what might the nature of those "goods" be? In the context (see Matthew 12:22-24) Jesus had delivered someone from a demon that caused blindness and dumbness, and in their comments the scribes and Pharisees include other instances where Jesus had expelled demons—it seems clear that the "goods" are people who are subject to Satan's power, in one way or another. Thus we have the same essential truth as that declared in Acts 26:18—we have to do something about Satan's power over a person so that he or she can be saved![1] So just what

---

[1] I have been asked why Paul himself is not recorded to have done this; and if this is so important why were not the other Apostles told as well. I would say that the other Apostles were indeed told, and three of the Gospels mention it (Matthew 12:29, Mark 3:27, Luke 11:21-2). As for Paul, he did not merely preach and teach, he gave visible demonstrations of God's power (1 Thessalonians 1:5). The first recorded example of his procedure is in Acts 13:6-12. Elymas was presumably demonized, but in any case was being used by Satan to keep Sergius Paulus from the truth. Paul discerned what was involved and took appropriate action, with the result that the proconsul believed, "when he **saw** what had been done". That this was not an isolated case may be seen from Acts 14:3, 16:18, 19:11-20, 2 Corinthians 12:12 and especially Romans 15:18-19. Paul declares that he made the Gentiles obedient "by word and **deed**", "by mighty signs and wonders, by the power of the Spirit of God", and on that basis he claimed to have "fully preached the Gospel of Christ". Which leads to the question of how the other Apostles understood their commission.

Paul did not share with them the advantage of observing the three years of Jesus' ministry at close range. Christ's preaching was inextricably mixed with His healing the sick and expelling demons. He knew exactly what was involved (cf. Luke 13:16). When He sent them out two by two His orders were explicit: "As you go, preach, . . . heal the sick, cleanse lepers, expel demons" (Matthew 10:7-8; cf. Mark 6:7-13 and Luke 9:1-6). In Mark 16:15-18 healing and expelling are expressly included in the Great Commission (I am prepared to demonstrate that verses 9-20 are of

can or should we do? Since the point of handcuffs ('bind') is to keep someone from acting, I believe that in so many words, aloud or in thought, we must forbid Satan (who will usually be using demons) from interfering in the minds of our hearers, before we witness, preach or teach. Consider what Sovereign Jesus said in Luke 10:19.

"Take note, I am giving[1] you the authority to trample on snakes and scorpions, and over all the power of the enemy, and nothing at all may harm you." In Matthew 28:18 Sovereign Jesus affirms that He holds "all authority in heaven and on earth", so He is clearly competent to delegate some of that authority to us. Now then, just how does "authority over all the power of the enemy" work, in practice? Authori-

---

necessity the original ending of Mark, and therefore Scripture), and verse 20 affirms that the Lord confirmed their preaching "through the accompanying signs". Hebrews 2:4 repeats that their ministry was characterized by "signs, wonders and various miracles". The Apostles demonstrated the truth of John 14:12, where Jesus affirmed: "he who believes into me, the works that I do he will do also". The Gospel as preached by Jesus and His Apostles was with word and **deed**, miraculous deed, supernatural deed. How about the Gospel we preach?

I wonder sometimes if we evangelicals do not regard the Apostles, especially Paul, as virtually divine. Scripture makes clear that the OT writers did not understand the full implications of what they wrote. They were kept from error while writing, but not when interpreting to themselves what they had written. I see no reason for supposing that the NT writers were treated differently. The Sacred Text itself records some of their failures. Why should we assume that Paul and the others had a full grasp of the complete range of options for spiritual warfare? Certainly no detailed procedure or technique is spelled out in the Bible. Why not? I suggest the following. This area of truth is so powerful that if an infallible procedure had been spelled out in an unmistakable way, Satan and his angels would have been wiped out long since. But that would have frustrated the purpose of God in allowing them to continue in operation even though defeated and with their final destination defined. Also, it seems to be God's purpose that our walk with Him not be easy or automatic—He is a rewarder of those who "**diligently** seek" Him (Hebrews 11:6). Further, to wield the power of God is a demanding privilege; it requires clean hands and a pure heart (James 4:8), it demands humility (James 4:6). God does not give up His secrets to the lazy and uncommitted (Proverbs 25:2).

[1] Instead of 'am giving', perhaps 2.5% of the Greek manuscripts, of objectively inferior quality, have 'have given' (as in NIV, NASB, LB, TEV, etc.)—a serious error. Jesus said this perhaps five months before His death and resurrection, addressing the seventy (not just the twelve). The Lord is talking about the future, not the past; a future that includes us!

ty controls power, but since we have access to God's limitless power (Ephesians 3:20), we should not give Satan the satisfaction of our using his (and he could easily deceive us into doing things we shouldn't). We should use our authority to forbid the use of Satan's power, with reference to specific situations—in my experience, we must be specific. (I have tried binding Satan once for all until the end of the world, but it does not work; presumably because God's plan calls for the enemy's continued activity in this world. We can limit what the enemy does, but not put him completely out of business, or so I deem.) But just how should we go about it?

In the armor described in Ephesians 6 we find "the sword of the Spirit" (verse 17). A sword is a weapon for offense, although it is also used for defense. The Text tells us that this sword is "the rhma of God"—rhma, not logoj. It is God's Word spoken, or applied. Really, what good is a sword left in its sheath? However marvelous our Sword may be (Hebrews 4:12), to produce effect it must come out of the scabbard. The Word needs to be spoken, or written—applied in a specific way.

In the Bible we have many examples where people brought the power of God into action by speaking. Our world began with a creative word from God—spoken (Genesis, 1:3, 6, 9, 11, 14, 20, 24, 26; and see Hebrews 11:3). Moses did a lot of speaking. Elijah spoke (1 Kings 17:1, 18:36, 2 Kings 1:10). Elisha spoke (2 Kings 2:14, 21, 24; 4:16, 43; 6:19). Jesus did a great deal of speaking. Ananias spoke (Acts 9:17). Peter spoke (Acts 9:34, 40). Paul spoke (Acts 13:11; 14:3, 10; 16:18; 20:10; 28:8). In short, we need to speak!

The Strategic Effect

It seems obvious to me that whoever does not take this truth into account will be condemning himself to produce little effect in the spiritual realm, to work hard and achieve little. And is that not exactly what we see? We preach, we evangelize, we speak and do so much, and yet the results are usually sparse, especially the lasting ones. So much so that we easily become discouraged and think of quitting. Is that not so? But my friend, before preaching or talking did you take the trouble to forbid the enemy's interference in the thoughts of your hearer? If not, what do you expect? It was Jesus Himself, God the Son here in this world, who made it clear that we must bind Satan in order to be able to remove people from his 'house'. We must bind Satan so as to avoid his interference in the minds of those who are being evangelized, as also those who are being taught. (I will explain how to bind Satan later when I discuss the weapons that are at our disposal.) Now then, this 'coin' has two sides: our efficiency and our success depend upon our binding the enemy; but if we **do not** bind him we become his accomplices, because by permitting his interference without doing anything about it we cooperate with him! Can you imagine that? Actually, I suspect that few have in fact so imagined since these truths receive little or no mention in our churches, institutes and seminaries, at least so far. But really, people, the time has come, don't you think?

I went to the Amazon jungle in 1963 in order to begin our ministry among the Apurinã people (along the Purus River in the state of Amazonas, Brazil). So far as I know I was the first one to challenge Satan's dominion over that people, a total domination down through the centuries. My basic purpose in being there was to see if I could remove that people from Satan's house and take them to Jesus' house, if I could transfer them from the kingdom of darkness to the kingdom of light. But unfortunately, in spite of a Master of Theology degree and having read the Bible through several times, I was not aware of these truths. I got clobbered! I got it without mercy, until I had had enough. Satan wiped the floor with me. He did not think that my idea was the least bit funny, and I did not know how to defend myself—actually, I did not really understand what was happening. You see, I was skeptical about the activity of the demons. Oh yes, I knew that Satan and the demons exist, because the Bible is clear and emphatic on that score, but I knew very little about how they operate and virtually nothing about the use of our weapons, whether for defense or offense. My theological background, both formal and informal, was strictly 'traditional'—casting out demons and things of that sort was 'pentecostal'. My professors transmitted the idea that a servant of Christ was untouchable or exempt from demonic attack; that sort of thing would not be a problem for us.

Anyhow, I got clobbered. First, my wife and I were attacked—in the mind, in the body. Second, being skeptical on the subject I was not able to hide my skepticism. Such peoples have to deal with demons; that relationship is central to their culture. Since they know that the demons both exist and attack them in various ways, as in fact they do indeed exist and attack, my skepticism disqualified me. I was there proposing to teach them about spiritual truth, about supernatural things, but was obviously ignorant about the central reality of their existence. I lost my credibility. Third, in consequence (of my skepticism and ignorance) I was unable to help or liberate them, giving proofs of Christ's power and therefore of the value of the Gospel, while I was still learning the language and culture (which takes several years).

Fourth, when you finally control the language and culture to the point where you can explain about Jesus—what He is like, what He did, what He taught—then, sooner or later, you will say that He expelled demons and cured the effects of their activity. At last you said something that the people really want to know. (As I have already explained, they 'worship' the demons out of necessity, not because they enjoy it, because they do not know of any benevolent power great enough to free them.) Now you have their attention and can expect this query: "Jesus has power over the demons?!" At this point you have a choice: are you going to say that Jesus **has** power, or that He **had** it? What are you going to affirm? I imagine that you would say, "Yes, He has!" Right? Only at that point a demon will challenge you to your face, attacking someone in the village. So now what do you do? You do not know how to cast out demons, you are skeptical about such things, and yet you affirm that Jesus **has** power over them. If you do not know how to impose the victory and power of Christ in that hour, if you cannot **prove** that Jesus is greater, then you were just beating your gums. You will be demoralized. You lied! Worse yet, Jesus is demoralized too! Of course—you are His only spokesman in that place and if you cannot demonstrate His power the people will certainly conclude that He does not have such power. Any doubt about that? Well, I got clobbered. I weep when I think on the little that I achieved among the Apurinã people, on behalf of Christ's kingdom, compared with what I could and should have achieved had I understood this missionary strategy of Christ: free the peoples from the power of Satan.

And that is not all. The great majority of the missionaries actually working (and that have already worked) among the animistic peoples of the world are skeptical about these things, like I was. Sadly, our missionary organizations have not concerned themselves about this matter, as a rule. The missionaries are out there suffering, as I did, producing much less effect than they could produce. What a tragedy! What a waste, in every sense of the term! The strategic importance of this matter is tremendous. If one day we reach the point of sending out workers who are adequately prepared in this area and of having churches full of people who know how to conduct spiritual warfare, then we will finish reaching the world. (Even the Islamic world, which I believe to be the most difficult challenge that we face, should be reachable in this way, because they too are troubled by demons.) There is another consequence that is even worse: **evangelical syncretism**.

As evangelicals we do not mind commenting on the syncretism that often follows the Roman Catholic Church, but no one says anything about the syncretism that follows our missionaries. Well, it exists. In June of 1992 I learned of the situation in an indigenous group in the state of Rondônia, Brazil. Missionaries had been there for over 35 years and there had been believers and a church for at least 25. However, to that day, when the villagers performed their ceremonies to pacify the demons the believers also participated (all of them). Since the missionaries did not offer a solution for demonization the believers found themselves obliged to resort to the ancient rites—evangelical syncretism. That is not an isolated case; it is routine!

In April of 1991 I listened to Mark Bubek, author of *The Adversary* and several sequels. He had just returned from Africa where he had addressed a conference of African pastors. The topic had been spiritual warfare. He related that after the standard greetings he started out more or less like this: "My brothers, I am here to ask your forgiveness. In the name of all the American missionaries who came here and preached a Gospel that did not give you a solution to the demons, and so you felt obliged to resort to syncretism, I am here to ask your forgiveness." As one man the 300 African pastors stood up and applauded, for several minutes. Pastor Bubek wept as he spoke, and I wept as I listened. Africa, Asia, Latin America, indeed the world, are full of **evangelical syncretism.**

We have yet to comment upon the last phrase of Paul's commission, "a place among those who are sanctified". I would say that the primary reference of this phrase is to final sanctification, our position in Christ. It happens, however, that it could easily refer to our experience as well, because what Satan and the demons do has a definite influence on our spiritual life and on the effectiveness of our ministry, as well as on our life in general. My how the enemy messes up our lives, spoils our homes, dilutes our efficiency in the work! If we would convince ourselves about the extent of this activity and learn how to handle the spiritual weapons that Christ gives us we could simply transform our lives, our homes and our ministries. The majority of the people that God calls to transcultural mission are defeated by Satan right here—they never get to the field. Of the few, relatively speaking, who do get to the mission field half are removed from the running within four years—they return defeated to their home countries, and never venture out again. Such have been the statistics of modern missions, but I sincerely believe that we can improve the picture dramatically. All we have to do is get serious about this missionary strategy of Christ: liberate people from the power of Satan. It is absolutely necessary that we recognize that **we are at war**.

The Spiritual War

We are in a war whose sphere is universal and which provides the context from which everything we do derives its deepest importance. In Luke 11:23 Sovereign Jesus said: "Whoever is not for me is against me; and whoever does not gather with me scatters". Jesus does not allow neutrality—you are either for or against, one or the other. Either we are gathering or else we are scattering and therefore there is no neutral ground. We may grant that a given object is presumably neutral in itself, but the **use** that we make of it will not be neutral. At the deepest level we either do things with a view to God's kingdom and glory or we do them for some other reason, and be that other reason what it may, it will serve the interests of the enemy. "Whoever does not gather with me, scatters." It follows that everything we do is invested with importance. Even the ordinary things that we usually do without thinking have consequences in the spiritual realm. We are at war, whether we know it or not and whether we like it or not.

We can state the problem more precisely. Not only are we at war, we are on the front line. That is to say, there is lead flying around on all sides. To walk around on a field of battle without taking due precaution is simply stupid, too stupid; it is to guarantee that you will be hit. The more so when we are precisely the ones who are in the enemy's sights because we belong to Jesus.

One of the principal passages on the spiritual war is Ephesians 6:10-19.

> 10 Finally, my brethren, be strong in the Lord and in the power of his might.
> 11 Put on the whole armor of God, so that you may be able to stand against the wiles of the devil.
> 12 For we do not wrestle against flesh and blood, but against the principalities, against the powers, against the world-rulers of the darkness of this age, against wicked spirits in the heavenlies.

13 Therefore put on the whole armor of God, so that you may be able to stand firm in the evil day, and having done all, to stand.

14 Stand therefore, having girded your waist with truth, having put on the breastplate of righteousness,

15 and having shod your feet with the preparation of the gospel of peace;

16 above all, taking the shield of faith with which you will be able to quench all the fiery darts of the wicked one.

17 And take the helmet of salvation, and the sword of the Spirit, which is the word of God;

18 praying always with all prayer and supplication in the Spirit, being watchful to this end with all perseverance and supplication for all the saints;

19 and for me, . . .

It states plainly that our fight is not against people ("flesh and blood") but against evil spirit beings that are organized in a hierarchy, a veritable army. It speaks of "the wiles of **the devil**"; it speaks of "the fiery darts of **the wicked one**". But I wish to call attention to a crucial detail in verse 12. "Wrestle" is actually a noun in the Greek text, "our wrestling match"—now as you know, wrestling is a very physical, direct, even violent sport. The whole idea is to pin your opponent to the mat! So if you find yourself in a match and do not know how to fight you will certainly be thrown, inescapably. As often as you try to get up you will be thrown down, until you learn. Now then, the Apostle Paul, inspired by the Holy Spirit, writing to believers and including himself ("our"), declares that we are in a wrestling match with evil spirits. We, believers. This means that we are attacked by demons every day, attacked and hit—unless you know how to protect yourself. So, do you know how? Most Christians do not, and are constantly defeated—they have never received adequate orientation on the subject. It is urgent that we know the enemy, but first I want to mention another factor.

The Guarantee of the Strategy

In Hebrews 2:14 we find the truth that renders this strategy viable. "Since, then, the children partake of flesh and blood, he also himself [Jehovah the Son] likewise shared in the same things so that through his death he might destroy the one who had the power of death, that is, the devil." Why did Jesus die? To destroy Satan! Did you know that? Well it is true, and He succeeded! Hallelujah! Colossians 2:15, Ephesians 1:20-22 and John 16:11 speak of the defeat suffered by Satan and his angels, the demons. That is why we read that he "had" the power of death (Hebrews was written after Christ's victory). In Revelation 1:18 the glorified Jesus declares: "I <u>have</u> the keys of Death and Hades". Jesus won! It is Christ's victory that guarantees this strategy and makes it viable. We can, yes we can, liberate people from the power of Satan! Shall we go for it? On the way we will be well advised to know the enemy and understand how he operates.

Who Is the Enemy?

It is of interest to any military commander to know as much as possible about the enemy, including about the opposing commander. **The** enemy is Satan. In 1 Peter 5:8 he is expressly stated to be our adversary. "Be sober, be vigilant, because the devil, your adversary, goes about like a roaring lion seeking whom he may devour." Please note that this word is addressed to believers—we must keep vigilant at all times because Satan is prowling around us just waiting for any carelessness on our part.

As a matter of fact the Bible says a great deal about our enemy. Satan "deceives the whole world" (Revelation 12:9), he presents himself as "an angel of light" (2 Corinthians 11:14), he is "the tempter" (1 Thessalonians 3:5), "the accuser" (Revelation 12:10), "the prince of the power of the air" (Ephesians 2:2), "the god of this age" (2 Corinthians 4:4), "the ruler of this world" (John 12:31, 16:11). 1 John 5:19 informs us that "the whole world lies in the wicked one", as though the world is in Satan's arms or on his lap, a graphic figure that speaks of the massive control or influence that he exercises over this world.

The Bible says so much about Satan and the demons, and the Lord Jesus was so clear in His teaching about them, that I cannot understand those Christians, including pastors and theology professors, who affirm that they do not believe in the existence of such beings. If someone wishes to present himself as a follower of Jesus, and all the more so if it be as His **representative**, he should receive what He taught. Otherwise he should be consistent and present himself as a humanist, a marxist or whatever. A warning needs to be sounded at this point: God's people need to be on their guard against the wolves in sheep's clothing (Matthew 7:15) that infiltrate our churches, beginning with our theological seminaries. This strategy must be dear to the enemy's heart for it has certainly paid off handsomely. "And no wonder, for Satan himself masquerades as an angel of light" (2 Corinthians 11:14).

His Origin

But who is this Satan? Where did he come from? What is his nature or essence? I believe there are two passages that answer these questions, Isaiah 14:12-15 and Ezekiel 28:12-17. The word in Isaiah is directed against "the king of Babylon" while the word in Ezekiel is against "the king of Tyre". But it happens that the language in both passages becomes such that it cannot be referring to a mere man, no matter what kingdom he ruled. The tenth chapter of Daniel makes perfectly clear that angelic beings are presented as kings and princes of kingdoms and peoples of this world. "The prince of the kingdom of Persia" (Daniel 10:13) has to be a high ranking demon because a mere man would not even know that there was an angel nearby and certainly would not be able to hinder him. (That particular demon was of such high rank that it took the archangel Michael to overcome him so that the first angel could get through to Daniel. Since Persia was the most important empire in the world at that time, it seems logical to me to assume that Satan would entrust his interests in that kingdom to one of his most important lieutenants, say a four star general.) Verse 13 also refers to "the kings of Persia". In verse 20 the angel states that besides the "prince of Persia" he will also have to fight the "prince of Greece". In verse 21 Michael is presented as "your prince"—that is to say, of the people of Israel.

Now let us look at Ezekiel 28. The lament concerning the "king of Tyre" takes up verses 11-19, but it is verses 12-17 that are of special interest for our present purpose:

> *12 Son of man, take up a lament upon the king of Tyre and say unto him: Thus says the Lord GOD: You were the model of perfection, full of wisdom and perfect in beauty.*
>
> *13 You were in Eden, the garden of God; every precious stone was your covering: sardius, topaz and diamond, beryl, onyx and jasper, sapphire, emerald and carbuncle, and gold; the workmanship of your settings and mountings was prepared in you on the day that you were created.*
>
> *14 You were the anointed cherub that covers, for so I established you; you were on the holy mountain of God; you walked among the stones of fire.*
>
> *15 You were perfect in your ways from the day that you were created till iniquity was found in you.*
>
> *16 Through your widespread trade you were filled with violence, and you sinned; therefore I will cast you out of the mountain of God as profane, and I will expel you, O covering cherub, from among the stones of fire.*
>
> *17 Your heart was lifted up because of your beauty; you have corrupted your wisdom on account of your splendor; I cast you to the earth, I made a spectacle of you before kings.*

It is clear that such statements cannot refer to the man who was sitting on the throne of Tyre when Ezekiel penned these words. The personage described was "in Eden"; he had his beauty and perfection "from the day that he was created"; he was the "anointed cherub" and had a very high position and function in Heaven. His position was so high that one day he decided that it was not enough; he became filled with pride and resolved to supplant the very Creator. The account is in Isaiah 14.

The prophecy against "the king of Babylon" occupies verses 4-23, but let us confine our attention to verses 12-15 for the moment:

> *12 How you have fallen from heaven, O morning star, son of the dawn! How you have been cast down to the earth, you who weakened the nations!*
>
> *13 For you said in your heart: "I will ascend to heaven; I will exalt my throne above the stars of God; I will sit upon*

the mount of the congregation, in the utmost heights of the north;

14 I will ascend above the heights of the clouds; I will be like the Most High."

15 But you shall be brought down to Sheol, to the depths of the Abyss.

The personage we are discussing was called "morning star" (in Hebrew). (That name was translated into Latin as "Lucifer" and came down to us in that form. But "Lucifer" is a has-been. That name refers to what the enemy used to be before his fall. God's people should no longer refer to him by that name—now he is "**the** devil", or else, Satan.) His crime was that he determined to become "like the Most High". Obviously he did not succeed. How could a created being ever overpower his own creator? He will be "brought down to hell". We are informed in Matthew 25:41 that the Lake of Fire has been prepared precisely for Satan and his angels.

His Fall

Judging from the language of both passages, Ezekiel 28 and Isaiah 14, it appears that the being we now know as Satan was created as the first in the hierarchy of the angelic hosts. He was the most intelligent, the most powerful and probably the most beautiful. His was the highest office among created beings, sort of like God's prime minister. The only One greater than he was the Creator Himself. One day he resolved to usurp the place of the Creator. (There are those who have wondered if it was not the creation of the human being, who is essentially superior to the angelic being, that filled Lucifer with jealousy and spite and lead him to rebel.) He evidently convinced about a third of the original angels (Revelation 12:4) to join his cause. It is hard to understand how such an intelligent being could attempt something so stupid, but he did, and he lost. Lucifer became Satan, the enemy, the leader of the opposition to God (an opposition completely underhanded and perverse). The angels that followed him became the demons, evil spirits who are now active on this earth. We do not know how many there are, but since the number of angels that remained faithful to the Creator is greater than one hundred million (Revelation 5:11) the demons must number **at least** fifty million. What a calamity!

And so what? Well, I would have imagined that when he was defeated and deposed from his functions in Heaven—he still has access before the Throne of God (Job 2:1, Revelation 12:10)—Satan would have been demoted, have lost his rank; he would no longer be the first in the hierarchy of angelic beings. Unfortunately such imaginings are unfounded. Consider verse 9 of Jude (Jude is one of five books that have only one chapter). "Even Michael, the archangel, when he was contending with the devil about Moses' corpse, did not dare to bring a slanderous accusation against him, but said: The Lord rebuke you!" What a strange account! I confess that to this day I have not found a satisfactory explanation for this scene: the two highest ranking angels of the original creation quarreling over a corpse, even if it was **Moses'** corpse! It is truly a perplexing picture. I conclude that Michael, who took over the office once held by Lucifer and now leads God's faithful angels (Revelation 12:7), must have been second in the original angelic hierarchy and remained faithful to the Creator when Lucifer rebelled. However that may be, there are Satan and Michael contending over a corpse. As already stated, I would have thought that Michael would now be greater than Satan, that he could easily overpower him, but no! Instead of ordering Satan off the premises; instead of saying something like—"Get lost, you rascal, I don't even want to see your ugly face!"—he had to be content with saying, "The Lord rebuke you!" Michael was not in a position to impose his will on Satan; he could not say, "I rebuke you". (Now then, what Michael could not do, we can—I will tell that story in a bit.) In other words, Lucifer was created greater than Michael and **continues** to be greater, even though he is now Satan. I am obliged to conclude that Satan did **not** lose his rank. And neither did the other fallen angels—he who was a general, still is; he who was a colonel, still is; he who was a major, still is, and so on. That is why Ephesians 6:12 speaks of "principalities, powers and rulers" and Ephesians 1:21 speaks of "principality, authority, power and dominion"—it is the hierarchy of the officers in the army of the fallen angels. Apparently the fallen angels lost none of their original capabilities, aside from exchanging a predisposition toward good for one toward evil. Because now they are malevolent, perverse, terrible.

Consequences for Us

So what? What does all this have to do with transcultural missions? It has everything to do with it. Please recall what has already been said about Paul's commission, about Acts 1:8, Mark 3:27, 2 Corinthians 4:4 and Mark 4:15. When you try to snatch a people, or a person, from the power of Satan all you have to face is the most powerful, the most intelligent and now the most malevolent created being in the universe! That is all. Whoever confronts a wild animal without recognizing and respecting the danger that it represents, without knowing how to proceed so as to overpower it, will certainly get the worst of the encounter (as I did!).

I believe this is the place to examine a question that is frequently raised. Why does not God protect His servants? For example, why did He permit that I should be clobbered so much? Well, we have to understand the rules of the game. When He created a type of being capable of making choices, God had to accept the consequences of the choices they would make, as also to oblige them to take those consequences. (Unfortunately we must suffer the consequences not only of our own choices but of those made by others as well. Our life is spent victimizing and being victimized.) God cannot and will not perform a continuous miracle so as to protect me from the consequences of my own ignorance, the more so since it is culpable. The Bible furnishes the basic information that we need to know about the spiritual war. If I close my eyes, if I do not pay attention to the Sacred Text, if I attach more value to my religious culture than to the Word of God, then I must suffer. I deserve it! Why would or should God protect me? In order to encourage my blindness, my stupidity, my idolatry? Not much! As a matter of fact, I understand that God permitted my defeat precisely to get my attention, to make me open my eyes and research the subject. What you are reading is the result, what I have learned so far.

Another question comes to the fore. What about Christ's victory? Was Satan not defeated? Yes he was, completely (Colossians 2:15). So, how come he is still such a threat to us? For His own sovereign reasons (which He has not explained) God permits that Satan and the demons continue their activity in this world, even though they have been defeated and their final destination defined. They are bluffing, pretending that nothing happened. ('Bluffing' is not really satisfactory because the enemy still has his power; perhaps 'impostor' or 'usurper' would come closer. Satan is now a false pretender to the throne of this world.) It is up to us to call their bluff. It is up to us to oblige them to respect Christ's victory. As long as no one calls his bluff the enemy keeps on 'winning'.

It is time to wake up, folks. It is time to take appropriate action, people. It is time to stop suffering unnecessarily! To that end we need an adequate understanding of how the enemy operates.

How do Satan and the Demons Operate?

Let us go directly to the Sacred Text. We will begin with Luke 9:18-22:

> 18 It came to pass that as He was alone praying His disciples came to Him, and He asked them, saying, "Who do the multitudes say that I am?"
> 19 Answering they said, "John the Baptist; others say, Elijah; still others say that one of the ancient prophets has resurrected."
> 20 He said to them, "But you, who do you say that I am?" Peter answered and said, "The Christ of God."
> 21 Warning them He ordered them not to tell anyone, saying,
> 22 "It is necessary that the Son of man should suffer many things, that he be rejected by the elders, the chief priests and the scribes, that he be killed and that he rise from the dead on the third day."

I wish to call attention to the grammatical structure of this passage. Note the present participles: 'answering', 'warning' and 'saying'. The effect of this structure is to signal continuous action. Verses 18-22 contain a single conversation. Having registered this fact let us move to the parallel passage in Matthew 16:13-23, which gives us some more detail. Rather than transcribe the whole thing I will just comment on the added details. In verse 16 Peter answers, "You are the Christ, the Son of the Living God", to which He responds, "You are blessed, Simon, son of Jonah, because it was not flesh and blood that revealed this to you but my Father who is in Heaven" (verse 17). Skipping to verse 21 we have Jesus' declaration that He must suffer and die. With that Peter began to rebuke Him: "Far be it from you, Lord; this shall never happen to you!" (verse 22). To which initiative Jesus answered, "Get behind me, Satan! . . ." (verse 23).

Well, that scares me; that sends shivers up my spine. Within three minutes, or five at the most (we saw in Luke that this was a single conversation), Peter spoke two times. The first time it was God who put the words in Peter's mouth. It was Jesus Christ, God the Son on earth, who explained the true nature of the transaction—Peter did not speak on his own but moved by the Father. So far so good; that God can do something like that comes as no surprise. It is the second time that is bothersome because this time it was Satan who put the words in Peter's mouth! Again, it is Jesus Christ, God the Son on earth, who explains the true nature of the transaction. When He uses the enemy's proper name, Satan, His meaning is inescapable. It really was Satan. Once again we are face to face with the most terrible truth that there is in this life, at least as I see it. The enemy has access to our minds, he can put words in our mouths. I wish in the worst way that it was not true, but my wishes do not change reality.

They Attack our Minds

When I finally awakened to this truth I began to understand several things that used to happen to me. More than once I would be talking with someone, a serious conversation about the things of God, when all of a sudden words would come from my mouth that were simply unacceptable, words that destroyed the situation. As soon as I had spoken I knew it was bad, but it was too late; the other person would turn his back and leave. I was left dismayed and perplexed. How could I say something like that? Note well, it was not something I had been thinking about, that had been in my mind; no, I became aware of it only after I had spoken. For years I never found an answer, I could not figure out what happened to me, but now I know. Some demon put those words in my mouth, and since I did not realize such a thing was possible I fell into the trap. Now that no longer happens to me. Now I know how to defend myself.

I know. You do not like this idea, you do not want to accept it. Let us go slowly. Maybe you yourself never experienced anything like I just described but perhaps you have observed the following. It is routine, you can virtually count on it; in any meeting where the progress of the work is being handled (be it of the deacons, elders or trustees; of the board of a mission or a school; of a presbytery, synod or conference; in short, be it a small or large gathering) you can observe the following. Everything is going well, the blessed communion of the saints seems to be functioning, when all of a sudden someone says something he shouldn't, gratuitously, to no good purpose. The climate of the meeting is ruined; you may as well go home for all the constructive progress that will now be made. Have you never seen that happen? I bet you have; it is routine. You can even call that person aside, after the meeting, and ask: "Tell me, please, why did you ever say that?" And if he is sincere, as he often is, he may answer something like this: "To be perfectly frank with you, I don't know!" And it will be the truth, for he was simply an instrument in the hand of the enemy— a demon put those words in his mouth, and that was it!

Some 30 years ago a certain young pastor was taking a linguistics and missiology course in Brazil (I was the academic director). About the second week I observed that he was walking with his head down, apparently very discouraged. So I asked if anything was wrong and if I could help. His answer went something like this: "Oh Dr. Wilbur, you know that I am a university student, that I have always enjoyed studying, have always gotten good grades. But since I came here it seems like my head is full of cotton—I can't retain anything; during a whole lecture I can't take a single note; if there is a pop quiz I hand in a blank piece of paper. It is no good, I've had it; I am going home." Whereat I said, "It seems to me that you are being demonized; you have a mental block caused by a demon. But we have 'medicine' for that sort of thing, so here goes!" Right there on the sidewalk I rebuked that demonic interference in the authority of Christ, also forbidding any recurrence. From then on he was able to study normally, caught up and finished with good grades. That sort of interference in our minds is very common. Have you ever wondered why your mind went blank while you were taking a test, or standing in the pulpit?

Nor should we forget the "sifting" that Peter suffered (Luke 22:31). As a direct result of that satanic invasion in his mind Peter reached the point of denying the Lord Jesus, in fact the first time was right in front of John (John 18:16-17)! (The difference between Peter and Judas was that Jesus prayed for Peter—Luke 22:32.)

Against prayer

You still do not like it? You are still resisting the idea? Then let us think about prayer. Please tell me, when you set yourself to pray, to intercede, to really seek God's face (let us say when you plan to spend at least fifteen minutes), does everything go well? Are you able to concentrate your thoughts in prayer without problem? I bet not. Don't your thoughts wander? All of a sudden you think of a conversation you had, about an unfinished job, about something that happened six months ago—no? Let us analyze this together. Your thoughts were concentrated on God, right? You did not have idle thoughts that were free to go looking for those things. So where did they come from? Is it not obvious? It was demonic interference in your mind. Those extraneous thoughts do not have to be dirty or vile—if our thoughts are diverted away from prayer then the enemy has achieved his objective.

We need to understand something else about prayer. As soon as we start to pray we enter the spiritual sphere and with that the enemy gets busy. It is primarily in prayer that we wage spiritual war and the enemy feels a direct threat. So he goes into immediate action to distract us. You can put this down: no one remains alone when he prays—the moment you begin to pray in a serious way you will be 'covered' or opposed by at least one demon (depending on how dangerous the enemy thinks you are). This opposition may take various forms. If it is not extraneous thoughts it is sleepiness. (When I was a boy we had a sure cure for insomnia. If I could not sleep my mother would say, "Just pray and you will go right to sleep". Sure enough! I would start praying and in a few minutes I was snoring. Counting sheep isn't in it.) If it is not sleepiness it is discouragement, or your mind goes blank or you feel fear. A homemaker finds a few moments and kneels to pray, and guess what happens. The telephone has not rung for a week but now it will not stop. She has not had any visitors for the longest time but at that exact moment the doorbell sounds. The children were playing quietly but all of a sudden a loud fight breaks out. If there are any dogs in the neighborhood they all start barking. Is that not so? Remarkable, don't you think? We are at war, friend, we are at war!

Nor should we forget the case of Daniel (Daniel 10:12-13). As a direct consequence of demonic interference the answer to his prayer was delayed for three weeks. The angels are also involved in the war and apparently it is not always easy going for them either.

Against life

The access that the enemy has to our minds can have drastic consequences. Consider the case of Ananias in Acts 5. Let us review the context. "The multitude of those who believed were of one heart and one soul; neither did anyone say that any of the things he possessed was his own, but they had all things in common. . . . Nor was there anyone among them who lacked; for as many as were possessors of lands or houses sold them, and brought the proceeds of the things that were sold and laid them at the apostles' feet; and they distributed to each as anyone had need" (Acts 4:32-35). That was the situation that gave rise to the case of Ananias. Please stop here and read Acts 5:1-10.

As Peter explains, they did not have to bring anything; or they could bring half, if they wished, as long as they did not claim it was everything. Their problem was that they lied, wishing to receive credit as if they had brought the full amount. The Apostle Peter affirms that it was Satan (again the proper name is used) who placed the idea in Ananias' mind, or heart. What was the result for Ananias? Death. Right? This is really heavy, people! A little later in comes the wife: "Is that the way it was, Sapphira?" "That is right." Flop—she died on the spot! This access that the enemy has to our minds can result in physical death—recall that he "had the power of death" (Hebrews 2:14) and by bluffing (or usurping) he continues to do virtually as he pleases. I suspect that we might go into shock if we knew how many people have died as a direct result of demonic activity. But that is not the worst of it. Consider the case of Judas.

In John 13:2 we read: "Supper being ended, the devil having already put into the heart of Judas Iscariot, Simon's son, to betray him . . ." While in John 13:27 we read: "After the morsel Satan entered into him [Judas]. Then Jesus said to him, 'What you are going to do, do quickly'." (Cf. Luke 22:3.) The idea of betraying Jesus was put in Judas' heart by the devil. But at the crucial moment Satan, by name, "entered" into him, took control of him to guarantee that he would execute it. What was the result for Judas? Physical death, because a little later, overtaken by remorse (not repentance, which is different), he hanged himself. What further result did he receive? Spiritual death, because while praying to His own Father Jesus said, "Those whom you gave me I have kept, and none of them is lost except the son of perdition, that the Scripture might be fulfilled" (John 17:12). Note also Matthew 26:24: "The Son of man goes as it is written of him, but woe to that man by whom the Son of man is betrayed! It would have been good for that man if he had not been born." Judas was lost!

Too often we do not stop to really reflect upon what God caused to be written. We tend to look down on Judas, don't we? We only have bad things to say about him. But does he really deserve so much revulsion? That same night, there in the upper room, at a certain point Jesus became distressed in spirit and declared: "Most assuredly I say to you that one of you will betray me!" At that the disciples looked at each other, not knowing to whom He was referring, and in perplexity began to ask, one by one, "Lord, is it I?" "Lord, is it I?" Jesus answered, "It is one of the twelve who dips with me in the dish." Then Judas asked, "Rabbi, is it I?" To which Jesus responded, "You said it". Evidently the others were still confused because Peter signaled to John to ask who it was. So John leaned back on Jesus and asked, "Lord, who is it?" He answered, "It is the one to whom I will give the dipped morsel." Then, dipping the morsel He gave it to Judas. At that Satan entered him and Jesus said, "What you are going to do, do quickly". I must confess that what follows surprises me, because we read: "Now no one at the table knew for what reason He said this to him; because Judas was the treasurer some of them supposed that Jesus had told him, 'Buy what we need for the feast', or that he should give something to the poor." (See Matthew 26:21-25, Mark 14:18-21 and John 13:21-30.)

Frankly, that account surprises me. Recall that during two years the twelve disciples had walked together, eaten together, slept in the same place. The point is, there was no way Judas could deceive the others as to his character and personality. In church, on Sunday, we can act very pious and deceive those who only see us in that context, but those who live with us or work with us know the truth. So then, I would have expected that as soon as Jesus said, "One of you will betray me", the others would look at Judas out of the corner of their eye and say, "I knew it!" Don't you think? If Judas had been different, not of the same spirit, the others would certainly have perceived it. But the Sacred

Text is very clear: not one of the others even imagined that it could be Judas; so much so that even after Jesus had clearly declared **twice** that it was Judas, it did not register. It seems that they just could not believe that it would be Judas. I am obliged to conclude that until that day he had been an exemplary disciple, perhaps even better than some of the others. To be treasurer is a sign of confidence, isn't it? (John's editorial comment, given in 12:6, was presumably based on hindsight.) Judas was like the rest, until the day that Satan invaded him. Help!

The enemy's interference in people's minds not only can result in physical death, it can also result in spiritual death. Judas is not the only one. If it were just Judas, perhaps we could dismiss it—after all, Judas! Alas, no! We have already seen from 2 Corinthians 4:4 (also Mark 4:15 and Luke 8:12) that multitudes are going to hell as a result of Satan's interference in people's minds. (Since he is not omnipresent he works through a chain of command, using his angels, the demons.) This is a most serious matter—anything that results in the salvation of the soul, or the forfeiting of that salvation, is of maximum importance. To close our eyes to this issue is treason against our King.

Other evidences

I know, you still do not like it. Well, let us look at the Text some more. In 2 Corinthians 11:3 we are informed that "the serpent" (Satan) corrupts our minds; in the context it is the minds of **believers**. That is the interference in our thoughts. In James 3:2-12 we find a very interesting description with respect to our thesis.

> 02 In many things we all stumble. If anyone does not stumble in word the same is a perfect man, able also to bridle the whole body.
> 03 Behold, we put bits in horses' mouths so that they may obey us, and we turn their whole body.
> 04 Behold also the ships; though they are so large and are driven by fierce winds, they are turned by a very small rudder, wherever the pilot wills.
> 05 Even so the tongue is a little member and boasts great things. See how great a matter a little fire kindles!

06 The tongue also is a fire, a world of iniquity; that is how the tongue is among our members, defiling the whole body and setting on fire the whole course of our existence, being itself set on fire by hell.

07 For every kind of beast and bird, of reptile and marine animal can be tamed and has been tamed by mankind;

*08 but the **tongue** can no man tame, incorrigible evil that it is, full of deadly poison!*

09 With it we bless God, even the Father, and with it we curse men, who are made in the likeness of God.

10 Out of the same mouth proceed blessing and cursing. My brethren, these things ought not to be so.

11 Does a spring send forth from the same opening both sweet water and bitter?

12 Can a fig tree, my brethren, yield olives, or a grapevine figs? Likewise no spring can give both salt water and fresh.

We know that in nature a spring never gives both sweet and bitter water, alternately; it is not possible. But let us imagine that one day we came across such a spring: one minute the water was sweet, the next it was bitter, and so on. How could we explain such a thing? There would have to be two sources or veins feeding the spring, and they would have to meet just under the surface, taking turns. This is just what God's Word affirms happens with our mouths: first blessing and then cursing proceed from them. How can this be? In fact, the language in verses 2, 6 and 8 could strike us as peculiar—not to offend in word is to be perfect; the tongue contaminates the body and inflames the course of life; the tongue is a fire, a world of iniquity, an incorrigible evil, a deadly poison! How can we explain such language? Whatever is going on? I believe that the answer may be found at the end of verse 6.

What are we to understand when the Text says that the tongue "is set on fire by hell"? At the very least it must mean that the tongue receives its capacity or ability to inflame from "hell", and therefore owes its inflammatory activity to "hell". But who or what is "hell"? I believe this is an instance of metonymy (a figure of speech where a word is used in place of another which is intimately associated with it). With whom is hell most closely associated? With Satan, since it has been prepared precisely for him and his angels

(Matthew 25:41). I take it that this passage attributes a large share of the damage that results from the wrong use of the tongue to the activity of Satan and the demons, influencing the thinking and speaking of human beings. To be sure, we can make wrong use of our tongues all by ourselves, no doubt about it, but the language of the Text demands a further explanation. There are two sources contributing to our speech, our own will and malignant interference. Be not deceived!

When you find yourself beside a stranger on a bus, train or plane, do you find it hard to converse with him? Say about the weather, fashions, politics or sports? Well, an introvert would presumably have difficulty, but most of us have little or no trouble. But if you shift the topic of conversation and start to talk about Jesus, then what happens? Do you speak as freely as you were? As a matter of fact, no. Correct? Don't you feel fear, get nervous, your mind goes blank, your palms get clammy? Why, do you suppose? Where does that fear come from? In 2 Timothy 1:7 we read: "God has not given us a spirit of fear, but of power, of love and of self-control." It goes on to say, "therefore do not be ashamed of testifying to our Lord." The spirit of fear that attacks us when we want to witness about Christ does not come from God. The Text is clear. So where does it come from? Whose interest does it serve if we do not talk about Christ? Is it not obvious? When a believer finds it hard to talk about Jesus, instead of calling him a coward and loading him with guilt we should first rebuke the spirit of fear. Obviously we can be cowards without demonic assistance. Of course. Still, you may be sure that many times we are attacked by an evil spirit.

Then there are those terrible nightmares. Often the person feels that he is being suffocated. (Actually, 400 years ago the word 'nightmare' referred precisely to a demon that came and suffocated people while they slept.) If the demons can attack our minds while we are awake, how much more so while we are asleep and helpless (protection does exist—we must forbid any such interference before going to sleep; we can do this for others as well as for ourselves).

Besides what happens in the mind, sometimes you can feel, or even see, an evil presence in the room.

Surrounded as we are by the practice of spiritism of every sort (the criminal practices of satanists are getting more and more attention in the news media; more and more movies deal with the occult; go to the library of your local high school and just see how many books on occult practices are available to the students; the growing 'New Age' movement has significant components of spiritism; converted spiritists/ satanists declare that they have infiltrated our churches, our schools, the whole society to an alarming extent), it becomes hard to understand how there can be disciples of Jesus who still do not believe in the existence of the demons, and in their activity, including an interference in our minds. I would not be surprised if in a not too distant future almost the only people to remain skeptical about these things will be the members of certain protestant churches. What a tragedy!

The charismatic gifts

Another area where the enemy takes advantage of the access which he has to our minds is falsifying the gifts of the Spirit. The damage that he does in this area is terrible! The Lord Jesus said in John 10:10, "the thief comes only to steal and kill and destroy". Well, there is a thief in the 'sheepfold'. Alas for the wreckage! Now then, let us proceed calmly—I know that this is a controversial subject which tends to call forth more heat than light—let us proceed calmly, very calmly. I ask that the reader not jump to conclusions about my position, thereby closing his mind. Let us see if we can manage to humble ourselves before THE WORD OF GOD.

The use of the word 'falsify' necessarily implies that the genuine article exists—you cannot imitate a non-existent something. If Satan falsifies or imitates the gifts of the Spirit it is because they exist. Consider 1 Corinthians 13:8-12.

> 08 Love never fails; but as for prophecies, they will pass; as for tongues, they will cease; as for knowledge, it will pass;
> 09 for we know and prophesy only in part.

10 But when the perfect comes, then the "in part" will pass away.

11 (When I was a child I spoke like a child, I understood like a child, I thought like a child; but when I became a man I put away childish ways.)

12 For now we see in a [metal] mirror, dimly, but then face to face; now I know in part, but then I will know fully even as I am fully known.

The key to the proper interpretation of this passage is furnished by the temporal adverbs "when" and "then". To begin, we note that the reason given in verse 9 for the ceasing or passing of the gifts mentioned in verse 8 is that they are "in part". Those gifts are deficient in that they are partial, and therefore imperfect. Now let us look carefully at verse 10. **When** "the perfect" comes, **then** the "in part" will pass away. What we have to know is whether "the perfect" has already come—right?—because only then will the "in part" pass. To whom or to what might "the perfect" refer? It cannot be the completed Canon of the Bible because in that case the "in part" would refer to the Old Testament, which certainly has not "passed away" yet. Nor will it, for we read in Psalms 119:89: "Forever, O LORD, thy word is settled in heaven." (If I wanted to be difficult I would suggest that the "in part" would also include the New Testament books written before 1 Corinthians, or even before Revelation!)[1]

The solution is in verse 12. (Verse 11 is parenthetic—in the Greek text the "when" of this verse is different from that of verse 10.) Can we say that the "now" of verse 12 has al-

---

[1] Now and again one hears the argument that the expression "that which is perfect" is neuter in gender (in the Greek text), which is true, and therefore does not refer to Christ, but rather to the Canon. However, it is also true that no vocabulary item normally used to refer to the Sacred Text (like 'word', 'scripture' or even 'canon') is neuter in gender either; they all are either masculine or feminine. So by the same reasoning "that which is perfect" cannot refer to the Canon either. It is necessary to note that the opposite expression, "that which is in part", is also neuter in gender, but it refers precisely to "prophecy", "tongues" and "knowledge"—each one of which is feminine in gender! What we have is a Greek idiom—expressions like "the perfect" or "the in part" are normally in the neuter no matter what the gender of the referents. In any case, "the perfect" could refer to the whole package represented by Messiah's return to reign over this earth.

ready passed? Would any of us venture to say that he no longer sees "dimly", that he has perfect understanding? Should he dare to do so he would be contradicted by the Text, for it continues, "**Then** face to face". What is the antecedent of "then"? It is the same as that of the "then" in verse 10, namely, "when the perfect comes". So, when will we see "face to face"? When will we know fully just as we are fully known? The answer is in 1 John 3:2. "Beloved, now we are children of God; and it has not yet been revealed what we shall be, but we know that when He is revealed we shall be like Him, for we shall see Him as He is." It is when Jesus returns that we will see "face to face". Since He has not returned yet the gifts are still with us. Okay?[1]

The gifts of the Spirit exist, but to deal with them requires **discernment**. As already mentioned, God has allowed me to minister in all sorts of churches, including many that recognize the gifts. I have also visited many others. I have observed something disquieting: there is much lack of discernment in the use of the gifts. Satan's thing is to be like God (Isaiah 14:14). So then, if God gives prophecy, so does Satan; if God gives tongues, Satan does too; if God gives healing, Satan ditto. How many false prophecies there have been! How many lives have been ruined by them!

False prophecies are of two types: pre-arranged and demonic. The pre-arranged ones have nothing to do with a demon; they come from people who want to manipulate others, abusing their confidence and exploiting their lack of spiritual discernment. Such prophecies may cause some damage, but demonically inspired ones are much worse—

---

[1] One often hears or reads the affirmation that the 'miraculous' gifts ceased with the Apostles, that they were a phenomenon limited to the first century. But that is a matter of historical record. We have documents written by the early Church Fathers: one or two from the first century, a dozen or so from the second, many more from the third, even more from the fourth, etc. I invite the interested reader to check out those documents with attention. He will discover that those early Christian authors attest the presence of the miraculous charismatic gifts in the second century, in the third, in the fourth (at that point the amount of material is so large that I stopped reading). Who in our time is competent to show that all those eyewitnesses were mistaken?

they always harm their victims. Frequently they have to do with a person's private life—"Jack is to marry Jill" and things of the sort. (Many in Brazil know of the case of the leader of a certain spiritual renewal movement; he received a 'prophecy' saying that he should marry a certain sister of that church—only he was already married, as was she! They left their legitimate spouses and got married. And that was the end of a servant of Christ—he later committed suicide!) We cannot be too careful, friends. I would never accept a prophecy directed to me without checking with the Holy Spirit immediately, I myself, to know if it came from Him. Actually, I would normally expect God to tell me directly that which pertains to me. However, He might well make use of prophecy to confirm something He had already told me, or perhaps to jog me if I am not paying attention. I must say that I doubt the legitimacy of depending on a 'prophet' or 'prophetess' to receive direction for each day. Whoever has the Holy Spirit should be guided directly by Him—any believer may, and should, discern the will of God for his own life (provided he is a true disciple).

The gift of an unknown tongue (i.e. a language unknown to the one who receives it) also may be genuine or falsified. The falsified gift is of two types: feigned and demonic. In churches that teach that the gift of tongues is the **necessary** evidence of the 'baptism in the Spirit' the feigned gift is very frequent. The believers are placed under great pressure; until they speak in tongues they are second class citizens, if indeed they are citizens at all. They become distressed: "What does the Holy Spirit have against me that He won't baptize me? Why did He baptize the other person but not me? Can it be that I am not even saved, that God doesn't want me?" Many cannot stand such pressure and wind up pretending. I am a linguist; I know when someone is pretending—it is usually an endless repetition of a limited number of syllables, which almost always come from the person's mother tongue (such persons generally lack the linguistic sophistication to invent different syllables).[1]

To fake the gift solves the problem of being seen as inferior—since many others are also faking it, and since the leaders accept it, it works—but it does not solve the basic problem (the person knows that he is pretending and that the Spirit has done nothing). What is more, God never lies or accepts a lie; inevitably any lie brings spiritual harm to the liar. If this is true at the personal level, just imagine how much spiritual damage results when the whole church embraces a lie! But that doctrine (that tongues is the necessary sign of the baptism) has a more serious consequence. People become desperate and want a 'tongue' at any price, without worrying about the source (where the spiritual climate is such there seems to be little discernment, apparently, and they do not guard against the demonic 'gift'). Some people receive a real language—it has phonological and grammatical structure (and semantic too, for those who understand it)—only it is demonically inspired.

On several occasions I have witnessed the manifestation of a demonic tongue in a service—it usually comes at the climax of the message, or at some other point when God is really moving, and destroys the atmosphere—but I have yet to see the one who was directing the service rebuke that malignant interference. How can this be? (At times somebody present may have discernment, but the prevailing climate in the church is such that he lacks the courage to stand up and protest.) To deal with the gifts of the Holy Spirit demands **discernment**. Where it is lacking Satan has a picnic, he goes on a roll, and the resulting damage to the cause of Christ is incalculable.

The genuine gift also exists, without doubt, but God will never give the same gift to everybody. It seems to me that

---

[1] In answer to this some claim that the language is 'angelic' and therefore does not obey the rules of normal language. But does not that insult the angels? Surely they could do better than that pitiful sequence of sounds. And without mouths and tongues they evidently do not communicate using sound.

the Sacred Text is sufficiently clear on that score. The basic passage is in 1 Corinthians 12.

> 04 Now there are diversities of gifts, but the same Spirit.
> 05 And there are different ministries, but the same Lord.
> 06 And there are diversities of operations, but it is the same God who works all in all.
> 07 The manifestation of the Spirit is given to **each one** for profit.
> 08 For to one is given the word of wisdom, by the Spirit; to another the word of knowledge, by the same Spirit;
> 09 to another faith, by the same Spirit; to another gifts of healing, by the same Spirit;
> 10 to another the working of miracles; to another prophecy; to another discerning of spirits; to another tongues; to another the interpretation of tongues.
> 11 It is one and the very same Spirit who works all these things, distributing as He wills to each one his gift.

Frankly, the Text is quite clear: the Spirit does not give the same gift to everyone. It would not make sense. Verses 4 and 5 may suggest some connection between gift and ministry, which seems logical enough. Since we have differing ministries our gifts should correspond to them. Beginning with verse 12 the apostle uses the figure of the diverse members of a body, with their distinct functions. Can you imagine a body made up only of tongue, a tremendous, monstrous tongue? Can you? The finishing touch is supplied in verses 29-30 (1 Corinthians 12), which we may be used to reading like this: "Are all apostles? Are all prophets?" etc. As it stands a negative response is evidently called for (are you an apostle?), but the Greek text is clear; a negative response is required. We may legitimately translate as follows: "Are all apostles? No. Are all prophets? No. . . . Do all speak in tongues? No." It is a clear declaration that all do not have the same gift.

Dear people, we could avoid the excesses of both sides if we would obey the commands in 1 Corinthians 14:39 (since the Author brings the main biblical treatment, three chapters' worth, of the charismatic gifts to a close in this way, this must be His intention). "Wherefore, brethren, earnestly desire prophecy, and do not forbid speaking in tongues." One side blatantly disobeys the second command, forbidding any manifestation of tongues and even denying the existence of the gift since the apostolic age; it also disobeys the first command, since far from "desiring" the gift of prophecy (to desire it "earnestly" is out of the question) it denies its existence too. But the other side also has difficulty with these commands. Far from "not forbidding" the gift of tongues, it reaches the point of **requiring** it. Instead of desiring prophecy, or "the best gifts" (1 Corinthians 12:31), it emphasizes the least of the gifts elevating it above the others. (To say that one is being humble before God, and man, by asking for the least of the gifts will not work, because that would be disobedience to a divine order—that is not humility, it is rebellion.) Friends, our spurious polarization only helps the enemy. Let us return to the Sacred Text. Let us bow to the Word of God. The worship of our own ideas and traditions is a form of idolatry. Idolatry is idolatry!

A word about the "gift of healing". In 1 Corinthians 12:9 the Text does not say "the gift of healing" but "gifts of healings"; we might translate it "charismatic healings". I know a number of brethren through whose ministries miraculous healings occur (they really do), but I never heard tell of anyone who could heal **all**. If **the** gift of healing existed then whoever had it could heal everybody, indiscriminately. But that does not happen. (Sometimes a brother who sees miraculous cures occur through his ministry gets carried away and begins to think that all he has to do is lay on hands and pray—when nothing happens there can be various negative consequences, some quite far-reaching.) As the Sacred Text says, some people receive divine presents of healing, some more some fewer.

Since our underlying concern is missionary strategy, I do not want to pass up the command that we find in 1 Corinthians 12:31, "seek earnestly the best gifts". It is an **order** not an optional point. Do you suppose we are obeying this command? I have to say, "No". Otherwise there would not still be some 1,000 ethnic nations without a spokesman for Christ. The point is that the best gift of all is the gift of apostleship: "first, apostles; second, . . . third, . . ." (1 Corinthians 12:28). If everyone asked for the gift of apostleship then the ones that God chose would be sent to the unreached ethnic peoples of the earth. Pioneer missionary work is essentially an apostolic work. Whoever takes the Gospel to an ethnic group for the first time is the apostle of Jesus Christ to that nation. Verse 11 (1 Corinthians 12) makes clear that the Holy Spirit distributes the gifts according to His own sovereign will; we may ask (we are commanded to ask), but we will not necessarily receive it. Not everybody will be an apostle, nor should they be. However, if everyone asks, then God can make the best choices and every nation will be discipled. Now if that prospect doesn't turn you on, what will!?

They Influence Physical Objects

Returning to the subject of the enemy's activity, he not only attacks people's minds, he also attacks their bodies. Whoever reads the Bible with even a little attention will be aware of this truth. One thinks of Job. It was Satan, by name, who caused the boils all over Job's body (Job 2:7). He it was who sent Sabeans, Chaldeans, fire and wind to make an end of Job's goods and children (Job 1:12-19). Paul called his physical problem "the messenger of Satan" (2 Corinthians 12:7).[1] One day Jesus cured a woman who had "a spirit of infirmity eighteen years" and said that it was Satan who had bound her (Luke 13:11-16).

Physical problems are repeatedly linked to demonic activity: Matthew 8:16, 10:1 and 12:22; Mark 1:26, 5:2-13 and 9:17-27; Luke 6:18, 7:21 and 8:2; Acts 5:16 and 8:7, among other passages. I have personal knowledge of many cases, including in my own family. Without question there is illness that is of organic origin; a case of malaria will not be cured by trying to expel a demon. It is equally true that a

---

[1] I have been asked why Paul did not repel this satanic attack on his body. It is possible that he tried, but God was using this attack to keep Paul from getting puffed up because of the revelations he had received. He pleaded with God for relief three times, but God said no.

problem that is of demonic origin will not be solved with medicines. It is also possible to have a mixture of symptoms of both origins. One case had me going round and round for two and a half years. There was an organic problem that caused certain symptoms, but a demon complicated the issue introducing other symptoms. I would rebuke the demon but the relief was only partial; the person would take medicine and again the relief was only partial. It was necessary to move adequately on both fronts.

We really must understand that demons do indeed influence physical objects. We suffer a good deal, uselessly, when we do not pay attention to this fact. For example, it is common to have problems with the lighting or the public address system during large evangelistic meetings, which can be solved by rebuking the enemy's interference (only too often they **are not** solved because those involved do not understand what is happening). Any believer who was once a spiritist, the more so if he was a medium, can give emphatic testimony to the fact of demonic interference in objects: doors slam without wind, electric appliances work without being plugged in, objects move without visible cause, strange sound effects, etc. It is not superstition; it is plain fact. We have experienced demonic interference in a computer! (Just think about the implications of that for a minute.)

I heard the following account from a missionary who used to work with an indigenous tribe in Rondônia, Brazil. He and a colleague were in a hut less than a kilometer from the village. One afternoon a man came and said: "You had better get out of here, because tonight the shaman is going to tell the demons to make that huge tree fall on this house and kill you; run for your lives!" They thanked the man for his goodwill but decided to stay. They went to their knees and prayed all night, crying to God for protection. Near dawn there was a sudden wind storm that felled precisely that huge tree, only it fell to one side without touching the hut. The noise of the crash went reverberating through the jungle and presently the people came running to see the result. Imagine their surprise when they found the two men safe and sound! From that day onward that people began to take the Gospel seriously because they had seen proof that the power of God was greater than that of the evil spirits. Although God protected His servants, the demons did in fact fell that big tree. Since neither a warning nor specific prayer is always forthcoming we are frequently harmed. We are at war, whether we know it or like it or not. To wander on a battlefield without taking due precaution is really too stupid!

Temptation to Evil

I make a distinction between the types of interference already discussed and temptation to do evil. Those hit us directly and effectively but without our perceiving or understanding it (many times). Temptation is something that is presented to our conscious mind, as an option. If the Lord Jesus was tempted by Satan (see Matthew 4:1-11 and Luke 4:1-13), we need not think that we will escape. I am sure there is no need to belabor this point since presumably everyone recognizes that he suffers temptation. Which makes 1 Corinthians 10:13 a precious promise. "No temptation has overtaken you except such as is common to man; but God is faithful, who will not allow you to be tempted beyond what you are able, but with the temptation will also make the way of escape, that you may be able to bear it." That is to say, the way out exists, but we do not always use it.

We need to pay attention to the truth stated in James 1:13. "Let no one say when he is tempted, 'I am tempted by God', for God cannot be tempted with evil, nor does he himself tempt anyone." The Text is very clear, God **never** tempts us to do evil. So then, when we are tempted we don't need to hesitate even one second—there is no need to roll it around on your tongue or wonder if maybe it comes from God—we should reject the idea immediately, knowing that it cannot be from God and therefore must be from the enemy. It is not smart to play with fire.

Implications

If we would wake up, really and truly, to how much the demons interfere with our lives, we could simply transform them, provided we also learned how to use the weapons that the Lord Jesus puts at our disposal. However, two warnings are in order: first, not to see a demon behind every bush and under every stone; second, not to blame the enemy for everything bad that we do. Sometimes when a person wakes up to these truths he goes overboard and starts seeing demons in everything. That is not the case—there must be **discernment**. Others think they can avoid responsibility for their own sins. It will not work—we are sinners by choice and God will hold us accountable. I, all by myself, without help from anyone, am capable of thinking or doing all sorts of evil. I was born with a tendency to sin. Even in the things that we do under malignant influence we have a share of the blame and must give an accounting to God.

Still and all, having made those allowances I again insist that we are attacked in a wide variety of ways, we believers. Recall that Ephesians 6:12 says that **we** are in a wrestling match against wicked spirits. (Have you ever watched a wrestling match? Kind of physical, isn't it?) What happens out there in the world probably exceeds our wildest imaginings. The extent of demonic involvement in the suicides, the violence, the crime, the immorality, the drug scene, the homosexual scene, the rock, the pornography, etc. that characterize our society has never been told.

One other thing: we may be attacked indirectly. The enemy moves someone to write a letter, send an email or to phone and the message distresses us. We are put in a turmoil through another person and do not discern the true source of the attack. Another thing that the enemy likes to do is attack a child to get at the parents, and it works very well. If my son comes down with a strange illness this will obviously distract and preoccupy me, and my ministry will suffer; to say nothing of the time and money that are spent without result. Watch out for indirect attacks.

I have spent all this time talking about the enemy **not** in order to build him up, and much less to worship him, but so that God's people will wake up and realize the extent of the danger that we face. If you take on a tiger without respecting the danger that he represents, without knowing how it is done, you will lose. I do not know about you, but personally I am tired of 'losing'. Enough! We are indeed faced with a terrible enemy, but our Master, Jesus, has placed at our disposal weapons that are perfectly adequate, not only to defend ourselves but to impose defeat on the enemy. However, before we discuss the weapons themselves I think we will be well advised to take up a preliminary question: Why is there so much ignorance about these things in evangelical circles?

Why So Much Ignorance?

As soon as we begin to realize the implications of this subject, a question comes naturally to mind. How is it that these truths are not taught in our churches and theological schools (with a few exceptions)? Is it not strange? Thinking in terms of practical, daily effect this area of truth is virtually without equal in its direct impact on our lives. It should occupy an important place on our church menus, but instead it can scarcely be found. Why? I believe there are several factors that contribute to this situation.

The Surrounding Culture

We are influenced by our culture, which is very materialistic, skeptical of and uncomfortable with the supernatural. We have already noted that Satan exerts a strong influence on the cultures of men (1 John 5:19). I take it that materialism is one of the "sophistries" (2 Corinthians 10:5) that Satan has cooked up to keep people from coming to an adequate knowledge of the true God. (Besides Materialism there is Islam, Marxism, Hinduism, Buddhism, Animism, Humanism, Confucianism, and so on—world views all that separate men from God.) It seems clear to me that a disbelief in the very existence of the enemy is what will help him most (especially when it is on the part of those who say they are Christians). If someone does not even believe that Satan and the demons exist then they can do just as they please since the skeptic will never understand what is really happening. The enemy has a field day without opposition.

Things have taken a very serious turn in recent years. Materialistic researchers in the social 'sciences' have been studying evidences of demonic activity while rejecting the existence of anything supernatural. Since demons do indeed produce observable phenomena, such researchers ascribe the phenomena to hidden or latent powers of the human mind, subconscious, soul or whatever. In the name of 'science' they then open themselves up to demonic influence. The wedding of Spiritism with 'science' poses a most serious threat to our society.

It is nothing less than a tragedy that 'Christian' people allow themselves to be influenced by the surrounding culture to the point that they reject the clear teaching of the Word of God. In Europe and North America materialistic humanism has become virtually the state religion. It dominates the educational system at all levels. It predominates in the media—television, cinema, theater, advertising, newspapers, magazines, whatever. So I guess it is not surprising that the fundamentals of this worldview are invading and influencing our churches, though it is certainly sad. Dear people, we must open our eyes! We must wake up to the terrible danger that surrounds us. Humanism, Materialism and even Marxism are infiltrating and penetrating our churches more and more—yes, and even Spiritism in the guise of 'positive thinking', 'possibility thinking', 'visualization' and things of the sort. They are satanic sophistries that only bring harm. They may offer certain features that imitate features that belong to God's Kingdom, thereby deceiving the undiscerning and doing more damage in the end.

A False Notion of Blame

In some circles there seems to be a false notion of blame that inhibits them from talking about this. That is, they understand that demons exist and do attack people but they seem to have the idea that it is a shameful thing to be so attacked—presumably because the individual invited or facilitated the attack. The subject thus becomes impolite or embarrassing and is consequently avoided. Such a situation also favors the enemy. The victims receive no help. On the

contrary, a feeling of guilt is added to the other consequences. People are not instructed. Our defensive weapons
are not explained. In short, the enemy has things his way
almost as much as when there is unbelief.

In the numerous Gospel accounts it is never intimated that
the victims of demonic attack were to blame. They were
simply assaulted, victims of acts of violence. If you are
walking down the street and suddenly a total stranger as-
saults you, would you feel shame as if it were your fault?
There is no reason to. Even if the nature of the attack causes shame, silence favors the criminal and encourages other
attacks. To be sure, it is certainly possible to invite attack.
If you get involved with ouija boards, with horoscopes, with
seances, with rock, with things that belong to Satan, brace
yourself! You will be opening yourself up to attack. However, I believe that the great majority of the attacks that we
suffer come because we belong to Jesus and have an enemy
that hates us. However that may be, my purpose here is to
argue against silence. We must reject the taboo. We must
discuss the problem openly. We must warn and prepare
people against the danger. We must unmask the enemy and
teach people how to defend themselves.

Our Versions of the Bible Mislead Us!

Strange as it may seem, our versions of the Bible mislead
us on this subject. The noun 'demon' is simply a transitera-
tion of the Greek δαιμονιον or δαιμων. I wish they had done
the same thing with the corresponding verb, δαιμονιζω. In
that event we would have the verb 'demonize'. But no, the
translators put 'possessed' of a demon. As a result we have
tended to think of demon activity only in terms of possession. Well, so what is the problem? I suggest the following.

By 'possession' the translators presumably intended to con-
note 'control', but the more common meaning denotes
'ownership', and most people seem to take the second
meaning. This has serious consequences. First, the concept
is wrong, since demons do not and cannot 'own' human be-

ings (although a demon will often claim that its victim "belongs" to it).[1] Second, it has fostered a misunderstanding about Christians and demon 'possession'—since a believer belongs to God it is presumably impossible that a demon should own him as well. We need to stop using the word 'possessed' in this connection altogether and replace it with the more precise term 'controlled'.

Demon control certainly exists, but it represents only a small part of the enemy's activity against mankind, precisely the most extreme cases. (Although organic insanity does exist it would not surprise me to verify that most cases of insanity involve at least some demonizing.) The vast majority of the demons' attacks should not be characterized as control. There are less severe forms that are sometimes called oppression or obsession. They also cause physical problems. But I believe that the most frequent attacks interfere with our minds in less obvious ways; so much so that most of the time we are not even aware of it. I suggest that we use the term 'demonization' to refer to any and all direct interference, whether in the mind or the body. The following continuum will help us to visualize the concept:

<u>minds | bodies | obsession | oppression | control</u>

Note that I have not included temptation to evil in this continuum. What **is** included in the concept of demonization, however, encompasses a world of suffering.

Let us now consider some consequences of the translation "possessed". I am not sure how far that rendering is at fault, but 'traditional' churches and schools scarcely touch the subject; perhaps because they think only in terms of ownership and conclude that believers are exempt. Whatever the explanation, you could attend certain churches during 20 years and never hear any teaching on Satan and the demons. On the other hand, 'pentecostal' or 'charismatic'

---

[1] Within Satanism there are 'robots', people who have turned themselves over to the complete control of a demon. For practical purposes a 'robot' is owned by his demon.

churches and schools do at least deal with the subject, even if only partially. During deliverance sessions they tend to deal mainly with cases of control—is that not so? When does the leader of the service expel a demon? Only when it manifests itself—right? Someone begins to scream, foam at the mouth, roll on the ground or give some other evidence of foreign control, at which the leader confronts the demon and commands it to leave. But if the demon keeps still, what happens? Nothing, usually—nobody bothers it; its presence is not discerned. I know that some order the demons to show themselves, but do all obey? How do we know? Or if the manifestation is not of a type that we recognize as 'possession', who will identify and repel it? It seems clear to me that even in the churches where there is expulsion of demons the greater part of the enemy's activity against us goes unrecognized. They are focusing only on control.

I see another consequence that can be rather serious. When we conceive of demonic activity only in terms of ownership, and when a church teaches that a believer cannot be 'possessed', the following occurs. A believer is demonized. In terms of the continuum I am suggesting it is not a case of control, yet the person knows he is being attacked. But the only terminology he knows for talking about demonic attack is 'possession' and the church teaches that a believer cannot be 'possessed'. So the person is plunged into anguish— he knows he is saved but a believer cannot be 'possessed'; yet he is being attacked and knows it. What is the explanation and how can he escape? He cannot say anything to the church because if he admits that he is being 'possessed' then they will no longer accept him as a believer. He does not dare talk and so he cannot receive help. Even if he did talk, he would not receive adequate help because the leaders think only in terms of ownership. As a result of all that, the poor believer may even reach the point of doubting his salvation! The worst of it all is that such suffering is simply unnecessary. We must learn to speak in terms of demonization, understand that believers certainly are demonized, and explain the use of the spiritual weapons that are at our disposal.

The Idea that We Are 'Untouchable'

In many evangelical circles there exists the catastrophic notion that we are, so to speak, exempt or untouchable—i.e. that a demon may not touch a believer. Indeed, there is a verse that seems to say just that, 1 John 5:18. "We know that whoever is born of God does not sin; but he who has been born of God keeps himself, and the wicked one does not touch him." There you have it, "the wicked one does not touch him"—could anything be clearer? Well, let us slow down a bit. What might the semantic content of "touch" be here? It cannot refer to temptation to evil, because the Lord Jesus was tempted (Matthew 4:1-11) and if He could be, then obviously we can too. It cannot refer to an attack against the physical body, because the Apostle Paul was thus attacked (2 Corinthians 12:7), and if he could be, then clearly we can also. It cannot refer to interference in the mind, because the Apostle Peter suffered such interference (Matthew 16:22-23), and if he could be victimized in that way, why should we imagine that we will escape? If our verb 'touch' does not include those three things, then what is left? However, the real solution here is different.

What is the antecedent of the pronoun "him"? Just who is it that the wicked one cannot touch? The context is clear—it is "whoever is born of God". Right? Now then, are you born of God? Who among us will say that he is born of God? I will. And if you have been regenerated by the Holy Spirit, you may too. But when did it happen, when your mother gave birth to you? No. Only Jesus was born that way; He was literally begotten by God in the virgin Mary. But what about us? We are born of God the moment we are regenerated. Yet we do not lose our identity; everyone who knew us before we were born again still knows us afterwards. So then, just what is it in me that is "born of God"? It cannot include anything that I, Wilbur, was before the new birth. What then? I take it to be the new nature or 'new man' that the Holy Spirit begets in me. We cannot equate the 'new man' with the Holy Spirit, exactly, but there is a close connection between the two. So much so that in Galatians 5:17 it is "the Spirit" that fights against the flesh. That which in me is born of God is the new man, and this it is, aided by the Holy Spirit in me, that the wicked one cannot touch. It happens that I, Wilbur, am now (after conversion) a mixture of two natures and as a whole being am most certainly 'touchable'. The enemy probably attempts to attack me every day.

Our principal versions render 1 John 5:18 rather differently, offering two serious discrepancies. Where NKJV has "does not sin", NIV has "does not continue to sin". Here it is not a problem of textual variants; they are both rendering the same Greek phrase. The verb 'to sin' is a simple present indicative, but negated—the natural, normal meaning is "does not sin". So where did NIV get the verb "continue"? From their theological presuppositions. (In all fairness, they would give a different answer. They would probably tell us that the present tense in Greek has 'linear' force. Well, sometimes, up to a point; sort of like English. If I ask, "Do you drink coffee?" and you answer, "Yes I do"—what should I understand, that you continually drink coffee? Probably not; just now and again, perhaps every morning for breakfast. But if you say, "No I don't"—now what is the meaning? That you do not continually drink? No, you do not drink at all, period. Even if the present tense has linear force when <u>affirmative</u>, it does not have it when negated—negation changes the rules.) The point is, "does not touch" at the end of the verse has precisely the same grammatical form; it is a simple present indicative, negated. So NIV should have rendered "does not continue to touch", to be consistent, but of course they did not. They (and all) render, correctly, "does not touch". NKJV has it right: "does not sin" and "does not touch".

The second discrepancy does involve a textual variant, the difference of one letter—with the extra letter the relative pronoun is reflexive, without it, it is not. Thus, NKJV, following over 95% of the Greek manuscripts, reads "he who has been born of God keeps <u>himself</u>" while NIV, following a small minority of manuscripts, reads "the one who was born of God keeps him safe." In the NIV the one being kept and the one doing the keeping are two different entities. I give it as my considered opinion that the reflexive form is original (for the theory see my book, *The Identity of the New Testament Text IV*). Are we really capable of "keeping ourselves"? Is the Holy Spirit? How about the new nature, with the Holy Spirit is help?

However all that may be, Ephesians 6:12 is crystal clear. In verse 10 Paul makes very clear that he is writing to believers and in verse 12 he includes himself. "**We** wrestle . . . against . . . wicked spirits . . ." Have you ever watched a wrestling match? Pretty physical, pretty direct, isn't it? If someone is trying to wrestle you down and pin you to the floor and you do not struggle, you do not defend yourself, what happens? You get knocked down. How many times? As often as you try to stand up! Stop and think of the implications for a minute. We have an enemy that hates us and is going for our throat. He prowls around us like a lion (1 Peter 5:8). If we are not vigilant, if we do not defend ourselves, what will happen? We will be "devoured"—we, **believers**.

In short, we are vulnerable to demonic attack—be not deceived! To the extent that I suppose that I understand the subject, and I recognize that it may not be very much, I believe that while my thoughts are **consciously** subject to the Holy Spirit my mind should be free from malignant interference, but as soon as that submission ceases to be conscious, and worse yet if it simply ceases, then my mind is vulnerable. Even when the mind is free the body continues to be vulnerable. At least Paul suffered from a physical problem that was satanic in origin during a considerable space of time and I would not venture to suggest that he was not subject to the Spirit all that time.

I imagine that many readers are struggling with these suggestions. I know they contradict certain ideas that have enjoyed wide dissemination and acceptance in evangelical circles. But what can I do? I have a commitment to the Word of God and feel obliged to do sound exegesis. Let us analyze the question a bit more. If you were Satan, where would you concentrate your fire? Sometimes, when I am lecturing at a theological seminary, I scandalize the class by asking what place in the city they think has the heaviest concentration of demons. They usually mention the prison, a brothel, an important spiritist center, etc. "Not at all", I answer, "it is right here". "What? You can't mean that, professor!" "Why of course! What place in this city represents the greatest danger to the enemy? This is a 'factory' producing soldiers for Christ's army—it is certainly here that Satan will concentrate his fire. There is nothing else in the city that threatens him more." Can there be any doubt? Is it not obvious? That drunk in the gutter, a prostitute or a drug addict, they are already 'in the bag'. The demons do not have to spend more effort on them. You may be sure, my brother, that the more useful you become in God's hand, the more stature you gain in the Kingdom, so much more you will be attacked. Whatever else he may be, Satan is not a fool.

Well, I guess I cannot put it off any longer—we must deal with the 'chestnut'. After all, can a believer be 'possessed', or not? (I have already stated that demon 'ownership' is a false issue; not even an unbeliever can be owned [with the possible exception of 'robots']. So the real question is: Can a demon 'control' a believer or must its attacks stop short of control?) Please try to keep your cool! Let us go slowly. Is God not omniscient and omnipresent? Well then, wherever Satan is God is too—it has to be so if God is omnipresent. Job 2:1 makes clear that Satan appears before the very Throne of God! Revelation 12:10 seems to indicate that he still has access there and evidently spends a lot of time there since he accuses us "day and night". The point is this: it is common to argue that if God is in my life then Satan cannot enter at the same time. But how does that follow? If the enemy can enter the very Sanctuary in Heaven, to enter my life is 'small potatoes'—it should not be any problem at all. Let us think of our life as if it were a house. Anyone who is genuinely converted has the Holy Spirit in his life, or 'house'. Unfortunately, however, many believers keep Him in the parlor. He is in the house (which is of maximum importance) but He does not control the house—there are closets locked with seven locks! There are areas of the life that have never been opened up and turned over to Him. So then, if the Spirit is confined to the parlor, if He does not have access to the whole house, Satan can easily install himself in the kitchen. Easy. With reference to the specific problem under discussion here, the basic question is not whether I have the Holy Spirit but whether He has me! It is not the Spirit's presence but His **control**. We must turn over all the keys to our 'house'.

I know, you still are not satisfied. Then let us think a little more. If I sin knowingly in some area I am rebelling against God in that area. Correct? But if I rebel against God I am joining hands with Satan, because rebelling against God is his thing. In other words, I am handing that area of my life to him on a silver platter. And if I rebel in a second area; there go two areas on the silver platter. And a third, or a fourth? Very frankly, my friend, if you turn three or four areas of your life over to Satan he can mess it up to such an extent that I do not much care what name you choose to give to your condition; I am concerned about the reality.

Let us look again at the continuum suggested above. The division and distinctions are arbitrary. Who told me to draw the lines where I did? How do we know that the line between 'control' and 'oppression' should not be more to one side or the other? Since such distinctions are arbitrary, things that come from people's heads and not the Sacred Text, I judge that we should not attempt to base doctrine upon such distinctions. They may be useful for discussing specific cases, but as soon as we start talking about doctrine we should leave them aside, returning to the Text. The Text speaks of demonization which, for the various reasons I have given, I believe to include everything from mere interference in the thoughts to control of the person. I know of cases where a believer really became controlled; to try to deny that such a person was saved will not work; there are cases where I would say, "If he isn't a believer, neither am I". To elevate our preconceived ideas above reality is a form of idolatry.

Here I want to make an appeal: even if you still feel that you must reject the idea that a believer may be 'controlled', please do not reject the concept of demonization as well. Actually, if God's people will learn to recognize and repel the lesser forms of demonic activity the problem of control (for believers) should not arise. I felt that this discussion would be incomplete if I did not take up the question of 'possession', but I repeat and insist that it is to the lesser forms of demonization that we must pay special attention.

To conclude, we must walk full of the Spirit, consciously controlled by Him. Someone who lives like this will never be controlled by a demon. But, if you give the enemy an opening he will not lose it. We, Christ's soldiers, are certainly the preferred target. We are at war, a war without quarter or cease-fire. As we have already observed, God will not work a continuous miracle to free us from the consequences of our culpable ignorance. We have to pay for our negligence.

The Intimidated

Some (many?) preachers and teachers seem to be **afraid** to touch on the subject. It is not a problem of unbelief or ignorance; they know that Satan and the demons exist and are active, but they are cowed. One day the young pastor preached a dandy message against the enemy, he really lowered the boom, but the counter-attack did not delay! Since the preacher did not know how to defend himself he got the worst of it, and now he is intimidated. Never again has he spoken about the enemy, and as a result of his silence his hearers remain in ignorance. Now then, 2 Timothy 1:7 makes it clear that God does not give us a spirit of cowardice. It seems clear that any cowardice on our part will only help the enemy. But no matter how afraid someone may be of Satan, should he not be more 'afraid' of God? (Well, but we tend to take God for granted, do we not? When I lived among a jungle tribe in the Amazon, I noted that although they believed that good spirits exist, since those good spirits did not bother them they did not spend time on them; they gave their attention to the evil ones, in the effort to appease them.)

In Psalms 78:9 we find a sad commentary. "The men of Ephraem, though armed with bows, turned back in the day of battle. They did not keep God's covenant . . ." What a shame! From God's point of view they betrayed the Covenant; God was not pleased. Remember that at that time the bow was a superior weapon (firearms did not exist yet) and so their cowardice became even greater. Jeremiah 48:10 has a yet stronger word. "Cursed is he who does the work of the Lord negligently; cursed is he who keeps back his sword from bloodshed!" **Cursed**! **Cursed!** That is how God feels about the person who refuses to fight, being armed. **Cursed**! To be a pacifist in the spiritual war is treason against our King. **CURSED!** It is high time that we learn about our weapons and how to use them. First, defensive weapons.

Defensive Weapons

Jesus would not send us against Satan without adequate defense, nor does He. We are facing a terrible enemy, but we also have the best weapons. But what good is it to have such weapons if we do not use them? I may have the best shield in the world but if I leave it in the closet when I go out, what good does it do? Even if I have it on my arm when I go out I must keep alert, so as to stop any arrows with the shield and not my body. Let us begin with the armor described in Ephesians 6.

The Armor in Ephesians 6

It seems to me that the pieces of armor described here serve mainly for defense. Further, there is nothing to protect the back—if you turn your back to the enemy you have had it. We must face the enemy, and beyond that we must keep alert. (That is one aspect of the business that makes me mad! We can never rest. You doze just a little and "Wham!" We get tired but the spirits, since they do not have bodies, do not have that problem.) Since the passage was given in full at the beginning of the chapter I will now merely discuss the armor.

First the belt and the breastplate (verse 14): it seems evident that any lack of truth or justice in one's life gives an opening to the enemy (and he does not miss any chances). Then the boots (verse 15): I would say that lack of preparation is like going out barefoot; any sharp stone or shard of glass will cut you and then you will limp (for a soldier that can have serious consequences).

The shield deserves special mention (verse 16). What a tremendous weapon, able to quench "all the fiery darts of the wicked one"! But what might the precise nature of this weapon be? It is not the mere fact of having faith, for everyone has it. In fact, nothing is done in this life without faith. Have you ever paused to consider that? While seated I am trusting in the chair, that it will not collapse under me—there have been chairs that did not deserve that trust. While standing I am trusting in my legs to hold me up—they have betrayed me on occasion. To drink your coffee today was an act of faith—there have been those who drank coffee seasoned with arsenic! In short, nothing is done without faith. The question is, in what or in whom is my faith deposited? I believe that our shield must be faith in God, but faith in Him as being **The Greatest**—it is this certainty that enables us to face the enemy and ward off all his darts.

Then we have the helmet and the sword (verse 17). It seems clear that without salvation we will not even be in Christ's army, but since it is precisely the head that a helmet protects it may be conviction or certainty of salvation that is in view. Without such a certainty our inner man is not prepared to take on the enemy. As for the sword, the Lord Jesus illustrated the defensive use of the Word of God when He repelled Satan's temptings (Matthew 4:1-11). We will doubtless use the Word in offensive action against the enemy as well.

It is in prayer that we enter the spiritual realm and it is primarily in this realm that the war is waged, since it is essentially a spiritual war. Let us look again at verse 18. It speaks of "supplication" and "always"; it speaks of "watching" and "perseverance". Evidently it is to be an activity that we take seriously, that takes time and in which we persist. It is not a matter of praying just once and then forgetting or stopping. We are to pray for "all saints", which means it must be very important, since everyone needs it. But Paul continues, "and for **me**"—well now, if Paul needed prayer imagine the rest of us! It is my habit to say to any missionary candidate that he should not leave for the field until he has a good number of people who have promised to pray for him. Since the use of our spiritual weapons is almost always expressed through prayer, I will still be talking about prayer as I discuss those weapons. That being the case, let us move on to the other weapons.

The Greatest Defensive Weapon[1]

In James 4:7 we find the greatest and best defensive weapon, at least in my opinion. "Therefore submit to God. Resist the devil and he will flee from you." This verse contains two verbs in the imperative mood, two commands. The first one is "submit"—it is absolutely necessary that we be effectively subject to God before we take action against the enemy (nothing better than to be a radical disciple of Jesus). Do not even think of taking on Satan in your own strength; you will be crushed—do not forget that he is simply the most powerful, intelligent and malevolent created being in the universe! In order to use God's power and impose Christ's victory upon the enemy it is essential that we be in submission to God. But as soon as we fulfill the first command we face the second, "resist". It is an order, not an option. Whenever a servant of Christ suspects that the enemy is at work in a given situation he has the duty, the obligation to resist him. It is a command.

Let us think a bit about this verb "resist". First, it refers to a conscious attitude. Next, it refers to a negative reaction. Finally, one must be aware of whatever is inspiring the reaction (or else you will not react). I believe that is exactly what is involved in "resisting" the devil: we must consciously react against his attacks. We must reject or repel them. When I left the Amazon jungle in 1972 I wanted an answer. I was tired of getting clobbered; how could such a thing happen to a servant of Christ, especially one with as much theological training as I had? I finally concluded that I was

---

[1] I first wrote this some thirty years ago, and I have learned a few things since then. I would now say that Luke 10:19 offers us a still better weapon than James 4:7, but I will leave this discussion as it is, with the promise that I will take up Luke 10 in a bit.

in the dark about some important truth. So I set myself to find out. I read, listened to and observed those who claimed to have understanding and experience in this area. I never accept anyone's experience as being normative; I listen respectfully but then I go straight to the Sacred Text to see if it follows, if the idea has biblical support. Indeed, it is worth saying in passing that doctrine should never be based on experience; doctrine must be based on the Word of God. Experiences may serve to illustrate a truth or doctrine, but they must be evaluated—experiences may be deceiving because Satan is a veritable factory of experiences (if you want 'experiences' he will cheerfully give you a bundle!). But to return to my search.

I was informed that the "resisting" in James 4:7 consists in recognizing the enemy's activity in a given case and rebuking him in the name of the Lord Jesus. This agrees with the semantic content of the term. I tested it in my own experience in this way. I was working on a doctorate at the University of Toronto, Canada. At the time we were driving a long station wagon. We would collapse the rear seat and put down a foam slab for the children to play (and sleep) on, we would pile the baggage behind the front seat to serve as a bit of buffer between us and the kids (if you have children you will understand). One day we went to visit my wife's parents, an eight-hour drive. Our two daughters, who at the time were ten and six, were in the back, I was at the wheel and my wife at my side. It was a beautiful day, not much traffic, a limited access highway, a powerful car—I was probably doing about 70 mph. The point is that at that speed the car is noisy. So then, I was driving serenely, the girls were playing nicely and quietly, when all of a sudden a noisy fight broke out. I mean to say it was sudden, with no advance warning. It is normal for children who have been cooped up for a while to begin to become irritable, but in that event things follow a normal course and you can cut it off. Not this time; I was taken completely by surprise. It took me several seconds to react and before I spoke I received a clear impression, a word from God: "That is not natural". I had been researching James 4:7 and so was ready. I said: "Satan, it is you. I rebuke you in the name of Jesus!"

Now then, let us review the situation: the car was noisy and the kids were yelling; although I spoke out loud I did not raise my voice, and I was facing forward driving the car. The point is, there was no way the girls could hear what I said, and in fact they did not. So then, as soon as I spoke, immediately, the two girls stopped fighting; the fight stopped abruptly and they went back to their quiet play. Praise be to God!

That taught me two things. First, resisting the devil works in just that way: I recognized an attack of the enemy and repelled it in the name of Jesus. In passing I should say that I certainly do not imagine that it was Satan himself that attacked my children, he presumably has more important things to do. It was some pip-squeak demon. I used the enemy's proper name because that was the orientation I had received; and it worked. But how could it work if it was not really Satan? Well, I suppose that when I rebuked the boss I rebuked by extension the subordinate that was the operative in my case—since it is God who forces the enemy to obey He takes advantage of our intention. Second, the enemy has no shame. To attack two children in that way was a low-down, dirty, cowardly trick. The dirtier and more cowardly something is the better the demons like it. I have become convinced that their preferred targets are the weak and helpless, especially small children and the mentally handicapped. Note that my daughters were attacked in their **minds**, provoking that fight.

I believe that we must associate this resisting with the concept of demonization. It is incumbent upon us to repel **any and every** attack of the enemy against us, and not merely cases of control. In the example I just gave it was an interference in the thoughts. As I see it, to expel a demon is the same as to 'resist' him, only the term is usually reserved for cases of control. When will someone expel a demon? When it manifests itself—right? In other words, the demonic activity is recognized as such and is thereupon rebuked. It is to **resist**.

Returning to our Text, we find a promise: "he will flee from you". The first time I explained these truths to my family, my older daughter—she was fifteen at the time—listened carefully. She is the enthusiastic, bouncy type but when she came home from school the next day she was almost jumping up and down. "Daddy, Daddy, it worked!" "What do you mean, 'It worked'?" "Daddy, I resisted the devil and he left!" I wept with joy that afternoon; the enemy had to flee from a 15-year-old girl! Hallelujah! But I must register one detail—that daughter was already a true disciple of Jesus and so was in shape to confront the enemy. It needs to be emphasized again: it is really necessary to be effectively subject to God before you take action against Satan, directly or indirectly.

As we have already said, Satan prefers to keep people in unbelief or ignorance in this area. However, when a person, or a church, decides to wake up and begin to act, then he really bestirs himself. He wants to keep the damage he incurs to a minimum. So he tries to confuse people, to take them to abuses and extremes, to mystify and create erroneous ideas about the subject. In this way he achieves two ends. First, he undermines the efficiency of those who are awake, thereby diminishing the damage he must suffer. Second, those who are skeptical see the abuses and are confirmed in their unbelief. The result is two opposing camps that become increasingly radical in their positions, moving farther and farther away from the truth, which is left alone in the middle. And Satan laughs at us!

My dear friends, I wish to affirm that I do not consider myself an expert on this subject. I know that many were working in this area long before I woke up. I cheerfully acknowledge that I may be mistaken. However, I do believe that God has allowed me to learn and understand a few things and that He wants me to share them. That being the case, I will now evaluate various notions where it seems to me that the enemy has succeeded in peddling ideas that diminish our efficiency in spiritual warfare.

Some Misconceptions

Not a gift but an order

Certain evangelical circles seem to have the idea that casting out demons is a gift, or something to be done only by the pastors. I have searched all the lists of the spiritual gifts and it is not there. The expelling of demons is not a gift, it is a **command**. We are commanded to "resist" not only in James 4:7 but also in 1 Peter 5:9. It is clear that it is in Satan's interest to peddle the idea that it is a gift. If expelling demons is a gift, then the enemy's loss will be limited by the time and disposition of the few gifted ones; when they tire, forget or sleep the enemy is left alone. But what if **every believer** was resisting the activity of Satan and the demons, what a tremendous loss we would inflict on the enemy! Can you imagine it? Well that is exactly what Satan wants to avoid at all cost—it must be his worst nightmare. A gift is only for the gifted, but a command is for **all**.

There is another misconception that is similar. When someone begins to wake up to these things, he sometimes lacks the courage to confront Satan directly. So, when he recognizes an attack he asks God to resist it. One hears prayers like this: "Oh God, please rebuke the demon that is troubling 'Jack's' life." Only He often does not do it. And why not? He does not do it because it is our job, He has ordered us to do it. With the order He also gave us the power, the wherewithal so as to be able to obey. To ask God to do the resisting is not an expression of spiritual humility, it is disobedience to a divine command. He commands that **we** resist the devil.

Here I wish to elaborate a point mentioned earlier, that we can do what Michael could not (Jude 9). In essence the human being is superior to the angelic being. In Genesis 1:26 we learn that we were created in God's image and likeness, which presumably is not true of the angels. According to Romans 8:17 we are heirs of God and co-heirs with Christ, a privilege the angels do not have. 1 Corinthians 6:3 tells us that we will judge the angels, which implies that they are inferior to us. Hebrews 1:14 says that they are our ministers, they are to serve us. The AV misleads us in Hebrews 2:7 with the rendering, "a little lower than the angels"; it should be "for a little" or for a little while, which is presumably the correct interpretation of Psalms 8:5 as well. While we are limited by these physical bodies here on earth our superiority does not appear.[1] Finally, Ephesians 1:20-21 and 2:6 permit us to understand that in Christ we are seated at the Father's right hand, a privilege that Michael does not have. So then, because of our position, of our authority, of everything that we have in Christ, it is our responsibility to resist the enemy. God will demand an accounting of that command.[2]

Do not ask permission

Strange as it may seem, I have encountered the idea that one must ask permission before expelling a demon. Can you imagine a soldier on a battlefield calling out, "Hey mister enemy, is it all right if I shoot you?" He would have to be crazy! Before he finished he would himself be shot at; his voice would guide the enemy. War is war! When you see an enemy, shoot! Even if you do ask permission it is obvious that the demon will not agree. No, we do not have to ask permission. Furthermore, we do not even have to be physically present.

Some years ago I took part in an international conference in Dallas, Texas. Upon arriving I went to visit some friends

---

[1] And with reference to those that Satan succeeds in taking to the Lake with him, that superiority will never appear. Which is at least partly why Satan does all that he can to take as many as he can with him.

[2] It is true that "rebuke" in Jude 9 and "resist" in James 4:7 come from different Greek verbs. The "rebuke" of Jude 9 also occurs in Matthew 17:18, Mark 1:25 and 9:25, Luke 4:35, 4:41 and 9:42 (among other places) and in each case describes how Jesus expelled demons. (In Matthew 10:8 the disciples were commanded to expel demons.) In Mark 8:33 Jesus "rebuked" (same word) Satan, who was speaking through Peter. Since in John 14:12 the Lord Jesus said we would do what He did, if we believe, I submit that He is expecting **us** to rebuke Satan and the demons. The verb "resist" of James 4:7 can be quite strong, as illustrated by Acts 13:8, Galatians 2:11, 2 Timothy 3:8 and 4:15 (rendered "withstand" in the AV), but I cannot prove that it is to be taken as synonymous to "rebuke", with reference to the enemy. I give it as my considered opinion that it is.

who live there. During the meal I shared some things that I was learning about spiritual warfare. At that the lady of the house told me the following. Three days before she had gone to visit some good friends of theirs. When she entered the house she found the couple in distress. One of their four children is a daughter who was 16 years old at that time and she had just run off with a well-known criminal of the area. The man was about 30 years old, had been in and out of prison several times for a variety of crimes and was known for what he was. And yet the girl had run off with him, a girl brought up in the church and in an evangelical home. Well, you can imagine the parents' anguish: "How could it happen? What did we do wrong?" etc. As I heard the story I found it strange. That the girl should have an affair with a schoolmate would be regrettable but not particularly unusual in our society; but to take off with a known criminal twice her age—I became suspicious. So I said to my friends: "I suspect that there was demonic interference in this case and in that event there is something we can do; shall we give it a try?" "Yes, by all means." So right there in the kitchen I briefly explained the ground rules and then rebuked any and all demonic activity in the girl's life, commanding it to cease and forbidding any recurrence. While I was about it I did the same thing for the man in the case. I also rebuked the spirit of depression that was attacking the parents. Then I took my leave of my friends and went to the conference. Ten days later, at the end of the conference, I went to say good-bye to my friends before I left town. When the lady of the house opened the door and saw me she exclaimed: "Wilbur, do you know what happened?" "No, what is it?" "Do you remember your prayer the other Sunday?" "Yes." "Well three days later the phone rang over there and the mother heard her daughter's voice: 'Mom, I want to come home, is it all right with you?' 'Of course, come as soon as you can.' She arrived that same night." She was a changed person. Before, for some time she had been rebellious, agitated and difficult; now she was calm. The next day she went to the principal of her school to see what she had to do to catch up. In short, she set about putting her life in order.

Now then, nobody asked permission. We did not know where the girl was; we did not even know if she was still alive. We said nothing to the parents. We are talking about spiritual warfare which is waged in the spiritual realm. In the spirit world there are no barriers of space or matter. This gives rise to a tremendous truth which has a very great strategic value: in the spiritual realm we can wage war around the world! My body may be in Brazil but in spirit, in prayer I can bind Satan in China, in Nigeria, in Iran or wherever. Can you imagine it? How often one hears an elderly brother complain because he cannot get out of the house, he cannot do anything in the church anymore, etc. Such a brother could become a great warrior in the spiritual war. Precisely because he can no longer get out of the house he has a lot of time. He could wage war around the world, producing a great effect. Or a homemaker, with a number of small children, who complains because she can no longer go out with the evangelism teams, or whatever. In the first place, to be a mother is one of the most important roles in our society, but she can also be an effective warrior. I myself have washed tons of dishes (really and truly) and I know how it is—your hands work almost by themselves, leaving your mind essentially free; you can wage spiritual war while you wash. I have swept miles of floor (really and truly) and I know how it is—again, your hands can do it virtually by themselves; you can wage war. Our range or radius of action can be virtually limitless.

Prayer and <u>fasting</u>

I am concerned to demythologize our subject. We should treat it in a lucid, objective and serious way. I cannot believe that God would place us in a battlefield such as we are in without explaining the ground rules in a way both recognizable and explainable; He would not leave us groping in the dark, at the mercy of our imaginations, each one holding a different opinion without any way of settling the question. 1 Corinthians 14:33 declares that God is not a God of confusion.

So I have asked God to help me recognize and isolate basic principles to guide our conduct in spiritual warfare. I believe that the fundamental fact is the victory of Christ. Colossians 2:15, Ephesians 1:20-22 and John 16:11, among other texts, show that that victory was complete. James 4:7 affirms that the devil will flee when I resist him, but why does he flee? What is the active ingredient? Is he afraid of me? I doubt it. It is the power of God, liberated by Christ's victory (of course I have to know how to unleash that power, and be prepared to do so, which would give Satan cause to fear me). That must be why Ephesians 6:10 says, "be strong in the Lord and in the power of his might". Further, expressions like "in the name of Jesus" or "the blood of Christ" presumably do not produce a magical effect; the mere pronouncing of that sequence of sounds will not work. We must consciously claim the reality of Christ's victory. If that is what we are doing as we use such expressions, that is fine. And now for fasting.

In Mark 9:29 Jesus said that a certain kind or rank of demon would only leave through prayer and fasting. Before considering the effect of fasting as such, we are obliged to take up a different problem. Most modern versions omit the words "and fasting". And why do they do that? Because four Greek manuscripts omit those two words, four against over 1,700 that have them! How come? During the past 130 years it has been the fashion in the scholarly world to ascribe an exaggerated value to two of those manuscripts (Vaticanus and Sinaiticus), since they are the most ancient that contain most of the New Testament. Many scholars have declared that they are also the best, but I disagree emphatically. Those two manuscripts are full of errors; they disagree **between themselves** over 3,000 times just in the four Gospels, etc. (For more on this subject the reader may consult my book, *The Identity of the New Testament Text IV*, 2014.) The reader may rest assured that the words "and fasting" belong to the Original Text. Most modern versions omit Matthew 17:21, the whole verse, for the same reason (now there are six manuscripts, still against over 1,700, but if it were not for the two the verse would be uncontested). The reader may accept the verse with full confidence. Since Jesus did in fact say "prayer and fasting", what is the interpretation?

Starting from the basic premise that it is the victory of Christ that is operative, that makes the devil run, I then ask: does my fasting add anything to Christ's victory? Can I say that Christ's victory was incomplete? If we were to countenance the hypothesis, on what basis could we argue that we are competent to perfect that victory? As far as I can see the Text is clear: Jesus won a complete victory; Satan suffered a total defeat. If the very chief of the demons was defeated how can we argue that any rank below him escaped? Is not the point of Ephesians 1:21 that Jesus is now over their whole hierarchy?

I know that many experienced brethren will disagree with the interpretation that follows, and I offer it with humility, but I ask the reader to evaluate it carefully. What Jesus said in Mark 9:29 was said before His death and resurrection, before the victory was won, therefore. In other words, the rules of the game were different. When Jesus began to cast out demons it caused a tremendous sensation. Later He, God the Son on earth, gave the same authority to the twelve and to the seventy (Luke 9 and 10), but it must have been on the basis of the sovereignty of God since Satan was still on his feet as the god of this world (in John 12:31 the Lord Jesus said, "now the ruler of this world will be deposed", shortly before the crucifixion).

Given that in Christ we are seated at the right hand of the Father in Heaven, and consequently "far above every principality, and power, and might and dominion" (Ephesians 2:6 and 1:20-21), I believe that God expects us to impose upon Satan and the demons, all of them, the defeat they have already suffered. To that end it should not be necessary to fast, if we are effectively subject to God. Now then, in saying that, I am not trying to make light of fasting; I believe it to be of value. It adds nothing to Christ's authority but it may well increase my courage in making use of God's power. Fasting increases my sensitivity to the spirit world. That is why many shamans and other professional spiritist mediums are thin—they fast a lot. Why? To increase their sensitivity to the demons. We fast to increase our sensitivity to the Holy Spirit. As far as I can see fasting has this value, but it adds nothing to the victory of Christ.

There are other practices that can be evaluated in the same way. There are those who like to yell when they expel a demon. I wonder; a demon may cause deafness but is not itself deaf, at least to my knowledge. Does a yell add anything to Christ's victory? At times I have wondered if the person was not insecure and was yelling to bolster his own courage. At other times it seemed to me that the person was trying to be sensational. Which leads me to make an appeal—let us avoid sensationalism! The simple demonstration of God's power, healing or liberating, is in itself a wonderful thing that will produce an impact on the people; it is not necessary to embellish it. To be more precise, it is not wise! The miracle by itself draws attention to God and glorifies Him; any effort at embellishment, at sensationalism draws attention to the person, and that is dangerous. First, God is jealous and will not share His glory with anyone (Isaiah 42:8). Second, it is easy for the person to become proud and fall into the snare of the devil. The more proud a person becomes the farther he departs from God and the more surely his ministry will wind up in the swamp. In fact, there is one very sure way to turn God against you; it is to become proud. "God resists the proud, but gives grace to the humble" (James 4:6 and 1 Peter 5:5). Therefore, let us avoid sensationalism.

To conclude, I would say that to lay on hands or to burn objects likewise adds nothing to the victory of Christ. I see no need to touch, it is enough to speak. To burn or destroy an object associated with a demon can be an important way of rejecting that association on the part of one who is being freed, but it should not be necessary in order to expel the demon. I understand what is recorded in Acts 19:19 as being in the nature of a public break with the past. The importance given in the Old Testament to the destruction of places and objects associated with idolatry—the idols represented demons—seems to me to derive from different ground rules; Christ's victory was still future. I believe we have enough authority to isolate objects or houses; simply order the spirits to leave, forbidding any further use of them—our problem is not with the object, which is not at fault, but with the demon (however, perhaps certain objects, such as ouija boards and rock recordings, should be destroyed on general principles, assuming that there is no way they can be used for God's glory). Actually, there are already those who are closing down spiritist centers. They simply declare the area off limits to all demons, forbidding any further manifestations there; with that it closes, since nothing more happens.

Demons are con men

Demons will do anything to deceive, confuse or demoralize us. If you resist a spirit, he leaves, but another may immediately take the place of the first and produce the same effect, making you think that nothing happened, so that you feel demoralized. If you resist but do not forbid a return, he leaves but may come back, in an hour, a day or a week. If I have to rebuke the enemy I now rebuke not only the spirit actually at work but any and all others that might wish to attack the person in the same way. I also forbid any repetition of the attack. Actually, nowadays I send them to the Abyss (Luke 8:31), a procedure that will receive attention presently.

One tactic they frequently use to deceive us is to strike up a conversation. There are those who make a point of chatting with the enemy. I confess that I do not get it. Can you imagine on a battlefield: "Hey mister enemy! Come here, let's have a little chat, drink some coffee together; then I'll kill you. Okay?" What do you think? I know that some think they need to know the name of a demon in order to expel it, and therefore they can only expel one at a time. Sometimes a demon imposes some requirement. Some really absurd things have happened. I heard of a case where a man tried to cast out a demon. The demon said he would only leave if the man went home and put on a tie. So the man ran home for the tie. But when he returned the demon laughed in his face: "You just obeyed me, so how do you think you can cast me out? Go jump in the lake!"

One night after I had lectured on this subject several people came to me and gave me the following account. In a certain city in the interior of Brazil a certain pastor had this experience. He was called on to handle the case of a severely demonized woman. He took a few others with him and tried to cast out the demon. It did not leave. After several tries and some effort the demon said, "I won't leave because she has something of mine". Finally it divulged that the 'thing' was a mattress that had belonged to an old spiritist medium and had come to her when he died. At that the pastor jumped in his car and took off toward the woman's house. On the way a motorcycle came out of a side street and ran into his car. Nervous and in a hurry the pastor said he would take care of everything (it was the cyclist's fault but the pastor wanted to get clear so he could finish off the mattress) and went on. He entered the house, found the mattress, took it out to the yard and burned it! He then returned to the house where the demonized woman was and the demon left. Was it a victory for Jesus? Maybe, but let us hear the rest of the story. It happens that the woman had a husband and he figured that he had some right to that mattress. In short, the pastor wound up paying for the mattress and the motorcycle (besides the damage to his car). He was considerably out of pocket, not to mention the wear and tear. Was all that song and dance necessary? I think not. Certainly Jesus would not have believed the demon and gotten involved in such a situation.

In the Gospels we find several occasions where the demons tried to strike up a conversation with Jesus, but none where He took the initiative. Only once did He ask their name, in the case of the Legion (Mark 5:9). Why do you suppose He asked, because He did not know? Of course He knew! I understand that Jesus did it so that the fact of demon infestation would be recorded for our instruction. Observe that He did not expel them one by one, He cast out all thousand at once. You do not need to know the name of an enemy soldier to kill him; just send an accurate bullet. Demons are liars by nature. Satan is the father of lies (John 8:44). Sure, a demon may speak a truth now and again, but how do you recognize a truth among a hundred lies? There is a denomination in Brazil that began in the liberty of the Spirit but then moved into a strict legalism. A pastor that was involved in that movement told me that some of the rules came about in the following manner: when dealing with a demon controlled person they would ask the demon whether such and such a thing was not of the devil; when the demon answered that it was then the church made a rule against it! Satan must be laughing yet.

Demons love to peddle 'experiences'. I have heard that there are churches where demons are vomited; every Sunday there is a puddle of vomit in front of the pulpit (at least the janitor earns his wages). Really, folks, don't you think Satan is making God's people look ridiculous? Isn't he making fun of Christ's victory? And many times it is the same people being 'liberated' every Sunday, and from the same problem. What is this? Did Jesus win or not? We must keep alert, folks! We cannot be too careful; demons are con men.

Suggestions for Research

I wish to state that there is a great deal that I do not yet understand. There are things that leave me perplexed. I am still researching them and asking God to elucidate them. I will now outline some of these problem areas in the hope that others will be able to help me. Someone else may already have the answer to some of these things. Please share your insights with me. If we work together at researching these things perhaps the solutions will become clear to us more quickly.

I will begin with a question to which I think I already have the answer but would like to hear from others. It often happens that a sermon is reaching its climax when suddenly a baby begins to cry violently. I am reasonably sure it is a demonic attack but I do not want to rebuke it openly (it might offend the parents and cause perplexity among others; in other words, it might cause more distraction than the crying). So I rebuke the attack silently but nothing happens. Why not? Perhaps my hypothesis was wrong and it was not a demon at all. But if I was right, then I suggest the following answer: since the challenge was public the rebuke must be also. If I succeed in stopping the crying just with my thoughts no one else will understand what happened, they will think it was a natural crying and that the child just decided to stop. For the enemy's defeat to be public he must be rebuked openly (what is in view here is only the response to a public challenge; we may still wage war around the world in our thoughts, in prayer).

There are those who say that all rebuking of demons must be done audibly, on the assumption that demons cannot read our thoughts. So far as I know, the Bible says nothing about this question. However, the reading of thoughts should not be equated with omniscience. To be omniscient is to know everything in the universe simultaneously. To read my thoughts a demon must be where I am and therefore cannot be anywhere else observing anything else at the same time. Since spirit beings are not hindered by matter, what is there to stop a demon from tracing the electrical impulses in my brain?[1] Further, since it is God who makes the demons obey us, presumably, and since the Text does affirm that **He** reads thoughts (Revelation 2:23, etc.), I see no basis for the idea that all rebuking of demons should be audible.

Another thing that eludes me is the question of duration. Can I free a person or isolate a place for a lifetime? Are there limits? Only for a month or a year? I confess that I am in doubt. I would really like to hear from others on this subject. (I have observed a number of instances that point to a week as being a relevant time frame, but I recognize that they could have been orchestrated by the enemy precisely to lead me to accept a fiction.) Just to be sure, I try to remember to protect my family every morning when I wake up and every night when I go to bed.

---

[1] Modern technology now realizes that thoughts can be read outside the cranium by a computer; if a computer can do it, why not a demon?

The problem that abuses me the most is the matter of re-calcitrant demons. I imagine that everyone has heard of cases where someone struggled for hours (or days) trying to expel a demon; it finally left, but the person was exhausted, really wrung out. In 1987 I learned of a case where a whole church struggled for weeks trying to liberate a teenage girl who was seriously demonized (the pastor insisted that she was converted at the time). They fasted, plenty; they prayed, a great deal; experienced workers from other churches came to help—and nothing happened! Well, there it is, folks, what are we to think when faced with such a situation? Did Jesus win or not?

First, we must never forget that our God is the Sovereign of the Universe. **He** is the one in command, and if He permits some demon to disobey me, He is presumably trying to get my attention; there is something that I need to learn or understand. At times there is some specific difficulty: unconfessed sin in my life, a pact exists between Satan and the person I am trying to help, some fetish, curse or other form of witchcraft, etc.[1] It may be that God is testing my faith or my humility. Returning to the case of the teenage girl, as he was relating the case to me the pastor said that he had told the girl's parents that if **he** did not succeed in liberating the girl he would resign from the ministry. So I said, "Brother, if I am not mistaken, that is where you goofed. You introduced your own person into the equation as if it was your name, your honor, your victory that was at stake." I suggested that he turn the case over to God from

---

[1] Recently the question of hereditary curses has become a 'hot potato'. I do not have the slightest doubt about the reality of such curses. In fact, something very similar may be found right in the Ten Commandments. "I am a jealous God, visiting the iniquity of the fathers upon the children to the third and fourth generation . . ." (Exodus 20:5). But the real question is if that can happen to a believer. It is argued that Jesus bore our curse on the cross. To be sure, but He also bore our sins and our sicknesses. So, do we no longer sin? Do we no longer get sick? The solution for those problems is available, but is not automatic. 1 John 1:9 makes clear that forgiveness exists, but we must confess. Healing exists, but we must claim it. It is not automatic. Curses also need to be treated specifically. Just as we go through life suffering the consequences of other people's sins, we can also suffer from their curses. Really and truly—we believers.

the pulpit, telling the people to stop praying and fasting about that case. Some months later he told me that he followed my advice and the girl was freed. God was testing his humility.

In various places and from different people I have heard a proposed solution for a recalcitrant demon: it is to call down fire from heaven to burn it. Those people told me that the demon takes off screaming! I must confess that when I first heard that story I smiled. I figured it was some more sensationalism, but, as is my custom, I went to the Sacred Text to see if by any chance the idea might have some backing. Imagine my surprise at finding that perhaps it does. In the presence of God the Son here on earth the demons repeatedly expressed a certain concern: "Have you come to destroy us?" (Mark 1:24), "Have you come here to torment us before the time?" (Matthew 8:29). They know only too well that they are destined for hell (Matthew 25:41), they just do not want to arrive early! It might be that by threatening a demon with fire from heaven it is made to think of the Lake of Fire and gets scared; it might be. But if it is fear of the Lake that is functioning, why not appeal directly to it?

A colleague had a set to with one of the recalcitrant ones and at a certain point called for fire from heaven—the demon yelled but said, "Even so I won't leave". Could it be that some of them flee (seemingly) at the threat of fire to distract us and keep us from discovering a devastating resource (like a mother bird that pretends to be crippled to lead danger away from her nest)?

With all due respect to contrary opinions, I will not converse with a demon; I will not implore it to leave nor will I struggle with it hours on end. The more you do things like that the more advertising you give the enemy and the more doubt is cast on Christ's victory and power. I obey all the instructions that God has given us for such situations, to the extent of my understanding. Then, if the demon does not obey I turn the case over to God—that is right, if I have done everything that was within my range of responsibility and even so the enemy will not obey then the appropriate course of action is to turn the problem over to God. After all, it is not my name, it is not my honor that is at stake; it is of the victory and authority of Christ that the demon is making light. (This is what I suggested to the pastor in the case of the teenage girl just mentioned—he tried it and told me later that it worked.) However, there is one more thing that we may do, precisely the devastating resource I just alluded to.

In Luke 8:31 we read that the demons begged Jesus "not to order them to go into the Abyss" ("the Abyss" is the same phrase that the AV renders as "the bottomless pit" in Revelation 20:1). That means that He could have—I conclude that He refrained from doing so because He had not yet won the victory, at that time. But now it is different. In John 14:12 the Lord Jesus said to His disciples: "Most assuredly I say to you, he who believes into me, the works that I do he will do also; even greater works than these he will do, because I go to my Father." What does "because I go to my Father" imply? I conclude that it must be His victory—could He have returned if He had failed, if He had not succeeded in destroying the devil (Hebrews 2:14)? That is why we are supposed to be doing "**greater**" works—like ordering demons into the Abyss, for instance.

C. Fred Dickason, who had personally ministered to over 400 demonized believers (by 1987), says that his experience indicates that once a demon is ordered into the Abyss it does not come back (*Demon Possession & the Christian*, Moody Press, 1987). Paul E. Billheimer says much the same in *Destined to Overcome* (Bethany House Publishers, 1982, p. 46). Can you imagine if God's people really got a hold on this? We could continuously **reduce** the number of demons opposing us! Hallelujah! So then, why not order all recalcitrant demons into the Abyss? In fact, why not do the same for any and all that intrude upon our notice?[1]

Once again I wish to emphasize humility. God is Sovereign and will not give His glory to another. It seems to me perfectly possible that God might allow a demon to be recalci-

---

[1] I assume that God Himself will not allow us to decimate the enemy's forces to the point where prophesied events cannot occur.

trant precisely to teach us something, even to reprimand us for some reason (in fact, at times the demon itself will do the job—if there is some sin in the life of the would be expeller the demon may declare it for all to hear, in order to humiliate the person and make him withdraw). It is easy to get puffed up, to get carried away when you verify that you can make demons run. It is easy to start intruding yourself into the picture, thinking that **you** are doing something. At that God takes offense and sooner or later you will fall on your face. I know of someone who became impressed with himself because he could "bind" demons (the demonized person would become stiff), but was he really solving the problem? Demons are con men, you cannot be too careful. I believe it is most important, in fact necessary, that we maintain an attitude of humility before God, that we not intrude our selves, because then we may reasonably hope that He will take us by the hand and teach us what we need to know. Oh Lord, please illumine us!

I am aware of evidence that points to two further factors that may be involved, praise and forgiveness. It may be that praising God could make a difference in some recalcitrant case—it is a good way of reaffirming our confidence in Him even when faced with perplexing circumstances. A lack of forgiveness may well hinder God's working. If He conditions His forgiving on ours (Matthew 6:12 and 14-15), it must be a most important factor (cf. Job 42:10).

Some cautions

If you liberate someone it is not wise to leave a vacuum; Matthew 12:43-45 explains why. Even though it is perfectly possible to expel a demon from an unbeliever without explaining or even being present, I believe we should explain what is going on and try to lead the person to commit himself to Jesus. That way he acquires the possibility of defending himself. But I believe it is possible to do even more. Consider Matthew 18:18. "Assuredly I say to you, whatever you bind on earth will have been bound in heaven, and whatever you loose on earth will have been loosed in heaven." For many years I could not understand this verse. I just could not see how I could say of something I did that it had already been done in heaven, first. But now I think I understand it—it has to do with spiritual warfare. When we bind Satan down here we are doing something that has already been done in Heaven. If the first half of the verse refers to repelling a negative influence then the second half should refer to the opposite, to introducing a positive influence. Does not Hebrews 1:14 say that the angels are sent to serve those who will inherit salvation? Well, I believe that the "loosing" in Matthew 18:18 has in view our claiming positive and active effects of Christ's victory, like calling on the angels to work in the life of someone who has just been liberated, predisposing him to embrace the Gospel.[1] (The person's will is not violated, he must still choose.)

Now let us look at verse 19 (Matthew 18): "Again assuredly I say to you that if two of you agree on earth about anything you ask for, it will be done for you by my Father who is in Heaven." The "again assuredly" seems to me to link this verse closely to the previous one, which begins with "assuredly". In that event this verse should also have to do with spiritual warfare. I do not really see how the fact of two people agreeing will add anything to the victory of Christ such that they can claim something that one cannot. But I do not have to understand; if God's Word says something then it is so. So then, I wish to suggest a research procedure. Let us see if each one can find at least one other person who will agree to meet at least once a week in order to engage in warfare, in specific terms. It may make a difference and we may receive some added light. But watch out for the counter-attack; you may be assured before the fact that the enemy will not take it lying down. It should not

---

[1] We must not pray to angels; they are our servants (Hebrews 1:14). According to the rules they may not interfere with human beings unless properly authorized to do so (the demons do not obey the rules). I understand that in Christ we have the authority to authorize them to intervene in specific cases—when dealing with an unbeliever I habitually "loose" the spirits of truth, faith and obedience to work in the person's mind to help him to understand and believe. However, neither we nor the angels can oblige anyone to believe; each one must make his own decision—we can help, but only up to a certain point.

cause surprise, but I have seen people taken unawares—apparently they imagined that the enemy would be passive. War is war! Cowardice is not a valid option. So let us go into battle, but prepared and alert.

At this point I must issue a warning. Virtually the whole exposition up to here has been about demonic activity, demonization, attacks leveled against the human being without his knowledge (most of the time). I have not mentioned voluntary relationships with demons. It should be clear that a spirit medium (witch or warlock) who deliberately relates to evil spirits may well have a variety of different experiences, that I have not covered. I do not wish to take up that area here, I am just alerting you.

And then there is satanism! The satanists have been boasting for several years that they have in place a network of thousands of human 'robots' (in the U.S.). These are people who voluntarily turned themselves over to the complete control of a demon. I confess that I am not sure just what the consequences of this new twist will be; we must research the matter. Remembering that the human being is essentially superior to the angelic, if a human being joins his abilities and qualities to those of a demon the result will probably be more dangerous than either one of them alone. At the moment all I can do is warn you of the danger—it is going to get worse before it gets better. We need to take care, but not despair. The Lord Jesus has already won the final victory. Still and all, we urgently need some orientation from God to know how to destroy this new threat.

Luke 10:19—Defense that shades into offense

Luke 10:19—"Take note, I am giving[1] you <u>the</u> authority to trample on snakes and scorpions,[2] and over all the power of

---

[1] Instead of 'am giving', perhaps 2.5% of the Greek manuscripts, of objectively inferior quality, have 'have given' (as in NIV, NASB, LB, TEV, etc.)—a serious error. Jesus said this perhaps five months before His death and resurrection, addressing the seventy (not just the twelve). The Lord is talking about the future, not the past; a future that includes <u>us</u>!

[2] The Lord gives us the authority to "trample snakes and scorpions". Well now, to smash the literal insect, a scorpion, you do not need power from

the enemy, and nothing at all may harm you." In Matthew 28:18 Sovereign Jesus affirms that He holds "all authority in heaven and on earth", so He is clearly competent to delegate some of that authority to us—note that He has given us the authority, the Greek Text has the definite article. We may have any number of enemies, but the enemy is Satan. The phrase, "all the power", presumably includes his works, followed by their consequences. Now then, just how does "authority over all the power of the enemy" work, in practice? Authority controls power, so can we command Satan to do things? Perhaps, but I would not recommend it (Satan is so much smarter than we are that he could easily trip us up, get us to do wrong things). More important, we have access to a power that is far greater; consider Ephesians 3:20.

"Now to Him who is able to do immeasurably more than all we ask or imagine, according to the power that is working in us,[1] 21 to Him be the glory in the Church in Christ Jesus, to

---

on High, just a slipper. To trample a snake I prefer a boot, but we can kill literal snakes without supernatural help. It becomes obvious that Jesus was referring to something other than reptiles and insects. I understand Mark 16:18 to be referring to the same reality—Jesus declares that certain signs will accompany the believers (the turn of phrase virtually has the effect of commands): they will expel demons, they will speak strange languages, they will remove 'snakes', they will place hands on the sick. ("If they drink . . ." is not a command; it refers to an eventuality.) But what did the Lord Jesus mean by 'snakes'?

In a list of distinct activities Jesus has already referred to demons, so the 'snakes' must be something else. In Matthew 12:34 Jesus called the Pharisees a 'brood of vipers', and in 23:33, 'snakes, brood of vipers'. In John 8:44, after they claimed God as their father, Jesus said, "You are of your father the devil". And 1 John 3:10 makes clear that Satan has many other 'sons'. In Revelation 20:2 we read: "He seized the dragon, the ancient serpent, who is a slanderer, even Satan, who deceives the whole inhabited earth, and bound him for a thousand years." If Satan is a snake, then his children are also snakes. So then, I take it that our 'snakes' are human beings who chose to serve Satan, who sold themselves to evil. I conclude that the 'snakes' in Luke 10:19 are the same as those in Mark 16:18, but what of the 'scorpions'? Since they also are of the enemy, they may be demons, in which case the term may well include their offspring, the humanoids [see the essay, "In the Days of Noah"]. I am still working on the question of just how the removal is done.

[1] I sadly confess that I have not yet arrived at a spiritual level where I can unleash this power—I have yet to make the truth in this verse work for

all generations, forever and ever. Amen."[1] Ephesians 1:19 spoke of "the exceeding greatness of His power **into** us who are believing"—note that the verb is in the present tense; having believed yesterday will not hack it, we must believe today. This tremendous power that God pours into us, as we believe, exceeds our powers of imagination. Well now, my personal horizon is limited and defined by my ability to imagine. Anything that I cannot imagine lies outside my horizon, and so obviously I will not ask for it. But for all that we <u>can</u> imagine we should use Christ's limitless power, not Satan's.

Since He goes on to say, "nothing at all may harm you", I suppose that we are to forbid Satan (and his servants) from using his power against us. This I am doing. We can protect ourselves, our families, our ministries—anything within Christ's Kingdom. I do this every day, so as not to forget and not to get careless. A defense that stops attacks from reaching us is obviously a great defense! But why stop at defending ourselves? Why not forbid the use of Satan's power in other ways? How about forbidding any use of Satan's power in our government, in our schools, in our hospitals, in the media? And why limit our activity to our country? How about forbidding any use of Satan's power in Iraq, in Iran, in North Korea, in Kenya, etc.? Well, well, well, am I getting carried away? Perhaps, but have I given you food for thought?

Seriously, there may be a significant difference between defense and offense. For defense we have the Lord's promise, so we can bank on that. As to offense, some other factors probably enter in.

---

me. But I understand that the truth affirmed here is literal, and I only hope that others will get there before I do (so I can learn from them), if I keep on delaying. The whole point of the exercise (verse 21) is for God to get glory [not for me to have a good time, although if I ever get there I will certainly have a great good time!], and to the extent that we do <u>not</u> put His power in us to work we are depriving Him of glory that He could and should have.

[1] The glory that God gets from the Church will go on forever.

1) The consequences of sin: we should not try to protect people from such consequences. This includes the religion and the government that people choose.
2) God sovereignly allows Satan and the demons to continue operating in this world, and presumably He will not allow us to frustrate His purpose in so doing.
3) A word of caution occurs to me: we are at war, and the more we expand our radius of operation, the more effort the enemy will expend to hinder us (be prepared).

We will be well advised to maintain a conscious submission to the Holy Spirit. More precisely, we need to try to follow the example of Sovereign Jesus. In John 5:19 He said: "Most assuredly I say to you, the Son is not able to do anything from Himself, except something He sees the Father doing; because whatever things He does, precisely these the Son also does." I find this statement to be amazing, revealing and challenging. Jesus only did what He saw the Father doing; so how about us? I would say that my main 'ministry' problem is that I often do not know what the Father is doing, and so I waste a lot of time and effort. But with reference to taking the fight to the enemy, we most certainly need the Father's backing.

Conclusion

In sum, our defensive weapons are the best and perfectly adequate (once you know how to use them) but it is not wise to remain only on the defensive, always waiting for the next blow, always leaving the initiative to the enemy. Let us go on the offensive, let us attack, let us dictate the direction of the battle!

Unfortunately the idea is defended in certain circles that we should be passive. There are some who speak of 'power encounters', referring to situations on the mission field where a missionary is challenged by the enemy in some way and is thereupon obliged to demonstrate that God's power is greater. But the way the idea is presented it is the enemy that provokes the encounter; the missionary should not go looking for trouble but content himself with defensive action. It is a siege mentality. But the commands of Christ do not permit a siege mentality. If we are going to take the Gospel throughout the world, preaching to every person, making disciples in each ethnic group, we need a different mentality, a mentality of conquest. Of necessity we must take the offensive. 2 Corinthians 10:4 affirms that our weapons "are not carnal but mighty through God for **demolishing strongholds**". That implies offensive action, taking the battle to the enemy. We have already noted Psalms 78:9 and Jeremiah 48:10. In the second passage, when it says "cursed is he who holds back his sword from bloodshed!", it seems clear that God is demanding an active stance. We must take our swords in search of the enemy's blood (to follow the figure). So let us consider how to take the offensive.

Taking the Offensive

Before anything else we must have complete certainty about the victory that our Commander has already won and about the power, the authority that is available to us.

Our Position and Authority

Our position and authority are described in Ephesians 1:19-22 where the apostle is praying for us that we may know several things, including:

> *19 what is the exceeding greatness of his power toward us who believe, according to the working of his mighty power*
> *20 which he worked in Christ when he raised him from the dead and seated him at his own right hand in the heavenly places,*
> *21 far above all principality and power and might and dominion, and every name that is named, not only in this age but also in the one to come;*
> *22 and he has placed everything under his feet, . . .*

When we read that Jesus is now above all principality, power, might, etc. (see also 1 Peter 3:22) the terminology makes us think of the similar list in Ephesians 6:12 which refers to the hierarchy of the demons, headed up by Satan. The point is that Jesus did in fact win. He achieved the purpose of the incarnation as stated in Hebrews 2:14. "Since the children partake of flesh and blood, he himself likewise shared in the same, so that by his death he might destroy him who had the power of death, that is, the devil." Jesus came to destroy the devil and succeeded. Hallelujah! Consider also Colossians 2:15: "Stripping the principalities and powers he exposed them to public humiliation, triumphing over them by the cross." Satan and his hosts suffered a complete defeat. In John 16:11 the Lord Jesus said that "the ruler of this world has been judged". (It was still a few hours before His death, but Jesus was speaking of what the Comforter would do when He came, see verse 8, and by the day of Pentecost Satan had indeed been condemned.) That is why 1 John 4:4 affirms that He who is in us is greater than he who is in the world.

Returning to Ephesians let us look at 2:6, "and raised us up together, and made us sit together in the heavenly places in Christ Jesus". There it is. If you are in Christ where are you now seated? In the "heavenly places"! Right? But comparing this verse with 1:20, if we are in Christ precisely where is it that we are seated? Well, where is Christ? At the Father's right hand! God be praised, what a marvelous truth! And if we are at the Father's right hand that means that we also are **above** all principality, power, might, etc. There you have our position and our authority. We are face to face with a tremendous truth, a greater than that terrible truth of an enemy that has access to our minds. In Christ we are greater than the enemy! It makes you feel like kicking up your heels, doesn't it?

The enemy was defeated, was deposed, was expelled from his position as "ruler of this world" (John 12:31). However, for His own sovereign reasons (which He has not revealed to us), God allows the enemy to keep on operating on the basis of bluff (or as an impostor or usurper), as if nothing had happened. It is up to us to call his bluff, to call his hand, to force him to acknowledge his defeat. When we resist him we are doing this, in part, but we may take the offensive, and for that there are other weapons.

Bind the Enemy

Our starting point here is Mark 3:27. "No one can plunder the strong man's goods, invading his house, unless he first bind the strong man; then he may plunder his house." This verse already received some comment at the beginning of the chapter. The Lord Jesus declares that we must "bind the strong man". Although the verb 'to bind' is not in the imperative, it winds up having the effect of an order. If He commands us to evangelize and make disciples, and if to achieve that end we must bind the enemy, as already explained, then the binding is equivalent to a command. So how does one 'bind', wherein does it consist?

In my understanding and experience the binding consists of taking your position in Christ, claiming His victory and authority, and in so many words forbidding any satanic or demonic interference or activity with reference to a given person, place or occasion. It appears that we must be specific. I have already tried to bind Satan once for all to the end of the world, but it did not work. Why not? Well, I do not know, but I suppose it was God Himself who would not allow it, because if He did I would have frustrated His purpose for leaving Satan loose—for the world to end in the way that the Bible foretells the activity of Satan and the demons is still required. We must be specific, and then it works.

The New Testament in the Munduruku language (an indigenous group of Brazil) was 'in press' in our print shop for three years. It seemed like everything that could go wrong did: machinery broke, people got sick, the computer disobeyed the program, brand new plates came out of the sealed package already oxidized—it was really something! Finally the plates were ready to put on the machine to print the book. I was about to leave on a three-week trip. I went to the man in charge of the shop and explained that I wanted to bind the enemy so that nothing further would happen to delay the printing of that New Testament. He agreed and gathered his crew. I explained the ground rules and we proceeded to forbid any further interference in that project. When I returned from my trip three weeks later I looked up the print shop foreman: "How did it go?" "Like a charm, the New Testament is printed." Praise the Lord!

As I explained a bit ago, I consider that Matthew 18:18 also refers to this 'weapon'. Satan has already been bound in Heaven and it is up to us to bind him down here.[1] I am aware that the immediately prior context (verses 15-17) deals with discipline in the church, but I ask: Whose interests are best served when a brother falls into sin, is it not the enemy's? Notice too that the Text foresees the possibility that the person will persist in his sin. Should we not see Satan at work in such a situation? In fact, when faced with two such cases the procedure that the Apostle Paul used was to give the impenitents over to Satan (1 Corinthians 5:5 and 1 Timothy 1:20). I am also aware that in some churches this passage is used to impose some practice upon the faithful. A leader gets up and says that he is 'binding' sleeve length—from then on everyone must wear long-sleeved shirts. I do not see how such a use of our text can be correct, because if one person can 'bind' something like that then someone else can 'loose' it, and we are back to zero. It sometimes happens that two churches take opposite views on a certain practice and each one insists that it has 'bound' that practice. Of course it is fun to impose our ideas on others, but do you really suppose we can impose our ideas on God? We know that God is not "the author of confusion" (1 Corinthians 14:33); we cannot impute to Him confusions that are of our own making. As I have already said, the only viable interpretation of Matthew 18:18 that I have seen is to link it to spiritual warfare.

On February 28, 1986 the Brazil government decreed zero inflation (down from over 200%). Retail prices of consumer

---

[1] I am not aware of any Scripture that says in so many words that Satan is now 'bound' (he will be, literally, during the Millennium, but we are not there yet). However, Colossians 2:15 says he has been "stripped", Hebrews 2:14 that he has been "destroyed", John 12:31 that he has been "deposed", Ephesians 1:22 that he is "under Christ's feet", and Romans 16:20 promised the believers that he would shortly be "crushed" under their feet. Within the context of my exposition I consider that it is perfectly reasonable to say that from God's perspective, "in heaven", Satan is bound.

goods were frozen but the paper money supply continued to increase at some 18% a <u>month</u>![1] The poor masses loved it, but soon food and merchandise became increasingly scarce—the producers were losing money. By July it was obvious that adjustments had to be made, but important nation-wide elections were coming up in November and the government wanted to cash in on the popularity of the 'zero inflation' program. The price freeze was maintained until the election; the government party won a smashing victory at the polls; a week later they lifted the freeze and made other changes in economic policy. The public outrage was general; the people felt betrayed; there was unprecedented rioting in Brasília, the nation's capital. A few days later the leading labor unions decreed a nation-wide strike to close down the country for one day, December 12, 1986. Given the explosive social climate at that time I feared that the enemy would take advantage of the situation and instigate violence and destruction around the country.

I suggested to a home Bible study group that we pray specifically forbidding any malignant interference of any kind throughout the whole country on that day, with special reference to violence and destruction. We prayed, binding Satan and the demons in those terms. Those who were in Brazil on that day will recall that it was an unusually tranquil day, even less crime than usual. Now then, I know that I cannot prove cause and effect in this instance. I know also that other brethren were in prayer on that day calling on God to preserve the nation. However, I believe that the 'binding' of the enemy works precisely in this way, and I would like to suggest that we try to use this weapon toward the solution of the problems that trouble our country.

In the first instance "bind the strong man" in Mark 3:27 certainly refers to Satan, but I believe the concept can be applied locally. We have already verified from Daniel 10 that high-ranking demons take charge of important or strategic nations on this earth. It seems obvious to me that this is how Satan controls the world. He is not omniscient or omni-

---

[1] We did not find out about that until later.

present. So then, each country, each state, each city and town has a resident demon in charge of that area—the rank of the demon presumably corresponds to the relative importance of the place. In lecturing on this subject I have suggested that any missionary, upon arriving in an area where he plans to work, should bind the 'strong man' of that place, thereby avoiding much unnecessary suffering and difficulty. Some students of a certain Bible Institute in Brazil's Northeast put this suggestion into practice and reported back to me that it works. They formed teams and set out to start evangelical congregations in towns and villages of the interior, a region both arid and difficult. They always encountered heavy opposition—the local vicar would give orders that no one should rent to them or have any dealings whatever with them—in short, a tough situation. Then some of them decided to bind the strong man of the place before they arrived. They told me the situation changed dramatically—the people were more open, they found cooperation, people responded to the Gospel sooner and in greater numbers. In short, it worked! Thank you, Jesus!

Now just consider what a difference this procedure would make if we applied it around the world! Up to now, speaking generally, we have sent missionaries to the peoples of the world without paying attention to this truth—the missionaries have not, the missions have not and the churches have not, with the following result. When the missionary arrives at the place where he intends to work, there is the enemy—set, ready and waiting to smash him. Since the missionary does not know how to defend himself he usually takes a beating, sometimes a severe one, and in any case will achieve less than he could. We must change that scene. Before a missionary even gets near the field the churches and individuals that are backing him should send heavy artillery fire to flatten the enemy. The missionary himself needs to bind the strong man of the area before arriving, and to be alert to resist him at every step. If he does this he will certainly encounter less difficulty and enjoy greater success. Things will go even better if the churches remain alert and fight the war along with the missionary, binding the enemy from a distance.

Destroy Sophistries

Now let us consider another offensive procedure or weapon; we find it in 2 Corinthians 10:3-5.

> 03 though we walk in the flesh, we do not war according to the flesh,
> 04 for the weapons of our warfare are not fleshly but mighty through God for destroying strongholds,
> 05 destroying sophistries and every pretension that sets itself up against the knowledge of God, and taking captive every thought to make it obedient to Christ.

The apostle affirms that we have these great weapons, but does not say what they are nor how they operate. I really wish we had a full explanation, but since we do not we must learn by trying. But first, I understand that all our weapons are based on the victory and the power of Christ. Next, the Holy Spirit should be willing to give us orientation. The Text explains that the weapons are good for destroying strongholds—presumably of the enemy, since nobody would destroy their own. Well, I take it that verse 5 offers some light—it is made up of two participial clauses that are subordinate to the last phrase of verse 4.

The entire content of verse 5 enlarges upon "destroying strongholds", but I wish to call attention to the "sophistries" because the strongholds that we must destroy are mainly based upon the sophistries that Satan has fostered in this world (1 John 5:19). I take it that any worldview or philosophy of life that opposes the worldview of the Bible is one such sophistry. We may define 'sophistry' as a fallacious argument prepared with the intent of inducing someone else to err. For our purposes a sophistry is precisely any system of thought that sets itself up "against the knowledge of God".

And what are some of those sophistries? They are Islam, Marxism, Hinduism, Humanism, Spiritism, Buddhism, Materialism, Animism, Xintoism, Confucianism, among others. I wonder if we should not take a careful look at certain other '-isms' also—Protestantism, Catholicism, Denominationalism, etc.—to see if they do not distract or mislead people with reference to a true "knowledge of God".

The apostle affirms that "we do not war according to the flesh". Well, at least we shouldn't, right? But how often our 'fighting' is in fact fleshly! Is it not so? That is why we achieve so little; that is why half the world continues to perish without any knowledge of Christ. The use of fleshly weapons in the spiritual war can only produce negative results; it helps the enemy. Our God demands that both the end and the means be worthy of Him. The doctrine that the end justifies the means is diabolic. The weapons of our warfare must be spiritual, for that is the only way they can be powerful, and even so they must be "in God" (the enemy also uses spiritual weapons). Now then, the weapons that God gives us are designed for destroying "strongholds", and I believe we can understand the nature of those strongholds by studying verse 5. Anything that lifts itself up against the knowledge of God is a 'stronghold', or at least forms a part of such a stronghold. The end result of the destruction of the strongholds should be that every thought become obedient to Christ.

But how does this destroying of strongholds work? I confess that I do not know, for sure. I am still studying the question. However, I will offer a few ideas. Let us consider the 'sophistry' that presents the greatest challenge in Brazil, Spiritism. How can we dismantle that sophistry and free that country from it? Well, when dealing with an individual we must take account of what he believes. For instance, an informed and convinced voodooist: he knowingly deals with demons because of the demonstrations of power that they give. To make fun of him, to call his rituals mere superstition, will not reach him; he is dealing with demon power and knows that it exists (as in fact it does). What is required is a power confrontation. We must prove to the voodooist that we have power greater than that of the demons, that we can overpower them, that we can free people from their power. Without such proof we will just be talking through our hats.

We can liberate people one at a time and in this way produce some effect, no doubt. But, our time is short, Jesus is
coming! So I suggest the following: let us organize a campaign to close down all the spiritist centers in the country
(for starters), in a systematic way. I have stated that there
are already those who have closed such centers. This is
done by literally sealing off the area where the sessions are
held; that is to say, by forbidding in Christ's authority any
further demonic manifestation in that place from that moment on. When the manifestations cease the center will
close down, since there will be no more reason to gather
there. At this point we need to anticipate a protest. By sealing off such centers we will not violate anyone's religious
freedom; they are entirely free to call on the demons all day
and all night, if they wish. By all means. Our action is
against the evil spirits, not the people; our concern is to
demonstrate that Jesus is the greatest; that is all.

Now let us consider the case of a spiritist who believes he is
dealing with 'white' magic and 'angels of light'. To accuse
him of dealing with demons will not work because he will
repel that statement and despise our 'ignorance' into the
bargain; in other words, we place ourselves at a disad-
vantage. So how do we convince him of the truth? Again, I
believe that the best procedure is to go after the spirits,
sealing off the centers. When every manifestation of the
spirits ceases at a given center it will lose its attraction. At
that the participants will want to know what happened.
Then we can explain that we sealed off the area in Christ's
authority, and the fact that the manifestations ceased is
presumptive proof that the 'angels' were not exactly of
'light'; in any case we proved that the power of Jesus is
greater. The result of such a campaign will be the destruction of that sophistry; the power of the system will be undone.

In Hinduism and Animism the people are also dealing with
evil spirits and the most efficient approach we can take is to
give indisputable evidence that Christ's power is greater. I
understand that the Muslim also has trouble with the demons, and his religion gives him no solution. So, instead of

arguing about Jesus versus Mohammed or the Bible versus the Koran, perhaps a better way would be to sidle up to a Muslim and ask: "How are the demons doing today?" The point is, we need to find an area of life where we can give a clear and immediate demonstration that Jesus solves the problem but Mohammed and Allah do not (for a well written discussion to the effect that Allah is not the God of the Bible see *The Unholy War* by Marius Baar [Nashville: Thomas Nelson Publishers, 1980, pp. 58-70]). To handle case by case will produce some effect, but how can we dismantle the sophistry, the system? I confess that I do not know, but I would like us to think some more about the implications of our text. When it speaks of destroying every "pretension" that sets itself up against the knowledge of God and of "taking captive every thought" to make it obedient to Christ, what are we to understand?

Since it all is part of the destroying of strongholds these procedures have to do with offense. It follows that the 'thoughts' in view here must belong to persons who oppose the Gospel. (Our own thoughts must already be subject to Christ before we attempt to wage war like this.) We are obliged to conclude that it is possible to influence the thoughts of such persons, altering them to the point of being able to say that now they are obeying Christ! Did you ever think of that? Really? Oh praise be to our God! What a tremendous weapon! If we only knew how to wield this weapon we could take the world by storm! No one would be able to stop the Church! But alas, euphoria aside, can it be that we do know how to use it? Since I never heard anyone speak of it, and since I never saw anyone else do it, I suppose that we do not. I myself am barely crawling in this area, trying to learn how to walk. But let us turn our imaginations loose a bit.

The first problems that a missionary encounters when he tries to enter some foreign country relate to the government. He must have a visa, he must explain his intentions, he has to go through customs, sometimes restrictions are placed on his movements, etc. And why so many problems? It is because of the mentality that pervades the government for religious, ideological or political reasons, or else because of the personal background and mind-set of the particular official that is handling the case. And what about Christ's spokesman, must he bow to the 'inevitable'? Must he lower his head and return in defeat? I say, "No!" They are 'pretensions' that we must destroy; they are thoughts that must change, and it is up to us to impose that change in the authority of Christ. But how does it work? I suggest the following: we must take our place in Christ at the Father's right hand and claim all the power and authority that that position represents or confers; then, in the name of Jesus and in so many words we should require a change in the thinking of the official or the government such that the barriers will be removed. I believe we can do this at any level. I ask the reader to let me know what you learn in this area.

The concept of destroying strongholds can be applied in a variety of ways—for instance, in personal evangelism. There are 'strongholds' of the enemy in the minds/hearts of individuals that hinder them from being saved—it could be an 'addiction' to alcohol, rock or whatever; it could be a philosophical bias, a cultural value, a private 'hang-up' of some sort.[1] Christian parents with rebellious teen-age children should take a careful look at this possibility. It just could be that Christ's followers also fall prey to such strongholds— like theological bias, arrogance, selfishness; in short, anything that keeps us from hearing and obeying the voice of the Holy Spirit. (The 'world' and the 'flesh' are Satan's natural allies.) A whole culture may have a value or feature that seems to be designed to make it difficult for them to receive God's Word. For instance, the Jamamadi people of the Purus River in Brazil have a taboo against an exact repetition of

---

[1] I believe there are three forces or wills that are involved and interact— God's, Satan's and man's. In a certain sense we can cast the deciding vote. Until a person is freed from satanic interference in his thoughts he can be virtually powerless to respond to the Gospel. But we can give him every chance by repelling the evil interference and introducing a positive influence. However, the person must choose and can still refuse. At times it seems like an unequal struggle—although our power is greater, by and large we haven't used it; in the mean time the enemy plays dirty while the angels are obliged to play by the rules.

any statement. This made language learning very difficult, because every request for a repetition was answered with a synonymous utterance. Worse still, the taboo was extended to written statements—so it is unacceptable to read the Bible aloud, for example, or to quote it in a sermon! I believe it should be possible to claim the destruction of all such strongholds in the authority of the Lord Jesus. In fact, this was done to the taboo in question and it is losing its hold on that people. Praise the Lord!

Returning to governments, why not do something for ours? We can and should make use of our weapons on behalf of the peace and well-being of our people. Indeed, is that not the thrust of 1 Timothy 2:1-4? We are exhorted to intercede for those in authority so that we may lead a peaceable life; verse 3 says this is good and acceptable to God, while verse 4 links all this to God's desire that all men be saved! The social and economic problems we are facing undermine our capacity for exporting the Gospel. We must do something about that! I believe we can forbid any and all interference by the enemy in the thinking of the President and his advisers, in the Congress, etc. But we should not content ourselves with that; we can introduce a benevolent influence in the thinking of those people, as I explain in the next section.

Impose the Authority of Christ

Here I invite the reader's attention to two passages that have already received comment, Matthew 18:18 and 2 Corinthians 10:5. The first speaks of binding and loosing things that are already so in Heaven. It is the 'loosing' that invites further comment now. I have already suggested that the loosing should be the opposite of the binding, but both procedures depend on or result from the victory of Christ. If the binding refers to repelling malignant activity then the loosing should refer to the introduction of benevolent or positive activity, from God's point of view of course. I believe that in certain circumstances we can impose the authority of Christ on other people, on animals, on nature.

While I was studying in Toronto I learned of the following case. A certain lady, a sister in Christ, was on foot and had to walk under the 401 to get home; I believe she used the Bayview underpass. I think the 401 has some 14 lanes at that point, so it was not a very inviting place even though there is a sidewalk and some lighting. About half way through the underpass she was accosted by two men with criminal intent. She said: "I take authority over you in the name of Jesus." At that they were immobilized and she went by and kept on walking. Presently they cried out: "Have mercy, don't leave us here like this!" (they could not move). So she turned back, explained the facts and freed them. I cannot recall whether the men were converted on the spot, but in any case they no longer constituted a threat.

I may be mistaken, but it seems to me that it should not be necessary for us to fear assault, a fierce dog or anything else that wishes to attack us; or does Luke 10:19 mean something else? Except with reference to the difficulties that God Himself prepares for our exercise and growth, we should be able to use the authority of Christ—but always on behalf of the Kingdom of God, not our own selfish interests. Let me reinforce this proviso: the power of God and the authority of Christ are **not** to be used for ego trips or personal agendas, but only under the sovereign direction of the Creator to reach His objectives.

Returning to the example given above, the Lord Jesus did something similar; it is in Luke 4:28-30. On a certain Sabbath He was teaching in the synagogue of Nazareth; He was not very diplomatic and the hearers became enraged. They forced Him to the brow of the hill on which the town was built "in order to throw him down over the cliff". But then, Jesus "passing through the midst of them" went His way. Now then, tell me please, how did that work? Jesus was surrounded by a furious mob with some of them holding on to Him. So how did he escape? The Text does not say, but obviously Jesus did something to the people—either they were blinded or paralyzed or something. He made use of supernatural power to free Himself from a suffering, or perhaps a death, that was not of God. In John 8:59 it appears that Jesus became invisible to avoid a stoning. In John 10:39 He escaped again, presumably by supernatural means. (Let us not forget that Jesus said that we who believe into Him **will** do what He did—John 14:12.)

Now let us look at 2 Corinthians 10:5 again. Let us think some more about "taking captive every thought to make it obedient to Christ". When I spoke of that nation-wide strike in Brazil and said that we bound the enemy, forbidding any of his interference, I did not mention something else that we did. Since people are capable of thinking violent thoughts without any demonic 'help', we also took authority, in Christ, over the thinking of all the inhabitants of the country, forbidding thoughts of violence and calling for thoughts of peace, respect and tranquility. That is the way it was. Again, I cannot prove cause and effect, but I believe we are looking at a 'weapon' that has tremendous potential. I believe it is the sort of thing that we can, and should, do on behalf of our government as also of the countries where we send missionaries. And why not do some thing about the violence in Lebanon, for example, or the hate in South Africa, etc., etc.? I believe that with a bit of 'sanctified imagination' we may be guided by the Holy Spirit to take the initiative on various fronts around the world.

Undo the Works of the Devil

The last 'weapon' to be discussed is in 1 John 3:8. "For this purpose the Son of God was manifested, that he might undo the works of the devil." What should we understand by 'undo' the works of the devil? It seems to me that it must include altering the **consequences** of those works. We are looking at another tremendous weapon, one that is able to undo the results or consequences of attacks already perpetrated upon us. I tested this in my own experience in the following way.

In November, 1984 I was in Teresina, Piaui (a state capital in Brazil) lecturing on the missionary strategies of Christ. One night, after speaking about spiritual warfare, I was about to go to bed when I gave my cheek a bad bite—I almost took a piece off, the blood began to run. It happened that for several months prior to that night I had been having a strange experience. Whether speaking, chewing, or for no apparent reason my lower jaw would go out of control and I would bite my cheek or tongue. Once a sore started it seemed like I kept hitting it, so it was slow in healing. It seems like a minor matter but for someone who was doing a lot of public speaking it was bothersome. So then, by the time I got to Teresina I had about decided that I was being demonized. And I had been meditating on 1 John 3:8. So when I gave my cheek that bite I got angry—"Enough!" I resisted the demonizing, but it was too late; I was already bleeding. What to do? Then I remembered about undoing the works of the enemy. No sooner said than done, I proceeded to claim in the name of Jesus that the consequences of that attack upon my body should be undone. For the glory of God I wish to state that immediately the blood stopped and the pain passed. I slept. By the light of the new day I looked in the mirror to check the place of the bite—it was smooth. Thank you, Lord!

Jesus did something similar; the account is in Mark 4:37-39 (see also Matthew 8:24-26 and Luke 8:23-24). They were crossing the Sea of Galilee. After a day of teaching and dealing with the multitude Jesus was tired and fell asleep in the stern. Then a violent windstorm came up and the waves beat into the boat so that it was nearly swamped. At that point, fearing death, the disciples woke Him up. Jesus got up and rebuked the wind and the sea: "Shut up! Be muzzled!" And there was complete calm. Personally I do not doubt that that storm was prepared by Satan. Being professional fishers the disciples had seen no end of storms on that lake; to really scare them required something unusual. However that may be, Jesus worked a double miracle. First, He stopped the wind. But, if that was all He did, the water would still be agitated for some time. When He produced an immediate calm He **undid the consequences** of the windstorm. There you have it.

You do not have to be a prophet to see that this weapon permits us to catch sight of marvelous effects. Here too I am barely crawling. There is much land yet to be occupied, but the potential that this weapon offers justifies almost any effort to learn how to really use it. If we can reverse tragedies that have already been perpetrated—it should be possible to cure emotional and psychological traumas in this way—how many transformed lives and healed homes shall we not see! Again, I ask the reader to share with me what you may learn in this area.

"Greater Works than These"

Perhaps some reader is feeling a little bit stunned by the audacity of my suggestions. Okay, I recognize that I have proposed things that in fact we have not been doing. But then, just what interpretation do you give to the words of the Lord Jesus recorded in John 14:12? "Most assuredly I say to you, he who believes into me, the works that I do he will do also; even greater works than these he will do, because I go to my Father." To be frank, I have always found it hard to think of **equaling** Jesus' works; to excel them was simply out of the question. But there is His declaration: He did not say "perhaps do", He said "**will** do"; He did not say "a few privileged or gifted ones", or "if the doctrine of your church will allow it", He said "**he who believes**". So now what do we say? Are we going to believe, or not? Are we going to do, or not? I understand that it is precisely the victory of Christ that makes possible our doing 'greater' things. In some sense Jesus had to restrain or limit Himself until He actually defeated Satan by His death and resurrection, and until He took up His place at the Father's right hand. Now the rules of the game are different; there is the victory of Christ waiting to be claimed and applied down here.

Although in this day and age we have television, computers, satellites, etc. that allow us to do things that were unknown in Jesus' time, I do not see how we can point to such things as the interpretation of our text—Jesus said, "because I go to my Father" (what does modern technology owe to Christ's ascension?); Jesus said, "he who believes into me" (there is nothing there about waiting until the invention of television). Even if someone were to persist in such a position it is still incumbent upon us to **do the works that He did**, namely raise the dead, cure the sick and free the demonized, for starters! Actually, it seems to me to be perfectly clear that Jesus was thinking of the unleashing of God's power, not modern technology, when He said "greater works than these". Past generations did not have the technology but the Text was written for them as well.

And what might some of those "greater works" be? Well, would precluding violence in an entire country [Brazil] during the 24 hours of a national strike be a reasonable candidate? Dismantling spiritism in Brazil would be another. I believe Luke 8:31 give us basis for consigning demons to the Abyss, thereby reducing the number of the enemy's forces (against us). And how about destroying sophistries, taking thoughts captive and punishing disobedience (2 Corinthians 10:5-6)? If we will ask the Holy Spirit, really placing ourselves at His command, surely He will show us further procedures. Just look at Ephesians 3:20—"Now to Him who is able to do exceedingly abundantly above all that we ask or think, according to the power that works in us, . . ." Wow! The Holy Spirit, using the apostle, affirms that God Himself is waiting to do **much** more than we can even imagine. In other words, the procedures I have suggested above are 'small potatoes'. "The power that works [present tense] in us" is just waiting for us to turn it loose, for us to act with courage and a holy imagination, for us to be audacious in the use of that power.

As I have already stated, I do not pretend to have a corner on the truth. There is a great deal that I do not understand. I hope to learn from others. All said and done it is to **Jesus** that we will have to give an accounting for all the abilities and resources that He has placed in our hands. So I make this plea: let us humble ourselves before God and His Word and in all sincerity ask the Holy Spirit to orient us with respect to the things presented in this essay. Oh God, may Your will be done, may Your name be glorified, may Your kingdom come in us and through us in this world!

Strategic Implications

To conclude and sum up the exposition of this strategy, let us review a few implications. The real world is the spiritual one (see Hebrews 9:8-9 and 22-24, 2 Corinthians 4:18, 1 Corinthians 9:11, Romans 15:27, Galatians 6:6)—this physical world that so fills our vision is nothing more than a 'shadow', a 'figure of the true'. That is why the real war is fought in the spiritual realm. We need to increase our sensitivity to the spiritual; our churches are full of wounded 'soldiers' who do not even know it.

We have a terrible enemy who hates us and is always after us. The servants of Christ are his favorite target; the more useful you become in God's hand the more you will be harassed. Too often Satan manages to use us as his instruments to knock down some colleague and then trample him to make sure he cannot get back up. One thinks of cases where a brother suffers violent and virulent attacks, beyond restraint, beyond measure, beyond reason, all out of proportion to the error he may have committed, attacks leveled by other believers. How can this be? Sometimes a spirit of hate is evident; the others do all they can to destroy the person so that he may never be restored. It is a work of Satan and we must open our eyes to this fact. And then there are the bitter fights over doctrinal minutiae, things that make no real difference; and yet they split churches and cause permanent estrangement between believers, as well as other types of damage. This too is a work of Satan. We must get wise, people!

Yet we have adequate weapons, in fact tremendous ones, both for defense and offense. We must instruct God's people about these things. We must become skilled in the use of our weapons. We need workers who know how to wage spiritual warfare, who know how to impose Christ's victory over Satan and the demons. If we manage to fill the world with that kind of worker we can finish reaching the world, fulfilling Christ's great commission, within a few years, relatively speaking. Yes, because that kind of worker will produce a great deal more than the others that do not know how.

We need churches full of disciples who also know how to wage war. We need sharpshooters, people who can hit a specific target. Up to now the prayers of God's people have usually been general, like shooting in the general direction of the enemy; it may make him duck down for a bit but does not cause many casualties. We will see much better results when we send accurate shots at the heads of the enemy.

We need to really believe what the Lord Jesus said in Matthew 16:18—". . . I will build my Church, and the gates of Hades will not withstand her." The verb rendered as "prevail" usually implies that its Subject has the initiative, and accordingly most English versions give the impression that Hades is attacking the Church. If this is the correct interpretation, we have the important promise that Hades will not win. However, that verb may also imply a defensive posture, and since "gates" do not attack but rather are the last line of defense of a city, I suggest that the correct interpretation is that the Church is attacking Hades—"the gates of Hades will not be able to withstand it". This gives us the even more exciting promise that the Church will indeed batter down the enemy's gates. Either way, we should take courage and fight with confidence!

I have left till last a truth that abuses me, that really makes me angry. It is this: with reference to 1,000 ethnic groups we are the ones who are bound; for those groups the victory of Christ is still worth very little! How can we bear such a thing?! For them the Gospel does not exist, there is no witness for Christ, and as a result there is little point in binding Satan with reference to them. Yes, we can bind him, but what good will it do? I suppose we could alleviate the physical suffering of such a people but we cannot solve the fundamental problem of their spiritual destiny and well-being until the Gospel is effectively within their grasp. It is altogether necessary that Christ have a spokesman for every ethnic group! **"Pray ye, therefore, the Lord of the harvest."**

Of all the missionary strategies of Christ that are discussed in this book the one treated in this essay seems to me to be the most important. To be sure, if God's people would really obey any one of them we would finish reaching the world in our generation. But if every believer learned to wage spiritual warfare in the terms herein presented we would mow Satan down. We would transform our lives, our families, our churches, our society and maybe even the world! What do you say? Shall we give it a try? Let us have at it! Let us go for it! May God help us!

BIBLICAL SPIRITUAL WARFARE[1]

The Christian Life as it Should Be!

We are here to undo the works of the devil!

A. **The Purpose of the Lord Jesus**: "Just as the Father has sent me, so I send you" (John 20:21)—just as . . . so. It is the Lord Jesus Christ, greatest of missionaries, our ultimate example, who is speaking. He expects, indeed demands, that we do like He did.

1. So then, what did He do? The Father decided and the Son obeyed: "I am here to do your will, O God" (Hebrews 10:7). (John 4:34—"My food is to do the will of Him who sent me, and to finish His work.") To any and all concerned Christians I say, we too must experience Hebrews 10:7. Any genuine, effective participation in the spiritual war begins with total commitment to the Lord Jesus, which needs to be renewed each day. Just like Sovereign Jesus, our life needs to revolve around the Father's will (John 5:19 & 12:49-50).

2. And what was that will, in specific terms? We find it in Hebrews 2:14—the Son took on flesh and blood in order to destroy the devil (and He succeeded, Revelation 1:18); He came to undo his works (1 John 3:8). So why was that necessary? Back in the Garden, Adam turned over the administration of this world to Satan, who continued through time as the god/prince of this world [recall that after the 40 days Jesus did not deny Satan's right to offer what he did]. That is why a Second Adam (1 Corinthians

---

[1] All interpretations are the responsibility of the author, who does not subscribe to any denominational 'package'. (To place any doctrinal package above the Text is a form of idolatry.) I attempt to handle the Sacred text with total respect, because I understand it to be our highest authority. In passing we may observe that the Truth is not democratic, does not depend upon human opinion or vote; the Truth is. (It should also be obvious that the Kingdom of God is not a democracy.)

15:47; or "last", verse 45) had to come to recover all that the first one had lost [a perfect man—the virgin birth was necessary because any human seed was now contaminated].

3. O.K., so why are we here? To continue the work of Christ. He came to destroy Satan, and He succeeded, hallelujah! (Colossians 2:15, John 16:11, Ephesians 1:20-21, John 12:31, 1 Peter 3:22,   1 John 4:4). In fact, Satan was indeed destroyed, his final destination has been decreed (Matthew 25:41), but for His own sovereign reasons, the Creator still allows the enemy to operate in this world. It is up to us to call his bluff—we have to oblige the devil to acknowledge his defeat in concrete terms (Matthew 18:18). Christ came to undo Satan's works, but since Satan continues to perpetrate all forms of evil, it is up to us to undo them, because as soon as He won the victory, Jesus went back to Heaven. Since the Church has been terribly remiss in this area, we are all obliged to live with the negative consequences of our omission. **We are here to undo the works of the devil**!

4. From the beginning the Lord Jesus knew who He was, and why He was here. From 1 Peter 1:18-21 and Revelation 13:8 we understand that the Lamb was known and slain before the creation of this earth. In Hebrews 1:10, John 1:3, 10 and Colossians 1:16 we see that the Son was the primary agent in the creation of this world. In other words, Jehovah the Son went ahead and created this world even though He knew beforehand that He would have to be the Lamb so as to rescue it. [Our understanding is limited, but it is clear that the human race represents something that is very important to the Creator.] Upon entering this world the Son said: "Sacrifice and offering were not what you wanted, but You prepared a body for me" (Hebrews 10:5). Jehovah the Son accepted the body prepared for Him [as any true disciple also must], knowing just what was in-

volved (John 12:27)—the Lord Jesus knew who He was and why He was here.

5. So what? Well, "just as...so". We too must know who we are and why we are here. So, who are we?

   a. We are human beings, created in the image and likeness of the Creator (Genesis 1:26) (a privilege and responsibility greater than we sometimes imagine). [Noah's ark; evolution is scientifically impossible; the earth is young.]

   b. In Christ we are accepted in the Beloved (Ephesians 1:6).

   c. In Christ we are at the Father's right hand, in Heaven, far above the whole army of fallen angels (Ephesians 1:20-21, 2:6).

   d. "I give [as in some 98% of the Greek manuscripts] you **the** authority . . . over all the power of the enemy" (Luke 10:19). "All authority has been given to me in heaven and on earth" (Matthew 28:18). If the One who holds all authority has delegated to us the authority over Satan's power, then we can give orders to that power—we need to learn how to do this! However, since Luke 10:19 goes on to say, "nothing will by any means hurt you", the focus appears to be on defense—defending ourselves, and others, from Satan's attacks. But since we have access to Christ's limitless power (Ephesians 3:20), we do not need Satan's, and we should not give him the satisfaction of seeing us use it. Further, he is so crafty that the distinct possibility exists that he could deceive us into doing things that we should not. We need to ask God for an adequate understanding of just how we are to exercise our authority over the enemy's power.

   e. "As He is, so are we in this world" (1 John 4:17). The Church is the Body of Christ, so it is mainly through her that He deals with the world. (When you look at someone what you see is his body.) We are the Creator's spokesmen on this earth. (John 20:21, Luke 4:17-21/Isaiah 61:1-2, Matthew 28:20—"teaching them to observe <u>all things</u> that I have commanded you.") (In fact, we are spokesmen for the Trinity!—1 John 4:13-14, Genesis 1:26.)

    f. <u>Attention</u>: Believers, it is time to wake up! We must realize and accept that we represent the Creator down here and He is expecting from us a posture and behavior that are worthy of our office.

6. "As He is so are we in this world"—in this world, not the next. "Just as the Father sent me, so send I you." Let us think a bit about our Lord's example. We have already said that He knew who He was and why He was here. At twelve years of age He knew that He was about "my Father's business" (Luke 2:49). He was always in control of the situation, He never showed fear. In Luke 4:28-30 He made use of God's power to avoid a premature death. In John 8:59 we find another instance where He extracted Himself in a sovereign way (see also John 10:39). In Mark 4:35-41 Satan used nature in an effort to kill Him. Even in the garden, when Judas brought the guards to take Him, Jesus, hearing that they were looking for Him, said, "I am He"—and they fell to the ground (John 18:6). He was only taken prisoner because He permitted it. As He said to Peter, He had only to ask and the Father would immediately send "more than twelve legions of angels" (Matthew 26:53). But the hour had come for Him to die, as He well knew before He came (John 12:27). Everything was under control. [John 19:11—Pilate; Matthew 27:34—gall; He shouted τετελεσται (John 19:30); John 10:18, 19:30 (Matthew 27:50)—He dismissed His spirit; Mark 15:37-39—centurion] {2 Timothy 1:7, Proverbs 25:26,28, 29:11, 29:25 X Proverbs 28:1} We must recover a principle that was known in the O.T. (Elijah—fire [2 Kings 1:9-15]; Elisha—bears [2 Kings 2:23-24], blinded Syrians [2 Kings 6:18]). Paul also (Acts 13:8-11).

7. That was then, but this is now, so how about us? The example of Jesus is precisely to the point, because what He did He did as a man. In John 14:12, in the upper room, that last night before the crucifixion, the Lord Jesus said to the Disciples: "Most assuredly I declare to you that he who **believes** into Me will also do the works that I do; he **will do** even greater than these, because I go to my Father." Note well, Jesus did not say, "you the Apostles", but rather, "he who believes". ("Believe" is present tense; if you believed yesterday it is not enough, you must believe today.) He did not say, "perhaps do", but rather, "will do". He did not say, "if the doctrine of your church allows", but rather, "will do". It follows that if I am not 'doing' I am not believing. That conclusion is inescapable. I used to think that to actually do the same works that Jesus did would be great, so I would have been satisfied if I could manage it. But **Jesus** would not be satisfied, because He now expects "greater" things. The secret is in the final phrase, "because I am going to my Father". With that phrase He was foreseeing His victory, because if He had sinned on His own account He would have had to pay the "wages of sin" and thus could never return to the Father. But He won, Hallelujah, and is now really and truly at the Father's right hand, "far above every principality, power, might," etc. (Ephesians 1:20-21). But Ephesians 2:6 gives us to understand that whoever belongs to Jesus is there too. That is why we can and should be doing the "greater things".

   a. Although He was indeed God, He walked this earth as a human being submissive to the Holy Spirit. [The 2nd Adam, a perfect man, had to recover everything as a human being.] It follows that we too can do the works that He did; if we are submissive to the Holy Spirit. "**Just as. . .so**"—we can and we should do as He did (Luke 10:19).

   b. But the Lord Jesus expects and demands "greater things"; because now He is at the Father's right hand, and **we are too** (Ephesians 1:19-22, 2:6). Ephesians 3:20—the power **at work** in us is practically unlimited, potentially; so we have all we need in order to walk as Jesus walked, wielding the power of God on behalf of God's Kingdom.

   c. Matthew 17:17-20—"perverse and faithless generation", "like a grain of mustard seed *has*". To go against known truth is to be perverse.

   d. Luke 16:10-12—"faithful in the unjust riches" → will receive the true riches (it is wise to get rid of any financial debt before taking an active role in the war). (Romans 13:8; Leviticus 19:13)

   e. John 20:21, John 14:12, 1 John 4:17—if we fail to do the "greater things" we will be cheating the Lord Jesus out of what He deserves = to see His victory being used and applied on behalf of the salvation of the world.

   f. (Our own participation in the administration of the Kingdom is at stake [Revelation 2:26-27].)

   g. Before taking up the "greater things", as such, let us consider the Apostle Paul's missionary commission.

B. **Paul's Missionary Commission** (Acts 26:17-8).

   1. Jesus came back from Heaven to commission Paul— he was to carry on with the war against Satan (see Isaiah 42:7).

     a. Open eyes—light does not help the blind; one must open their eyes first (by prohibiting the satanic blinding, 2 Corinthians 4:3-4).

     b. Rescue people from Satan's power; bring them back to God—"so that they may receive remission of sins and a place among the sanctified".

     c. Handcuff the strong man so as to steal his goods (Mark 3:27).

     d. Because he interferes in the thought processes of those who are being evangelized (2 Corinthians 4:3-4, Mark 4:15, Luke 8:12). (To my mind, this access of the enemy may well be the most terrible reality that exists in this life.)

N.B.—to remove people from Satan's house is a principal way to "undo the works of the devil".

2. The strategic effect—anyone who fails to take account of these things will produce little effect, make little difference (accomplice of the enemy).
   a. I got clobbered, being skeptical; in spite of a ThM I did not know how to bind the enemy. I was demoralized, and since I was Christ's representative He was too! (Jesus sent me to the Amazon jungle to an indigenous people to try to extract them from Satan's house.)
   b. Most of the ethnic groups of the world are animists or otherwise concerned to coexist with evil spirits, waiting for a power able to free them from the demons. Lamentably, the large majority of missionaries working with such peoples are also skeptical (as I once was)—they do not know how to impose the victory of Christ upon the enemy. The general result has been **evangelical syncretism**.
   c. "A place among the sanctified"—in the first place this presumably refers to our position in Christ (final sanctification), but I believe it also refers to our daily experience—most of those who are called to transcultural work are defeated by the enemy before they leave home; of those who do reach a mission field, half return home defeated within four years—we must understand that we are at war!
3. The spiritual war (Ephesians 6:10-19)—we are in a war universal in sphere, and everything we do acquires its main significance in the context of that war (Luke 11:23); actually we are on the battlefront—it is necessary to take all due precaution. To be more precise, we are in a wrestling match with malignant spirits (Ephesians 6:12) [1 Peter 5:8].

4. The guarantee of the victory—Jesus died in order to destroy Satan, and succeeded! (Hallelujah!) In any war it is normally an advantage to take the offensive and maintain the initiative. The wars that the USA fought in Korea and Vietnam illustrate clearly the calamitous consequences of fighting a war of containment, only [the Persian Gulf war was far better in terms of strategy]. We should learn from such examples. We should attack the enemy at his base of supply, his backyard, his headquarters. The idea is to get rid of him, if possible. Satan and his angels, the demons, are totally bad, malignant, incurable, irrecoverable—there is absolutely no way to help them, improve them, save them. They hate us and are becoming ever more aggressive against us. Knowing that they are condemned (Matthew 25:41), their only 'pleasure' is to do as much damage as possible, dragging the 'image of the Creator' in the mud. We need to get it into our heads that we are in a war without truce, quarter, pity or compassion. So now let us take up the "greater things".

C. **Taking the Offensive—the "greater things"** (John 14:12, Ephesians 3:20-21). Things that the Lord Jesus refrained from doing until He won the victory (got to the cross without sinning) we now can and should do, on the basis of the victory already won.
   1. Our position and authority.
      a. We are in Christ at the Father's right hand (Ephesians 1:19-22, 2:6, 1 John 4:4) and therefore (far) above Satan and all the demons, in all their ranks.
      b. Satan is already defeated (Colossians 2:15, John 16:11, 1 Peter 3:22, Hebrews 2:14, John 12:31, Ephesians 1:21). But God, for His own sovereign reasons (which He has not revealed very clearly), permits the enemy to continue operating here, on the basis of bluff or usurpation, as if nothing had happened. It is up to us to call his bluff, to impose his defeat upon him.

2. Bind Satan (Mark 3:27, Matthew 18:18). Jesus declares that it is necessary, but does not explain how it is done. In our experience it works like this: you take your place in Christ (consciously), claim His victory and authority, and in so many words forbid any satanic or demonic interference or activity with reference to a specific person, place, occasion, etc. (Do not forget those who are being evangelized.)
   a. It appears that we must be specific. I have tried to bind Satan once for all until the end of the world, but it did not work. Why? I suppose that if it should work it would frustrate God's sovereign purpose whereby He still allows Satan to work, and obviously He will not permit that; also, He is training us for our future responsibilities.
   b. Bind local 'strongmen'—territorial demons (Daniel 10). Pound the enemy with heavy artillery before the arrival of the missionary. [war in the Persian Gulf]
      i. Pacts with demons made by ancestors. Spiritual mapping.
      ii. Injustices perpetrated in the past (2 Samuel 21:1-6, 14). Identificational prayer.
      iii. Local curses/maledictions: Matthew 10:14-15 (Acts 13:51, Matthew 11:21-24)—missionaries and pastors who left defeated/bitter (John 20:23).
3. Send demons to the Abyss (Luke 8:31, Revelation 9:1-11).
4. Destroy strongholds and "sophistries" (2 Corinthians 10:4-5). Retaking areas from territorial spirits (cardinal points).
   a. At the level of countries or regions: religions / worldviews / ideologies. We can wage war around the world, in the spiritual realm, fighting beside our missionaries.
   b. At the level of the individual: strongholds (beachheads) in people—curses, pacts, fetishes (Exodus 20 X Ezekiel 18). [2 Corinthians 5:17 "everything became new" = potentially. Neither

the blood of Christ nor the grace of God will necessarily or automatically free us from the consequences of our sins in this life (just in the hereafter).] Jeremiah 17:5—to confide in man brings a curse.

5. Impose the authority of Christ (2 Corinthians 10:5-6, Matthew 18:18b) (activate angels—Hebrews 1:14; Matthew 26:53, 18:10; Acts 12:15).
   a. Influence governments—"take thoughts captive". (Influence the thoughts of government officials.)
   b. Influence people and nature (Luke 10:19 and Mark 16:18) (Jesus—Luke 4:28-30, John 8:59, 10:39; Mark 4:35-41—He quieted wind and water).
   c. "Punish disobedience"—2 Corinthians 10:6 (judgment begins at House of God); Psalm 149:7-8.

6. Undo the works of the devil (1 John 3:8; Luke 10:19).
   a. In society (1 Timothy 2:1-4). The Church, "pillar and foundation of the truth" (1 Timothy 3:15). Proverbs 25:26 X Proverbs 28:1; Proverbs 28:4, Zechariah 5:1-4. (Psalm 149:5-11)
   b. Consequences in specific cases (disease, etc.)—(Jesus—Mark 4:37-9).
   c. In nature, especially in human bodies. [Some years ago Dr. Ralph Winter suggested that all pathogens are the work of Satan—he alters good bacteria created by God. The hypothesis is plausible; since he manages to alter human beings (who are infinitely more complex) to alter a microbe is 'small potatoes'. By all means, let all of us work at testing the thesis—the potential is staggering.] See my essay, "Concerning Pathogens—Origin and Solution".

7. Order Satan to return what he has stolen from us, directly or indirectly ("four/five times as much"—Exodus 22:1; or even "seven times"—Proverbs 6:31). The 'goods' that we are to plunder, Mark 3:27, include more than the persons that are in Sa-

tan's 'house'; they also include the money and material goods that he has stolen from God's servants and the Cause of Christ over the years. [I am not yet sure as to just how to go about this; if you know, please tell me.]

8. "As He is, so are we in this world" (1 John 4:17). The Church is the body of Christ. The prerogative to judge the world—John 5:22, 27; Psalm 149:5-9; 1 Corinthians 6:2-3; Zechariah 5:1-4. [dominion of the world: God → Adam → Satan → Christ → us]

9. (Careful with competition against 'saints' and shamans—take care that <u>God</u> will receive the glory for a healing, etc.)

Now then, be not deceived. We are at <u>war</u>, and the enemy will certainly fight back, retaliate. It is absolutely necessary to be alert and prepared, and to know how to defend yourself.

D. **Weapons of Defense**: God does not send us against Satan without defense—we have the best weapons, but we must know what they are and be prepared to use them.

1. Free yourself from aftereffects of the past—'interior healing'.
   a. Be baptized (break your link with the world and the devil). Invoke the Lord (1 Peter 3:21).
   b. Pacts and curses that come through others (Exodus 20:5). Leviticus 26:40 teaches explicitly, Jehovah speaking, that it can be necessary to confess the iniquity of our forebears. (But against current attacks we should bind the enemy.)
   c. Contamination by 'transferred' spirits (Ness). If you embrace a lie, you invite Satan into your mind.
   d. Pacts and curses for which we ourselves are responsible (Jeremiah 17:5, 48:10 [against 'pacifism'], Revelation 3:16, Malachi 1:8,13-14, 3:8-9).

e. "I won't accept that!" If resisted, the Holy Spirit withdraws, and Satan takes advantage—that area may become a stronghold of Satan in one's life. Our ignorance of the Bible and of spiritual realities is an open door inviting Satan into our minds. When someone is more concerned to defend his point of view than to hear God's Word, it is quite possible that his point of view is in fact a stronghold of Satan in his mind.

f. Snares of the devil (masonry—John 8:12, transcendental meditation, theory of evolution, pornographic material, etc.)—2 Timothy 2:26, Acts 8:23, Exodus 23:33, Joshua 23:13, 2 Timothy 2:26, 1 Timothy 3:7, Acts 19:19.

g. Alliances with sin—Hebrews 12:1 (fornication, abortion, divorce) (Judges 2:23, 3:4) (Psalm 109:17-18). (Satan exploits trauma, any and all trauma.) Idolatry—the doctrine of the church is placed above the Word of God, Mark 7:7-8 (Isaiah 29:13). (Like a dog on a leash, with Satan holding the other end.)

h. Capital sins—God decrees death: witchcraft (Exodus 22:18,20, Leviticus 18:21,29, 20:27); bestiality (Exodus 22:19, Leviticus 18:23,29, 20:15-16); homosexuality (Leviticus 18:22,29, 20:13, Romans 1:26-27); incest (Leviticus 18:6-17,29, 20:11-12); adultery (Exodus 20:14, Leviticus 18:20,29, 20:10, Proverbs 6:32-33—it destroys the soul, the reproach lasts until the grave). Romans 1:32 makes clear that those who practice such things (among others) "**are** deserving of death"—it does not say "were", but "are", now, in this time of grace (Romans was written after Pentecost). God's moral standards do not change, because His character does not change— with "the Father of lights" there is "no variation or shadow of turning" (James 1:17); "Jesus Christ is the same yesterday, today, and forever" (Hebrews 13:8). It would not surprise me if such crimes against the Creator were to require special procedures so as to become liberated to really get involved in the war. (See chapters 9 and 12 of *Becoming a Vessel of Honor in the Master's Service*, by Rebecca Brown.)

2. Free yourself from complications in the present.
   a. Do not give place to the devil—Ephesians 4:27.
      i. Ephesians 4:26—anger, hate, resentment if harbored and nurtured become Satan's saddle horses.
      ii. Lack of pardon—Matthew 6:14-15 (Ephesians 4:30-32).

      ("Your Father in heaven will <u>not</u> pardon you"—what did the Lord Jesus mean? Even if we choose a less troublesome interpretation— that there are two types or areas of divine pardon, the pardon that gives justification and eternal life to the regenerated and the pardon that reestablishes fellowship and depends on constant confession [1 John 1:9], and that the pardon here is of the second type—we are looking at a serious matter. If God does not pardon me, because I do not want to pardon, then I remain out of fellowship, which will certainly affect my protection—I am open to the enemy's attacks without understanding what is going on.)

      iii. Do not dally with Delilah (Samson). Do not set anything wicked before your eyes—Psalm 101:3 (Psalm 119:37, Philippians 4:8). (Television, videos, Internet—a diet of pornography, violence, perverted values, occult, destruction, etc., is guaranteed to subject you to satanic influence, because if you feed the flesh, the Spirit withdraws.)
   b. You must understand that we are not automatically free from curses and other attacks from witches and warlocks; they can project their spirits, etc. (See also Psalm 37:14-15.) Retaliation most certainly exists, and it will come against

anyone who gets involved in spiritual warfare, but there is protection—Joel 3:4.

    c. Inappropriate prayers and maledictions proffered against us by fellow Christians—Gal. 5:15 (Proverbs 28:9, John 20:23). A believer can curse just with his thought. (When God cannot use a prayer it plays right into the enemy's hand. Our churches are full of people who have been wounded by other believers.) (We need to keep alert, repel such attacks, ask for God's counter blessing [Psalm 109:28], take their thoughts captive [2 Corinthians 10:5], overcome evil with good [Romans 12:14, 17-21]—do not descend to their level.)

    d. Curses through the church—Malachi 2:1-3, 7; Hosea 4:6<u>b,c</u>; Jeremiah 23:14,17,22. ['the Lord's anointed'—only by direct command from God; that anointing is not for life; it does not exist in the NT] ['apostolic succession'—ordination by pastors who are masons, evolutionistic, arrogant sinners, etc.] When the hierarchy has an alliance with evil (Jeremiah 20:1-4)—when the head pastor persecutes a prophet sent by God, that pastor becomes a curse. See also Matthew 23:2,13,15,33, <u>15:9</u>. The spirit of impunity that pervades the society at large has invaded the churches; the same holds for the spirits of materialism, humanism, relativism. They curse lives.

    e. Protection/coverage lacking—irresponsible husband, etc. (1 Corinthians 11:9-10; Numbers 30:3-15.)

3. The armor in Ephesians 6:13-18 (there is nothing to protect the back—we must face the enemy).

    a. Truth—any lack of truth in my life will be an opening that the enemy will certainly take advantage of.

    b. Justice—any lack of justice in my life, likewise.

    c. Training—to go out to war without adequate training is like going barefoot; you step on something sharp and then have to limp. A wounded foot in a wrestling match is very serious.

d. Faith—in God (Ephesians 6:16). We must know that our God is the greatest! (Rebecca Brown, in *Becoming a Vessel*, says we can use the shield and sword literally against witches/warlocks.)

e. Assurance of salvation.

f. The Word of God (Ephesians 6:17)—Jesus illustrated the defensive use after the 40 days (repel fear, accusations, etc. on the basis of the Word).

g. Prayer (Ephesians 6:18-9)—since our war is spiritual it is mainly waged in the spiritual realm, that is, in prayer. (A missionary needs a good number who will pray for him, verse 19, and with perseverance.)

4. The greatest defensive weapon = "resist" (James 4:7).[1] One must submit to God first. "Resisting" works like this: recognize that the enemy is at work in a specific case and then repel him in the authority of the Lord Jesus Christ. 'Casting out' demons = "resist"; it works in the same way.

Now then, Satan prefers to keep people and churches in ignorance and skepticism about him, but when someone wakes up to this truth then the enemy works to confuse the issue, thereby reducing the damage he will suffer. Calmly and humbly I wish to discuss certain 'myths' in this area, at least as I see it.

a. "Resist" is not a gift; it is a command (1 Peter 5:9). A gift is for the few who receive it, a command is for all. (Protect your own family.)

b. Do not ask God to do it; He has ordered us to do it (on the basis of His victory / in His name). It would be disobedience, not humility. We can do what the archangel Michael could not (Jude 9)—

---

[1] I first wrote this some thirty years ago, and I have learned a few things since then. I would now say that Luke 10:19 offers us a still better weapon than James 4:7, but I will leave this discussion as it is, with the promise that I will take up Luke 10 in a bit.

in essence we are superior to the angels (Genesis 1:26, Romans 8:17, 1 Corinthians 6:3, Colossians 2:18, Hebrews 1:14, Ephesians 1:21, 2:6).

c. Do not ask permission—war is war. It is not necessary to be physically present; in the spiritual realm we can fight around the world.

d. Prayer and <u>fasting</u> (Mark 9:29, Matthew 17:21 [over 99% of the Greek manuscripts have "fasting"—the few that do not are of inferior quality]. Does my fasting add anything to the victory of Christ or the power of God? (The 'rules of the game' may now be different, since the Victory—Ephesians 1:20, 2:6.)

   i. if you have authority you do not need to yell (demons are not deaf)—avoid any semblance of sensationalism [religious culture].

   ii. it is not necessary to lay on hands or burn objects (except that fetishes and satanic artifacts should be destroyed). (In the O.T. things were different, but with Christ's victory the rules changed.)

   iii. do not destroy things without the permission of the owner.

e. Demons are 'con men'—they will try anything to mislead or confuse us.

   i. resist any and all and forbid their return—better yet, send them to the Abyss; also seal off the person or place against any other demons.

   ii. do not converse with them—they are liars by nature. Note Deuteronomy 18:9-14 and John 8:44. To be a spirit medium is sin; to interrogate a demon is to oblige the demonized person to serve as a medium. To listen to a demon speaking through a witch is to be an accomplice to sin.

   iii. you do not need to know its name—expel all at one time, like Jesus did (Luke 8:30-33).

   iv. careful with 'experiences'; Satan is a veritable 'factory' of experiences.

    f. What if the demon does not obey? (When a 'demon' does not obey our command, remember that it may not be a demon at all, but a projected human spirit; not being a demon the spirit does not obey; in such an event it is necessary to repulse the projected spirit, specifically.)

       i. start with the boss (James 4:7).

      ii. join forces (Matthew 18:19, Mark 9:29).

     iii. send to the Abyss (Luke 8:31, John 14:12).

     iv. God is sovereign—He wants to teach us something new. Or else, hear from <u>Him</u> if there is a pact or other complication.

        (a) praise.

        (b) forgive.

        (c) humility.

        (d) <u>faith</u>—"faith is the substance of things <u>not seen</u>" (James 4:7 "<u>will</u> flee"). Why keep repeating the order? It is God who makes it work, and **He** is not deaf (so why repeat?).

      v. activate angels—Hebrews 1:14, Matthew 26:53.

     vi. at times people pretend to be demonized (to get attention or to get even).

5. 'Cover with the blood of Christ', forbid attacks before they happen. (Bind Satan every morning and every night.)

6. Questions to be researched.

    a. Do certain cases require that you speak out loud? When the challenge is public the answer should also be.

    b. Are there time limits? For instance, with reference to forbidding new attacks. (A demon that has been sent to the Abyss should not return.)

    c. Satanism ups the ante. (demon + human = ?) ['astral projection'—possible biblical examples (2 Kings 5:26, 6:12 [Elisha]; Matthew 17:25, John 1:48 [Jesus]; 1 Corinthians 5:3-4, Colossians 2:5 [Paul]). [human robots, werewolves, humanoids, etc.]

7. Careful with 'gifts' that may be cursed; bless everything you eat, or that you bring into your home.
8. Dangers.
    a. Counter-attacks / retaliation [accidents, sickness, calamity, financial problems, child born with defect].
    b. Watch out for pride (James 4:6).
    c. Do not leave a vacuum (Matthew 12:44). When you repel an evil interference you should also introduce a positive influence (Matthew 18:18, 26:53).
    d. Spiritual pacifism (Psalm 78:9, Jeremiah 48:10).
9. **Luke 10:19—Defense that shades into offense**
    Luke 10:19—"Take note, I am giving[1] you <u>the</u> authority to trample on snakes and scorpions,[2] and

---

[1] Instead of 'am giving', perhaps 2.5% of the Greek manuscripts, of objectively inferior quality, have 'have given' (as in NIV, NASB, LB, TEV, etc.)—a serious error. Jesus said this perhaps five months before His death and resurrection, addressing the seventy (not just the twelve). The Lord is talking about the future, not the past; a future that includes <u>us</u>!

[2] The Lord gives us the authority to "trample snakes and scorpions". Well now, to smash the literal insect, a scorpion, you do not need power from on High, just a slipper. To trample a snake I prefer a boot, but we can kill literal snakes without supernatural help. It becomes obvious that Jesus was referring to something other than reptiles and insects. I understand Mark 16:18 to be referring to the same reality—Jesus declares that certain signs will accompany the believers (the turn of phrase virtually has the effect of commands): they will expel demons, they will speak strange languages, they will remove 'snakes', they will place hands on the sick. ("If they drink   . . ." is not a command; it refers to an eventuality.) But what did the Lord Jesus mean by 'snakes'?

In a list of distinct activities Jesus has already referred to demons, so the 'snakes' must be something else. In Matthew 12:34 Jesus called the Pharisees a 'brood of vipers', and in 23:33, 'snakes, brood of vipers'. In John 8:44, after they claimed God as their father, Jesus said, "You are of your father the devil". And 1 John 3:10 makes clear that Satan has many other 'sons'. In Revelation 20:2 we read: "He seized the dragon, the ancient serpent, who is a slanderer, even Satan, who deceives the whole inhabited earth, and bound him for a thousand years." If Satan is a snake, then his children are also snakes. So then, I take it that our 'snakes' are human beings who chose to serve Satan, who sold themselves to evil. I conclude that the 'snakes' in Luke 10:19 are the same as those in Mark 16:18, but what of the 'scorpions'? Since they also are of the enemy, they may be demons, in which case the term may well include their offspring, the humanoids [see my essay, "In the Days of Noah"]. I am still working on the question of just how the removal is done.

over all the power of the enemy, and nothing at all may harm you." In Matthew 28:18 Sovereign Jesus affirms that He holds "all authority in heaven and on earth", so He is clearly competent to delegate some of that authority to us—note that He has given us <u>the</u> authority, the Greek Text has the definite article. We may have any number of enemies, but <u>the</u> enemy is Satan. The phrase, "all the power", presumably includes his works, followed by their consequences. Now then, just how does "authority over all the power of the enemy" work, in practice? Authority controls power, so can we command Satan to do things? Perhaps, but I would not recommend it (Satan is so much smarter than we are that he could easily trip us up, get us to do wrong things). More important, we have access to a power that is far greater; consider Ephesians 3:20.

"Now to Him who is able to do immeasurably more than all we ask or imagine, according to the power that is working in us,[1] 21 to Him be the glory in the Church in Christ Jesus, to all generations, forever and ever. Amen."[2] Ephesians 1:19 spoke of "the exceeding greatness of His power **into** us who are believing"—note that the verb is in the present tense; having believed yesterday won't hack it, we must believe today. This tremendous power that God pours into us, as we believe, exceeds our powers of imagination. Well now, my personal horizon is limited and defined by my ability to imagine. Anything that I cannot imagine lies outside my horizon, and so obviously I won't ask for it. But for all that we <u>can</u>

---

[1] I sadly confess that I have not yet arrived at a spiritual level where I can unleash this power—I have yet to make the truth in this verse work for me. But I understand that the truth affirmed here is literal, and I only hope that others will get there before I do (so I can learn from them), if I keep on delaying. The whole point of the exercise (verse 21) is for God to get glory [not for me to have a good time, although if I ever get there I will certainly have a great good time!], and to the extent that we do <u>not</u> put His power in us to work we are depriving Him of glory that He could and should have.

[2] The glory that God gets from the Church will go on forever.

imagine we should use Christ's limitless power, not Satan's. Since He goes on to say, "nothing at all may harm you", I suppose that we are to forbid Satan (and his servants) from using his power against us. This I am doing. We can protect ourselves, our families, our ministries—anything within Christ's Kingdom. I do this every day, so as not to forget and not to get careless. A defense that stops attacks from reaching us is obviously a great defense! But why stop at defending ourselves? Why not forbid the use of Satan's power in other ways? How about forbidding any use of Satan's power in our government, in our schools, in our hospitals, in the media? And why limit our activity to our country? How about forbidding any use of Satan's power in Iraq, in Iran, in North Korea, in Kenya, etc.? Well, well, well, am I getting carried away? Perhaps, but have I given you food for thought?

Seriously, there may be a significant difference between defense and offense. For defense we have the Lord's promise, so we can bank on that. As to offense, some other factors probably enter in.

a. The consequences of sin: we should not try to protect people from such consequences. This includes the religion and the government that people choose.

b. God sovereignly allows Satan and the demons to continue operating in this world, and presumably He will not allow us to frustrate His purpose in so doing.

c. A word of caution occurs to me: we are at war, and the more we expand our radius of operation, the more effort the enemy will expend to hinder us (be prepared).

We will be well advised to maintain a conscious submission to the Holy Spirit. More precisely, we need to try to follow the example of Sovereign Jesus. In John 5:19 He said: "Most assuredly I say to you, the Son is not able to do anything from Himself, except something He sees the Father doing; because whatever things <u>He</u> does, precisely these the Son also does." I find this statement to be amazing, revealing and challenging. Jesus only did what He saw the Father doing; so how about us? I would say that my main 'ministry' problem is that I often do not know what the Father is doing, and so I waste a lot of time and effort. But with reference to taking the fight to the enemy, we most certainly need the Father's backing.

N.B.: Our defensive weapons are the best and perfectly adequate (once you know how to use them), but it is not wise to remain in a defensive posture, just waiting for the next blow, letting the enemy keep the initiative. Let us take the offensive; we should control the sequence of events. In any war it is important to know the enemy.

E. **Who is the Enemy?**—Satan, "your adversary" (1 Peter 5:8). The Bible has much to say about Satan and his angels (the demons), and the Lord Jesus gave clear teaching about them—so if you do not believe in them you are rejecting His Word. Satan "deceives the whole world" (Revelation 12:9), is our "accuser" (Revelation 12:10), is the "tempter" (1 Thessalonians 3:5), presents himself as an "angel of light" [he once was] (2 Corinthians 11:14), is "prince of the power of the air" (Ephesians 2:2), is "the god of this world" (2 Corinthians 4:4), is "the prince of this world" (John 16:11, but already deposed—John 12:31), and the whole world "lies" in him (1 John 5:19).

1. His origin and fall—the highest created (angelic) being (Ezekiel 28:12-17, Isaiah 14:12-15)—he did not fall alone (Daniel 10:12-13, Revelation 12:4)—he did not lose his rank (Jude 9, Ephesians 6:12, 1:21)—they number over 50 million (Revelation 5:11).
2. Consequences for us: So what? What does all this have to do with evangelism and transcultural mission? Everything (Mark 3:27, 2 Corinthians 4:4, Mark 4:15).

a. When you attempt to extract a people (or person) from Satan's power, all you have facing you is merely the most powerful, intelligent and now malevolent <u>created</u> being in the universe.

b. Why does not God protect His servants? He must allow us to take the consequences of our culpable ignorance. We have to learn.

c. Did not Jesus win? Was not Satan defeated? So why do we have such a problem? (They operate on the basis of bluff or usurpation—it is up to us to call their bluff; we must oblige them to recognize their defeat.)

F. **How do Satan and the Demons Operate?** Let us go directly to the Sacred Text (Luke 9:18-<u>22</u> and Matthew 16:13-23)—we are faced with a terrible truth, we have an invisible enemy who has access to our minds!

N.B. One needs to understand that the moment that he was born in this world, he was born in a battlefield. Satan and his demons hate people because we are in the image of the Creator (spite). But when you believe into Sovereign Jesus their rage increases, because now you are an enemy soldier (not a civilian). You will be attacked.

1. They attack our minds—Peter (Matthew 16:23; the "sifting"—Luke 22:31), my own experience, business meetings [blanks, inverted ideas].
    a. Against prayer (Daniel 10:12-13)—serious prayer attracts interference [sleep, phone, visitor, dogs, children].
    b. Against physical life—Ananias (Acts 4:32-5:10; cf. 1 Chronicles 21:1).
    c. Against eternal life—Judas (John 13:2 and 27; cf. John 17:12, Matthew 26:24)—and not only Judas (2 Corinthians 4:4, Mark 4:15).
    d. Other evidences—Satan "corrupts minds" (of <u>believers</u>, 2 Corinthians 11:3), the tongue "inflamed by hell" (James 3:2-12), fear in witnessing (2 Timothy 1:7), nightmares ('nightmare' 400 years

ago), Spiritism and Satanism (drugs, pornography, 'rock', homosexualism, abortion, etc.).

e. They falsify the gifts of the Spirit—to deal with the charismatic gifts demands <u>discernment</u>, because Satan also gives prophecy, tongues, healings, etc. The damage that the enemy produces in this area is terrible. (Casting out demons has no necessary connection with the charismatic gifts.) 1 Corinthians 14:39.

f. They deceive and give false doctrine (1 Timothy 4:1) ['brilliant' ideas]. They build up strongholds of the enemy in people's lives; and in churches, missions, ministries (you cannot be too careful).
   i. Systems of thought (evolution, relativism, humanism, 'free' sex, homosexualism, etc.)
   ii. More restricted theories (against the Sacred Text, against language).
   iii. Within the churches ('a demon cannot read one's thoughts'; 'a believer cannot be demon possessed').

g. They read our thoughts—it is not a big problem, but avoid a false 'security'. This has nothing to do with omniscience (advanced technology in aviation—our thoughts project beyond our skulls).

2. They influence physical objects.
   a. They attack health: Job, Paul (2 Corinthians 12:7), "daughter of Abraham" (Luke 13:11,16), personal experience, mixed symptoms.
   b. They manipulate objects: computers, haunted houses, ex-spiritists.
   c. They materialize themselves (werewolves, rape, UFOs).
   d. They use objects to plague lives and homes (fetishes, artifacts, cursed objects).

3. Within Spiritism.
   a. They imitate deceased persons.
   b. They can cure (for a price).
   c. A higher ranking demon can expel a lower ranking one (Matthew 7:22).
   d. They can cause supernatural phenomena.

e. By order of a medium they attack (and kill).

f. They assist a person in 'projecting' his spirit (and to materialize in another form [really!]).

4. They tempt us to evil (this is <u>not demonization</u>)—Christ (Matthew 4:1-11, Luke 4:1-13), us (cf. 1 Corinthians 10:13)—but God does <u>not</u> tempt (James 1:13).

5. Things attributed to Satan.

a. He influences human culture (1 John 5:19, "the world") and people (Ephesians 2:2).

b. He prepares "snares"—deceived Christians (2 Timothy 2:26), pastors (1 Timothy 3:7).

c. He tempts, deceives, accuses (see F).

6. Implications.

a. If we could really appreciate how much they disturb our lives (they also attack our finances) we could transform them (remember Ephesians 6:12). (Most of us cannot imagine what goes on out in the world—there is heavy demonic participation in suicides, drug addicts, homosexuals, pornography, rock music, crime, violence, etc.

b. However, there is not necessarily a demon under every stone or behind every tree—we must use <u>discernment</u>.

c. Do not try to blame the enemy for the evil that you do—we are sinners by nature.

d. Their attacks may be indirect (letters, telegrams, phone calls); they attack a child to trouble the parents, etc.

<u>N.B.</u>: My purpose in spending so much time on the enemy is not to exalt him or venerate him, assuredly, but to help the reader recognize and realize the danger that faces him. To deal successfully with a wild animal one must respect the danger it represents; if you do not, you will get the worst of the encounter. We have a terrible enemy that must be dealt with, but our Master, Sovereign Jesus, has placed at our disposal a variety of weapons that are entirely adequate, not

only for defense but also for offense, so as to impose on the enemy the defeat he suffered long ago.

There is still one question that demands attention: how is it that there is so much ignorance on this subject in evangelical circles?

G. **But, why is there so much ignorance among us?**
(To ignore the enemy is to give him a deadly advantage.)
1. We are influenced by the culture that surrounds us, which is very materialistic, skeptical of the supernatural. Recall 1 John 5:19. Materialism is one of the sophistries (2 Corinthians 10:5) that Satan has devised to remove people from the knowledge of the Creator (also Islam, Marxism, Hinduism, Buddhism, Animism, Humanism, Spiritism, etc.). (A materialist researcher who investigates parapsychological phenomena will almost certainly be demonized—he is asking for it.)
2. Certain groups have a false notion of blame such that they are ashamed to talk about the subject (but silence favors the enemy).
3. Our primary versions of the Bible have mislead us— we should read "demonized" instead of "possessed by a demon". The word 'possessed' does not exist in the Original Text; it was invented by the translators.
   a. The central idea of 'possession' is property, which is misleading on this subject. First, a human being cannot be the property of a demon (although they sometimes make that claim). Worse, it has given rise in the churches to an idea that brings serious consequences—since a believer belongs to God he presumably cannot belong to a demon at the same time. But the real question involves control, not property—we should retire the term 'possessed'. Demon control certainly exists, but represents only a small part of the enemy's activity against human beings, precisely the more ex-

treme cases. The following chart shows the areas included in 'demonization' (at least as I understand the term).

<u>our minds | objects | obsession | oppression | control</u>

    b. Consequences: In 'traditional' churches and schools the subject simply is not included in the menu, perhaps because they think in terms of 'property' and therefore imagine that the believer is exempt. Even in churches that have a ministry of liberation, they usually deal only with cases of control—the greater part of the enemy's action against us is never recognized. Thus, the idea that 'a believer can't be possessed' brings with it serious negative consequences.

4. There exists the catastrophic idea that we are exempt or 'untouchable'—1 John 5:18.
    a. Wherein might the "touch" in the Text consist? (Christ—Matthew 4:1-11; Paul—2 Corinthians 12:7; Peter—Matthew 16:22-23).
    b. The correct Text and translation is "does not sin" and "keeps himself"—but who is the "born of God"? Since only Jesus was literally born of God from His mother's womb, the rest of us receive the 'new man' at regeneration, so the believer as a whole person is not in view.
    c. Ephesians 6:12 is clear enough—"<u>our</u> wrestling match" is against wicked spirits (wrestling is direct, physical, violent—it is impossible to be in a wrestling match and not be 'touched'). Consider also 1 Peter 5:8—why "be vigilant" if that lion cannot touch us? You may be absolutely certain that believers can be and are demonized! The crucial thing is a **conscious** submission to the Holy Spirit (while controlled by the Spirit you will never be controlled by a demon).
    d. But can a believer really be controlled ('possessed')?

i. First, it is a question of control, not just presence. God is omnipresent and therefore coexists with Satan and the demons, inescapably (Job 2:1, Revelation 12:10). Have you turned all areas of your life over to God? If not . . . .

ii. Next, when we sin deliberately (=rebellion) we make common cause with Satan. When a believer remains in sin he gives a beachhead or foothold to the enemy—he enters the life and sets about increasing the area that he influences; you get obsession, then oppression, and finally, control. A believer who lives in sin becomes progressively weaker, and may reach the point where he is too weak to help himself; he must then be helped by others, but if that help does not arrive . . . .

iii. **Exception**: retaliation that comes against a warrior of Christ who is conducting offensive action against Satan is totally different—it is not because of sin in the life (although any lapse will surely be exploited).

iv. In any case, I must make an appeal: even if you feel that you cannot accept the idea of a believer being controlled by a demon, please do not reject the plain biblical truth that a believer can be demonized. The best thing is to live controlled by the Holy Spirit, then you will never be controlled by the enemy.

5. The cowed—some (many?) preachers and teachers seem to be afraid to touch on the subject. Perhaps early in his ministry he preached a dandy sermon against Satan, but there was a prompt counterattack and the preacher got the worst of it, so now he remains silent about the enemy. Yet 2 Timothy 1:7 makes it clear that any spirit of fear or cowardice does not come from God. (Recall Psalm 78:9 and Jeremiah 48:10.) [Here in Brazil many pastors are masons, and they are forbidden to teach on the subject.]

H. **Putting into Practice—Some Prerequisites**. "It is enough for a disciple to be like his Master" (Matthew 10:25). It is important to follow our Savior's example in the following items.
1. Maintain fellowship with the Father. An effective participation in spiritual warfare begins with total commitment to Jesus Christ and His Kingdom, a commitment that must be renewed each day (Hebrews 10:7, Romans 12:1-2, Luke 9:23). We need to keep short accounts.
    a. Humility—God requires humility on our part (James 4:6).
    b. Holiness (1 Peter 1:15-16; Hebrews 12:14)—God requires pure hands and a pure heart (James 4:8), that we walk in communion with Him and submissive to the Holy Spirit—in this way we can walk clothed with the authority He gives us and wielding His power. (Dirty hands cannot grasp God's power.)

    c. Intimacy—friends, neither horses nor yet mere slaves (Psalm 32:9, John 13:13 & 16, 15:15 & 20). The 'presence' of God upon us depends on intimacy VS 'grace' that all have. Intimacy → sensitivity (Psalm 32:8)—do what you see the Father doing (John 5:19); speak what you hear the Father saying (John 12:49).
2. Be radical in the defense of the authority of the Sacred Text. "If you abide in my Word then you will truly be my disciples" (John 8:31).
    a. In Matthew 24:35 the Lord Jesus declared: "Heaven and earth will pass away, but my words will never pass away." "My words" represents the word of the Creator (Jesus knew who He was). He declares the eternal authority of His own word. As for the O.T., He was no less emphatic—in John 5:45-47 He virtually equates the writings of Moses with His own word. After affirming that He came to fulfill the law and the prophets He affirms: "Assuredly I tell you that until Heaven and earth pass not one jot or one tittle will by any

means pass from the law until all is fulfilled" (Matthew 5:18). "It is easier for Heaven and earth to pass than for one tittle to fall from the Law" (Luke 16:17). "The Scripture cannot be broken" (John 10:35). Observe that He guarantees the <u>form</u> of the Text to the minimal detail (the "jot" is the smallest letter in the Hebrew alphabet). Jesus took the Sacred Text seriously— He sometimes increased the range or application of the Word, but never retreated an inch from its literal meaning (see Matthew 5:17-48).

b. As for Revelation, and by extension the N.T., the One seated upon the throne guarantees that <u>the words</u> written are "faithful and true" (Revelation 21:5). (The precise throne here is presumably the great white throne [Revelation 20:11], and since it is the Son who judges [John 5:22, 2 Timothy 4:1] we may understand that it is the glorified Christ.) The use of the plural, "words", includes each component that contributes to the whole—God guarantees **each** word.

c. In Matthew 4:4 the Lord Jesus affirmed: "Man shall not live by bread alone, but by every word that proceeds from the mouth of God." Now then, if we are to live by "every word" of God <u>today</u>, then each one needs to be in existence today—so we have a guarantee of the preservation of the Text through the centuries. See 1 Chronicles 16:15. Indeed, almost the last words in the Bible (Revelation 22:18-19) clearly reflect God's concern for the exact transmission of each word in the Book.

So, what do you say? Shall we be like our Master?

3. Rise above culture. 1 John 5:19 and Ephesians 2:2— every human culture has aspects that come from the enemy and do not mesh with the values of the Kingdom. (1 Thessalonians 5:21, Romans 12:1-2, 1 John 2:15)

    a. The Lord Jesus criticized His own culture (of the Jews)—Matthew 23:13-28, 11:21-24, 5:33-48; He always did things on the Sabbath that the Jewish leaders did not like. He was not afraid of contaminating Himself—He could deal with a prostitute or touch a leper.

    b. He criticized Samaritan culture—John 4:22 (verse 18).

    c. He criticized Gentile culture—Matthew 15:26 (the O.T. contains severe criticisms of Canaanite culture, etc.).

    d. And how about your culture? Matthew 5:37, 2 Thessalonians 3:10, Ephesians 4:28, Proverbs 22:15, 23:13-14, Hebrews 12:6.

    e. And how about our religious culture? John 3:8 (the Holy Spirit is unpredictable), 2 Timothy 3:5 (a form of godliness X power; 'image').

4. Hate evil. To hate evil is a <u>necessary</u> part of God's love, because of the **consequences** of sin.

    a. Hebrews 1:8-9 cites Psalm 45:6-7, declaring that it refers to the Son: among other things it affirms that He hates iniquity. The glorified Christ Himself declares that He hates the works of the Nicolaitans (Revelation 2:6). Jehovah hates stealing (Isaiah 61:8), divorce (Malachi 2:16) and seven other transgressions (Proverbs 6:16-19). "The fear of Jehovah is to hate evil" (Proverbs 8:13, 9:10). In Psalm 97:10 we have a <u>command</u>: "You, who love Jehovah, **hate evil**". Shall we obey?

    b. Psalms 5:5-6 informs us that Jehovah hates everyone who practices iniquity. We usually preach that God hates sin but loves the sinner. Presumably so, up to a point. But when someone teams up with Satan, insisting upon practicing evil, he incurs the wrath of God—Deuteronomy 7:10. (See Psalm 26:5, 31:6, 101:3, 119:104, 113, 128, 163—this helps us understand David's attitude in Psalm 139:21-22; it is those who act with "evil intent" [verse 20] that he hates.) We must learn to hate sin, evil in all its forms, Satan and his angels—since they cannot be recuperated (Matthew 25:41, 2 Peter 2:4, Revelation 20:10), we are in a war without quarter, to the death. [Remember that God only pardons **confessed** sin (1 John 1:9).]

c. Jehovah the Son came the first time as the Lamb, meek and lowly—a broken reed He did not crush, a smoldering wick He did not quench, until He made justice triumph (Matthew 12:20). But now, He has already won the victory; Satan has been judged. Jesus will return as the Lion, to judge and reign with a rod of iron. He who made the propitiation, alone (1 John 2:2, Hebrews 1:3), will also tread the winepress of the **wrath** of God, alone (Revelation 19:15) (cf. Acts 3:23). Albeit we are spokesmen for the Lamb, we are also spokesmen for the **Lion**, right now. The "greater things" depend on the victory **already won**.

d. Remove "snakes" (Mark 16:18, Luke 10:19) (they are people who have sold out to evil— "brood of vipers", "your father the devil"). I am reminded of Matthew 6:22-23, words of the Sovereign Creator while He walked this earth: "The lamp of the body is the eye. So if your eye is sound your whole body will be full of light. But if your eye is evil your whole body will be full of darkness. So if the light that is in you is darkness, how great is that darkness!" Of course we have two eyes, but the Text has "eye" in the singular. I take it that the reference is to the way we interpret what we see (which is our real "eye")—two people, one pure and one vile, observing the same scene will give very different interpretations to it. "Evil" here has the idea of malignant—aggressively evil. Someone with a malignant mind will give an evil interpretation to everything he sees, and in consequence his being will be filled with unrelenting darkness. That is

what it says in Titus 1:15; to someone who is defiled **nothing** is pure. With a defiled mind <u>and</u>
<u>conscience</u> such a person is simply incapable of
giving a decent interpretation to anything at all in
this whole wide world. That is why Paul goes on
to say in the next verse that such a person is
disqualified for any good work. Surely, if you are
full of evil how can you do good? (However, we
need to distinguish between two types of bad
men—those who deliberately scheme evil, who
have sold themselves to the devil, and those who
gradually lost the ability to distinguish good from
evil; for the second type there may be hope.)

5. Understand our function to judge. In John 5:22,27 (2
Timothy 4:1) the Lord Jesus affirms that the prerogative to judge is His, and in 1 John 4:17 He informs
us that "as He is so are we in this world"—<u>in this</u>
<u>world</u>, not the next.

a. When Paul asks, "do you not know that the saints
will judge the world?" (1 Corinthians 6:2-3) it is
clear that his readers should know. So it must be
something that had already been revealed. In
fact, it is in Psalm 149:5-9. It is up to the saints
to take the "two-edged sword in hand, to bring
vengeance on the nations and to punish the peoples, to bind their kings with chains, and their
nobles with bars of iron, to execute upon them
<u>the written judgment</u>; this is the glory [or 'hon-
or'] of all the saints." "All the saints"—if you are a
saint, to execute written judgment is within your
prerogative.

For example: in Zechariah 5:1-4 we find a
written curse against thieves. How about the
government of your country—are there no
thieves there, and big ones? Why not invoke upon them "the written judgment"? We should be
"bold as lions" and "fight against the wicked"
(Proverbs 28:1 and 4). (Revelation 18:6—God's
people will judge Babylon.)

b. The Lord Jesus granted to His disciples the authority to condemn a city (Matthew 10:14-15), and the Apostle Paul made use of the expedient at least once (Acts 13:51). The Lord Jesus Himself had given the example (Matthew11:21-4, 23:13-38). But *it is possible to reverse such a curse.* At least twice Paul delivered someone to Satan (1 Corinthians 5:5, 1 Timothy 1:20). The risen Christ granted to the disciples the authority to forgive or retain sins (John 20:23).

c. 1 John 4:3-4 affirms that we have already defeated the spirits of antichrist. One day we will judge the angels, presumably the good ones (1 Corinthians 6:3), but Satan and his angels, the demons, already stand judged (John 16:11, Ephesians 1:21), and we have authority over them (Ephesians 2:6). So then, disciples all, let us take our prerogative seriously—it has much to do with spiritual warfare.

6. Accept the "cup" prepared for us—John 12:27, Hebrews 12:1-3.
   a. The prepared "body"—Hebrews 10:5.
   b. The "cup" and the "baptism"—Mark 10:37-8.
   c. Endure "hardship" as a good soldier of Jesus Christ—2 Timothy 2:3, 1 Thessalonians 3:3-4.
   d. Complete the sufferings of Christ—Colossians 1:24.

7. Have the servant mentality—Matthew 20:26-28, John 13:14-15. Jesus worked with His hands.

I. **Strategic Implications for Missions:**

1. The true world is the spiritual world (Hebrews 9:8-9, 22-24; 2 Corinthians 4:18 [1 Corinthians 9:11, Romans 15:27, Galatians 6:6]); it follows that the real war takes place in the spiritual realm. We need to increase our sensitiveness toward the spiritual—our churches are full of wounded 'soldiers', who do not realize it.

2. The majority of those who are called to be missionaries are defeated by Satan at the beginning—they never leave their home land. Of those who do manage to reach a foreign field, half are removed from action within the first four years—it is a matter of statistics.
3. We need workers who know how to conduct spiritual warfare, who know how to impose Christ's victory upon Satan and the demons. If we can fill the world with such workers we will finish reaching the world, fulfilling the Great Commission. And it will not take very long because such workers will produce far more, in much less time, than those who do not understand spiritual warfare (most of those presently at work).
4. We need churches full of believers who also know how to conduct the war. We need sharpshooters, people who can hit a specific target. The elderly and homemakers can be great warriors. Protect your family daily.
5. With reference to 1,000 ethnic groups <u>we</u> are the ones who are handcuffed; with reference to 1,000 ethnic groups Christ's victory still makes no difference! Since the Gospel has yet to reach them there is little point in binding Satan with reference to them. (Another 1,000 may have heard superficially but have no disciplers.) It is necessary that each ethnic group receive its discipler, its apostle! "Pray the Lord of the harvest" (Matthew 9:38).
6. In Matthew 16:18 the Lord Jesus affirms, "I will build my Church and the gates of Hades shall not withstand it". This is an important promise that should encourage us. Let us fight with confidence!
7. If every believer would learn how to conduct spiritual warfare we could wipe the floor with Satan. We could transform our lives, our families, our churches, our society and maybe even our world. What do you say? Shall we go for it? Let us do!

"As were the days of Noah"[1]

Mathew 24:37—"Just as were the days of Noah, so also will be the coming of the Son of the Man"[2]—spoken by the Lord Jesus Christ.

According to Ezekiel 33:6-7, a watchman who sees danger approaching has the obligation to warn the populace. I believe that God has designated me as a watchman with reference to the matter in hand—most unpleasant but terribly serious—so I consider that I am obligated to sound the alarm. Unfortunately, I myself have taught error on this subject in the past (in Portuguese, if not in English).

The Fact

1. Sovereign Jesus declares that at the time of His second coming the situation in the world will be similar to what it was in Noah's day (Matthew 24:37-44, Luke 17:26-35). Many of us believe that the Second Coming is upon us, so let us consider the reality of our day.

2. The people were completely evil and perverse: "Jehovah saw that the wickedness of man was great in the earth, and that every intent of the thoughts of his heart was only evil continually" (Genesis 6:5). If a person is as he thinks in his heart (Proverbs 23:7), then in Noah's time a majority (evidently) of the people practiced only evil, were incapable of doing good. And what about our day? 2 Timothy 3:1-5—

---

[1] The author takes full responsibility for all interpretation herein, not being tied to any denominational 'package'. (To place any 'package' above the Sacred Text is a form of idolatry.) I approach the Text with rigorous respect, as having maximum objective authority. In passing we may observe that the Truth is not democratic, does not depend on opinion or vote; the Truth **is**. (It should also be obvious that the Kingdom of God is not a democracy.)

[2] That is what the Text says, "the Son of the Man", which appears to be a phrase coined by the Lord Jesus to refer to Himself; the phrase does not make very good sense in English, at first glance, but if "the man" refers to pristine Adam and "the son" to an only pristine descendent, it makes great sense. It seems to indicate a perfect human prototype, like Adam was before the fall—the human side of the God-man.

"Now understand this: <u>In the last days</u> there will be griev-
ous times; because people will be self-lovers, money lovers,
boasters, arrogant, blasphemers, disobedient to parents,
ungrateful, unholy, without family affection, unforgiving,
slanderers [or, 'devils'], without self-control, brutal, despis-
ers of good, betrayers, reckless, conceited, lovers of pleasure rather than lovers of God; wearing a form of godliness
while having denied its power! You must avoid such people."[1] Now is that not a faithful picture of our present day
society at large? (See also Romans 1:28-32.)

3. Sovereign Jesus affirmed that marriage would be similar.
So how was that marriage? "The sons of God saw the
daughters of men, that they were beautiful; and they took
wives for themselves of all whom they chose" (Genesis
6:2). The phrase, 'the sons of God', is a translation of the
Hebrew phrase, *bene-haelohim*, that in the other places
where it occurs—Job 1:6, 2:1 and 38:7—clearly refers to
angelic beings, apparently of high rank. The inspired commentary in the New Testament, Jude 6-7 and 2 Peter 2:4-7,
makes clear that they were in fact angelic beings, albeit in
rebellion against the Creator.[2] (In Luke 20:36 the Lord Je-

---

[1] Note that the order is to avoid such people. But, wait a minute—how can
we evangelize them if we are ordered to avoid contact with them? Could
it be that they have passed a point of no return, or might they be a type
of being that is not an object of salvation? Matthew 7:6 comes to mind.
This verse may be a chiasmus, ab,ba. But just who are 'the dogs' and
'the pigs'? A pig will sniff the pearl and perhaps think it a stone—it not
being edible the pig will ignore it and it will get trampled into the mud. So
a 'pig' is someone who is incapable of recognizing or appreciating the
'pearl' (perhaps a materialist with a completely closed mind) —the reaction will be one of total indifference. So do not waste your time. In contrast a 'dog' reacts in an aggressively hostile manner against what is
'holy'. So a 'dog' is presumably someone who is committed to evil and
will therefore attack what is holy. So do not innocently offer what is holy
to a 'dog'—you will get chewed up! Anyone who has sold out to Satan will
almost certainly have a resident demon, and we have the authority to
bind such.

[2] Jude makes clear that the phrase in Genesis 6:2 is not an exception. "And
the angels who did not keep their proper domain but deserted their own
dwelling He has kept bound in everlasting chains under darkness for the
judgment of the great day. So also Sodom and Gomorrah and the surrounding towns—who gave themselves up to fornication and went after a
different kind of flesh [Greek ἑτερος] in a manner similar to those angels—stand as an example, undergoing a punishment of eternal fire"

sus said, with reference to the resurrected, that "they are equal to angels and are sons of God".) Note that the fallen angels acted on their own initiative, taking 'whom they chose'. And what was the result of those 'marriages'? "There were giants [Hebrew *Nephilim*] on the earth in those days, <u>and also afterward</u>,[1] when the sons of God came in to the daughters of men and they bore children to them"

(Jude 6-7). The author, inspired by God, affirms that the people of Sodom did what certain angelic beings had done; they wanted sex with a different kind of flesh. Recall that the men of Sodom, old and young, from every quarter, wanted to rape the angels that were with Lot (Genesis 19:4-5). Whatever kind of flesh an angel has (when he materializes), it is not human flesh; it is precisely "a different kind of flesh". The parallel text in 2 Peter 2:4-6 links the crime of those angels to the Flood. (In Matthew 22:30 [Mark 12:25, Luke 20:35-36] the Lord does not say that angels do not have a sex/gender. Evidently no baby angels are born [whether good or bad], but if angels are of only one gender then they cannot reproduce in kind. In the Bible, whenever an angel materializes it is in the form of a man, not a woman.)

The argument that 'the sons of God' would be a reference to the male descendents of Seth, while 'the daughters of men' would be a reference to the female descendents of Cain, is totally unfounded. Genesis 6:1 says that the men (Hebrew *haadam*, 'the man' or 'Adam', but in 5:1 we find *adam* twice without the article, referring to 'Adam' and 'the man' respectively) began to multiply, which included daughters. It should be obvious that the reference is to the human race as a whole, not just to the descendents of Cain—surely, otherwise there would be no male descendents of Seth to take the female descendents of Cain (on that hypothesis). Verse 2 goes on to say that 'the sons of God' saw those daughters of men (Hebrew *haadam*, just as in verse 1) —if *haadam* in verse 1 refers to the human race as a whole, then the identical vocabulary item in verse 2 ought to have the same meaning. Further, in verse 3 Jehovah declares that He is not going to strive with man (*adam*) forever and in verse 7 further declares that He will destroy man (*haadam*) from the face of the earth. It is clear that the Flood destroyed the descendents of Seth just as much as those of Cain. So then, the Hebrew word *haadam* refers to the human race as a whole. (Will anyone argue that the female descendents of Seth were not also 'daughters of men'?)

[1] Unfortunately, I once taught all over Brazil that apparently God had changed the rules after the Flood, with the result that we no longer see that happening; at least we no longer have giants, and although demons are certainly having sexual relations with women, we do not hear of anything being born as a result. But, just a minute, how would I know that no offspring of demons were being born? In Brazil we have a great many single mothers (and presumably that is not just here), and are they going to trumpet to the world that their baby's father is a demon? How can we know? [And what about the babies found in the trash or in the brush; might they be demonic offspring that the mother did not want?] But the Text is clear, "and also afterward", and I am to blame for having ignored this plain statement.

(Genesis 6:4). A race of 'humanoids' was born, half-breeds of demon and woman, beings that were totally perverse, malignant, and of impressive size. And what about our day? Is our society at large not replete with beings that are totally perverse and malignant? The impressive size is lacking, but I think I can explain why.

4. An objection will probably be raised: "But, but, but, didn't Jesus say that angels don't marry?" Let us check it out; the text is: "When they rise from the dead, they neither marry nor are given in marriage, but are like angels in heaven" (Mark 12:25; see also Matthew 22:30 and Luke 20:35-36). Jesus was answering the captious question posed by the Sadducees, who denied the existence of resurrection; He affirms that in Heaven marriage, as we know it, does not exist; once there we will no longer procreate (since no one will die, there will be no need to produce new people to replace the old). In Heaven the angels do not procreate either, but that could be the consequence of there being only one sex (Jesus did not say that angels do not have gender, or a sex). Whenever an angel materializes in the appearance of a human being in the Bible, it is always as a male or man, never as a woman.[1] The lack of females among them could explain why angelic beings are fascinated by the female of our species (see 1 Corinthians 11:10, that I will discuss below).

5. Before proceeding, let us go back to the "and also afterward" to check out what happened after the Flood. Based on Deuteronomy 2:10-12 and 20-21 we may understand that already in Abraham's day, and even before, other mongrel races had appeared, and of impressive size. Deuteronomy 3:11 states overtly that Og, king of Bashan, was the last of his race, the *Rephaim*, that were similar to the *Anakim*; it states further that his bed was some 4½ meters in length, which allows us to deduce that Og himself was around four meters tall. Thirty-eight years before, the spies,

---

[1] The women in Zechariah 5 are part of a vision, not materializations; what Zechariah saw was women, not angels. In contrast, the Text says plainly that it was an angel who was talking with him.

wishing to badmouth the land, spoke of a number of giants, sons of Anak, that are overtly called *Nephilim* (Numbers 13:33). Four hundred years later David still had to face Goliath, and others of his race (1 Chronicles 20:4-8), but his height was 'only' three meters, no longer four (1 Samuel 17:4). As soon as God promised the land of Canaan to Abraham, it was entirely predictable that Satan would attempt to louse things up.[1] So much so, in fact, that although all the fallen angels who married women before the Flood had been confined in Tartarus (2 Peter 2:4), which would have been a rather severe warning to the rest, Satan obliged (so I imagine) a number of others to repeat the stunt. The severity used by God in the case of Sodom and Gomorrah indicates that the level of perversity there had reached uncommon proportions—Genesis 13:13 affirms that "the men of Sodom were exceedingly wicked". Although the Text does not make direct mention of giants in Sodom, we may deduce that yes there were, because Deuteronomy 2:10-12 says that Moab, that occupied what was left of the area controlled by Sodom and Gomorrah (that was not under the Dead Sea), took the area away from the *Emim* (who were the same size as the *Anakim*—it becomes evident that there were several mongrel races). God's severity with reference to the Amalekites, commanding Saul to annihilate them, including babies and even animals (1 Samuel 15:3), is probably to be explained by a massive demonic infestation of some sort. Just as we destroy animals and poultry to keep an epidemic from spreading, perhaps the contamination of the Amalekites was such that the only solution was destruction. (Cancerous cells cannot be recovered, returned to normal; they need to be destroyed in order to save the organism as a whole.)

6. And now about the size: why do we not have giants in our day? To begin, the phrase 'sons of God' evidently referred to angelic beings of high rank. Next, in Noah's day the women would have numbered in the thousands, or tens

---

[1] And with the reappearing of Israel as a nation in that land, will anyone suppose that Satan is doing nothing?

of thousands, certainly not more than hundreds of thousands; but there are over 50 million fallen angels (Revelation 12:4 and 5:11).[1] There simply were not enough women to go around! So then, it seems to me to be perfectly logical that it would be the biggest/strongest demons that got the women. However, all that gang was imprisoned in Tartarus as punishment for their incredible crime; so all of a sudden thousands of high-ranking demons are removed from the scene, which would open up the opportunity for the lesser ones. I cannot prove it, but it seems to me logical that the size of the offspring would reflect the size of the 'father', just as with us. (However, everything was bigger before the Flood than after—people, animals, plants—so the pre-Flood women were much larger than women today.) In any case, Goliath was certainly smaller than Og, who was probably smaller than the *Nephilim* destroyed by the Flood. Although the Text is silent, it would not be strange for God to keep on sending to Tartarus any other high-ranking demons that perpetrated the same crime. Since Satan needs his high-ranking subordinates for other purposes, he himself would tell them to stop.[2] It could be that lesser demons are allowed to escape, and their offspring would not be of abnormal size. Further, with the return of Christ bearing down

---

[1] We understand that 'the dragon' (12:3-4) refers to Satan. The term 'star' frequently refers to an angel, and in the context it should be obvious that the reference cannot be to literal luminaries—since the stars are many times larger than our planet, just one would have blown it to smithereens, and the Text refers to a third of them. Therefore we understand that Lucifer managed to recruit a third of the original angels to join him in his rebellion against the Creator. In 5:11 the Greek Text says that the angels around the throne of God numbered ten thousand times ten thousand and thousands of thousands. Well, 10,000 X 10,000 = 100,000,000 (one hundred million), but there were more than that. It follows that if the two thirds that remained true to the Creator number a hundred million, then the one third that went with Satan must number over 50 million. What a calamity!

[2] There is another possibility. Jude 6 affirms that the *bene-haelohim* of Genesis 6 "deserted their own dwelling". The idea of deserting or abandoning implies that there is no return. It may be that those fallen angels, in order to be able to procreate with women, had to make an irreversible choice. Upon taking on human form they could never return to their former condition. Following this hypothesis, again Satan would command them to stop, since he needs his high-ranking subordinates for other purposes.

upon us, God may be permitting a renewing of that activity. In any case, based on the declaration of the Lord Jesus, something similar to what precipitated the Flood must exist in our world today. He who hath an ear, let him hear!

Implications

1. Consider Jude 18-19: "<u>In the end time</u> there will be scoffers who live according to their own godless desires; these are the division-causers;[1] they are soulish [characterized by soul], not having a spirit." That is what the Text says. Our Bibles generally read, "not having the Spirit", but there is no article with 'spirit' in the Greek text; translators have supposed that the reference is to the Holy Spirit, and in that event the 'soulish' people would be the unconverted. But the description of such persons that occupies verses 8-16 is almost violent—they are totally perverse. One is reminded of Genesis 6:5 and 2 Timothy 3:1-5. The crucial question is precisely this: would the offspring of a demon have a human spirit? The Sacred Text informs us that the human spirit is transmitted by the sperm of the father, in which event that hybrid race would have lost the human spirit, and presumably the 'image of God' as well. Let us check it out.

In Genesis 5:3 the Text affirms that Adam "begot a son in his own likeness, after his image", that reminds us of Genesis 1:26. "Then God said: Let us make man in our image, according to our likeness." In all the genealogies it is always the man who begets; women conceive and gestate. I take it that Hebrews 7:9-10 is clear enough. "Even Levi, who receives tithes, paid tithes through Abraham, so to speak, for he was still in the loins of his father when Melchizedek met him." When Abraham paid the tithe to Melchizedek, not even Isaac had been begotten, much less Jacob and Levi. Still, the inspired author affirms that the person of Levi was in Abraham's reproductive system. It follows that it is the sperm of the man that transmits the human spirit and the

---

[1] The 'divisions' they cause would be in the society at large, not in the church.

image of the Creator. That is why Romans 5:12-21 teaches that Adam's sin was transmitted to all his descendants, and death as well.[1] As David explains, "Behold, I was brought forth in iniquity, and in sin my mother conceived me" (Psalm 51:5). (It should be obvious that the reference is not to the reproductive process itself, since the Creator Himself commanded them to "be fruitful and multiply"—Genesis 9:1.)

Consider also Genesis 38:8-10. The Text affirms that God killed Onan. Why? It was not because he did not want to perpetuate his brother's name—even under the more stringent demands of the Law of Moses the penalty for that was 'only' public humiliation, not death (Deuteronomy 25:5-10). In Onan's day there was no Law of Moses. Up to that point only one crime carried the death penalty, precisely murder (Genesis 9:6). Since the life is in the seed, when Onan spilled the seed on the ground, before having intercourse with the widow, he was deliberately killing the human life in the seed—it was murder. And God exacted the penalty![2] We

---

[1] When Eve sinned, she sinned alone. When Adam sinned, we did too, because we were in his reproductive system. It was Adam who degraded the race.

[2] To be sure, the life latent in the sperm is only set in motion when a spermatozoon joins an ovum. Since a man produces many billions, if not trillions, of spermatozoa during his life, almost all of them are wasted, one way or another. It is mainly a perverse intention that the Creator punishes. However, if I am not badly mistaken, He is not pleased when people go after pleasure without assuming the accompanying responsibility.

Leviticus 18:6-30 prohibits certain practices because they contaminate the earth, and the situation can reach a point where the earth 'vomits' the people. Now there is a dramatic picture for you: the very ground gets nauseated at the people that walk it! And what are those practices? Every kind of incest (verses 6-17), sex with a woman in menstruation (verse 19), adultery (verse 20), human sacrifice (verse 21), homosexualism (verse 22) and sex with an animal (verse 23). Verse 29 decrees the death penalty for all those practices. Leviticus 20:1-22 is a parallel passage. The Text states plainly that innocent blood shed without punishment contaminates the ground, and God demands the death penalty for murderers. But why does the Creator react the same way to the practices listed above? I suppose for the following reason: sex with an animal, anal sex and sex with a menstruating woman destroys the man's seed, and it is the seed that transmits 'the image of God', human life. So they are kinds of homicide—remember the case of Onan. Human sacrifice is obvi-

may add Exodus 21:22-23 here as well. A human fetus is a person, and whoever caused the death of a fetus was liable to the death penalty.[1] It is the seed of the man that transmits the human spirit; so the offspring of a demon will not have one. The essence of a woman being her soul, the offspring has the mother's soul. Not having spirit, it most probably will not have any conscience either.[2] Here in Brazil, where I live and work, the papers and newscasts are full of cases where the criminals appear to have no conscience at all—they say they would do it again, and with pleasure![3]

2. 1 Corinthians 11:9-10—"Nor was man created for the woman, but woman for the man. For this reason the woman ought to have authority upon her head, because of the angels." Our Bibles generally add 'a symbol of' before 'authority'—there being nothing of the sort in the Text, it is an unwarranted addition. The woman needs the protection of male authority, precisely because of the angels. In Numbers 30:3-15 Jehovah makes clear that the man exercises spir-

---

ous murder. Incest and adultery degrade the seed. In short, the Creator attaches considerable importance to His 'image'!

[1] In verse 22 the correct rendering is a premature birth, not a miscarriage. The baby lives. In verse 23 the baby dies.

[2] Down through the years many Christian writers have affirmed that every human being has a 'space' in the soul that only the Creator can fill. Analogously, humanoids probably have a demon-specific 'socket', being open to demonic influence at any moment.

Modern medicine informs us that each person has the father's blood, not the mother's; so the mixed race mentioned in Genesis 6:4 had demonic blood in their veins, not human. Had Satan succeeded in contaminating everyone, the Messiah, the second Adam, could not have been born, and Genesis 3:15 could not have been fulfilled. The maneuver that Satan devised against God's plan was so incredible, and came so close to succeeding, that the response was to destroy everything and start over, using eight human beings not yet contaminated.

[3] Please note, I am not suggesting that every perverse and violent individual is a humanoid. Persons who turn themselves over to Satan grow progressively worse. And then, there are the 'robots', people who voluntarily and deliberately turn themselves over to the complete control of a demon; they become under 'remote control'. Over fifteen years ago I was informed that at that time there was a network of thousands of 'robots' distributed around the United States (we also have them in Brazil). I must confess that I never troubled myself to study the problem and find a way to neutralize such 'persons'—it would be a welcome asset toward the subject in hand.

itual authority over the woman. Recall that in Genesis 6:2 the angelic beings simply took the women that they wanted, at their own initiative. A woman without male protection is an easy target. In our day, the feminist women who peremptorily reject any semblance of male authority are asking for a demon (and what little demon is going to object?). [It would not surprise me in the least if 100% of such feminists have a demon.] And what about the lesbians that want sex, but without a man—are they not an open invitation? Well, and so what? Well, our society ought to be full of single mothers, and many of the children would be humanoids.[1] I understand that the return of Christ is upon us, and He Himself declared that things would be like they were in Noah's day. In that event, a significant percentage of the population today is probably made up of humanoids, that mongrel race of demon with woman. All of a sudden we are faced with an urgent necessity—we need to be able to distinguish the imitation. We need the gift of discerning spirits! On the way, let us think about the probable characteristics of such beings.

The females, not having a spirit, will be very sensual, and will be used by Satan to ruin men. A human male who has sex with one of them will certainly be demonized, and if he marries her he will be tormented; he can never be happy, and any children will be perverse. As for the males, without a spirit, they will also be sensual, as well as given to violence, to lying and to corruption. The Lord Jesus affirmed that Satan is a murderer and a liar (John 8:44), as well as a thief and a vandal (John 10:10).[2] The description of Lucifer in Ezekiel 28:13 includes musical instruments, and I think it is obvious that Satan uses music as a favorite tool to destroy young people. Some time ago there was a rock group called KISS (Knights in Satan's Service) whose 'music' was openly satanic, and so on. The description given in 2 Timothy 3:1-5 is precisely to the point. They will be beings with-

---

[1] Of course married women can also produce humanoids.

[2] "Brood of vipers", "your father is the devil"—like father, like son; if the father is a 'snake', the children are too.

out conscience, without remorse. They will kill their parents without any emotion, etc. etc.

3. "As it was in the days of Noah"—never before had I paused and tried to imagine the emotions of Noah and the other 'decent' people of his time as they saw their world being taken over by those *Nephilim*, as they watched their culture being destroyed, apparently without being able to do anything to stop, much less reverse, the trend. There would be frustration, anger, perplexity, melancholy and at last despair and panic. So how about us in today's world—are we not beginning to have the same emotions as we observe a world without the political will to confront the organized Islamic terror, organized crime running loose, violence rampant in the streets, corruption at home in all levels and all areas of society, the growing lack of shame and modesty in customs and culture, in short, a 'church' that is absent and unable to promote biblical values in the public sector and society at large?

For some time now Canada has had a law whereby if you voice a criticism of the homosexual life style you go to prison. I believe similar laws are in place in several European countries. The militant 'gay' lobby is hard at work to get similar laws in the US and here in Brazil—a similar law has been passed by the House of Representatives here and is presently being debated in the Senate. According to the proposed law, moral or religious objections to homosexualism will not be tolerated; a church would not be able to fire a pastor for being 'gay', and so on. The 'gay' lobby is openly working for an inversion of cultural values, the destruction of any moral principles left over from our former civilization. Those who study the militant 'gay' agenda are telling us that the movement is no longer concerned for the person, but rather with the pleasure derived from their destructive program itself—the pleasure of perverting what is natural, of transforming the right into wrong and the wrong into right (see Isaiah 5:20), of destroying the human being as a whole.[1] It is simply satanic.

Our turn to live Hebrews 13:12-13 is coming, something that Christians in China, North Korea, Islamic countries and those persecuted elsewhere have known for some time. "Jesus also, so that He might sanctify the people by His own blood, suffered outside the city gate. So then, let us go out to Him, outside the camp, bearing His disgrace." I doubt that even 5% of the so-called evangelicals here in Brazil are prepared to actually suffer physical persecution for Jesus Christ. Do you suppose that the percentage in North America will be any higher? Martin Luther wrote the following:

> "If I profess with loudest voice and clearest exposition every portion of the truth of God except precisely that little point which the world and the devil are at the moment attacking, I am not confessing Christ, however boldly I may be professing Christ. Where the battle rages, there the loyalty of the soldier is proved, and to be steady on all the battlefield besides, is merely flight and disgrace if he flinches at THAT point."

Well then, I would say that the "little point" that the world and the devil are presently attacking in Brazil, and elsewhere, is the position on anal sex.

The position of the Bible is clear enough. God created two sexes, male and female, and He expects that they be respected. Homosexualism is not a work of the Creator—so much so that He decrees the death penalty for the practice (Leviticus 18:22 & 29, and to this day, Romans 1:32). Whose work is it then? Romans 1:18-32 is to the point; homosexualism is a result of denying the existence of the Creator (Romans 1:26). Since God wants adoration that is in spirit and truth (John 4:24), He will not force us to adore; when people reach the point of actually denying His existence (the ultimate stupidity), He removes His hand, abandoning them to their disgraceful passions, that Satan knows how to manipulate very well.

---

[1] I have used material from an e-mail written by Rozangela Justino.

I believe that Hebrews 2:7 is relevant here: "You made him [man, verse 6] lower than the angels, for a little while" (quoting Psalm 8:5). The human being is superior to the angelic being in essence; we bear the Creator's image and they do not, and once glorified that superiority will be obvious, but only for the redeemed. Those who serve Satan subordinate themselves to him, and thus can never rise above him. If Lucifer's rebellion was provoked, as I suppose, by the creation of a being superior to himself, he is doing very well at getting his 'revenge', by depriving the vast majority of humanity of that superiority [and so verse 8 would not apply to them]. Now Satan is controlled by spite; he was demoted. Since he is unable to create, he gets his satisfaction by degrading and destroying. His greatest 'pleasure' must be to drag the image of the Creator through the mire, and for that purpose anal sex is just the ticket. Since it is a man's seed that transmits the 'image', anal sex mixes the image of God with feces—a monstrous insult! The practice of anal sex is the equivalent of spitting in the face of the Creator; it is an extremely serious offense (worse than a buck private spitting in the face of a four star general). So then, as soon as God removes His hand, Satan pushes men toward anal sex.[1]

Several years ago Dr. James Dobson, founder and president of Focus on the Family, on the television program Larry King Live, said that he never taught that the homosexual tendency was a choice of the person. That made me stop and think. If the tendency is not a choice (just supposing), where would it come from? I see two possibilities: either someone is born with it, or he gets it from a demon. Going on from there, in a society dominated by a relativistic humanism, starting from pluralistic presuppositions, there will be no perceived basis for combating homosexualism.

But, can it be that someone is actually born with the tendency? By an act of the Creator, no. Well, how about by an

---

[1] Here in Brazil, people who come out of the various forms of spiritism affirm that most of the men in those groups are homosexual; Satan pushes them in that direction—they teach that anal sex gives power, and it becomes necessary for those who wish to climb the hierarchical ladder.

act of evolution? I owe to Dr. Ney Augusto de Oliveira (a surgeon) the following observation: Even for someone who believes in evolution as an explanation of origins [even though it is scientifically impossible], it would be a contradiction for the organism to evolve a homosexual gene, because that gene would condemn the organism to extinction. It should be obvious to all that anal sex will never produce life—if during 50-60 years not a single woman gave birth, our race would disappear from this planet. Bye, bye. So then, if neither God nor evolution has produced, or would produce, a homosexual gene, how can someone be born with the tendency? Only as a work of Satan, that I understand to be entirely possible.[1] Actually, the ambush that the enemy has prepared for us is a whole lot worse than we have gotten around to imagining. Consider.

The inspired commentary links Sodom to the Flood. The Sodomites were known for their appetite for anal sex. If there was a mixture of humanoids in Sodom, as I understand (Deuteronomy 2:10), they were probably born with the tendency. It seems to me obvious that many (if not all) of the humanoids in our day will have been born with the tendency, precisely in order to create a social climate where approval for the practice becomes irresistible. Which, of course, will cause the Creator to abandon that society more and more, which will turn that society over to Satan more and more. It is a vicious cycle of evil, a downward spiral. Since we do not know how to distinguish between human beings and humanoids, the sexual acrobatics of the humanoids become part of the culture at large and influence the behavior of the real humans. Such perversity![2]

I was recently informed that soybeans (if not fermented) contain a good deal of female hormone, so that too much soy represses the masculine libido, reducing the virility. During centuries, if not millennia, Buddhist monks have taken soy precisely to smother their sexual desire. There

---

[1] See my essay, "Concerning Pathogens—Origin and Solution".

[2] Freud's theory that sex is the mainspring of human life has been, and continues to be, a most useful fool for Satan.

are no end of articles available on the internet telling about the bad effects of soy, that go beyond sex. (The Japanese make their soy sauce and tofu out of soy that has been properly fermented, that removes the harm.) In North America and Europe soy is sold to the public as 'health food', and the negative effects are beginning to appear.[1] Here in Brazil the vast majority of the population cooks with soybean oil, including the bars and restaurants.[2] So then, the negative effects of soy will not result in sodomites, those who take the male role in anal sex. Since soy inhibits precisely that capacity, it will be the number of catamites that increases, those who take the female role in anal sex. A catamite tendency could come from soy, rather than a demon. Obviously such a person can refuse to participate in anal sex, but it becomes difficult to blame him for the tendency (he could be the victim of an irresponsible mother).

4. Jude 22-23: "Now be merciful to some, making a distinction; but others save with fear, snatching them out of the fire."[3] The implication is clear: there is a third category, the without-mercy ('some' plus 'others' does not equal 100%; in fact, one gains the impression that the third category could be sizeable). 1 John 5:16-17 speaks of fatal sin, such that there is no point in praying for the culprit. Such culprits would presumably be among the 'without-mercy'. (See Solution, point 5, with special attention to the discussion of Deuteronomy 7:10, Psalm 34:16 and 2 Peter 2:17.)[4] We

---

[1] Women who do not wish to be bothered with breastfeeding their babies and fill the poor things with soy milk do special harm to the boys. And it might be that the girls reach puberty sooner—the number of eleven-year-olds that get pregnant seems to be growing.

[2] Every so often the local press comments on a growing level of impotence among the men, now approaching 40% (which would help to explain the increase in lesbianism among the women).

[3] I confess that I do not understand how it could be possible to rescue someone who is already in the fire, but that is what the Text says.

[4] It may be that the 'without-mercy' category includes two types: the mortal sin in 1 John 5:16-17 is presumably committed by a human being; but the third class in Jude 22-23 may be made up of humanoids, since a major share of the letter is describing them (as I see it).

A theological question presents itself: can a humanoid without a human spirit be saved? The demons cannot be recovered; their final destiny is

need discernment in order to do the triage. Yes, but, what can or should we do after that. According to the Sacred Text, Jehovah the Son took on flesh and blood in order to abolish Satan (Hebrews 2:14) and to undo his works (1 John 3:8). To undo a work one needs to also undo its consequences—is that not so? If someone crumples a fender of my car, how can we undo that 'work'? Someone has to take out the wrinkles, re-paint, restore the fender to its former condition. If someone kills my son, how can we undo that 'work'? Only by bringing him back from the dead, restoring his life. If someone rapes my daughter, making her pregnant, how can we undo that 'work'? I doubt that even God could restore her virginity, but the fetus could be aborted.[1] A son of a demon is an obvious work of Satan; so, how can we undo that 'work'?

A more or less literal translation of the Hebrew Text of Psalm 92:7 would be: "When the wicked flourish like grass, and all the workers of iniquity blossom, it is for them to be destroyed forever." The preceding verse speaks of persons

---

sealed (Matthew 25:41). So, will the son of a demon fare any better? A type of being with soul, but without spirit, would be very similar to an animal (mammal), that also has soul but not spirit. As far as I can understand the Sacred Text, when an animal dies it simply stops existing. Since a humanoid did not choose to be so born, and is not a candidate for salvation (as best I can see), would it not be unjust to condemn it to spend eternity in the Lake? The angels who fell chose to rebel against the Creator, and so have guilt. A human being has the option of submitting to the Creator and receiving salvation. But a humanoid, ... A rabid animal needs to be destroyed, for the benefit of the rest. Just as we have the option of sending a demon to the Abyss, so I understand the Text, stopping it from continuing with its evil around here, perhaps we can find a way to get rid of a humanoid as well, with the same objective, precisely. The question of discernment becomes crucial. Why waste time 'evangelizing' a humanoid? It would be like offering something holy to a dog, that will respond by attacking you (Matthew 7:6). (Actually, I believe the Holy Spirit has confirmed to me that the 'dogs' in Matthew 7:6, and possibly in Philippians 3:2 and Revelation 22:15, can include humanoids.) If there have always been humanoids, throughout human history, there must have been some in Jesus' day. In that event, it would be strange if He never touched on the subject, and dangerous for His followers. See Asides, item1.

[1] If the rape was perpetrated by a demon or humanoid, might aborting the result not be an obligation to society? Why give birth to a being that will only do evil in this world, and only be extinguished in the end anyway?

who ignore and despise the Creator—for such there is no cure, only destruction. Since a humanoid is not a candidate for salvation, and is in this world for the sole purpose of doing evil, it is like a gangrene in the body—if the gangrene is not excised, it will kill the body. But, what if we get to the place where we can identify a humanoid with certainty? So far as I know, there is no country in the world whose civil law distinguishes between human beings and humanoids. And many countries no longer have capital punishment. So then, we must find a solution in the spiritual realm. (If God removes someone, there is nothing the law of the land can do.)

Consider also Matthew 6:22-23—"The lamp of the body is the eye. So if your eye is sound your whole body will be full of light. But if your eye is evil your whole body will be full of darkness. So if the light that is in you is darkness, how great is that darkness!" Of course we have two eyes, but the Text has "eye" in the singular. I take it that the Lord Jesus is referring to the way we interpret what we see, which is our real 'eye'—two people, one pure and one vile, observing the same scene will give different interpretations to it. Someone with a malignant mind will give an evil interpretation to everything he sees, and in consequence his being will be filled with unrelenting darkness. (Cf. Titus 1:15.) Such persons reach a point where they are beyond help, beyond recovery, and should be removed, for the good of society.[1]

Solution

1. First, let us consider our incumbency, what Sovereign Jesus intends for us to do: "Just as the Father sent me, I also send you" (John 20:21)—just as. It is the Lord Jesus Christ, our Commander-in-chief, who is speaking. He is expecting, rather requiring, that we do as He did. So, **what** did He do? The Father ordered and the Son obeyed: "I have

---

[1] Perhaps we should distinguish between two types of bad people: those who deliberately devise evil and those who gradually lost the ability to distinguish between good and bad; perhaps these might still have a chance.

come to do Your will, O God" (Hebrews 10:7). (John 4:34—
"My food is to do the will of Him who sent me and to complete His work.") Brothers, we too must experience Hebrews
10:7. An effective participation in the spiritual war begins
with a total commitment to the Lord Jesus, and that needs
to be renewed daily. Just like the Lord Jesus, our life must
revolve around the Father's will. And what was that will, in
specific terms? It is stated in Hebrews 2:14—the Son took
on flesh and blood in order to abolish the devil; also to undo
his works (1 John 3:8).

So then, why are we here? To give continuity to the work of
Christ. He came to abolish Satan, and He succeeded, Hallelujah! (Colossians 2:15, John 16:11, Ephesians 1:20-21,
John 12:31, 1 Peter 3:22, 1 John 4:4). Yes indeed, Satan
has been defeated, his final destination has been decreed
(Matthew 25:41), but for His own sovereign reasons the
Creator still allows the enemy to operate in this world. It is
up to us to 'pay to see'—we must impose the defeat on the
devil, in practice (Matthew 18:18). Christ came to undo Satan's works, and since he continues to produce evil in this
world, it is up to us to undo it. As soon as Jesus won the
victory He returned to Heaven, leaving the undoing on our
plate. Since the Church has been calamitously absent in this
area, we are all obliged to live with the negative consequences of that neglect. **We are here to undo the works
of the devil!**

"Just as He is, so are we in this world" (1 John 4:17)—in
this world, not the next. The Church is the body of Christ,
and so it is mainly through her that He deals with this
world. (When you look at someone what you see is the person's body.) We are the Creator's spokesmen in this world.
(That could include the Trinity!—1 John 4:13-14, Genesis
1:26.) Attention please: it is time to wake up. It is time to
really understand that we represent the Creator down here,
and He expects us to conduct ourselves in a manner worthy
of our office.

2. Second, let us consider our competence, as stated in
Psalm 149:5-9.

"Let the saints exult in glory; let them sing for joy on their beds. Let the high praises of God be in their mouth, and a two edged sword in their hand, to execute vengeance upon the nations, and punishments upon the peoples; to bind their kings with chains, and their nobles with fetters of iron; to execute upon them the written judgment—this honor is for all His saints."[1]

Here are some observations based on the Text:

a) we are looking at commands (not optional points);

b) the commands are to be obeyed in bed—the point being, presumably, that we operate in the spiritual realm;

c) the battle is allied with praise, and the praise comes first (see 2 Chronicles 20:21-22);

d) the 'honor', a consequence of the positive results of obedience to the commands, is for "all His saints". It follows that if you are one of those saints, to obey those orders is on your plate, within your competence (so they will be required);

e) since our activity takes place in the spiritual realm, the 'kings' and 'nobles' presumably refer not only to the men who occupy positions of authority but also to the fallen angels (demons) who are behind them. In fact, a thorough job must get rid of the demons, as well as the men;

f) the scope includes entire nations, whole peoples; in short, any geographic or political entity that has a ruler;

g) since the battle is part of worshipping God, the 'vengeance' and 'punishment' need to be in accord with His character. It is where norms established by the Creator are being blatantly rejected that we should concentrate our action. NB: the point is to impose the Creator's norms, not our pet peeves;

h) since we operate in the spiritual realm, the authorities we bind may not literally wind up in the penitentiary, but

---

[1] The type of warfare ordered in Psalm 149 is at the highest level, including against fallen angels of high rank, 'world rulers'. A woman should not attempt it unless she is under the spiritual protection of a competent man (an unbelieving or backslidden husband will not hack it; nor a pastor who does not understand the subject [and does not want to learn]). (See 1 Corinthians 11:9-10 and Numbers 30:3-15.)

~ 237 ~

they will be removed from power; being bound hand and foot they cannot function;

i) there is no lack of 'written judgment'—Zechariah 5:2-4, against thieves and perjurers; Proverbs 20:10 against diverse weights and measures; Isaiah 10:1-2, against whoever makes unjust laws; Romans 1:26-32, against homosexualism and a sad list of other perversities (note that verse 32 says that they **are** deserving of death, by the righteous judgment of God; 'are', not 'were'—and this within the age of Grace, since Romans was written decades after Pentecost). (See also 1 Corinthians 6:9-10, Revelation 21:8 and 22:15.) Since humanoids are here to do evil, they come within our jurisdiction, without doubt.

Further, 1 Corinthians 6:2-4 affirms that saints judge the world; the verb 'judge' is in the present tense (the first occurrence is ambiguous with the future, but not the second one). Verse 3 adds that our jurisdiction includes angels. Well now, if we can judge an angel, then we can judge the son of an angel. Conclusion: judging humanoids is within our jurisdiction, our competence.

3. Third, let us consider our authority and power. In Luke 10:19 the Lord Jesus said:

> "Behold, I _give_ [so 98% of the Greek manuscripts] you **the** authority to trample on snakes and scorpions, and over all the power of _the_ enemy, and nothing shall by any means hurt you."

The Lord is addressing the Seventy, not the Twelve, and others were doubtless present; further, this was said perhaps four months before His death and resurrection. It follows that this authority is not limited to the apostles, and there is no indication of a time limit. The Lord Jesus affirms that He gives us **the** authority over all the power of the enemy. In Matthew 28:18 He declares that He holds "all authority . . . in heaven and earth", and so He has the right and the competence to delegate a portion of that authority to us. We may have any number of enemies, but _the_ enemy is Satan. The phrase, "all the power", presumably includes his works, followed by their consequences. Someone with authority can forbid an action, and therefore we can stop Satan from acting in a specific case.[1]

I link Ephesians 3:20 to Luke 10:19. "Now to Him who is able to do immeasurably more than all we ask or imagine, according to the power that is working in us, . . ." "Is working" is in the present tense; so it is valid for us today. There exists a power in us (the redeemed) that even surpasses our ability to imagine. It follows that to bring about something written should be easy.

Returning to Luke 10:19, the Lord gives us the authority to "trample snakes and scorpions". Well now, to smash the literal insect, a scorpion, you do not need power from on High, just a slipper. To trample a snake I prefer a boot, but we can kill literal snakes without supernatural help. It becomes obvious that Jesus was referring to something other than reptiles and insects. I understand Mark 16:18 to be referring to the same reality—Jesus declares that certain signs will accompany the believers (the turn of phrase virtually has the effect of commands): they will expel demons, they will speak strange languages, they will remove 'snakes', they will place hands on the sick.[2] ("If they

---

[1] Can we command Satan to undo his own works (including those of his servants)? I know a pastor here in Brazil whose car was stolen, so he ordered Satan, by name, to return it within 24 hours, and within the stipulated time it was parked in front of his house. But what about disease, would it not be better to use God's power (Ephesians 3:20)? I gather that the Lord Jesus always used God's power (not the enemy's), and we should follow His example. Since we have access to Christ's limitless power, we do not need Satan's, and should not give him the satisfaction of seeing us use it. And, recalling how subtle he is, there is the distinct possibility that he could deceive us and have us doing what we shouldn't.

(There are those who argue that Satan was stripped of his power, based on texts like Hebrews 2:14, Revelation 1:18, Colossians 2:15 and Matthew 28:18. The cruel facts of life that surround us and fill the world would seem to weigh inconveniently against that thesis, but the Text itself goes against it—what Satan will yet do through the Antichrist and the false prophet reflects considerable power. I understand the texts above to refer to the fact of Satan's having been demoted and deposed from his position as god/prince of this world, along with the privileges and perks that go with the office. Now he is obliged to act as a usurper, bluffing his 'rights'.)

[2] 1 Corinthians 12:29-30 leaves clear that no gift is given to everybody; we need the community, where all the gifts should be present.

drink . . ." is not a command; it refers to an eventuality.) Your Bible probably reads "they will take up serpents", or something similar. It happens that the Greek verb 'take up' covers a fairly wide semantic area, and one of the main meanings is 'to remove'—a garbage collector picks up a bag in order to remove it, get rid of it, not to keep it (he holds on to it only long enough to throw it into the truck). I believe that is the intended meaning here in Mark 16:18, but what did the Lord Jesus mean by 'snakes'?

In a list of distinct activities Jesus has already referred to demons, so the 'snakes' must be something else. In Matthew 12:34 Jesus called the Pharisees a 'brood of vipers', and in Matthew 23:33, 'snakes, brood of vipers'. In John 8:44, after they claimed God as their father, Jesus said, "You are of your father the devil". And 1 John 3:10 makes clear that Satan has many other 'sons'. In Revelation 20:2 we read: "He seized the dragon, the ancient serpent, who is a slanderer, even Satan, who deceives the whole inhabited earth, and bound him for a thousand years." If Satan is a snake, then his children are also snakes. So then, I take it that our 'snakes' are human beings who chose to serve Satan, who sold themselves to evil—the term could also include 'humanoids', who are literally devils' children. I conclude that the 'snakes' in Luke 10:19 are the same as those in Mark 16:18, but what of the 'scorpions'? Since they also are of the enemy, they may be demons, in which case the term may well include their offspring, the humanoids.[1] So then, whether as snakes or as scorpions, humanoids will be included, and therefore Luke 10:19 grants us the authority over them, explicitly so.[2]

---

[1] Since a snake is more dangerous than a scorpion (usually), and since a human being is superior to an angelic one in essence, and a human being in Satan's service can produce more damage in the world than a demon can, to associate scorpion with demon in this context is not unreasonable. I understand the Text to affirm that we have the authority to free ourselves from demons, humanoids, 'robots' and 'snakes' (human beings given over to evil).

[2] Yes, but the authority is to trample them; the intent is to kill or destroy. Evidently the Lord Jesus is talking about eliminating those things.

In Matthew 8:5-13 the centurion understood about authority—he gave orders and they were obeyed, without question or delay (but only within the sphere of his competence). But the Lord Jesus said that he had great faith, to an unusually high degree—but faith in what? Faith in Jesus' spiritual authority; all He had to do was give an order and it would happen. Perhaps we should understand this type of faith as being an absolute confidence, beyond a shadow of a doubt or a fear. In Matthew 21:21 the Lord said, "Assuredly I say to you, if you have faith and do not doubt" (see Mark 11:23, "and does not doubt in his heart") you also can dry up a tree, and even transport a mountain into the sea. See also Hebrews 10:22, "full assurance of faith" and James 1:6, "ask in faith, with no doubting". Mark 5:34 and Matthew 15:28 offer positive examples, and Matthew 14:30-31 the opposite.

If an authority gives a commission to someone, he will presumably back that commission up to the limit of his capacity. Since Christ's capacity is without limit, His backing should be so as well (as far as He is concerned). In Matthew 28:18 He said: "All authority in heaven and on earth has been given to me." Then comes the commission: "As you go make disciples . . . teaching them to obey everything that I commanded **you**"—the pronoun refers to the eleven apostles (verse 16). Very well, so what commands had Jesus given to the Eleven? Among others, "heal the sick, cleanse the lepers, cast out demons" (in Matthew 10:8—perhaps 94% of the Greek MSS do not have "raise the dead"). The Eleven also heard John 20:21. Knowing that we have the backing of the Sovereign of the universe, who has all authority and all power, we can and should do our duty with tranquil confidence.

4. Very well, we have the incumbency, the competence and the authority to face and solve the problem posed by humanoids in our world. It remains to know how to proceed, in terms both specific and concrete. I really cannot imagine that it could be God's will for His Church to be defeated or humiliated in this matter. So there must be a solution, and we need to keep calling out to God until He gives us a clear answer on this. Still, I believe that a few observations may already be made.

In the armor described in Ephesians 6 we find "the sword of the Spirit" (verse 17). A sword is a weapon for offense, although it is also used for defense. The Text tells us that this sword is "the ρημα of God"—ρημα, not λογος. It is God's Word <u>spoken</u>, or applied. Really, what good is a sword left in its sheath? However marvelous our Sword may be (Hebrews 4:12), to produce effect it must come out of the scabbard. The Word needs to be spoken, or written—applied in a specific way.

In the Bible we have many examples where people brought the power of God into action by speaking. Our world began with a creative word from God—spoken (Genesis, 1:3, 6, 9, 11, 14, 20, 24, 26; and see Hebrews 11:3). Moses did a lot of speaking. Elijah spoke (1 Kings 17:1, 18:36, 2 Kings 1:10). Elisha spoke (2 Kings 2:14, 21, 24; 4:16, 43; 6:19). Jesus did a great deal of speaking. Ananias spoke (Acts 9:17). Peter spoke (Acts 9:34, 40). Paul spoke (Acts 13:11; 14:3, 10; 16:18; 20:10; 28:8). In short, we need to speak!

The centurion did not say, "In the authority of Rome . . ."; he just said, "Do this; do that". The Lord Jesus did not say, "In the authority of the Father . . ."; He just said, "Be clean! Go!" In Luke 10:19 He said, "I give you **the** authority over all the power of the enemy"—so we have the authority; so let us speak!! Just like Jesus!

In Luke 17:6 we have a 'contrary to fact' condition, that in a literal translation would be: So the Lord said, "If you had faith [but you don't] like a mustard seed *has*,[1] you would

---

[1] I rather doubt that the Lord is commenting on the size of the faith; rather it is a quality of faith. But, what type of 'faith' might a mustard seed have? Although so small, it responds to the climatic circumstances without hesitation, and grows to a remarkable size. If we would respond without questioning to the nudges of the Holy Spirit, our 'climatic circumstances', we could literally transport a tree, just with our word. In Matthew 17:20 the Lord Jesus said, "If you have faith as a mustard seed *has*, you <u>will</u> say to this mountain, 'Move from here to there,' and it <u>will</u> move; and nothing will be impossible for you." That is what He said, but we just don't believe it.

say [but you don't] to this mulberry tree, 'Be pulled up by the roots and be planted in the sea,' and it would have obeyed you." The second apodosis is in a past tense, whereas the protasis and the first apodosis are in the present tense.[1] It is a curious grammatical construction, but I suppose that the Lord is emphasizing the certainty of the response—if they would only speak!!

I would translate Hebrews 11:1 like this: "Now faith is a realization of things being hoped for, an evidence of things not (being) seen." The concept of 'hope' in the New Testament includes an element of certainty (it is not mere wishful thinking). To declare as fact something we do not see is difficult for many (including myself), but I believe that to be the meaning of the Text. True faith is able to declare the existence of something before seeing it. When the centurion gave an order he was declaring what was going to happen, before the fact. He spoke, and it happened.[2] Of course the Lord Jesus did precisely the same thing; He would speak and it happened. I cannot help but wonder if some day people will say about me, "Of course he did the same thing; he would speak and it happened."

5. Perhaps someone will say: "Sure, sure, we have to speak; but exactly what are we going to say, and how and when and where?" Good questions. On the way to an answer we need to consider the following. Among all the sacrifices and burnt offerings in the Old Testament there is nothing for premeditated sin—something done with the intention of challenging or disdaining the Creator ('with a raised fist' in Hebrew), in short, rebellion. Thus, Deuteronomy 17:12 imposes the death penalty for rebellion; there was no sacri-

---

(But why then did Jesus emphasize the size of the seed? However small a seed may be, it can germinate and produce. However small a person may be [or appear to be] in the Kingdom of God, if he has the faith of a seed he will produce marvelously.)

[1] Well, actually some 30% of the Greek manuscripts, including the best line of transmission, have the protasis in the imperfect tense.

[2] We do well to remember, however, that it only worked, or would work, within the reach of his authority. That is why he appealed to Jesus—he himself could not heal the servant.

fice for that. According to Numbers 15:27-28, there was indeed sacrifice for unintentional sin, but now notice verse 30: "But anyone who sins defiantly, whether native-born or alien, blasphemes Jehovah, and that person must be cut off from his people." To insult Jehovah carried the death penalty, there being no sacrifice for that. Exodus 21:12-17 determines that those guilty of certain crimes must be executed. Notice especially verse 14: "But if a man schemes and kills another deliberately, you must take him away from my altar and execute him." Imagine that! At that time the altar represented precisely the means for expiating sins. To run to the altar was a way to plead for God's mercy and protection, but the Creator does not allow this recourse to a murderer—a murderer must be executed. People can object all they like, but the Creator is resolute—whoever deliberately kills the image of God (without due cause) must be killed in his turn; there is no indemnity. I have already commented on Leviticus 18:6-30 and 20:1-22, where incest, adultery, human sacrifice, homosexualism and sex with an animal received the death penalty. To be sure, since it was the society that applied, or was to apply, the penalty, it would only happen in the community of God's people. Pagan peoples were ignorant of God's laws. But none of that alters the fact that there was no sacrifice for such practices.

But how about the New Testament, does not the age of Grace change the picture? To try to argue that God's grace annuls His moral law will not work. Note Romans 1:18-32, where it is clear that the application is current. In verse 32 'the righteous judgment of God' is that those who practice the things mentioned (including the list in Leviticus 18) "**are** deserving of death". "<u>Are</u>", not "were"—the verb is in the present tense, as in the original Text. In other words, Paul affirms that the penalty has not changed; even in the Church age, the age of grace, certain persons continue to be subject to death—by divine sentence. 1 Corinthians 10:6-12 declares that the experiences of Israel in the desert are "examples for us" and "were written for our admonition" (verse 11), and concludes with: "Therefore let him who thinks he stands take heed lest he fall." All the examples given resulted in physical death, and if they were recorded for our admonition, it is because we may face something similar. We cannot be too careful! 1 Corinthians 6:9, Revelation 21:8 and 22:14-15 were also written after the day of Pentecost. And notice Hebrews 10:26, "For if we sin willfully after we have received the knowledge of the truth, there no longer remains a sacrifice for sins" (see verses 26-31). We cannot be too careful!

As for blood guiltiness (see Deuteronomy 21:1-9, 19:13 and Numbers 35:33), 1 Corinthians 11:27-30 makes clear that the New Testament does not change the Creator's position regarding it. According to verse 27, whoever drinks the cup of the Lord in an unworthy manner will be <u>guilty of the blood</u> of the Lord. And what is the consequence? The answer is in verse 30: "For this reason . . . many sleep." 'Sleep' means they are dead; in other words, God executed them. The apostle Paul, inspired by the Holy Spirit, declares that with reference to "many" the Creator had exacted the penalty of blood guiltiness, literally—the culprit died. I confess that God's severity in this case surprises me, but there it is. Let no one kid himself; the Creator is still punishing blood guiltiness!

The Bible declares that God created man in His own image, and from then till now men have tried to return the favor, creating their own 'god' in their minds (of course any god you create will be smaller than you are, inescapably—totally worthless). Something similar happens to God's love, concerning which the vast majority of people, including believers, have a mistaken view. "Whom the Lord loves He chastens, and **scourges** every son whom he receives" (Hebrews 12:6; see also Revelation 3:19). [I myself have been on the business end of a horsewhip, and can assure the reader that it isn't pleasant.] In Deuteronomy 33:2-3 the "fiery law" is an expression of God's love for the people. Precisely because He is concerned for our true wellbeing, the Creator imposes the earthly consequences of our sins. The love of God **necessarily** includes hating evil, because of the <u>consequences</u> of the evil that will harm His 'image'.

Hebrews 1:8-9 cites Psalm 45:6-7, declaring that it refers to the Son: among other things it is affirmed that He hates iniquity. The glorified Christ Himself declares that He hates the works of the Nicolaitans (Revelation 2:6). Jehovah hates stealing (Isaiah 61:8), divorce (Malachi 2:16) and seven other transgressions (Proverbs 6:16-19). "The fear of Jehovah is to hate evil" (Proverbs 8:13; and see 9:10). In Psalm 97:10 we have a <u>command</u>: "You who love Jehovah, hate evil!" Are we going to obey?

Psalm 5:5 informs us that Jehovah hates all workers of iniquity. We are in the habit of teaching that God hates sin but loves the sinner. It seems so, up to a point. But when someone decides to join Satan, and makes a point of practicing evil, he attracts God's wrath—Deuteronomy 7:10. (See Psalm 26:5; 31:6; 101:3; 119:104, 113, 128, 163—these help us to understand David's attitude in Psalm 139:21-22; it is because they act with wicked intent [verse 20] that he hates them.) We must learn to hate sin, evil in any and all forms, Satan and his angels—since they are beyond recovery (Matthew 25:41, 2 Peter 2:4, Revelation 20:10), we are in a war without pity, without quarter, to the death.

The Sacred Text is clear: the character of God does not change, cannot be altered. In Malachi 3:6 Jehovah Himself declares that He does not change. James 1:17 affirms the same thing in other words. Hebrews 13:8 affirms something similar about Jesus Christ. Let us give special attention to 2 Timothy 2:13. "If we are faithless, He remains faithful; He cannot deny Himself." <u>He cannot deny Himself</u>—is it not obvious? He cannot go against His very nature, His own essence; it is one thing that God cannot do. He is Truth, and so cannot be unfaithful. It is precisely for that reason that He is incapable of lying (Titus 1:2).

Now let us consider Deuteronomy 7:9-10: "Therefore know that Jehovah your God is **God**; He is the faithful God who keeps covenant and mercy for a thousand generations with those who love Him and keep His commandments; and He repays those who hate Him to their face, to destroy them. He will not be slow to repay to his face the one who hates

Him." If God repays hate with destruction, and without delay, then He does not offer salvation to that hater.[1] Obvious. Palm 34:16 reads like this: "The face of Jehovah is against those who do evil, to cut off the remembrance of them from the earth" (quoted in 1 Peter 3:12). Well now, to erase the memory of someone you must begin by erasing that someone himself. Any question? When a person chooses to become an ally of evil, he is challenging the Creator to kill him, literally. 2 Peter 2:17 affirms this about the allies of evil described in verses 9-17: "for whom the blackest of the darkness has been reserved forever".[2] We find the same expression in Jude 13. With an eternal reservation like that, what are their chances? John 3:16 declares that giving His Son was an expression of God's love for the world. So He offers salvation to those He loves, not those He hates. Whoever decides to hate God receives the hate back, and remains without salvation. In John 6:44 (and verse 65) the Lord Jesus declares, "No one can come to me unless the Father who sent me draws him", and it should be obvious that the Father is not going to draw someone whom He hates.[3] Actually, when you stop and think about it, for someone who hates God, being in Heaven would really be a sort of 'hell'.

In Matthew 10:25 the Lord Jesus affirms: "It is enough for a disciple that he be like his teacher, and a slave like his owner." 1 John 4:17 says that "just as He is, so are we in this world". So then, if He hates those who work iniquity, Psalm 5:5, we have the obligation to do the same thing. To permit

---

[1] In Joel 3:4 Jehovah expresses Himself like this: "Indeed, what have you to do with me, O Tyre and Sidon and all the coasts of Philistia? Will you retaliate against me? But if you retaliate against me, swiftly and speedily I will return your retaliation upon your own head." God demonstrates the same attitude as in Deuteronomy 7:10—He does not tolerate perversity.

[2] This darkness is associated with Satan's kingdom, because "God is light and in Him is no darkness at all" (1 John 1:5). Peter is affirming that they will share the same destiny as their boss.

[3] John 3:36 is also to the point: "The one believing into the Son has eternal life, but the one disobeying the Son will not see life, but the wrath of God remains upon him." Will the Father 'draw' someone who remains under His wrath? How? The Text declares that the person **will not see life**—not ever.

a malevolent person to continue doing damage in this world, when it is incumbent upon us to remove him, turns us into his accomplices. An accomplice to a crime is a criminal. In Luke 10:19, when the Lord Jesus gives us the authority to trample snakes and scorpions, it follows that He is also giving us the incumbency—otherwise, why give the authority? To 'trample' involves hostile intent. Just to step on a scorpion, even without wanting to, will crush the insect, will kill it. How much more if you do it with hostile intent! The purpose of trampling a snake is also to kill it. Conclusion: it is up to us to rid the world of 'snakes' and 'scorpions'; it is our responsibility; it is our incumbency! So, God is waiting on us—**we** are the ones who have to do it! And we will do it by speaking.

6. Conclusion: Humanoids are not candidates for salvation, do only evil, and therefore need to be eliminated, for the public good. Human beings who have chosen Satan, who have sold themselves to him to devise and do evil, are haters of God and therefore cannot be saved—they need to be eliminated for the public good. The partisans of the militant 'gay' agenda are a case in point; they are in open rebellion against the Creator and His values. Since it is their declared intention to destroy our culture, making it impossible for decent people to live in peace, we are facing a question of life or death. If we do not react adequately, we will lose the game.

At least three times the Lord Jesus referred to the Holy Spirit as being "the Spirit of the Truth" (John 14:17, 15:26, 16:13). It follows that to deliberately reject the Truth is to blaspheme the Holy Spirit, the unpardonable sin (Mark 3:29). It adds to our case. The enemies of God are without pardon, without salvation, do only evil, and are therefore a type of cancer or gangrene in society—if the society does not get rid of it, the society will be killed. Since the society at large does not have the slightest idea of the danger it faces, and even less of the solution, it is up to us to save the day, we who know and can. Recalling the exposition of Psalm 149 (Solution, 2.), I understand that all the texts that speak of the divine intention to eliminate partisans of evil enter the list of texts that state a 'written judgment'. And it is up to us to impose written judgment.

I invite attention to Psalm 91. The context is one of war. Since God offers protection to those who take refuge in Him, the terror, the arrow, the pestilence, the destruction come from the enemy. Verse 13 says: "You shall tread upon the lion and the cobra, the young lion and the serpent you shall trample underfoot", which reminds us of Luke 10:19. Verse 7 speaks of a thousand falling on our left and ten thousand on our right. Why the difference? Most people being right handed, a sword is normally held in the right hand. So a soldier would normally kill more to the right than to the left.

2 Corinthians 10:4 teaches us that "the weapons of our warfare are not carnal". So we must do our duty in the spiritual realm, using God's power. I understand that this is done verbally in the presence of the Righteous Judge of the whole earth (2 Timothy 4:8, Genesis 18:25, Hebrews 12:23), citing the written judgments specifically and applying them by name to those who deserve them. I myself am claiming before God the removal of eleven thousand of Satan's servants, and I am not alone in this.

Asides

1. More than one person has asked: "If humanoids were a reality that the Christians would have to face, why did not the Lord Jesus teach about them, why did Paul not write about them, nor any of the other authors of the New Testament?" The question is based on a false premise, that the New Testament is silent on the subject, but I will argue that it is not. Let us see.

It is a simple fact that the Bible frequently uses the term 'man' to refer to a materialized angel. In Genesis 18:2 Abraham saw three 'men', two being angels and the third Jehovah Himself (and the three ate the meal he prepared). As the story goes on, 19:1 says plainly that they were angels, but in verses 5, 10, 12 and 16 they are called 'men'. Once more in Genesis 32:24 the term 'man' refers to Jehovah Himself (see also Joshua 5:13). In Judges 13:6 Samson's mother refers to the Angel of Jehovah, who had appeared to her, as a 'man' (also in verses 8, 10 and 11). See also Daniel 3:25 and 28, 8:15-16, 9:21, 10:5 and 16, 12:5-7; Ezekiel 2:26; Zechariah 1:8-11, 2:1-3. In the New Testament angels had an important role at Jesus' empty tomb, sometimes appearing as angels, sometimes as men (Matthew 28:2-7, Mark 16:5-8, Luke 24:4-7, John 20:12-13). See also at the ascension of Jesus, Acts 1:10-11. Well now, if an angel can be called a 'man', why not, and all the more, the offspring of an angel? Quite so.

In Genesis 6:4 the hybrid race, the half-breeds, are called 'men', as also in the description that follows. Since the description in 2 Timothy 3:1-5 parallels the description in Genesis 6, the 'men' here presumably includes humanoids. The same holds for the description in Jude 10-19 and in Romans 1:28-32. Consider also 1 John 2:18—"Children, it is the last hour, and just as you have heard that the Antichrist is coming, even now many antichrists have appeared, by which we know that it is the last hour." Well, the Lord Jesus was a hybrid being, Holy Spirit with woman. I do not doubt that the actual Antichrist will also be a hybrid, Satan with woman (his 'thing' is to be like God). So what about the 'many antichrists' to which John refers, what might they be? It seems to me to be perfectly possible that they also were hybrids, precisely our 'humanoids'.

Once we start 'chewing' on this subject, I think we are obliged to conclude that humanoids themselves will marry and procreate—perhaps with another humanoid, but I imagine that the preference would be with a human. In that way the miscegenation would become increasingly diluted, and such subsequent generations would certainly be called 'men'. If we stop and think, the cultures where the parents choose a mate for their children may not be so 'stupid' as some might like to imagine. Really, to check out the lineage of a prospective mate is an important proceeding, in fact necessary (an impulsive marriage with a humanoid equals disaster).

Further, as I have already maintained, the 'snakes' in Mark 16:18 and Luke 10:19 and the 'scorpions' in Luke, presumably include humanoids. Also, I understand that the Holy Spirit has confirmed to me that the 'dogs' in Matthew 7:6 (and probably in Philippians 3:2 and Revelation 22:15) include humanoids.[1]

Over twenty-five years ago, when I started ministering on the subject of biblical spiritual warfare, I soon realized that not a single text that treats of our 'weapons' or procedures explains how to do it. For example: Mark 3:27 teaches that we must bind Satan; but does not say how! In James 4:7 we have the command to resist the devil; but it does not say how. 2 Corinthians 10:4 says we have some great weapons; but does not identify them—if they are the gerundive clauses in verses 5 and 6, again we are not told how to do it!! I take it that God uses Satan and his angels (the demons) to test and train the successive generations of people, and if all the procedures were clearly laid out, God's people would have wiped out the enemy long since. So, it is cheerfully foreseeable that the references to humanoids in the New Testament will be veiled, none of which justifies the claim that the New Testament does not mention the subject.

2. In John 14:12 the Lord Jesus said: "Most assuredly I say to you, the one believing into me, he too will do the works that I do; in fact he will do greater works than these, because I am going to my Father. "Most assuredly" is actually "amen, amen"—rendered "verily, verily" in the AV. Only John registers the word as repeated, in the other Gospels it is just "amen". In the contemporary literature we have no example of anyone else using the word in this way. It seems that Jesus coined His own use, and the point seems to be to call attention to an important pronouncement: "Stop and listen!" Often it precedes a formal statement of doctrine or policy, as here.

---

[1] Although the Jews were in the habit of referring to Gentiles as 'dogs', the context here calls for a different meaning.

"The one believing into me, he too will do the works that I do." This is a tremendous statement, and not a little disconcerting. Notice that the Lord said, "will do"; not 'maybe', 'perhaps', 'if you feel like it'; and certainly not 'if the doctrine of your church permits it'! If you believe you **will do!** The verb 'believe' is in the present tense, 2nd person singular; if you (sg.) are believing you will do; it follows that if you are not doing, it is because you are not believing. 2 + 2 = 4. Doing what? "The works that I do." Well, Jesus preached the Gospel, He taught, He cast out demons, He healed all sorts and sizes of sickness and disease, He raised an occasional dead person, and He performed a variety of miracles (water to wine, walk on water, stop a storm instantaneously, transport a boat several miles instantaneously, multiply food, shrivel a tree—and He implied that the disciples should have stopped the storm and multiplied the food, and He stated that they could shrivel a tree [Peter actually took a few steps on water]). So how about us? The preaching and teaching we can handle, but what about the rest? I once heard the president of a certain Christian college affirm that this verse obviously could not mean what it says because it is not happening! Well, in his own experience and in that of his associates I guess it isn't. But many people today cast out demons and heal, and I personally know someone who has raised a dead person. Miracles are also happening. So how about me? And you?

"In fact he will do greater works than these." Well now, if we cast out demons, heal and perform miracles, is that not enough? Jesus wants more, He wants "greater things" than those just mentioned [do not forget what He said in Matthew 7:22-23]. Notice again that He said "will do", not maybe, perhaps, or if your church permits. But what could be 'greater' than miracles? This cannot refer to modern technology because in that event such 'greater things' would not have been available to the believers during the first 1900 years. Note that the key is in the Lord's final statement (in verse 12), "because I am going to my Father". Only if He won could He return to the Father, so He is here declaring His victory before the fact. It is on the basis of that victory that the 'greater things' can be performed.

Just what are those 'greater' things? For my answer, see my outline (essay), "Biblical Spiritual Warfare". Now I would add to the list 'get rid of humanoids' ('robots' and 'snakes' should also receive appropriate attention).

In verse 12 the verb 'will do' is singular, both times, so it has to do with the individual. Please note that the Lord did **not** say, 'you apostles', 'just during the apostolic era', 'only until the Canon is completed', or whatever. What He did say is, "the one believing", present tense, and so it applies to any subsequent time including the present day. To deny the truth contained in this verse is to call the Lord Jesus a liar. Not a good idea![1]

3. In Luke 4:18-21 Jesus includes "to set at liberty those who are oppressed" (Isaiah 8:6) among the things He was sent to do. Turning to Isaiah we find that Jehovah is declaring what type of 'fast' He wants to see: "To loose the fetters of wickedness [a], to untie the yoke thongs [b]; to set the oppressed free [a], and that you break every yoke [b]." As is typical of Hebrew grammar, the two halves are parallel. "To loose the fetters of wickedness" and "to set the oppressed free" are parallel. Who placed the fetters and who is doing the oppressing? Well, although people can certainly forge their own chains through a sinful lifestyle, it seems to me that in this context it is evil beings putting the fetters on others. "To untie the yoke thongs" and "that you break every yoke" go together. First we should untie the thongs/cords that bind the yoke to the neck, and then we should break the very yokes. It seems clear to me that this text treats of the activity of Satan's servants: men, demons, humanoids. Using culture, worldview, legal maneuvers, threats, blackmail, lies, deceit and plain demonization and witchcraft, they bind individuals, families, ethnic groups, etc. with a variety of fetters and instruments of oppression.

---

[1] One other point: to affirm that the miraculous gifts ceased when the last clod of dirt fell on the Apostle John's grave is an historical falsehood. Christians who lived during the 2nd, 3rd and 4th centuries, whose writings have come down to us, affirm that these gifts still existed in their time. No Christian of the 20th or 21st century, WHO WAS NOT THERE, is competent to contradict them.

Well, but so what? What does that have to do with our subject? Well, fasting was an important/obligatory component of their worship of God. It follows that this kind of 'fasting' is something that Jehovah overtly wants; it is His declared will. And so, whenever we see the work of Satan in someone's life, it is God's will that we undo it. If we know that it is God's will, we can proceed with complete confidence. It is also included in our commission (John 20:21).

Well, and what if we do nothing?

James 4:17—"Therefore, to the one knowing to do good and not doing it, to him it is sin." So, if I do not undo Satan's works, it shows up on my bill as sin, and I will have to answer for it. Ezekiel 22:30-31—"I sought for a man among them who would make a wall, and stand in the gap before me on behalf of the land, that I should not destroy it; but I found no one. Therefore I have poured out my indignation on them; . . ." The Text is clear: just one person could have made the difference, and averted the destruction. See also Malachi 1:10, that asks for just one person to act. So then, if I do not undo Satan's works, people will continue to suffer, without need. If I reject the plain meaning of the Text, I am closing my mind against the Truth, and thereby condemning myself to continue living with error and its consequences. Condemning myself and any others who depend on me or follow me. Help!

We need the gift of discerning spirits! [Note that 'spirits' is plural.][1]

---

[1] I regret that I must confess that during 20 years of ministering on Biblical spiritual warfare around Brazil I never taught this gift, and I never heard anyone else explain it. We must try to diminish the damage. To deny the existence of cancer, AIDS, aviary flu, etc., would be to guarantee that a solution would never be found. Analogously, to deny the existence of humanoids will carry the same guarantee. Not a valid option! To ignore the word of Sovereign Jesus can only bring negative consequences—it was He who said, "As were the days of Noah"!!

CONCERNING PATHOGENS— ORIGIN and SOLUTION

The Origin of Pathogens[1]

1. We have no record of diseases before the Flood. As a consequence of the Fall, God cursed the soil, but nothing suggests the creation of bad bacteria. (Actually, it appears that all animals were herbivorous until after the Flood.)[2] Before the Flood the "firmament" filtered out the destructive rays from the sun. But that "firmament" was destroyed at the time of the Flood, so from then on the planet has received the negative effects of those rays. After the Flood there was a progressive reduction in longevity and size, of both living beings and plants. We understand that the planet is considerably less congenial to life (human, animal, plant) now than before. And the Flood was God's devastating answer to a terrible attack by Satan against the "seed".[3]

---

[1] Pathogens are organisms that produce pathology or disease.

[2] When placed in a hyperbaric chamber simulating pre-flood atmospheric conditions, snake venom is neutralized.

[3] The phrase 'sons of God' in Genesis 6:2,4 translates the Hebrew, *bene-haelohim*. In the other places where this phrase occurs, Job 1:6, 2:1, 38:7, it refers to angelic beings. Jude makes clear that Genesis 6:2 is no exception. "And the angels who did not keep their proper domain, but left their own habitation, He has secured in everlasting chains under darkness for the judgment of the great day. Just as Sodom and Gomorrah, and the cities around them, in the same way as these [angels], having fornicated and gone after a different kind [ετερος] of flesh, are exhibited as an example, undergoing a punishment of eternal fire" (Jude 6-7). The author, under inspiration of God, affirms that the people of Sodom did what certain angelic beings did; they wanted sex with a different kind of flesh. Recall that the men of Sodom, old and young, from every quarter, wanted to rape the angels that were visiting Lot (Genesis 19:4-5). Whatever kind of flesh an angel has (when he materializes), it is not human flesh; it is precisely "a different kind [ετερος] of flesh". The parallel passage in 2 Peter 2:4-6 links the crime of those angels to the Flood. (In Matthew 22:30 [Mark 12:25, Luke 20:35-36] the Lord does not say that angels do not have sex/gender. Evidently no baby angels [good or fallen] are born, but if angels are of only one gender they cannot reproduce in kind. Whenever an angel takes on human form in the Bible it is always the form of a man.) [And do not forget 1 Corinthians 11:10.]

2. In Deuteronomy 7:15, as a consequence of keeping and obeying Jehovah's commandments, statutes and judgments, God promises: "Jehovah will take away from you all sickness, and will afflict you with none of the terrible diseases of Egypt . . . ." On the other hand, if they do not obey, God promises exactly the opposite, Deuteronomy 28:59-60. Repeatedly the Bible affirms that God uses disease and calamity to punish those who disobey and do evil; He also uses Satan himself, fallen angels (demons), and evil men.[1] He uses evil to punish evil, so it follows that He can use pathogens, even if they are made by Satan and not God.

3. With respect to Jehovah, Psalm 103:3 affirms: "who forgives all your iniquities, who heals all your diseases." Neither activity is automatic, but the potential is there. Would He heal a disease that He Himself caused? "God is not the author of confusion" (1 Corinthians 14:33). Since He did not commit the iniquities that He forgives, it is presumably also true that He did not cause the diseases that He heals.

So what? We know from modern medicine that every human being carries the father's blood, not the mother's, so the mixed race mentioned in Genesis 6:4 carried demon blood in their veins, not human; and we know from the Sacred Text that the human spirit is transmitted by the male sperm, so that mixed race had lost the human spirit and presumably the "image of God". If Satan had succeeded in corrupting everybody, it would have been impossible for the Messiah, the second Adam, to be born, and Genesis 3:15 could not have been fulfilled. Satan's challenge to God's plan was so incredible, and came so close to succeeding, that God's response was to destroy everything and start over, using eight humans that had not yet been contaminated.

I offer the above as a possible historical background. If Satan got the clue that he was not going to be able to frustrate the plan of redemption, then all that was left to him was spite—do as much damage to "the image of God" as he could (his only way of 'getting back' at the Creator, besides taking as many with him to the Lake as possible). Having said all that, however, please note that if pathogens existed before the Flood, it makes no practical difference to the subject in hand: the origin of pathogens and the solution to them.

[1] Obviously evil men play right into Satan's hand. The greed that leads men to put hormones in meat, make and sell 'medicines' that are damaging, put aspartame in drink, etc. etc., plus certain life styles and eating habits, all contribute to set us up, to make us more susceptible to pathogens.

4. Consider the description that Jehovah gave of Himself to Moses on that rarest of occasions: "Jehovah, God, merciful and gracious, longsuffering, and abounding in goodness and truth; keeping mercy unto the thousandth generation, forgiving iniquity and transgression and sin; and that will by no means clear the guilty, visiting the iniquity of the fathers upon the children and the children's children unto the third and the fourth generation" (Exodus 34:6-7). He keeps mercy to the 1000th generation, He punishes to the 4th; the proportion is 250:1. The chances that Goodness and Truth would cause pathogens are probably no better than one in 250, if that.

5. With reference to the Messiah, Isaiah 53:4 says: "Surely He bore our diseases and carried our pains." Both of the Hebrew terms here have to do with physical sickness, not merely emotional 'griefs' or 'sorrows'. The inspired commentary in Matthew 8:17 makes this clear: "He Himself took our infirmities and bore our sicknesses." If He has already taken them, would He turn around and put them back on us?

6. We understand that Jehovah the Son took on human flesh in order to destroy Satan (Hebrews 2:14) and to undo his works (1 John 3:8); in other words, to recover what the first Adam lost. "As all in Adam die, even so all in Christ shall be made alive" (1 Corinthians 15:22). "The last Adam became a life-giving spirit" (1 Corinthians 15:45). In John 10:10 the Lord Jesus contrasts Himself with Satan: "**The** thief does not come except to steal, and to kill, and to destroy. I have come that they may have life, and that they may have it more abundantly." In John 8:44 the Lord Jesus said that Satan "was a murderer from the beginning". Well now, does 'more abundant' life include pathogens? Do pathogens produce life or death? If death, then they must be of Satan—murderer, thief, destroyer, father of lies—and not of the Author of life (Acts 3:15). "Every good giving and every perfect gift is from above, coming down from the Father of the lights" (James 1:17). So where do bad givings and nasty 'gifts' come from?

7. There are those who doubt the possibility that Satan could create pathogens, but it is not a question of 'creating' from nothing, but of deforming. The Creator made good bacteria (billions of them, invisible but necessary to our physical existence) and Satan deforms/degrades them, altering the DNA. Surely, if people are now cloning, playing with genetic engineering, messing with DNA, why not Satan? Is he less intelligent than we are? Does he have less power than we? Actually, 2 Peter 2:11 says that angels "are greater in power and might" than unjust human beings; and Satan was created as the number one angelic being (Ezekiel 28:12-16, Jude 9). If unregenerate people can do it, then Satan and his angels can too.

8. Repeatedly the Lord Jesus expelled a demon of blindness, deafness or paralysis and thereupon the person was healed. So the problem was caused by a demon, which means that the demon had altered the molecular structure of the victim. In Luke 13:10-17 the Lord heals a woman who had been "bound by Satan" for eighteen years; the Lord cites Satan by name, but verse 11 speaks of "a spirit of infirmity". Severely demonized people are visibly altered and degraded. If Satan can degrade a human being, infinitely more complex than a microbe, to alter a mere bacterium would be the essence of simplicity.

9. On more than one occasion the Lord said that if we ask anything "in His name" He, or the Father, will do it. To ask "in His name" is to ask something He is asking, or would ask. If Jesus would do it, then it is in His name, or in His will. We have repeated statements that He healed everyone who came to Him, and of every kind of malady, including congenital defects.[1] Perhaps He healed everybody because, whatever their problem, Satan was involved somewhere. In Acts 10:38 Peter says that Jesus "went about doing good and healing all who were oppressed by the devil." The devil

---

[1] Congenital defects are presumably the result of the effects of sin upon the gene pool down through the years and succession of generations; this would include allergic weakness and immune deficiency. Aside from his role in the Fall, Satan has a direct participation in much of the sin in the world.

is Satan. Did Peter mean that every time Jesus saw an oppressed person He healed them, or did he mean that everyone whom Jesus healed was oppressed, or both? The episode at the pool of Bethesda (John 5:2-13)[1] would appear to eliminate the first option, that every time He saw an oppressed person He healed them, because there was a "great multitude" of oppressed people there, and Jesus obviously saw them, but He did nothing to help them.[2] This leaves us with the clear conclusion that it is the second meaning that is correct, everyone whom Jesus healed was oppressed, which means that Satan is involved in all maladies.

We conclude that pathogens are a work of Satan.[3]

The Solution for Pathogens

1. The Son of God was manifested for the purpose of "undoing the works of the devil" (1 John 3:8), and it is incumbent upon us to continue His work here in this world (John 20:21). How can you undo a work without undoing its consequences as well? The Father sent the Son to undo Satan's works, and the Lord Jesus Christ is sending us to undo Satan's works.

------

[1] Less than 1% of the Greek manuscripts, of objectively inferior quality, omit the last clause of verse 3 and all of verse 4 (as in NIV, NASB, LB, [TEV], etc.). But obviously all those people would not stay there (in discomfort) day in and day out, year in and year out, if nothing was happening. Obviously people got healed, and verse 7 makes clear that it had to do with the stirring of the water—so why did those manuscripts not omit verse 7 as well? The UBS editions do us a considerable disservice by following a very small minority of manuscripts and making the angel "of the Lord". Since angels can be good or fallen, it seems most likely to me that the angel involved was fallen. A capricious, occasional healing condemned all those people to added suffering (being at the pool instead of the comfort of home), including the frustration and despair of those who never made it (like the man Jesus healed). A sadistic procedure is just like Satan.

[2] Why did not Jesus heal everybody? I do not know, I was not there. From the Record it appears that the Plan involved His healing only those who came to Him, in person or by proxy, except for an occasional strategic healing that was unsolicited. The Father is seeking those who will worship Him in spirit and truth—you have to want Him, you have to come.

[3] I owe the idea that pathogens could be Satan's work to Dr. Ralph Winter, founder of the US Center for World Mission.

2. Indirectly, if not directly, Adam's Fall was a work of Satan, and it follows that the consequences of that fall are consequences of that work. This includes the sin nature in man and Satan's control of the 'world'; it includes sin, sickness and disease.

3. In Luke 10:19 the Lord Jesus said: "Behold, I give [so 98% of the Greek manuscripts] you the authority . . . over all the power of the enemy."[1] The phrase, 'all the power' presumably includes his works, and therefore their consequences. Someone with authority can forbid action, so we can prevent Satan from doing things. Verse 19 goes on to say, "and nothing shall by any means hurt you", so it may be that the primary focus here is upon defense—defending ourselves, and others, against Satan's attacks.[2] So, are we going to use our authority, or not?

4. After His resurrection, with the victory won, the Lord Jesus said: "These signs will follow those who believe, in my name . . . they will lay hands on the sick and they will re-

---

[1] The Lord is addressing the Seventy, not the Twelve, and there were doubtless others around; also, this was spoken perhaps four months before His death and resurrection. It follows that this authority is not only for apostles, and there is no indication of a time limit.

[2] The Text must mean at least that, but can we also command Satan to undo what he (or his servants) has done? I know a pastor in Brazil whose car was stolen; he commanded Satan (he addressed him directly, by name) to return the car within 24 hours, and before the time was up the car was parked in front of the pastor's house [he told me this as an example of how to spoil Satan's goods]. But what about sickness, would it not be better to use God's power (Ephesians 3:20)? I understand that the Lord Jesus always used God's power, so we had better follow His example. Since we have access to the limitless power of Christ, we do not need Satan's power and should not give him the satisfaction of seeing us use it. (Considering how slippery he is, there is the distinct possibility that he would deceive us and get us to do things that we shouldn't.)

(There are those who argue that Satan has been divested of all power, based on texts like Hebrews 2:14, Revelation 1:18, Colossians 2:15 and Matthew 28:18. The cruel facts of life that surround us and fill the world would appear to weigh inconveniently against that idea, but the Sacred Text itself disavows such a view—what Satan will do through the antichrist and the false prophet reflects considerable power. I understand the texts listed above to refer to Satan's being divested of and deposed from his position as god/ruler of this world, along with all privileges and perquisites pertaining to that office. He is now obliged to function as a usurper, bluffing his 'rights'.)

cover" (Mark 16:17-18). The term "sick" translates the Greek, αρρωστος, which covers a fairly wide area of meaning—it includes a variety of maladies, even death dealing epidemics (so it includes pathogens).[1]

5. In John 14:12 the Lord Jesus said: "Most assuredly I say to you, the one believing into me, he too will do the works that I do; in fact he will do greater works than these, because I am going to my Father." "Most assuredly" is actually "amen, amen"—rendered "verily, verily" in the AV. Only John registers the word as repeated, in the other Gospels it is just "amen". In the contemporary literature we have no example of anyone else using the word in this way. It seems that Jesus coined His own use, and the point seems to be to call attention to an important pronouncement: "Stop and listen!" Often it precedes a formal statement of doctrine or policy, as here.

"The one believing into me, he too will do the works that I do." This is a tremendous statement, and not a little disconcerting. Notice that the Lord said, "will do"; not 'maybe', 'perhaps', 'if you feel like it'; and certainly not 'if the doctrine of your church permits it'! If you believe you **will do!** The verb 'believe' is in the present tense; if you are believing you will do; it follows that if you are not doing it is because you are not believing. 2 + 2 = 4. Doing what? "The works that I do." Well, Jesus preached the Gospel, He taught, He cast out demons, He healed all sorts and sizes of sickness and disease, He raised an occasional dead person, and He performed a variety of miracles (water to wine, walk on water, stop a storm instantaneously, transport a boat several miles instantaneously, multiply food, shrivel a tree— and He implied that the disciples should have stopped the storm and multiplied the food, and He stated that they could shrivel a tree [Peter actually took a few steps on water]). So how about us? The preaching and teaching we can

---

[1] Only three Greek manuscripts, of objectively, demonstrably inferior quality, omit Mark 16:9-20, against 1,700 that have the passage; so it is certainly part of the inspired Text. Mark wrote 1:1-16:20. For an exhaustive treatment of this question please see Appendix E in my book, *The Identity of the New testament Text IV.*

handle, but what about the rest? I once heard the president of a certain Christian college affirm that this verse obviously could not mean what it says because it is not happening! Well, in his own experience and in that of his associates I guess it isn't. But many people today cast out demons and heal, and I personally know someone who has raised a dead person. Miracles are also happening. So how about me? And you?

"In fact he will do greater works than these." Well now, if we cast out demons, heal and perform miracles, is that not enough? Jesus wants more, He wants "greater things" than those just mentioned [do not forget what He said in Matthew 7:22-23]. Notice again that He said "will do", not maybe, perhaps, or if your church permits. But what could be 'greater' than miracles? This cannot refer to modern technology because in that event such 'greater things' would not have been available to the believers during the first 1900 years. Note that the key is in the Lord's final statement (in verse 12), "because I am going to my Father". Only if He won could He return to the Father, so He is here declaring His victory before the fact. It is on the basis of that victory that the 'greater things' can be performed. Just what are those 'greater' things? For my answer, see my outline(essay), "Biblical Spiritual Warfare".

In verse 12 the verb 'will do' is singular, both times, so it has to do with the individual. Observe that the Lord did **not** say, "you apostles", "only during the apostolic age", "only until the canon is complete", or whatever. He said, "the one believing", present tense, so this applies to any and all subsequent moments up to our time. To deny the truth contained in this verse is to make the Lord Jesus Christ out to be a liar. Somehow I do not think that is very smart.[1]

---

[1] Also, to affirm that the miraculous gifts ceased when the last shovel of dirt fell on the Apostle John's grave is an historical falsehood. Christians who lived during the 2nd, 3rd and 4th centuries, whose writings have come down to us, affirm that the gifts were still in use in their day. No 20th or 21st century Christian, WHO WAS NOT THERE, is competent to contradict them.

6. Now consider 1 Thessalonians 5:23-24: "Now may the God of peace Himself sanctify you completely; and may your whole spirit, soul, and body be preserved blameless at the coming of our Lord Jesus Christ. He who calls you is faithful, who also will do it." Well, when we think of sanctification, the first thing that comes to mind is the spirit. But if we want to live a holy life, then the sanctification must include the soul as well; that much seems reasonable enough. But for the whole **body** to be sanctified, not to mention "completely" and "blamelessly", is a more difficult concept; how can it? However difficult the idea may seem to us, there is the Text, and it goes on to say that it is God who will do it. We know that the resurrection and glorification of our bodies are on the way; but if those bodies are to be sanctified here and now, and if pathogens are Satan's thing, then to free the bodies from those pathogens must be part of the process, and therefore must be within God's will.

7. In Luke 4:18-21 Jesus includes "to set at liberty those who are oppressed" (Isaiah 58:6) as one of the things He was sent to do. Turning to Isaiah 58:6 we find Jehovah stating what kind of 'fast' He would like to see: "To loose the fetters of wickedness [a], to undo the yoke-ropes [b]; to let oppressed ones go free [a], and that you (pl.) break every yoke [b]." As is typical of Hebrew grammar, the two halves are parallel. "To loose the fetters of wickedness" and "to let oppressed ones go free" are parallel. Who placed the "fetters" and who is doing the oppressing? Well, although people can certainly forge their own bonds through their own wicked life style, I take it that the point here is that wicked beings have placed the fetters on others. "To undo yoke-ropes" and "that ye break every yoke" go together. First we should untie the ropes that bind the yoke to the neck, then we should break the yokes themselves. I gain the clear impression that this text is talking about the activity of Satan's servants, men and angels. Using culture, world-view, legal devices, threats, blackmail, lies, deception and just plain demonizing and witchcraft, they bind individuals, families, ethnic groups, etc., with a variety of fetters and instruments of oppression.

So what does this have to do with our subject? Well, fasting was an important/required component in their worship of God. So this kind of 'fasting' is something that Jehovah overtly wants to see; it is specifically His will. So when we see any work of Satan in someone's life, it is God's will that we undo it. If we know it is God's will, we can proceed with complete confidence. And it is part of our commission (John 20:21).

8. Notice also Psalms 149:5-9. "Let the saints exult in glory; let them sing for joy in their beds. Let the high praises of God be in their mouth, and a two-edged sword in their hand—to execute vengeance upon the nations and punishments upon the peoples; to bind their kings with chains and their nobles with fetters of iron; to execute upon them the written judgment. This honor is for all His saints." Note that the saints are in their beds, so the activity described in the subsequent verses must take place in the spiritual realm. I assume that the 'kings' and 'nobles' include both men and fallen angels. The activity described is the prerogative of "all His saints"—if you are one of those saints, it is up to you.

We conclude that it is our responsibility to undo pathogens.[1]

---

[1] So how are people going to die, if we heal everything? How about dying in your sleep? Obviously everyone the Lord Jesus healed had to die; poor Lazarus had to die all over again! The wages of sin is death, physical and spiritual. The blood of God's Lamb can save us from spiritual death, but not the physical. Also, if we heal someone today, that does not make them immune to future attacks. We have two Gospel accounts of Jesus healing Peter's mother-in-law. Careful attention to the respective contexts convinces me that they were distinct occasions. If so, even if it is Jesus Himself who heals you, that does not mean that you will never get sick again.

Nothing in this study should be interpreted as a put-down of the people in the medical and scientific communities who are working to alleviate human suffering and even eradicate certain diseases. I would say they are trying to undo Satan's works by natural means, which is fine; and they have had considerable success. I wish them well; more power to them. On one occasion Paul recommended a home remedy, and for Luke to be called a physician he must have practiced medicine.

Faith = Basic Prerequisite

The theological training I myself received programmed me not to expect supernatural manifestations of power in and through my life and ministry. As a result, I personally am finding it to be difficult to exercise the kind of faith that the Lord Jesus demands. Consider:

1. In Matthew 8:5-13 the centurion understood about authority—he gave orders and they were obeyed, promptly and without question. But the Lord Jesus said he had unusually great faith—faith in what? Faith in the Lord's spiritual authority; He could simply give an order and it would happen. Perhaps we should understand this sort of faith as an absolute confidence, without a taint of doubt or fear. In Matthew 21:21 the Lord said, "Assuredly . . . if you have faith and do not doubt" (see Mark 11:23, "does not doubt in his heart") you can (actually "will") shrivel a tree or send a mountain into the sea. See also Hebrews 10:22, "full assurance of faith", 1 Timothy 2:8, "pray . . . without doubting", James 1:6, "ask in faith with no doubting". Mark 5:34 and Matthew 15:28 offer positive examples; while Peter blew it (Matthew 14:31, "why did you doubt?").

2. If someone gives a commission, they will presumably back it up to the limit of their ability. Since Christ's ability has no limit, His backing has no limit (on His end). In Matthew 28:18 He said, "All authority has been given to me in heaven and on earth." Then comes the commission: "As you go, make disciples . . . teaching them to obey all things that I have commanded you"—the pronoun refers back to the eleven apostles (verse 16). So what commands had Jesus given the Eleven? Among other things, "heal the sick, cleanse the lepers, cast out demons" (in Matthew 10:8 perhaps 94% of the Greek manuscripts do not have "raise the dead"). The Eleven also heard John 20:21.[1] Knowing that

---

[1] In recent years a spate of books has appeared on the subject of present day apostles and apostolic ministry. On the question of the 'signs' of an apostle, one sometimes encounters the assertion that certain things (like miracles) are exclusive to apostles. For starters, Stephen and Philip were deacons, not apostles. But John 14:12 makes clear that anyone believing

we are being backed by the Sovereign of the universe, who has all authority and power, we can and should act with complete confidence.

But, Just How Should We Go About Doing It?

1. How did the Lord Jesus undo Satan's works? He never touched a demonized person—just spoke to the demon. Others he healed by word or touch. When He turned water to wine or shriveled a tree He altered molecular structure. When He healed the demonically lame or blind He reversed the demonic alteration. All of this was done with God's power.[1] We ought to be able to follow His example.

2. The centurion did not say, "In the authority of Rome . . .", he just said, "Do this; do that." The Lord Jesus did not say, "In the authority of the Father . . .", He just said, "Be clean! Go!" In Luke 10:19 He said, "I give you the authority over all the power of the enemy"—so we have the authority, so it is up to us to speak!! Just like Jesus did.

3. In Luke 17:6 we have a contrary to fact condition, which rendered literally would be: So the Lord said, "If you had faith [but you don't] like a mustard seed *has*,[2] you would

---

into the Lord Jesus can and will do what He did; so dealing with pathogens will not be limited to 'apostles'.

[1] The point is, Jesus used God's power to undo Satan's works; He did not command Satan to undo his own works. However, Christ's example comes from before the Victory, and Satan was working within his rights, so to speak. But now he has lost those rights, and works on the basis of bluff and usurpation. Just as we oblige a child to clean up a mess he made (hoping that it will teach him not to repeat), perhaps we should oblige Satan to clean up his mess, thereby forcing him to acknowledge his defeat. (Since he is very proud, that humiliation may encourage him to go somewhere else.)

[2] I very much doubt that the Lord is talking about the size of their faith; rather He is talking about a quality of faith. What kind of 'faith' might a mustard seed have? Albeit so small, it reacts without question to the climactic circumstances, and grows to remarkable proportions. If we reacted similarly, without question, to the Holy Spirit's promptings, our spiritual 'climactic circumstances', we should indeed uproot trees, literally. In Matthew 17:20 the Lord said, "If you have faith like a mustard seed *has*, you will say to this mountain, 'Move from here to there,' and it will move; and nothing will be impossible to you." That is what He said, but we just do not believe it.

say [but you aren't] to this mulberry tree, 'Be pulled up by the roots and be planted in the sea,' and it would have obeyed you." The second apodosis is placed in the past, whereas the protasis and first apodosis are in the present. It is a curious grammatical construction, but I imagine that the Lord is emphasizing the certainty of the response—if only they would speak!!

4. There are those who teach that we should not address Satan directly, but in Christ we are above Satan (Ephesians 1:20-21, 2:6). Further, James 4:7 gives a command, "Resist the devil . . .". It is not an optional point, we must resist him (there are many devils, but the devil is Satan). Surely one of the principal ways to resist someone is with words.[1] And we have the Lord's example; on at least two occasions He rebuked Satan directly, by name (Matthew 4:10, 16:23).

5. But what if God is punishing someone for their sin? In James 5:14-15 the prayer for the sick is followed by healing and "if he has committed sins, he will be forgiven". In the context this forgiveness of sin presumably has to do with the immediate punishment that is being dealt with, not eternal destiny. I submit for consideration the possibility that when we are prepared to undo Satan's work, wherever we may find it, God is prepared to suspend whatever use He may be making of that work.[2] Or what does Matthew 18:18

(But why did the Lord emphasize the size the mustard seed? No matter how small a seed is, it can germinate and produce. No matter how small a person may be [or seem to be] within the Kingdom of God, if they have the faith of a seed they will produce wonders.)

[1] However, I recognize that addressing Satan is not necessarily the only way of controlling his power (Luke 10:19). Presumably we can call on God to do it (but since He gave us the authority, He is likely to tell us it is up to us). But in either event we have to open our mouth and say something! We have to speak!!

But, since Satan is not omnipresent, how can we address him? Speaking in Jesus' name/authority, in obedience to His commission, it is in His interest to make sure our message is delivered, and obeyed. Since the good angels are here to serve us (Hebrews 1:14), that may be one of the things they do.

[2] This will not apply in rare (presumably) cases such as Paul's where, because of the tremendous revelations he had received, God used the "messenger" to keep Paul's head from swelling (2 Corinthians 12:7). This

mean? "Assuredly I say to you, whatever (pl.) you (pl.) may bind on earth will have been bound in heaven, and whatever you may loose on earth will have been loosed in heaven."[1] So how do we bind or loose if not by our word?

6. But what if God is perfecting one of His servants, like He did with Job?[2] I believe Paul Billheimer (*Don't Waste Your Sorrows*) has given us a handle on a basic truth—the only way a human being can learn αγαπη love is through suffering. And the mainspring of God's Kingdom is αγαπη love, and God wants to prepare His servants for their responsibilities in the next world. So the lessons God wants us to learn come wrapped in unpleasant circumstances; but if we refuse a given lesson our spiritual growth stops. Further, sooner or later that lesson will return, and will keep on returning until we learn, or die (which is why Billheimer says, "don't waste your sorrows", because if we do not learn the first time we will have wasted that suffering).

So what? Well, if God is giving one of His servants a lesson, we should not interfere. So how do we know when a given situation is a lesson in progress, as opposed to a work of Satan? Ah, there is the rub. How do we know? Well, who knows for sure? God does, obviously. So we should ask

---

situation was sufficiently strange so that God explained to Paul the what and why.

[1] I am aware that this verse is often understood as somehow having to do with discipline in the church, because of verses 15-17; but verse 18 begins with "Amen", which normally signals a new subject. There is a change of subject between 14 and 15, and I believe there is another between 17 and 18.

[2] I was taught that Job was just a pawn in a contest between God and Satan, and in the end God said, "Look, I am bigger than you are and you are not competent to question me." So Job knuckled under and was blessed. I now understand that something very different was going on. If someone is the very best there is in a given field, they tend to stagnate—there is no one they can learn from; the others learn from them. God Himself declared that Job was His star pupil down here, he was the very best that there was. But Job had stagnated, and God knew that he had the potential to grow in his knowledge of Him, but for that to happen Job's theological package had to take a beating. The lesson was severe, but Job was exercised by it and learned, and moved up to a higher level of spiritual understanding. In his own words: "I have heard of You by the hearing of the ear, but now my eye sees You." Yes indeed, Job grew, Job moved up to a higher plane. And God's expectation was vindicated.

Him. If the Holy Spirit says it is a lesson, we should encourage the person to learn the lesson and move up. If it is not a lesson, then we undo Satan's work.

Hebrews 12:7-11 deals with this subject. God disciplines His sons so that they may be partakers of His holiness. Though it be unpleasant, even painful, if we are <u>exercised</u> by it, then we grow, then we move up. Like Job, we must interact with what is going on, not sit passively and say, "God is doing His thing and I just have to grin and bear it". So if we see a servant of God just passively enduring a situation, we need to urge them to learn the lesson and grow.

7. Related to item 6), but different, is "the fellowship of His sufferings" (Philippians 3:10). In Mark 15:30-31 we read: "Save yourself, and come down from the cross"; "He saved others, himself he cannot save". The chief priests and scribes were mocking, but without knowing it they stated an important truth. If Jesus had come down from the cross He could not have saved us—to save us, He could not save Himself. I take this to be a principle that still operates; to save others we may have to accept suffering (it will likely come regardless of our attitude). Consider Paul: "I now rejoice in my sufferings for you, and fill up in my flesh what is lacking in the afflictions of Christ, for the sake of His body, which is the Church" (Colossians 1:24). "In my flesh" is presumably physical. In 2 Corinthians 1:5-7 "as you are partakers of the sufferings" makes clear that the principle passes on to succeeding generations. So also 1 Peter 4:12-13: "Beloved, do not think it strange concerning the fiery trial which is to try you, as though some strange thing happened to you; but rejoice to the extent that you partake of Christ's sufferings." The "rejoice" bit I find to be difficult, but if suffering is the price we must pay to be used by God, and if we really desire to be so used, then maybe we will join Paul in his rejoicing.

8. I would translate Hebrews 11:1 like this: "Faith is a realization of things being hoped for, a declaration of things not being seen." The concept of "hope" in the New Testament includes an ingredient of certainty (it is not mere wishful thinking). To declare as fact something we do not see is difficult for most of us, but I believe that is the point of the Text. True faith is able to declare the existence of something before seeing it. When the centurion gave an order, he was declaring what was going to happen, before the fact. He spoke and it happened. Of course the Lord Jesus did precisely the same, He spoke and it happened. I wonder if someday people will say about me, "Of course he did the same thing, he spoke and it happened."

So, What Happens If We Don't?

1. James 4:17—"Therefore, to the one knowing to do good and not doing it, to him it is sin." So if I do not undo Satan's works it goes on my record as sin, for which I must answer.

2. Ezekiel 22:30—"So I sought for a man among them who would make a wall, and stand in the gap before me on behalf of the land, that I should not destroy it; but I found no one. Therefore I have poured out my indignation on them." The Text is clear: just one person could have made the difference, could have averted the destruction. So if I do not undo Satan's works people continue to suffer, unnecessarily.

I am asking for help in prayer to elucidate this subject. If God shows you something, please pass it on. Here is my email address: wilbur.pickering@gmail.com.

WHEN IS AN APOSTLE?
The beginning

The basic meaning of the term is 'sent one'; in John 13:16 it is used in that way. But within the incipient Christian Church it came to have a specialized meaning: an office or function characterized by special spiritual authority. It began with the twelve disciples who were personally chosen by Jesus; after His resurrection they received the designation, 'apostles' (but the Iscariot had lost his place, leaving eleven). With the exception of four verses (Luke 11:49, John 13:16, Acts 14:4 and 14) I would say that all the occurrences of the term in the four Gospels and Acts, about thirty-five, refer to that group, as do Galatians 1:17, 19; 2 Peter 3:2; Jude 17 and Revelation 21:14. The purpose of this note is to enquire whether the NT signals any further uses of the term.

Acts 1:13-26 records Peter's initiative to replace the Iscariot. The Text does not say that it was God's idea; and when they asked God to choose between the two candidates, they did not give Him the option of saying "neither". The Text affirms that Matthias was numbered with the Eleven apostles, but he receives no further mention.

Paul (erstwhile Saul of Tarsus) repeatedly refers to himself as an apostle: Romans 1:1, 11:13, 1 Corinthians 1:1, 9:1, 2, 15:9, 2 Corinthians 1:1, Galatians 1:1, Ephesians 1:1, Colossians 1:1, 1 Thessalonians 2:6, 1 Timothy 1:1, 2:7, 2 Timothy 1:1, 11 and Titus 1:1. Luke refers to Paul as an apostle in Acts 14:4 and 14. Jesus personally chose Paul, returning from Heaven to do so. Aside from the Eleven, Paul was the only one personally designated by Jesus.

Jesus Himself is called "the Apostle" of our confession in Hebrews 3:1. Peter calls himself an apostle in 1 Peter 1:1 and 2 Peter 1:1, but of course he is one of the Twelve.

James, the half-brother of Jesus, became the 'big boss' in Jerusalem, and evidently was regarded as an apostle—1 Corinthians 15:7 and Galatians 1:19. Luke refers to Barnabas as an apostle: Acts 14:4 and 14. Paul seems to refer to Silvanus and Timothy as apostles: 1 Thessalonians 2:6. It is possible to interpret Romans 16:7 in the same way with reference to Andronicus and Junias. I believe those are the only ones who are actually named.

The discussion up to this point was necessary to provide the background for the questions that are the occasion for this study: did 'apostle' become an established office or function for the ongoing life of the Church, until the return of Christ, and if so, how is an apostle to be designated or recognized? It is my intention to analyze every verse where the term is used, and I will begin with those that may be purely historical, going on from those already dealt with.

In 2 Corinthians 11:5 and 12:11 Paul compares himself to 'the most eminent apostles', which must be limited to his contemporaries. 1 Corinthians 9:5 also must be limited to his contemporaries. 1 Corinthians 15:5 and 7 refer to physical appearances of the resurrected Jesus before His ascension (of necessity historical). 1 Corinthians 4:9 is a little different: "I think that God has displayed us, the apostles, last, as men condemned to death; for we have been made a spectacle to the world, both to angels and to men " (read also verses 10-13). In the context, Paul is complaining about the way he has been treated by some in Corinth, but in this verse he seems actually to be blaming <u>God</u> for the way he has been treated! I suppose that the use of the word 'last' would be a comparison with God's servants in prior ages. Paul is not talking about the future of the Church in this passage, and if we only had this text on the subject, we would have to conclude that to be an apostle was not a good thing.

And now we come to Luke 11:49-51, a most interesting text. "Therefore the wisdom of God also said, 'I will send them prophets and apostles, and some of them they will kill and persecute,' that the blood of all the prophets which was shed from the foundation of the world may be required of this generation, from the blood of Abel to the blood of Zechariah who perished between the altar and the temple. Yes, I say to you, it shall be required of this generation." Jesus is speaking, deriding the lawyers. His citation of "the wisdom of God" appears to have no match in the OT, so what was His meaning? In 1 Corinthians 1:24 Paul refers to Christ as 'the wisdom of God'. In Matthew 23:34 Jesus said, "I send you prophets", so here Jesus may be referring to Himself as 'the wisdom of God'. However that may be, if the "required of this generation" was fulfilled in 70 AD, as I suppose, then the 'apostles' here are also historical.

I will now consider the other places where the phrase 'prophets and apostles' occurs, albeit with the terms in reverse order: Ephesians 2:20 and 3:5, and Revelation 18:20.

Ephesians 2:19-22—"So then, you are no longer strangers and aliens, but fellow citizens with the saints and members of God's household, 20 built upon the foundation of the apostles and prophets, Jesus Christ Himself being the chief cornerstone; 21 in whom the whole building, being joined together, grows into a holy temple in the Lord; 22 in whom you also are being built together to become a habitation of God in spirit." The truth that Paul is expounding is that in Christ Gentiles join Jews as "fellow citizens" and "members of God's household", part of "the whole building". In what sense can that "building" be built upon "the foundation of the apostles and prophets"? Presumably "prophets" is short for the writings that make up the Old Testament Scriptures, or Canon. **The Faith is based on revealed Truth, not individual people**. Analogously, presumably "apostles" is short for the writings that make up the New Testament Scriptures, or Canon. Again, the Faith is based on revealed Truth, not individual people. Our "growing into a holy temple" (verse 21) depends upon the Holy Spirit and His Sword (not individuals whom God used). Note that Paul mentions the 'apostles' first. In any case, the 'apostles' here are historical.

Ephesians 3:1-7—"For this reason I, Paul, the prisoner of Christ Jesus on behalf of you Gentiles—2 surely you have heard of the dispensation of the grace of God that was given to me for you, 3 how that by revelation He made known to me the 'secret'[1] (as I have written briefly already, 4 with reference to which, when you read, you can understand my insight into Christ's secret), 5 which in different generations was not made known to the sons of men, as it has <u>now</u> been revealed by Spirit[2] to His holy apostles and prophets: 6 that the Gentiles are joint-heirs, of the same body, and fellow partakers of His promise in the Christ through the Gospel, 7 of which I became a servant according to the gift of God's grace, the gift given to me according to the out-working of His power." The use of "now" in verse 5 indicates that Paul is referring to the NT Canon. An apostle, upon receiving a revelation, would also function as a prophet, but people like Mark and Luke were prophets without being apostles. I take the 'apostles' here to be historical.

Revelation 18:20—"Rejoice over her, O heaven, yes you saints and apostles and prophets, because God has pronounced your judgment against her!"[3] Perhaps this verse should be connected to 18:6-7, and in that event the judgment was pronounced in faith. But just who are these apostles? I take it that "saints and apostles and prophets" is in apposition to "heaven", and in that event, whoever they are, they are already in heaven. It follows that this text is irrelevant to the occasion for this study.

The hinge

As a hinge to link the past to the present, I will now consider the two texts that refer to 'false apostles'; they are 2 Corinthians 11:13 and Revelation 2:2.

2 Corinthians 11:12-15—"Further, I will keep on doing what I do in order to cut off the opportunity from those who de-

---

[1] I consider that 'secret' is a better rendering than 'mystery'. The truth about the Church is not all that mysterious; it just had not been explained before.

[2] There being no article with 'spirit', it could be either 'by Spirit' (used as a proper name) or 'in spirit' (referring to the manner). Both are true and legitimate, but I have chosen the first option in the translation.

[3] Instead of "saints and apostles", a small minority of the Greek manuscripts has 'holy apostles', as in AV and NKJV.

sire an opportunity to be considered equal with us in the things of which they boast. 13 Such men are really false apostles, deceitful workers, transforming themselves into 'apostles' of Christ.[1] 14 And no wonder, because Satan himself masquerades as an angel of light. 15 So it is no great thing if his servants also masquerade as ministers of righteousness, whose end will be according to their works." It is well to remember that neither Satan nor his servants are in the habit of appearing with horns and tails. Just because someone 'looks good' does not mean that he is. We need spiritual discernment at all times. Note that Paul affirms that such people are Satan's servants, and they evidently declared themselves to be 'apostles'. In our day we have a veritable plague of self-proclaimed 'apostles' (that I call 'apustles'); now whom do you suppose they are serving?

Going back to the title of this study, when is an apostle? In Galatians 1:1 Paul affirms that his apostleship was "not from men nor through a man", but through both the Father and the Son. Paul's apostleship did not depend upon human ordination or recognition. So what about apostleship today? In Romans 1:1 Paul says he is a "called apostle". I take the point to be that true apostles are not ordained by man; they are designated by God, who has a specific reason for doing so.[2] In the case of Paul, it was "to promote obedience of faith among all ethnic nations" (verse 5). Any genuine apostle will have a specific task to fulfil. Although God does not take back His gifts (Romans 11:29), a gift may be ignored (because the church's doctrine does not allow it), or neglected (1 Timothy 4:14), and hence aborted. Far worse, even an apostle that Jesus chose personally can be 'rejected' (1 Corinthians 9:27). If Paul recognized the possibility for himself, how about all the 'apustles' in our day?

---

[1] There have always been those who want to 'get on the band-wagon', to get a free ride; who traffic in spiritual things for personal, temporal advantage. Since such people only do damage, Paul's desire to expose them stems from his concern for the Corinthians' welfare.

[2] It follows that there is no 'apostolic succession', since an apostle is not 'ordained' by men. There is only 'discipolic' succession.

In Revelation 2:2 the glorified Christ is writing to the church in Ephesus: "I know your works, yes the labor, and your endurance, and that you cannot stand those who are evil. And you have tested those who claim to be apostles and are not, and found them *to be* liars." The glorified Christ Himself declares that there are false apostles (and this at the close of the first century), and that the church in Ephesus knew how to test them.[1] Unfortunately, at least from my point of view, we are not told how they did it, the criteria that they used. There is one text that speaks of the 'signs of an apostle', 2 Corinthians 12:12. "Truly the apostolic signs were produced among you with all perseverance, by signs and wonders and miracles."

Both Stephen and Phillip, 'mere' deacons, performed miracles, but evidently that did not transform them into apostles. And then there are the words of Sovereign Jesus Himself in John 14:12. "Most assuredly I say to you,[2] the one believing into me, he too will do the works that I do; in fact he will do greater works than these,[3] because I am going to my Father."

---

[1] Is there not an implication here that there were also genuine apostles? If there were no such thing as an apostle, there could be no candidates, and hence no need for criteria. When John wrote this he was the last survivor of the Twelve (also Paul), and he himself would soon die.

[2] "Most assuredly" is actually "amen, amen"—rendered "verily, verily" in the AV. Only John registers the word as repeated, in the other Gospels it is just "amen". In the contemporary literature we have no example of anyone else using the word in this way. It seems that Jesus coined His own use, and the point seems to be to call attention to an important pronouncement: "Stop and listen!" Often it precedes a formal statement of doctrine or policy, as here.

[3] Well now, if we cast out demons, heal and perform miracles, isn't that enough? Jesus wants more, He wants "greater things" than those just mentioned. Notice again that He said "will do", not maybe, perhaps, or if your church permits. But what could be 'greater' than miracles? This can't refer to modern technology because in that event such 'greater things' would not have been available to the believers during the first 1900 years. Note that the key is in the Lord's final statement (in verse 12), "because I am going to my Father". Only if He won could He return to the Father, so He is here declaring His victory before the fact. It is on the basis of that victory that the 'greater things' can be performed. Just what are those 'greater' things? For my answer, see my outline, "Biblical Spiritual Warfare", available from www.prunch.org.

This is a tremendous statement, and not a little disconcerting. Notice that the Lord said, "will do"; not 'maybe', 'perhaps', 'if you feel like it'; and certainly not 'if the doctrine of your church permits it'! If you believe you **will do!** The verb 'believe' is in the present tense, 2nd person singular; if you (sg) are believing you will do; it follows that if you are not doing, it is because you are not believing. 2 + 2 = 4. Doing what? "The works that I do." Well, Jesus preached the Gospel, He taught, He cast out demons, He healed all sorts and sizes of sickness and disease, He raised an occasional dead person, and He performed a variety of miracles (water to wine, walk on water, stop a storm instantaneously, transport a boat several miles instantaneously, multiply food, shrivel a tree—and He implied that the disciples should have stopped the storm and multiplied the food, and He stated that they could shrivel a tree [Peter actually took a few steps on water]). So how about us? The preaching and teaching we can handle, but what about the rest? I once heard the president of a certain Christian college affirm that this verse obviously could not mean what it says because it isn't happening! Well, in his own experience, and in that of his associates (cessationists all), I guess it isn't. But many people today cast out demons and heal, and I personally know someone who has raised a dead person. Miracles are also happening. So how about me? And you? But to get back to the 'signs of an apostle', if all of us are supposed to be producing miracles, that does not make us all apostles, so there must be further criteria. (Please notice the 'further', I am not denying the 'signs'.)

I suggest that we must consider the matter of spiritual authority, and I begin with 2 Corinthians 10:8 and 13:10. 10:8 reads like this: "Now even if I boast a little to excess about our authority (which the Lord gave us for building up, not to tear you down), . . ." 13:10 reads like this: "This is why I write these things while absent, so that when present I may not have to deal harshly, according to the authority that the Lord gave me, for building up and not tearing down." In both verses Paul states that the authority is for building up, not tearing down, although his mention of harsh dealing indicates that such may be included in the process, as circumstance may require. (In fact, on at least two occasions, Paul actually turned someone over to Satan!—1 Corinthians 5:5 and 1 Timothy 1:20.)

Is this not what we are to understand from 1 Timothy 1:3? "You recall that I urged you to remain in Ephesus, when I went into Macedonia, in order that you should command certain persons to stop teaching a different doctrine . . ." Now the church was well established in Ephesus, yet Timothy had authority to command; I suppose that Paul designated him as his deputy. And what about 1 Timothy 5:19-20? "Do not entertain an accusation against an elder except on the basis of two or three witnesses. 20 Those who are sinning rebuke publicly, so that the rest also may be in fear." Evidently Timothy had authority over the elders, being competent to rebuke them publicly.

Now consider Jeremiah 1:10—"See, I have this day set you over the nations and over the kingdoms, to root out and to pull down, to destroy and to throw down, to build and to plant." Of course this was before the Church, but there is a principle here that remains valid. If you plan to build on a site that is covered with ruins and rubble, where must you start? You must remove the wreckage. If God sent you to the church in Laodicea (Revelation 3:14-19), to try to straighten it out, where would you have to start? You might have to depose the leaders, as well as denounce the error. Presumably, also, you would have to be able to establish your authority over them. In Timothy's case, Paul presumably took care of that.

Something similar happened with Titus; consider: "I left you in Crete for this reason, that you should set in order the things that were lacking and appoint elders in every town, as I directed you" (1:5). "Because there really are lots of rebels, loudmouths and deceivers, especially those of the circumcision group, who must be silenced" (1:10-11). "Speak these things, whether you exhort or reprove, with all authority" (2:15). If Titus was to appoint elders, he evidently had authority over them. And to silence 'rebels' evidently requires authority. Now then, does anyone imagine that such situations, requiring apostolic authority, ceased to exist in 100 AD? History records no lack of such situations, and far worse, down through the centuries and millennia. In our day the degree of perversity in the churches is such that I don't know how God can stand the stench! We desperately need people with apostolic authority who are prepared to function.

But to get back to the Text, consider Ephesians 4:11-13. "Yes, He Himself gave some to be apostles, some to be prophets, some to be evangelists, and some to be pastors and teachers,[1] 12 for the equipping of the saints into the

---

[1] One might imagine that this list follows the chronological sequence of the several ministries. An apostle introduces the Gospel into an area or context; a prophet gets the people's attention and an evangelist urges them to believe; but once people are regenerated then pastors and teachers come to the fore—they are the ones who equip the saints. However, in practice, especially in a pioneer missionary situation, there are seldom that many people around. The missionary preaches the Gospel and it is up to him to teach the first converts; he is alone. A pioneer missionary, the first one to introduce the Gospel to an ethnic group or area, has an apostolic function (whether or not he himself is an apostle). But he must also function as an evangelist and as a teacher (whether or not he has those gifts).

However, most of us live and work where there are established, functioning congregations. So what would be the function of an apostle within an established, functioning congregation? If he lives and worships in that community, probably none at all, in that specific capacity—he might function as a teacher or a prophet. In a country, or area, where there is no more pioneer missionary work to be done, the exercise of the apostolic function would be itinerant, acting as God's special emissary, an official intervener, for disciplinary and correctional purposes.

I will take up evangelist next; what would his function be within an established congregation? Well, can you evangelize someone who is already regenerated? Evidently the function of an evangelist is directed to unbelievers, who should not be members of the congregation (although some often are). Of course an evangelist might also function as a pastor or teacher. A truly gifted evangelist will function beyond the limits of a local congregation.

As for the prophetic function, I will address the question of supernatural revelation of information not available through existing channels. (1 Corinthians 14:3 speaks of 'edification', 'exhortation' and 'comfort' as coming from a prophet, but I will not take up such activity here.) We understand that the Canon of Scripture is closed; God is no longer giving written revelation that is of general or universal application. But that does not mean that God no longer speaks into specific situations. Divine guidance is a type of prophecy; He is giving information not otherwise available. I myself have been contemplated with a prophecy delivered by

work of the ministry, so as to build up the body of Christ, 13 until we all attain into the unity of the faith and of the real knowledge of the Son of God, into a complete man, into the resulting full stature of Christ." If verses 12 and 13 are still being worked on, then the apostles, etc. are still necessary. Verse 13 emphasizes the truth in verse 12—every believer is supposed to grow into full stature. Just because we do not reach a goal does not invalidate that goal. I would say that one of the principal causes for the lamentable spiritual condition of most churches is the total lack of the apostolic function among us—itinerant, acting as God's special emissary, an official intervener, for disciplinary and correctional purposes. The idea of Christian or ministerial 'ethics', where one must not criticize a neighbor, is clearly designed to silence any prophetic or apostolic voice. It is designed to protect error.

Now consider 1 Corinthians 12:27-31. "Now you are the body of Christ, and members individually. 28 And those whom God has appointed in the Church are: first apostles, second prophets, third teachers; after that miracles, then presents of healings, helps, administrations, kinds of languages. 29 All are not apostles, are they? All are not prophets, are they? All are not teachers, are they? All are not miracle workers, are they? 30 All do not have presents of healings, do they? All do not speak languages, do they? All do not interpret, do they?[1] 31 But earnestly desire the best gifts."

---

someone who had no idea who I was, and not in the context of a local congregation. The function of a true prophet cannot be limited to one congregation. Indeed, God may use a prophet at city, state or country level. Our world desperately needs prophetic voices.

A teacher will normally reside in a specific community, but his ministry may range beyond it. A pastor's function is local, just as he is chosen and ordained locally. It is simply a fact of life that someone with a shepherd's heart is not necessarily a good teacher, and an honest to goodness teacher often lacks a shepherd's heart. The functions are supposed to be complementary, and the object is to get all true believers involved in the work of the ministry. Life in Christ is not a spectator sport!

[1] The Greek grammar of verses 29 and 30 is plain: no gift is given to everybody—not everyone is an apostle and not everyone speaks languages.

It should be observed that the terminology here is clearly hierarchical: '1st, 2nd, 3rd, then, then, . . .' (similar lists in other places lack this terminology) [the Kingdom of God is not a democracy]. Next, if God has appointed these functions, there must be a good reason for them, and to deliberately exclude any of them is to go against God. Here in Brazil, with a few exceptions, the churches have no place for a true teacher; they simply are not allowed. The consequences are not pretty.

Presumably even the most ardent 'cessationist' will grant that "teachers", "helps" and "administrations" are still around. But this letter was written around 55 AD, well into the Church Age, therefore. Why would God "appoint in the Church" things that would be extinguished in a few decades. If miracles come "after" teachers, how can miracles be gone if teachers are still here? We have the command to "earnestly desire the best gifts", so which ones are the best? Presumably those at the top of the hierarchical list. Why would God command us to earnestly desire a gift like apostleship, if He was going to extinguish it before the end of the first century? In such an event the command would be meaningless for the last 1900 years!

The present

Somewhere along the line, I heard this: 'the status quo' is Latin for 'the mess we're in'. Whether Latin or English, I

Those churches that teach that speaking in tongues is the <u>necessary</u> sign of being 'baptized in the Spirit' (and until you are 'baptized' you are a 2nd class citizen, if a citizen at all), have done untold damage to their people. Since the Holy Spirit simply does not give 'tongues' to everybody, those who do not get it are out in the cold. But the social pressure is intolerable, so many end up faking it. Since many of the leaders are also faking it, the social problem is solved; the person is 'in'. But since Satan is the source of all lies, someone who fakes it is living a lie and invites Satan into his life. I have been in many Pentecostal, neo-pentecostal, charismatic, whatever churches and have heard thousands of people 'speaking in tongues'—a large majority were faking it, while a few were speaking a real language, but under demonic control. (I am a linguist, PhD, and can tell when I am listening to a real language, even though I do not understand it, because real language has structure. To know whether or not a language is demonic requires spiritual discernment.) A church that teaches a lie invites Satan into the church, and he does not hesitate. Of course some had the genuine gift.

imagine that most of us would agree that the world is in a bad way, and that is at least partly because the Church is in a bad way. By and large, 'Christians' have ceased to be salt and light in the surrounding culture (Matthew 5:13-16); they are part of the problem, rather than part of the solution. As I have already opined, the lamentable spiritual condition of most churches is a direct result of the total lack of the apostolic function among us. It would appear that that 'lack' began early on.

In the writings of the 'church fathers' that have come down to us, there appears to be no mention of 'apostles' after the first century. Already in the second century, the concept of a 'bishop' came into being, an elder having authority over other elders in a given area—so a 'bishop' could exercise the apostolic function within his area (but all too often the bishop became part of the problem, since bishops were not chosen by God). It did not take long before the 'bishop of Rome' started to claim authority over other 'bishops', and then there were archbishops, and so on. If I am correct in defining the apostolic function as someone 'acting as God's special emissary, an official intervener, for disciplinary and correctional purposes', and if there has been a general lack of this function for 1900 years, then we should not be surprised at the 'status quo'.

In our day we have denominations, defined by different doctrinal and procedural 'packages', and there is no end of splitting within such denominations. Here in Brazil we have at least five 'Baptist' denominations, four 'Presbyterian' ones, and no end of 'Assemblies of God', plus any number of 'independent' ones. We have literally thousands of self-proclaimed 'apustles'; everywhere you turn there is an 'apostolic ministry'. It is a generalized ego trip; no one wants to be left behind, or to appear inferior to his neighbor. They are building private empires, and fleecing the sheep in the process. I am not aware of any theological seminary in this country that teaches the students how to study the Bible, and much less how to expound it; expository preaching is almost nonexistent. In consequence, the variety of abject stupidities promulgated from the pulpits appears to be without end, doing ever increasing damage to the hearers. I am not aware of any denomination here where the biblical Text has objective authority.

But it gets worse. We actually have self-proclaimed 'apostles' who pontificate like this: "I am an apostle on a level with Peter or Paul, so I can disagree with them; I can change what the Bible says." And they do; they reject plain biblical teaching and impose their own ideas on their flocks. It should be evident to any true subject of Sovereign Jesus that all such 'apustles' are in the service of Satan. We have already noted Ephesians 2:20, God's household is "built upon the foundation of the apostles and prophets, Jesus Christ Himself being the chief cornerstone." 1 Corinthians 3:11 says that "no one can lay any foundation other than what is laid, which is Jesus Christ." And Revelation 21:14 informs us that the foundations of the New Jerusalem are "the twelve apostles of the Lamb". No pipsqueak 'apustle' of our day is competent to alter the Sacred Text—they obviously do not believe what the glorified Christ said in Revelation 22:18-19.

To someone who intends to be totally committed to Christ and His Kingdom, the following question is obvious and necessary: What can be done to remedy, to correct the calamitous reality I have described? We must cry out to God to raise up true apostles; but this raises another question: How is an apostle to be recognized, and how can he establish his authority so as to be able to bring about necessary changes in actual situations? I see only one way, the use of supernatural power; and that power must be used to clear out wreckage before it can be used to build. I see a difference between a prophet and an apostle in this connection: a prophet warns; an apostle inflicts. In Acts 5 Peter simply executed Ananias and Sapphira, without warning and without chance for repentance. In Acts 13 Paul inflicted blindness on the sorcerer Elymas, again without ado.

It should be obvious that anyone who starts functioning in this way will promptly be declared to be 'public enemy number one'. Any and all leaders who are serving Satan will do all in their power to eliminate a true apostle, because of the threat to them personally and to the perverse structures they have created and maintained. It will be all out war. I am reminded of 1 Corinthians 4:11-13—"To this very hour we go hungry and thirsty; we are poorly dressed, brutally treated, and wander homeless; 12 yes, we labor, working with our own hands. Upon being reviled, we bless; upon being persecuted, we endure it; 13 upon being slandered, we exhort. We have been made as the refuse of the world, the off-scouring of whatever, to this moment." Well now, how many of the plague of self-styled 'apostles' in our day would maintain their pretentions if they had to experience the conditions described above? They would run and hide.

We need to understand what Paul is saying here. To be looked down on and criticized by believers among whom one has labored is one thing. Local people with personal ambition know how to do that. For God to make us "as the refuse of the world" is something very different. How should we understand this? If we insist on proclaiming a 'gospel' that the world considers to be stupid, abject foolishness, we will certainly be ridiculed. But if we insist on biblical values that the world has declared to be 'hate crimes', we will certainly be hated and persecuted, treated as refuse. The choice of Hebrews 13:13 is upon us: "So then, let us go out to Him, outside the camp, bearing His disgrace." The above applies to any true subject of Sovereign Jesus, but any true apostle will be the target of the total fury of the religious leaders as well. In short, to be an apostle is not for the fainthearted.

And now please consider 2 Thessalonians 2:8-12, noting especially verses 10 and 11. "And then the lawless one will be revealed, whom the Lord will consume with the breath of His mouth and abolish by the splendor of His coming; 9 that one's coming is according to the working of Satan with all power and signs and lying wonders, 10 and with all wicked deception among those who are wasting themselves, because they did not receive the love of the truth[1] so that they

---

[1] The use of the verb 'receive' clearly implies an act of volition on their part; that love was offered or made available to them but they did not want it; they wanted to be able to lie and to entertain lies told by others. But the consequences of such a choice are terrible; they turned their back on salvation.

might be saved.[1] 11 Yes, because of this God will send them an active delusion so that they will believe the lie[2] 12 and so that all may be condemned who have not believed the truth but have taken pleasure in wickedness."[3] Notice the sequence: first they reject the love of the truth; it is as a consequence of that choice that God sends the delusion. The implication is that there is a point of no return; God sends the delusion so that they may be condemned. The only intelligent choice is to embrace the truth!

Consider with me the consequences of the facts enunciated in verses 10-12 for a whole nation, like Brazil, where I now live. We have many thousands of local churches that call themselves Christian. But I know of almost none that could be characterized as 'loving the truth'. No one wants a Bible with objective authority. Humanistic, relativistic, materialistic values have taken over the churches. Biblical values are no longer acceptable. In consequence, Satan has control of the government, of education, of health services, of commerce, of the entertainment industry, in short, of the whole culture. The churches that have rejected biblical values are part of the problem—since they have rejected "the love of the truth", they have been taken over by "active delusion".

Note that God Himself sends that delusion with the declared objective of condemning all those who believed the lie. If God Himself visits "active delusion" upon a whole country, what possible escape is there? The only possible 'medicine' is "the love of the truth". Those of us who consider ourselves to be true subjects of Sovereign Jesus need to appeal to Him to show us how to promote the love of the truth to

---

[1] Since there are only two spiritual kingdoms in this world, that of Sovereign Jesus and that of Satan, "those who are wasting themselves", in this text, are still in Satan's kingdom and therefore wide open to his "wicked deception". The Text states plainly that they are wasting themselves "because they did not receive the love of the truth so that they might be saved". They are not saved.

[2] Perhaps "the lie" is best illustrated in our day by the theory of evolution: 'There is no Creator'—so there will not be any accounting; so you can do what you feel like. How terrible will be the awakening!

[3] "Taking pleasure in wickedness" involves rejecting the Truth of a moral Creator who will demand an accounting, or even overt rebellion against that Creator (like Lucifer/Satan).

the churches and to the society at large. Here in Brazil it may be too late, but if God's grace still offers us a window of opportunity, we must devote ourselves to promoting the love of the truth by all possible means. I imagine that the most effective means would be the exercise of the apostolic function, and that at more than one level. I am thinking of the following: local congregations, whole denominations, and the various levels of civil government. **Dear God, please send us apostles**!

JUDGMENT BEGINS AT THE HOUSE OF GOD

Let me begin by explaining why I am writing such an article as this. I am looking for a way (if it is still possible) to stop, and even turn back, the satanic steamroller that is destroying the culture and taking over all aspects of life in the country where I live, Brazil. (Of course the same is true of other countries as well.) The only possible 'medicine' is the love of the truth (2 Thessalonians 2:10, see below), so the bottom line is this: what can we do to promote the love of the truth? Lamentably, the vast majority of the churches are part of the problem, rather than being part of the solution. I venture to say that less than 1% of the churches want a Bible with objective authority.[1] The culture outside the church is totally dominated by relativistic humanism, and most church members have been heavily influenced by that worldview. On the way to promoting the love of the truth, we must defend the objective authority of the biblical Text,[2] and the place to begin is with the churches.[3] **To promote truth necessarily involves exposing lies**.

Any surgeon knows that for certain pathological conditions the only alternative to a premature physical death is radical

---

[1] In consequence, they are lacking in spiritual power and spiritual discernment.

[2] It is the biblical Text that defines and teaches the Truth, and in order to arrive at the Truth we must understand that the Text has objective authority. Relativistic humanism is inimical to objective authority, and any attempt to relativize the authority of Scripture only serves the enemy.

[3] Our only hope of correcting the national culture depends upon first correcting the churches.

surgery. The patient will not like the news, but if the surgery is successful, he will end up thanking the surgeon. Similarly, a brother probably will not appreciate being told that he has embraced a lie, but if he will stop and think, and change, he will end up thanking us. In desperate times 'business as usual' is not enough; it is necessary to take risks.[1]

Now consider 1 Peter 4:17—"Because the time has come for judgment to begin at God's house; now if it starts with us, what will be the end of those who keep disobeying the Gospel of God?" Although the 'publishing' of this letter is often stated to have been around 60 AD, or even later, I suspect it may have been at least ten years earlier. In any case, although the nation of Israel will yet return to center stage, beginning with the day of Pentecost Sovereign Jesus has been interacting with the world using mainly His body, the Church. Since Peter is writing to Christians, he is referring to them as "God's house". It is possible to translate the verse above as 'from God's house', that house being the point of departure. It seems clear that God's judgment does not stop with us; it goes on to the world.

God has always judged His people

Once the blood of God's Lamb had been shed, thus paying for the sin of the world, the judgment against those "who keep disobeying the Gospel of God" became more direct. But since judgment starts with God's house, the demands upon those claiming to belong to Christ also became more direct. The fate of Ananias and Sapphira is an emphatic case in point.[2] What I wish to emphasize is that God's judging His house began at the beginning, it began on the day of Pentecost, with reference to the Church. When we cry out to God to judge the world, the judging of God's house as a

---

[1] In order to try to save the 'patient', I must take the risk of being rejected and hated. On the other hand, Ezekiel 3:20-21 explains an even more serious risk.

[2] They were not given any warning, nor any chance to repent or explain.

prior condition is not a factor[1]—God has been judging His house right along.[2] However, I would say that judging is one thing, but correcting is another. The correcting of the culture begins with, and depends on, the correcting of the churches.

Consider what happened to the apostle Paul. The Holy Spirit had told him <u>repeatedly</u> **NOT** to go to Jerusalem, but he went anyway. When he got there he kowtowed to big boss James, who was well on his way back into Judaism. Do you remember his pitch to Paul? "You see, brother, how many tens of thousands are the Jews who have believed, and they are all zealous for the law; but they have been informed about you that you teach all the Jews who are among the Gentiles to forsake Moses, telling them not to circumcise their children nor to walk according to our customs" (Acts 21:20-21).[3] If his "many tens of thousands" was not a blatant exaggeration, as I suspect, then the whole church in that area was in a bad way (which it probably was anyway). Was Paul judged? He spent the next five years, at least, in chains.[4]

Was James judged? He was killed, not long after. Was the church in Jerusalem judged? The city was destroyed in 70 AD, and the Jerusalem church ceased to exist. The city was little more than a ruin for centuries.[5] And now consider 1 Corinthians 11:29-30: "He who eats and drinks unworthily eats and drinks judgment to himself, not distinguishing the Lord's body. Because of this many among you are weak and sick, and a good many have died." Paul declares that God had already visited sickness on many, and death on even

---

[1] For many years I had the idea that it was a prior condition that had not yet been fulfilled—don't ask me where I got it!

[2] Of course this has always been true. The O. T. is full of God's judgment upon His people, Israel. Adam was judged; Moses was judged. God has always required an accounting based on the benefits and blessings one receives.

[3] "The law", "Moses", "our customs" = Judaism.

[4] Try living in chains for just twenty-four hours, and see how you like it!

[5] References during the early centuries to especially good NT manuscripts in Jerusalem are probably just pious hogwash. The center of gravity of the Church had moved north.

more. God was judging His people. A variety of further texts could be mentioned, but Hebrews will do. Please read 2:1-3, 3:12-4:13, 6:3-8, 10:26-31, and 12:28-29. "It is a dreadful thing to fall into the hands of the Living God", "because our God is indeed a consuming fire!"

And then there are the seven letters that the glorified Jesus sent to the seven churches. Each letter ends with a promise to "the one who overcomes"; so what happens to you if you don't? Although He had some good things to say about the church in Ephesus, He said He would remove their 'lampstand' if they did not return to their first love. Indeed, in due time all seven of those churches lost their lampstand. Two of the letters refer to the doctrine and works of the Nicolaitans, that Sovereign Jesus says He hates. The etymology of the term suggests the beginning of the distinction between clergy and laity. It may have begun with James in Jerusalem.[1] Before the end of the first century, a certain Clement was the bishop of Rome. The term 'bishop' came to be used of a presbyter who had authority over the other presbyters in his area, the boss presbyter.[2]

Attempting to control someone else's spiritual life is forbidden

But the concept of special spiritual authority being vested in a 'bishop' soon ran afoul of Sovereign Jesus' words in Matthew 23:8-12 and John 4:23-24. First Matthew:

> "But you (pl.), do not be called 'Rabbi'; because your Teacher is <u>one</u>, the Christ,[3] and you are all brothers. 9 And do not call anyone on earth your 'father'; because

---

[1] The Jews were accustomed to a high priest, a single individual at the top of the religious pyramid. Evidently that attitude invaded the churches.

[2] In the writings of the 'church fathers' that have come down to us, there appears to be no mention of 'apostles' after the first century. This means that there was no 'apostolic succession'; the more so since apostles are designated by God, not ordained by men. Since the second century there has only been 'discipolic' succession. Any claims in our day based on apostolic succession are spurious (as were any such claims after the first century).

[3] Perhaps 4% of the Greek manuscripts omit "the Christ" (as in NIV, NASB, LB, TEV, etc.).

your Father is <u>one</u>, He who is in the heavens. 10 Neither be called leaders/guides; because your Leader is <u>one</u>, the Christ. 11 On the contrary, the greatest among you must be your servant. 12 And whoever exalts himself will be humbled, and whoever humbles himself will be exalted."

In verse 9, since the second person here is plural, the Lord is evidently referring to calling someone your spiritual father; He is not saying not to acknowledge your physical father. "Your (pl.) Father is <u>one</u>"—obviously they did not all have the same physical father. Verse 10 may be why we have no record in Scripture of a Christian calling someone his disciple; even in 1 Corinthians 3:4 Paul evidently avoids using the term. **I take it that our Lord is forbidding any effort by one Christian to control the spiritual life of another.** We may point the way, we may encourage, we may discipline when occasion warrants, but the rest is up to the Holy Spirit.[1] The Lord had already told the Samaritan woman that the Father must be worshipped "in spirit and truth" (John 4:23-24).

> "The time is coming, in fact now is, when the genuine worshipers will worship the Father in spirit and truth. Really, because the Father is looking for **such** people to worship Him. 24 God is <u>Spirit</u>,[2] and those who worship Him must worship in spirit and truth."

The Father "is looking" for those who will worship Him in spirit and truth.[3] It may be that we have here a window on the reason why God created a race such as ours—persons in His image with the capacity to **choose**. God "is looking" for something, which means He does not have it, at least not automatically, nor in sufficient quantity. I take it that He wants to be appreciated for who He is, but to have meaning

---

[1] It is normal, indeed inescapable, that a new Christian will receive his first ideas about spiritual things from the older Christians around him. But as he grows and matures, he should learn to depend directly upon Scripture and the Holy Spirit.

[2] Again the lack of the definite article presents us with an ambiguity; the rendering 'a spirit' is possible. But as I indicate by the underlining, I understand that the quality inherent in the noun is being emphasized, which is another use of an absent article (in Greek).

[3] See also 2 Chronicles 16:9, that tells you how to have God's help.

such appreciation cannot come from robots—it has to be voluntary. So He created a type of being with that capacity, but He had to take the risk that such a being would choose not to appreciate Him. Unfortunately, most human beings make the negative choice, and with that negative choice come all sorts of negative consequences. Ever since Adam human beings are born with an inclination toward sin,[1] so for someone to choose to appreciate God is definitely not automatic, nor even easy. No one can reasonably accuse God of having 'stacked the deck' in His own favor, of 'buying votes'—He seems to have done just the opposite. If a human being, against his natural inclination, chooses to appreciate God, then God receives what He is looking for.

"In spirit and truth" presumably means that it cannot be faked, cannot be forced or imposed, cannot be merely physical, cannot be merely emotional (though both body and emotions can, and often will, be utilized). The concept of 'bishop' (and in our day even of lowly pastors) as someone having the authority to control the spiritual life of others is an open rebellion against Sovereign Jesus, who forbids any such attitude or proceeding.[2] But rebellion against God is Satan's 'thing', and will certainly call down God's judgment (see the discussion of 2 Thessalonians 2:9-12 below).

Someone who wishes to control the spiritual life of others must develop a doctrinal 'package'; he must define what they may and may not believe, and/or do. But of course that gave rise to competing 'packages', and competition between 'bishops', to the point that they were mutually excommunicating each other, and so on. That gave rise to different 'churches', and in our day to different 'denominations'. This mentality guarantees the perpetuation of the falsehoods that have been incorporated into the denominational 'packages'. In some cases they reached the point of

---

[1] Babies have to be self-centered in order to survive, but self-centeredness is the essence of sin, which, however, is not charged to the account until the person can understand what he is doing.

[2] A typical proceeding is to dictate who may, or may not, participate in the 'Lord's Supper', as though the 'table' belongs to the leaders of the congregation, rather than to the Lord—after all, it is the 'Lord's Table'.

declaring that only those who were within their ranks could be saved. Anyone who embraces a 'package' elevates that package above God's inspired Word, and that is idolatry. Such idolatry offends the Holy Spirit, who has a special interest in that Word; such idolaters no longer listen to the Holy Spirit (if they ever did). Such idolaters condemn their 'package' to become an 'old wineskin', devoid of spiritual power.

I would say that the only way to avoid becoming an 'old wineskin' is to be constantly listening to the Holy Spirit and obeying what He says. Unfortunately, few Christians are in the habit of consulting the Holy Spirit, and those who do are marked for persecution. <u>No Establishment can tolerate anyone who listens to the Holy Spirit</u>. Surely, or have you forgotten John 3:8? "The wind blows where it wishes, and you (sg) hear its sound, but you do not know where it comes from or where it goes. So it is with everyone who has been begotten by the Spirit." Notice that the Lord is saying here that it is **we** who are to be unpredictable, like the wind, or the Spirit ("comes" and "goes" are in the present tense). If you are really under the control of the Spirit you will do unexpected things, just like He does, and that definitely will not please the 'bosses'.[1] (Since Satan is forever muddying the water with excesses and abuses, spiritual discernment is needed, but lamentably such discernment appears to be a rare commodity in the churches.) An Establishment is defined by its 'straightjacket' (or 'package'), and the Holy Spirit does not like straightjackets, and vice versa.

The love of the Truth

---

[1] But what about Hebrews 13:17? "Obey your leaders and submit, for they keep watch over your souls, as those who must give account." In the first place, I would say that the reference is to administrative matters, so that things be done 'decently and in order'. But the minute a leader attempts to impose a falsehood, he should not be obeyed; he is no longer listening to the Holy Spirit. As Peter said to the council, "We must obey God rather than men" (Acts 5:29). I treat 1 Peter 5:5 similarly. Some 4% of the Greek manuscripts, of inferior quality, omit "submitting to one another" (as in NIV, NASB, LB, TEV, etc.).

During the middle ages the Church all but died out, at least in the West. And why did the Church almost die out? It was because the Church became part of the problem, rather than being part of the solution. And how did it become part of the problem? It became part of the problem by rejecting the love of the truth (see the discussion of 2 Thessalonians 2:9-12 below). When the Church becomes part of the problem, the surrounding culture is condemned. Did you get that? **When the Church becomes part of the problem, the surrounding culture is condemned.** Surely, because salvation begins at the house of God.

Consider 1 Timothy 3:15—"so that you may know how it is necessary to conduct oneself in God's household, which is the Church of the living God, pillar and foundation of the truth." My first impression would be that the truth should be sustaining the Church, not vice versa. But it is the Church that has the responsibility to promote and defend the truth in the society at large—in education, health, commerce, government, everywhere. Salvation can come to an individual just by reading God's Word, all by himself, but to trans-form a whole culture requires the Church. Remember also what Jesus said to the Samaritan woman in John 4:22, "salvation is from the Jews". Quite so. The Lamb of God is a Jew, and the O.T. canon came through the Jewish people (for that matter, most, if not all, of the N.T. was written by Jews as well). As Paul says in Romans 3:2, "they were entrusted with the oracles of God". The Oracles of God are His written revelation to the human race.

Then came the Protestant Reformation, but because of its emphasis on reason it was born deformed. It was not long before 'packages' developed within the Reformation, and in the nineteenth century it was besieged by three satanic sophistries (2 Corinthians 10:5): 1) Darwin's theory of evolution, 2) the so-called 'higher criticism' of the Bible, and then 3) the text-critical theory of Westcott and Hort.[1] These

---

[1] The W-H theory did away with any notion of a NT text with objective authority. My demonstration that that theory is a tissue of falsehoods was first published in 1977 (the book having gone through at least six revisions since), and so far as I know, it has never been refuted. *The Identity*

were followed by materialism, humanism, relativism, etc. A biblical Text with objective authority barely limped into the twentieth century, but then came the onslaught of liberal theology.[1]

To understand the full impact of the onslaught of liberal theology, one must take account of the milieu. Reason has always been important to the historic or traditional Protestant denominations. In consequence, academic re-spectability has always been important to their graduate schools of theology. The difficulty resides in the following circumstance: for at least two centuries academia has been dominated by Satan, and so the terms of 'respectability' are dictated by him. Those terms include 'publish or perish', but of course he controls the technical journals. Since he is the father of lies (John 8:44), anyone who wished to tell the whole truth has always had a hard time getting an article published, no matter how good it was. To get an article published one had to toe the party line. 'Taking account of the existing literature' obliges one to waste a great deal of time reading the nonsense produced by Satan's servants, all of which was designed to keep the reader away from the **truth**—the 'reader' in this case being the students who in their turn would become pastors and church leaders, semi-nary professors, etc.[2]

The TRUTH—aye, there's the rub. Consider 2 Thessalonians 2:9-12:

> That one's coming is according to the working of Satan with all power[3] and signs and lying wonders, 10 and with all wicked deception among those who are wasting them-

---

of the New Testament Text (Nashville: Thomas Nelson Inc., Publishers, 1977); The Identity of the New Testament Text IV (self-published with Amazon.com, 2014).

[1] One response to liberal theology was the so-called Neo-orthodoxy; it holds that the Bible is made up of divine parts and human parts, so that the whole cannot be said to **be** God's Word. Since that view offers no way to know which parts are and which are not, it also does away with any notion of a NT text with objective authority.

[2] The systematic contamination of successive generations of future pastors inevitably resulted in the contamination of the congregations as well.

[3] When Satan fell he did not lose his power.

selves,[1] because they did not receive the love of the truth so that they might be saved. 11 Yes, because of this God will send them an active delusion so that they will believe the lie 12 and so that all may be condemned who have not believed the truth but have taken pleasure in wickedness.[2]

Although verse ten is in the context of the activity of the Antichrist, who will find an easy target in 'those who are wasting themselves' (my translation), it does not follow that no one will be wasting himself before that activity. Obviously, people have been wasting themselves all down through history, and the underlying cause for that 'wasting' has never changed—"they did not receive the love of the truth". (It began in the Garden.)

Consider Romans 1:18: "Now the wrath of God is revealed from Heaven upon all ungodliness and unrighteousness of the people who suppress the truth by unrighteousness." To 'suppress the truth' is a deliberate act, an evil choice that invites God's wrath. (Romans 1:24-25 and 2:8 give more detail.) To hear a sermon about 'the love of God' is easy enough, but how many have you heard (or preached) about 'the wrath of God'? 'God hates sin but loves the sinner' is standard fare, but consider Psalm 5:4-6.

> "For You are not a God who takes pleasure in wickedness, nor shall evil dwell with You. The boastful shall not stand in your sight; You **hate** all workers of iniquity. You shall destroy those who speak falsehood; the LORD <u>abhors</u> the bloodthirsty and deceitful man."

This is not an isolated text; there are a fair number of others in the same vein. Someone who deliberately chooses to

---

[1] The verb here, apwllumi, often rendered 'to perish' (John 3:16 in KJV), is used in a variety of contexts, but I take the core meaning to be 'waste'. The participial form here is ambiguous as to voice, either middle or passive, but the basic form of the verb is middle. Ephesians 1:5-14 makes clear that a basic objective of our redemption is that we be "to the praise of His glory", which was part of the original Plan (Isaiah 43:7). Only as we live for the glory of God can we realize or fulfill our potential, our reason for being. If you live for any other reason, you are wasting yourself.

[2] 'Taking pleasure in wickedness' involves rejecting the Truth of a moral Creator who will demand an accounting, or even overt rebellion against that Creator (like Lucifer/Satan).

be evil and to promote evil, having rejected the truth, thereby makes God his enemy, makes himself an object of His wrath.[1] God has been judging sin for six thousand years.

Consider also Luke 16:31 "He said to him, 'If they do not listen to Moses and the prophets, they will not be persuaded even if someone should rise from the dead'." Abraham states a disquieting reality: people who reject God's written revelation are self-condemned. As Jesus said in John 8:31-32, "If you abide in my word, you really are my disciples; and you will know the Truth, and the Truth will make you free." So what happens if you don't abide?

Consider further 2 Timothy 4:4, "They will turn their ears away from the Truth and be turned aside to fables." Notice the progression: first they choose to turn away from the Truth, but after that someone else takes over and leads them into ever greater stupidities—that someone else is Satan, using his servants.

But to return to Thessalonians, please notice carefully what is said there: it is God Himself who sends the "active delusion"![2] And upon whom does He send it? Upon those who do not receive the love of the truth—it is a direct judgment upon their rejection of the truth.[3] And what is the purpose of the strong delusion?—the condemnation of those who do not believe the truth. Dear me, this is heavy. Notice that the truth is **central** to anyone's salvation. This raises the necessary question: just what is meant by 'the truth'?

In John 14:6 Sovereign Jesus declared Himself to be 'the truth'. Praying to the Father in John 17:17 He said, "Thy Word is truth". Once each in John chapters 14, 15 and 16 He referred to the third person of the Trinity as "the Spirit

---

[1] A person who sells himself to evil will spend eternity in the Lake of fire and brimstone, but usually gets a taste of God's wrath in this life as well.

[2] I understand 'active' in the sense of 'aggressive'; it is not a passive delusion that lies quietly in your brain, allowing you to go your merry way. It is aggressive, it tries to control how you think, and therefore what you do and who you are.

[3] Please note that it is not enough to merely 'accept' the truth; it is required that we love the truth. Satan tantalizes us with fame and fortune (on his terms, of course), so to love the truth requires determination; since the love in question is agaph, it involves an act of the will.

of the truth". Since the Son is back in Heaven at the Father's right hand, and the Spirit is not very perceptible to most of us, most of the time, and since the Word is the Spirit's sword (Ephesians 6:17), our main access to 'the truth' is through God's Word, the Bible. The Bible offers propositional truth, but we need the Holy Spirit to illumine that truth, and to have the Holy Spirit we must be adequately related to Sovereign Jesus—it is Jesus who baptizes with the Holy Spirit (Matthew 3:11). If that is 'the Truth', then what is 'the lie'? I suggest that 'the lie' is short for Satan's kingdom and all it represents. In that event, we could also say that 'the Truth' is short for Christ's Kingdom and all it represents.

Now then, for something to be received, it must be offered; one cannot believe in something he has never heard about (Romans 10:14). A baby born to Satanist parents and dedicated to him may well grow to adulthood without ever having been exposed to 'the truth'. The same holds for cultures that have no knowledge at all of Christianity. In such circumstances a person can be serving 'the lie' because that is all he knows. He has not rejected 'the truth', because he has no knowledge of it. For such a person there is hope; if some day 'the truth' is presented to him, he has the option of embracing it, as has happened many times.

The use of the verb 'receive' clearly implies an act of volition on the part of those not receiving the truth; that love was offered or made available to them but they did not want it; they wanted to be able to lie and to entertain lies told by others. But the consequences of such a choice are terrible; they turned their back on salvation. Notice in verse 11 that God sends the active delusion so that they will believe the lie; God pushes them toward the lie! In John 8:44 Sovereign Jesus stated that Satan is the father of lying, there being no truth in him. So if God Himself sends delusion, He is turning the victims over to Satan. So if God turns you over to Satan, what are your chances?

Notice the sequence: first they reject the love of the truth; it is as a consequence of that choice that God sends the delusion. The implication is that there is a **point of no return**;[1] God sends the delusion so that they may be condemned. The only intelligent choice is to embrace the truth! If God offers you the truth and you reject it, your choice turns Him into your enemy—not a good idea!

A correct solution depends upon a correct diagnosis

Why did I write this article? I am looking for a way (if it is still possible) to stop, and even turn back, the satanic steamroller that is destroying the culture and taking over all aspects of life in the country where I live, Brazil. (Of course the same is true of other countries as well.) The only possible 'medicine' is the love of the truth, so the bottom line is this: what can we do to promote the love of the truth? Lamentably, the vast majority of the churches are part of the problem, rather than being part of the solution. I venture to say that less than 1% of the churches want a Bible with objective authority.[2] The culture outside the church is totally dominated by relativistic humanism, and most church members have been heavily influenced by that worldview. On the way to promoting the love of the truth, we must defend the objective authority of the biblical Text,[3] and the place to begin is with the churches.[4] To promote truth necessarily involves exposing lies.

The world hates the Truth

---

[1] However, since God is gracious and longsuffering, He may grant a number of opportunities to repent before a person reaches that point. In my own experience, I threw off a variety of falsehoods that I was taught one at a time over a period of years. That said, I should not assume that I am now totally free from false ideas; I need to keep listening to the Holy Spirit as I study the Scriptures.

[2] In consequence they are lacking in spiritual power and spiritual discernment.

[3] It is the biblical Text that defines and teaches the Truth, and in order to arrive at the Truth we must understand that the Text has objective authority. Relativistic humanism is inimical to objective authority, and any attempt to relativize the authority of Scripture only serves the enemy.

[4] Our only hope of correcting the national culture depends upon first correcting the churches.

Satan never quits with his attacks against the objective authority of God's Word; it began back in the Garden: "Yea, hath God said?" Satan hates the Truth, because as Sovereign Jesus said in John 8:44, "there is no truth in him". Satan is the father of lying (same verse), so whenever we tell a lie we are doing Satan's thing. And whenever we embrace a lie (like evolutionism, Marxism, Freudianism, Hortianism, humanism, relativism, etc.) we give Satan a foothold in our minds, which he usually turns into a stronghold. When Satan gets someone to sell himself to evil, having rejected the truth, that someone becomes what Jesus called a 'dog' in Matthew 7:6.[1] A 'dog' reacts in an aggressive and violent manner against any presentation of the Truth. The media and academia are filled with such dogs; they are sworn enemies of the Truth. Why did the Sovereign say **not** to offer anything 'holy' to such people? The implication is that it would be a waste of time; they are beyond recovery—their ongoing opposition will also get in the way. However, in order to save the people that they are damaging, it will be necessary to challenge and refute what they represent—before attempting to do this, you had better know how to wield God's power (Ephesians 3:20). To confront a 'dog' is not the same as offering him something 'holy'.

Consider our Lord's words recorded in Luke 17:2—"It would be better for him if a millstone were hung around his neck and he were thrown into the sea, than that he should cause one of these little ones to fall." What is worse than a horrible, premature physical death? Spiritual death. Whoever destroys the faith of a 'little one' is self-condemned. What about all the professors and pastors who make it their business to destroy the faith of their students and hearers?

Consider also 2 Peter 3:5—"This because they deliberately ignore that heavens and land (out of water and through water) had been existing from of old by the word of God." It appears to me that the term "deliberately" has a direct bearing on the intended meaning of the Greek term usually rendered as 'forget'. How can one 'forget' deliberately? To 'ignore' is deliberate; to 'pretend' is deliberate. When a professor, a scholar, or a scientist ignores the scientific evi-

---

[1] 1 Timothy 6:5 and 2 timothy 3:8 may refer to such 'dogs' as well.

dence for a worldwide flood, he is deliberately deceiving his students or readers. To do so is to be perverse, to do so is to serve Satan.

Comparing Romans 1:18: the wrath of God is upon those who suppress the truth, with Psalm 5:5: God hates all workers of iniquity, with what Jesus said in John 6:44: "No one is able to come to me unless the Father who sent me draws him", we may reasonably conclude that the Father will not draw someone whom He hates. So anyone who has become a 'dog' is condemned. Just by the way, have you not noticed that those who were brought up in a Christian environment but then turned their back on Jesus are often more virulent in their opposition to God's truth than those who were brought up as pagans? There is no way to save a 'dog', but we should work to save their students and readers—how can we do this apart from demonstrating that what the 'dog' teaches is wrong? To confront a 'dog' is not the same as offering him something 'holy'; we are not trying to save him, we are refuting him for the sake of his students and readers.

False doctrines in the churches

I suspect that not many Christians in the so-called 'first world' really believe what Sovereign Jesus said in Matthew 7:14: those who find the way of Life are **few**![1] We need to consider carefully Revelation 22:15; "whoever loves and practices a lie" is excluded from the heavenly City.[2] The

---

[1] Consider also Romans 9:27, "the remnant will be saved". The context is about Israel, but the statement is descriptive of all human history. At any moment during the last 6,000 years, only a very small percentage of the total population was seriously committed to God. The same is true of the Christian population during the last 2,000 years. What percentage of a wheat plant is edible grain (Luke 3:17)? And then there is Matthew 24:37—after 1,650 years of human procreation, how many people would there have been on the earth? Probably well over a million. And how many were saved? Sovereign Jesus said that at His coming it will be like it was in the days of Noah.

[2] Help! "A lie" is rather general, open-ended. What happens if I accepted a lie without realizing that it was one? But the text does not say 'accepts'; it says 'loves' and 'practices'. The implication is that the contrary evidence, to the lie, is available, but has been rejected, or deliberately ignored—the person sold himself to the lie.

Text has 'a' lie, not 'the' lie. The verb here is filew, that refers to emotional love; someone who sells himself to a lie usually becomes emotionally attached to it, and they react aggressively (often irrationally) if you challenge their lie. In contrast, in 2 Thessalonians 2:10 the love of the truth is agaph love, that refers to an act of the will whereby you align yourself with the truth.

Consider 1 Timothy 4:1-2—"Now the Spirit says explicitly that in later times some will fall away from the faith, paying attention to deceiving spirits and to things taught by demons—through hypocritical liars whose own consciences have been cauterized." Notice that one cannot "fall away from the faith" unless he was first with the faith. Be not deceived, the churches (with exceptions, of course) are filled with a variety of 'doctrines' of demonic origin. The enemy uses a certain type of person to 'sell' them. Whatever its origin, any false doctrine gives the enemy an entrance into the life of the church, and then into the persons who attend there.

But let us return to Revelation 22:15. The verb 'practice' indicates a value that orients your conduct. If you are practicing a lie, that lie has become part of what you are, part of your private 'package'. Depending on the nature of the lie, its contaminating influence could end up touching all areas of your life. A lie like 'God does not exist' touches everything. Obviously, the more lies that someone practices, the worse off that he will be. Notice, however, that the verbs "loves" and "practices" are in the present tense, which means that while there is life there is hope; it is still possible to repent and change and escape condemnation. Anyone who is overtaken by death while practicing a lie will be excluded from the City.[1]

Now notice what it says in Ezekiel 18; I encourage you to read the whole chapter with care. Each person is responsi-

---

[1] All of us have received false information that we assumed to be true, and in some cases may even have acted upon it, but if it did not become part of our ongoing practice, then it will not necessarily result in keeping us out of the City.

ble for his own destiny, and it is possible to change destinies. Verses 21-22 teach that someone who starts out wrong can change to right, and live. Verse 23: "Do I have any pleasure at all that the wicked should die?" says the Lord GOD, "and not that he should turn from his ways and live?" But verse 24 teaches that the reverse is true; someone who starts out right can change to wrong, and die. While there is life there is hope, except for certain irreversible conditions.[1]

If you consult the Holy Spirit on a given matter, He will not permit you to believe a lie. "He will guide you into all truth" (John 16:13). He is the Spirit of the Truth (John 15:26) and He cannot lie (Titus 1:2). It follows that He hates lies. "These six things the LORD hates, yes, seven are an <u>abomination</u> to Him: a proud look, **a lying tongue**, . . ." (Proverbs 6:16-17). "Lying lips are an abomination to the LORD" (Proverbs 12:22). And remember that liars cannot enter the New Jerusalem (Revelation 21:27, 22:15). The case of Joshua and the Gibeonites provides a negative example. The Text says explicitly that they did not seek the Lord's guidance (Joshua 9:14), and the negative consequences lasted for centuries.

I will now discuss some of the lies that Satan has succeeded in 'selling' to many Christians, precisely because they did not consult the Holy Spirit before embracing them. It may be that most people simply accept what they are taught because they trust the teacher, as well as not feeling competent to attempt an independent judgement—and many of them may stop short of 'loving' and 'practicing'. It is also lamentably true that very few churches teach how to consult the Holy Spirit, but none of this changes the consequences of a lie. Such lies often become strongholds of Satan in their minds, that they then defend emotionally. Have you never noticed that when you challenge certain doctrines the people simply explode? They are incapable of discussing the question rationally; they do not know all that the Bible says on the subject. <u>For all that, to promote the truth we</u>

---

[1] These will be discussed below in the section, "Sins that lead to death".

<u>must expose lies</u>. If the promoting of the love of the Truth is our top priority, then we must accept the consequences of exposing and denouncing lies. If all Christians were to throw off all of the eight cherished falsehoods discussed below, the world would see an outpouring of God's power unprecedented in human history.

Sovereign grace: The doctrine of 'sovereign grace' is obviously false. God is indeed sovereign, but no single one of His attributes can be, by simple logic, since it is constrained by all the others. God is certainly grace, but He is also love (which necessarily includes the hate of evil, because of the consequences to loved ones), truth, wisdom, power, justice, wrath, eternity, and doubtless others that our finite minds cannot comprehend. Nowhere does the Bible teach that grace is sovereign; the doctrine is an invention. Those who use the idea of sovereign grace to protect sin and comfort the sinner[1] are in for a terrible surprise. Anyone who has embraced the notion of 'sovereign grace' did not consult the Holy Spirit before doing so.

Unconditional love: The doctrine that God's love is 'unconditional' is also false. Since we have no way of deserving His love beforehand, presumably God offers His love without prior condition—it is unconditional only in that sense. But the minute someone receives God's love, then His expectations come into play. From John 4:23-24 it is clear that the Father is looking for a response to His love; He wants to be reciprocated. This is also clear from John 14:21 and 23. If God's love is unconditional, why then does He chasten us? "As many as I love, I rebuke and chasten" (Revelation 3:19). "Whom the LORD loves He chastens, and scourges every son whom He receives" (Hebrews 12:6). And why does He demand an accounting? "We must all appear before the judgment seat of Christ, that each one may receive the things done in the body, according to what he has done, whether good or bad" (2 Corinthians 5:10; see also 1 Corinthians 3:11-15). Those who use the idea of unconditional

---

[1] By 'comfort the sinner' I mean to tell a sinner not to worry about his sin, rather than confronting it.

love to protect sin and comfort the sinner are in for a terrible surprise. Anyone who has embraced the notion of 'unconditional love' did not consult the Holy Spirit before doing so.

Eternal security: The doctrine of 'eternal security', as usually understood, is also false, and even more dangerous to the souls of men than the two discussed above. A crass statement of the 'doctrine' would go something like this: Once saved, always saved, no matter what you do afterwards. When one mentions passages like Ephesians 5:5-6 and 1 Corinthians 6:9-10, that list practices that exclude from the Kingdom, the standard defense is to say that such people never were saved. But do they not beg the question? Both the passages above were written to <u>believers</u>, not unbelievers. Why would the Holy Spirit write such things to believers if it were simply impossible for them to fall into such practices? And why did the glorified Jesus say, "I will not blot out his name from the Book of Life" (Revelation 3:5)? Please note that <u>it is impossible to blot out a name that is not there</u>! To try to argue that the glorified Jesus was using an impossible 'bogey-man' to scare them would make Him out to be a liar, which He cannot be (Titus 1:2). And then there are all the passages that speak of enduring to the end, so as to be saved. But the definitive text on the subject is Hebrews 6:3-6. The descriptions given in verses 4 and 5 can only refer to someone who has been regenerated, as verse 6 makes clear. The only way to "crucify <u>again</u>" is if you have already done so, at least once. To say that the Holy Spirit is using an impossible 'bogey-man' to scare them would make Him out to be a liar, as well, also impossible.[1] Those who use the idea of eternal security to protect sin

---

[1] An appeal to John 10:28-29 reflects a basic misunderstanding of the Text; the crucial point is the semantic area of the verb "snatch". Being snatched is one thing; jumping out is another. You cannot 'snatch' yourself, it must be done by an outside force, and no such force is greater than God. But, if you don't want to go to Heaven, you won't; God will certainly not take you there against your will. Sovereign Jesus puts it very plainly in John 15:6, "If anyone does not abide in me, he is cast out as a branch . . ." 'Abiding' is up to us; we are not forced to do it. If we choose not to, we are out. Note that you cannot be "cast out" unless you are first in.

and comfort the sinner are in for a terrible surprise. Anyone who has embraced the notion of 'eternal security' did not consult the Holy Spirit before doing so.

Salvation without works: The Protestant Reformation correctly rejected the Roman doctrine of salvation by works, but to replace it with 'faith alone' is open to serious misunderstanding. Ephesians 2:8-10 gives us the truth on this subject in a nutshell:

> "For by grace you have been saved, through the Faith[1]—and this not of yourselves, it is the gift of God— 9 not by works, so that no one may boast. 10 You see, we are His 'poem',[2] created in Christ Jesus for good works, which God prepared in advance in order that we should walk in them."[3]

We are not saved <u>by</u> good works, but we are indeed saved <u>for</u> good works; we do not do good works in order to be saved, but we must do good works because we are saved. James is very clear on this point; a faith that does not produce <u>cannot</u> save (James 2:14). Faith without works is dead (James 2:17, 20, 26). If you are alive, you do things. The plan of redemption is not just about getting us to heaven, it is about our contributing to Christ's Kingdom down here. To tell someone that all he has to do is 'believe in Jesus'[4] and 'bang', he goes to heaven, is a cruel falsehood. Anyone who

---

[1] The Text has 'the' faith; the reference is to a specific Faith, presumably the body of truth that revolves around the person of Jesus.

[2] The English word 'poem' comes from the Greek word here, *poiema*, and is one of its meanings. Just as each poem is an individual creation of the poet, so we are individual creations, not produced by a production line in a factory.

[3] "Prepared in advance"—I imagine that this refers to God's moral code, the rules of conduct that everyone should follow (if everyone did, we would not need jails, rescue missions, etc.).

[4] Unfortunately, most versions do not translate the Greek text adequately with this clause; the Text never has 'believe <u>in</u> Jesus', it always has 'believe <u>into</u> Jesus', the point being that one must change location from being outside to being inside. To believe into Jesus involves commitment. It is also wrong to use 'accept Jesus' rather than the biblical 'receive Jesus'—one 'accepts' from someone who is inferior in rank, from someone superior in rank one 'receives'. A 'Jesus' that you merely accept cannot save you, since he would be smaller than you are.

has embraced the notion that he can be saved without working did not consult the Holy Spirit before doing so.

Substitutionism: The doctrine of 'substitution' holds that the Church totally replaces Israel as God's people and that never again will Israel receive any special attention from God. Adherents of substitution are obliged to ignore or mistreat the considerable percentage of the total biblical text that is prophecy relating to the end times. They must also reject plain biblical statements to the contrary, the equivalent of making the Holy Spirit out to be a liar (don't forget that to blaspheme the Holy Spirit is unforgivable). 1 Corinthians 10:32—"Give no offense, either to the Jews or to the Greeks or to the church of God." This text makes clear that during the Church Age there are three categories of people: Jews, non-Jews and the Church (made up of both Jews and non-Jews who are in Christ). Before Pentecost there were two categories: Jews and non-Jews. Substitutionists hold that after Pentecost there were still just two: Church and non-Church, wherein the Church replaced Israel. But it is not so; Israel still exists as a separate entity in God's plan. Chapters nine, ten and eleven of Romans go into some detail on this point. Romans 11:1-2—"I say then, has God cast away His people? Certainly not! . . . God has not cast away His people whom He foreknew."[1] Substitutionism contradicts this plain statement. At the end of Galatians 6:16 we find "the Israel of God". It is very common to hear this phrase used as a synonym for the Church, but it is not. According to Greek grammar, the repetition of the preposition 'upon' in two phrases joined by 'and' makes clear that the objects of the prepositions refer to distinct entities. Hence, "the Israel of God" cannot be a reference to the Church, assuming that "those who conform to this rule" refers to those who are "in Christ Jesus". I take "the Israel of God" to refer to sincere, devout Israelites. Anyone who has embraced the notion of 'substitution' did not consult the Holy Spirit before doing so.

---

[1] Recall that this was written decades after Pentecost and the beginning of the Church.

Idolatry: Idolatry is certainly sin, but in what sense is it a lie? Well, does it not replace something true with something false? 2 Timothy 3:16 says that Scripture is like God's breath. Psalm 138:2 says: "You have magnified your word above all your name", and a name represents the person. And John 17:17 says: "Your word is truth". To place church tradition above God's Word is a form of idolatry. To place a denomination's doctrinal 'package' above God's Word is a form of idolatry. To place a church leader's word above God's Word is a form of idolatry. Any of the above hinder spiritual growth, and may lead to ultimate loss, because they all contain falsehood. Anyone who has adopted any of those practices did not consult the Holy Spirit before so doing.

Cessationism: The doctrine of 'cessationism' is also false. Cessationism claims that the 'sign gifts' ceased when the NT Canon was completed, or when the last shovelful of dirt landed on the apostle John's grave.[1] The alleged scriptural basis for this is found in 1 Corinthians 13:8b-10. These verses have received more than their fair share of mistreatment, partly because commentators have not linked verse 12 to them (seeing verse 11 as parenthetical). Consider verse 10: "But whenever the complete should come, then the 'in part' will be done away with." If we can pinpoint the 'then', we will have also pinpointed the 'when';[2] and verse 12 pinpoints the 'then'. When will we see 'face to face', when will we know as we are known? 1 John 3:2 has the answer: "Beloved, now we are children of God; and it has not yet been revealed what we shall be, but we know that when He is revealed, we shall be like Him, for we shall

---

[1] To affirm that the miraculous gifts ceased when the last shovelful of dirt fell on the apostle John's grave is an historical falsehood. Christians who lived during the second, third and fourth centuries, whose writings have come down to us, affirm that the gifts were still in use in their day. No 20th or 21st century Christian, who was not there, is competent to contradict them. Any 'cessationist' will have a stronghold of Satan in his mind on that subject, because he has embraced a lie. Any doctrine that derives from reaction against excesses and abuses gives victory to Satan. Any argument designed to justify lack of spiritual power cannot be right.

[2] These two temporal adverbs work together.

see Him as He is." It is at the return of Christ that we will see 'face to face', so "whenever the complete should come" refers to Christ at His second coming. The problem with 'prophecy', 'tongues' and our present 'knowledge' is that they are 'in part', but after the return of Christ we will have no further need for them. Since Christ has not returned yet, these 'in part' things are certainly still with us. The claim that 'the complete' refers to the completed New Testament canon does violence to the Text. If it had really been the Holy Spirit's purpose to tell us that the *charismata* would disappear in a few decades, He presumably could have done a much better job of it. Cessationists also generally choose to ignore all that the Bible says about warfare with Satan and his angels, and in consequence they spend their lives in spiritual defeat, producing much less for the Kingdom than they could and should. They do not even do the same things that Jesus did, much less the greater things (John 14:12). Those who use the idea of cessationism in an attempt to explain and justify their lack of spiritual power are being foolish, if not worse. Anyone who has embraced the notion of 'cessationism' did not consult the Holy Spirit before doing so.

Prosperity gospel: While there may be variations on the theme, the basic 'pitch' is to the hearer's selfish interests, while any serious commitment to Christ and His Kingdom is severely ignored. The emphasis is upon blessings, not the Blessor, but the blessings are not free; to get them one must contribute heavily to the purveyors thereof. But Sovereign Jesus gave the definitive answer to this stupidity (or should it be 'perversity') in Matthew 6:24—"No one can serve two masters; for either he will hate the one and love the other, or else he will be loyal to the one and despise the other. You cannot serve God and mammon." 'Mammon' is sometimes translated as 'money', but it probably includes more than that, although money is central to it—a materialistic worldview. As Jesus said, someone serving mammon cannot be serving God at the same time. Anyone who wants to go to heaven must reject mammon. Anyone who has embraced any form of the prosperity 'gospel' did not consult the Holy Spirit before doing so.

The reader may well have tired of the refrain, "did not consult the Holy Spirit", but of course there is more to the story than that. Recall what Sovereign Jesus said to the Sadducees, "You are deceived, not knowing the Scripture nor the power of God" (Matthew 22:29). To be ignorant of both the Scripture and the power of God is to be spiritually bankrupt. Anyone who has embraced any of the falsehoods discussed above did not study the Scriptures sufficiently before doing so.

There are many, many more false things being taught in our churches,[1] but I consider that the short list discussed above is sufficient for my present purpose. **If all Christians were to throw off all of the eight cherished falsehoods discussed above, the world would see an outpouring of God's power unprecedented in human history.**[2] I am well aware that one painful consequence of taking Revelation 22:15 seriously is to consider the fate of people we loved and respected who passed on while embracing one or more of the falsehoods discussed above. That is a question that is in God's capable hands. For ourselves, 2 Corinthians 10:12 comes to mind: "But they, measuring themselves by themselves, and comparing themselves among themselves, are not wise." We had best base what we are and do on God's Text.

I now move on to a topic that has received very little attention, so far as I know. It underscores the importance of promoting the love of the Truth.

Sins that lead to death

Consider 1 John 5:16-17—"If anyone should see his brother sinning a sin not leading to death, let him ask, and He will give him life for those who do not sin unto death. There is sin leading to death; I am not saying that he should make

---

[1] All false teaching has a certain destiny; as Sovereign Jesus said in Matthew 15:13, "Every plant that my heavenly Father did not plant will be uprooted."

[2] The outpouring in Moses' time was limited to a small area, as was the outpouring in Jesus' time. Today there are Christians all around the world.

request about that.[1] 17 All unrighteousness is sin, and there is sin not leading to death." It should be obvious that John is not contradicting Romans 6:23—"The wages of sin is death, but the gracious gift of God is eternal life in Christ Jesus our Lord." Obvious, because the shed blood of God's Lamb delivers the true believer from that death (the spiritual part). Anyone who dies outside of Christ is condemned by his sin.

But notice that John is talking about Christians; "If anyone should see his **brother** . . ." John is saying that for <u>believers</u> there are sins that lead to death and others that do not. A necessary question presents itself; is he talking about a premature physical death (everyone dies sooner or later), or is it spiritual death? John clearly says that a sin leading to death is irreversible, there is no point in praying about it, God will not grant life. A premature physical death is not all that serious if the person still goes to heaven. I think of two possible candidates:

1) God sometimes kills those who participate in the 'Lord's Table' in an unworthy manner (1 Corinthians 11:29-30). The use of the verb 'sleep' indicates that they do not lose their salvation; I believe it is reserved for the death of believers.

2) Acting in an irresponsible manner (presumptuously) with the intent of obliging God to work a miracle to save you. Satan tried to get Jesus to do this, but did not succeed (Matthew 4:5-7). People who attempt this generally die prematurely.

That said, however, I rather doubt that John was writing about physical death. Consider what is said in Hebrews 10:26-31.

> "Because, if we deliberately keep on sinning after having received the real knowledge of the Truth, there no longer remains a sacrifice for sins, 27 just a certain

---

[1] I suppose that a request about a sin leading to death simply will not be granted. In that case it does no harm to take a chance, in the hope that you can still make a difference. We ignore this area of truth to our peril.

fearful anticipation of judgment and fierce fire that is ready to consume the hostiles. 28 Anyone who rejected Moses' law died without mercy on the testimony of two or three witnesses. 29 Of how much worse punishment, do you suppose, will he be deemed worthy who has trampled the Son of God under foot, who has regarded as unholy the blood of the covenant by which he was sanctified, and who has insulted the Spirit of grace? 30 For we know Him who said, '"Vengeance is up to me", says the Lord, "I will repay".' And again, 'The LORD will judge His people.' 31 It is a dreadful thing to fall into the hands of the Living God!"

Notice that verse 28 refers to a premature physical death, so the "how much worse punishment" in the next verse must refer to spiritual death. Notice further that from verses 19-25 (same chapter) it is clear that the author is addressing believers. This is confirmed by verse 26: "there no longer remains a sacrifice for sins" can only apply to someone who has already taken advantage of Christ's sacrifice. Notice also the 'after having received the real knowledge of the Truth' and 'by which he was sanctified' (verses 26 and 29).

I will now discuss some possible candidates for sin that condemns a Christian to spiritual death, that causes irreversible spiritual ruin.

1) Matthew 10:33 falls within the instructions that Jesus gave to the twelve apostles before He sent them out two by two: "Whoever denies me before men, him I will also deny before my Father who is in heaven". One possible reference is to a Christian who caves under persecution. Revelation 21:8 consigns 'the cowardly' to the Lake. A Christian who becomes a Mason (Freemason) is clearly condemned. During the initiation ritual the candidate is asked, "Where are you coming from?" and he must answer, "I am coming from darkness". Then he is asked, "What are you coming for?" and he must answer, "I am coming for light". At that moment the candidate has formally denied Jesus before men. Surely, because in John 8:12 Jesus affirmed: "I am the light of the world. He who

follows me shall not walk in darkness, but have the light of life." Further, such people generally do so for material gain, thereby switching from Jesus to mammon (Mathew 6:24).

2) Hebrews 10:29 refers to someone "who has trampled the Son of God under foot", evidently referring to a virulent rejection by someone who was once a Christian (sanctified). I can think of several modern day examples. Some years ago there was a very successful Canadian evangelist named Charles Templeton. His evangelistic campaigns filled football stadiums; many thousands of people responded to his invitations; at least one hundred Canadian foreign missionaries received their call under his ministry. But then someone convinced him that he needed more 'culture', more 'sophistication', and he went to a liberal theological seminary in the USA to get it. When he returned he was blaspheming God and cursing Jesus Christ; as a television host his favorite sport was to ridicule the Christian faith. Years later he told someone that he "missed Jesus", which indicates that he knew that he could not return (Hebrews 6:6).

3) And how about blasphemy against the Holy Spirit? Mark 3:30 defines it as ascribing to Satan something done by the Holy Spirit. Is it impossible for a Christian to do this? Have you never heard someone roundly condemn all things charismatic as being from Satan? I would suggest that to be careless on this point is not to be recommended—better safe than sorry.

Sins for which we may pray

Now then, having said all of that, what might be some sins about which we may, and should, pray? Well, how about the embracing of any one of the lies that I discussed above? If we can get a brother to abandon such a lie, we will be doing him a tremendous favor. I may not enjoy hearing a doctor tell me I have a life-threatening condition, but if I allow him to save me from a premature death, I will end up thanking him. Similarly, a brother probably will not appreciate being told that he has embraced a lie, but if he will stop and think, and change, he will end up thanking us. If we wish to save a brother from Revelation 22:15, it is a risk that we must take.

And then there is Hebrews 3:12-13. "Take care, brothers, that there not be a malignant heart of unbelief in any of you, so as to go away from[1] the living God; 13 rather, exhort yourselves every day, while it is called 'today', so that none of you be hardened through sin's deceitfulness." I rendered "exhort yourselves" because the pronoun here is reflexive, not reciprocal, but being plural it probably includes both ideas—each one should exhort himself, but we should also exhort each other. If we are attentive and vigilant, there will be no end of things to pray about, things where we can still make a difference.

All of this relates to the purpose of this article in the following way. To promote truth it is necessary to expose and combat falsehood. The obvious place to start with our promoting is with individual believers, and the more so if they are leaders and teachers within their communities. Although they may reject us and our 'impertinence', Ezekiel 3:20-21 bears directly on this question.

> "Again, when a righteous man turns from his righteousness and commits iniquity, and I lay a stumbling block before him, he shall die; because you did not give him warning, he shall die in his sin, and his righteousness which he has done shall not be remembered; but his blood I will require at your hand. 21 Nevertheless if you warn the righteous man that the righteous should not sin, and he does not sin, he shall surely live because he took warning; also you will have delivered your soul."

When we see a brother going in the wrong direction, it is incumbent upon us to warn him, even if he rejects us. Notice again, "his righteousness which he has done shall not be remembered"—how terrible! Allow me to insist that the question before us is not merely theoretical or 'pedantic'; it is terribly practical, it is of the essence. In the words of

---

[1] Notice the direction. The term 'malignant' implies satanic influence.

Deuteronomy 32:47, "It is not a vain thing for you, because it is your life." It is certainly life for each one of us individually, but it is also life for the churches, and then it will be life for the world.

Conclusion

In conclusion, I will review the 'building blocks' that make up the article.

1) Why did I use 1 Peter 4:17? There was a time when I thought that I could not ask God to judge the world because He had not yet judged the Church. But I was mistaken. God has always judged both His 'house' and the world. More to the point, the world is in the mess that it is because of failure in the Church. Further, judging is one thing, but correcting is another, and the correcting of the culture begins with, and depends on, the correcting of the churches. To correct a group of people begins with getting them to see where they are wrong, which involves denouncing error and showing a way out.

2) Why did I use Matthew 23:8-12 and John 4:23-24? I tried to trace a basic cause of failure in the Church—a correct solution depends upon a correct diagnosis. The Church became part of the problem, rather than being part of the solution, and it became part of the problem by rejecting the love of the Truth. The concept of 'bishop' (and in our day even of lowly pastors) as someone having the authority to control the spiritual life of others is an open rebellion against Sovereign Jesus, who forbids any such attitude or proceeding. But rebellion against God is Satan's 'thing', and will certainly call down God's judgment.

3) Why did I use 2 Thessalonians 2:9-12? This text gives the essence of the problem and the essence of the solution. The consequences of rejecting the love of the Truth are devastating, both to the Church and to the world. It is God Himself who sends the "active delusion"![1] And upon whom

---

[1] I understand 'active' in the sense of 'aggressive'; it is not a passive delusion that lies quietly in your brain, allowing you to go your merry way. It

does He send it? Upon those who do not receive the love of the truth—it is a direct judgment upon their rejection of the truth.[1] And what is the purpose of the strong delusion?—the condemnation of those who do not believe the truth. The only solution that I can see is to promote the love of the Truth, which necessarily involves denouncing error.

4) Why did I use Revelation 22:15? This text states plainly the terrible consequence of embracing a lie. To promote love of the Truth it is necessary to expose lies, and this is a necessary part of correcting the churches so they can be salt and light in the surrounding culture. A correct solution depends upon a correct diagnosis. Although they may reject us and our 'impertinence', Ezekiel 3:20-21 bears directly on this question. When we see a brother going in the wrong direction, it is incumbent upon us to warn him, even if he rejects us. Notice again, "his righteousness which he has done shall not be remembered"—how terrible!

5) Why did I use 1 John 5:16-17? This text emphasizes the possible terrible end result of being flippant about sin and the Truth. Anyone who is flippant about sin does not have the mind of Christ. We ignore to our peril the instruction given in Hebrews 3:12-13. And then there is 1 Corinthians 9:27—the Greek term *adokimos* is stronger than some commentaries would have you believe.

The future of the Church and of the world depends on the love of the Truth.

---

is aggressive; it tries to control how you think, and therefore what you do and who you are.

[1] Please note that it is not enough to merely 'accept' the truth; it is required that we <u>love</u> the truth. Satan tantalizes us with fame and fortune (on his terms, of course), so to love the truth requires determination; since the love in question is agaph, it involves an act of the will.

The Root Cause of the Continuous Defection from Biblical Infallibility and Consequent Objective Authority

That part of the academic world that deals with the biblical Text, including those who call themselves 'evangelical', is dominated by the notion that the original wording is lost, in the sense that no one knows for sure what it is, or was (if indeed it ever existed as an Autograph).[1] That notion is basic to all that is taught in the area of New Testament (NT) textual criticism in most schools. In an attempt to understand where that notion came from, I will sketch a bit of relevant history.

A Bit of Relevant History

The discipline of NT textual criticism, as we know it, is basically a 'child' of Western Europe and its colonies; the Eastern Orthodox Churches have generally not been involved. (They have always known that the true NT Text lies within the Byzantine tradition.) In the year 1500 the Christianity of Western Europe was dominated by the Roman Catholic Church, whose pope claimed the exclusive right to interpret Scripture. That Scripture was the Latin Vulgate, which the laity was not allowed to read. Martin Luther's ninety-five theses were posted in 1517. Was it mere chance that the first printed Greek Text of the NT was published the year before? As the Protestant Reformation advanced, it was declared that the authority of Scripture exceeded that of the pope, and that every believer had the right to read and in-

---

[1] There are those who like to argue that none of the books was written by its stated author, that they are forgeries, the result of editorial activity spread over decades (if not centuries) of time. Of course they were not there, and do not know what actually happened, but that does not deter them from pontificating.

terpret the Scriptures for himself. The authority of the Latin Vulgate was also challenged, since the NT was written in Greek. Of course the Vatican library held many Greek MSS, no two of which were identical (at least in the Gospels), so the Roman Church challenged the authenticity of the Greek Text.[1] In short, the Roman Church forced the Reformation to come to grips with textual variation among the Greek MSS. But they did not know how to go about it, because this was a new field of study and they simply were not in possession of a sufficient proportion of the relevant evidence.[2] (They probably didn't even know that the Mt. Athos peninsula, with its twenty monasteries, existed.)

In 1500 the Roman Catholic Establishment was corrupt, morally bankrupt, and discredited among thinking people. The Age of Reason and humanism were coming to the fore. More and more people were deciding that they could do better without the god of the Roman Establishment. The new imagined freedom from supernatural supervision was intoxicating, and many had no interest in accepting the authority of Scripture (*sola Scriptura*). Further, it would be naive in the extreme to exclude the supernatural from consideration, and not allow for satanic activity behind the scenes. Consider Ephesians 2:2—"in which you once walked, according to the Aeon of this world, the ruler of the domain of the air, the spirit who is now at work in the sons of the disobedience." Strictly speaking, the Text has "according to the Aeon of this world, according to the ruler of the domain of the air"—the phrases are parallel, so 'Aeon' and 'ruler' have the same referent, a specific person or be-

---

[1] Probably no two MSS of the Latin Vulgate are identical either, but that was not the issue. Indeed, so far as I know, there is no way to establish what may have been the original wording of the Latin Vulgate, in every detail.

[2] Family 35 (for an introduction to this family please see chapter seven of my *Identity IV*), being by far the largest and most cohesive group of MSS with a demonstrable archetype, was poorly represented in the libraries of Western Europe. For that matter, very few MSS of whatever text-type had been sufficiently collated to allow for any tracing of the transmissional history. Worse, the lack of complete collations made it impossible to refute an erroneous hypothesis within a reasonable time frame.

ing. This spirit is presently at work (present tense) in 'the sons of the disobedience'. 'Sons' of something are those characterized by that something, and the something in this case is 'the' disobedience (the Text has the definite article)—a continuation of the original rebellion against the Sovereign of the universe.[1] 'Sons of the disobedience' joined the attack against Scripture. The so-called 'higher criticism' denied divine inspiration altogether.[2] Others used the textual variation to argue that in any case the original wording was 'lost', there being no objective way to determine what it may have been (unfortunately, no one was able to perceive such a way at that time).

The uncritical assumption that 'oldest equals best' was an important factor, and became increasingly so as earlier uncials came to light.[3] Both Codex Vaticanus and Codex Bezae were available early on, and they have thousands of disagreements between themselves, just in the Gospels (in Acts, Bezae is wild almost beyond belief). **If** 'oldest equals best', and the oldest MSS are in constant and massive disagreement between/among themselves, then the recovery of a lost text becomes hopeless. Did you get that? **Hopeless, totally hopeless**! However, I have argued (and continue to do so) that 'oldest equals <u>worst</u>', and that changes the picture radically. The benchmark work on this subject is Her-

---

[1] Anyone in rebellion against the Creator is under satanic influence, direct or indirect (in most cases a demon acts as Satan's agent, when something more than the influence of the surrounding culture is required—almost all human cultures have ingredients of satanic provenance; this includes the academic culture). Anyone in rebellion against the Creator will also have strongholds of Satan in his mind. Since Satan is the 'father' of lies (John 8:44), anytime you embrace a lie you invite him into your mind—this applies to any of his sophistries (2 Corinthians 10:5) currently in vogue, such as materialism, humanism, relativism, Marxism, Freudianism, Hortianism, etc.

[2] The Darwinian theory appeared to be made to order for those who wished to get rid of a Creator, or any superior Authority, who might require an accounting. The 'higher criticism' served the purpose of getting rid of an authoritative Revelation, that might be used to require an accounting. Rebels don't like to be held accountable.

[3] Appeal was made to the analogy of a stream, where the purest water would presumably be that closest to the source. But with reference to NT manuscripts the analogy is fallacious, and becomes a sophistry.

man C. Hoskier's *Codex B and its Allies: A Study and an Indictment* (2 vols.; London: Bernard Quaritch, 1914). The first volume (some 500 pages) contains a detailed and careful discussion of hundreds of obvious errors in Codex B; the second (some 400 pages) contains the same for Codex Aleph. He affirms that in the Gospels alone these two MSS differ well over 3,000 times, which number does not include minor errors such as spelling (II, 1). [Had he tabulated all differences, the total would doubtless increase by several hundreds.] Well now, simple logic demands that one or the other has to be wrong those 3,000+ times; they cannot both be right, quite apart from the times when they are both wrong. **No amount of subjective preference can obscure the fact that they are poor copies, objectively so.**[1] They were so bad that no one could stand to use them, and so they survived physically (but had no 'children', since no one wanted to copy them).

Since everyone is influenced (not necessarily controlled) by his milieu, this was also true of the Reformers. In part (at least) the Reformation was a 'child' of the Renaissance, with its emphasis on reason. Recall that on trial Luther said he could only recant if convinced by Scripture and reason. So far so good, but many did not want Scripture, and that left only reason. Further, since reason cannot explain or deal

---

[1] John William Burgon personally collated what in his day were 'the five old uncials' (ℵ,A,B,C,D). Throughout his works he repeatedly calls attention to the *concordia discors*, the prevailing confusion and disagreement, that the early uncials display among themselves. Luke 11:2-4 offers one example.

"The five Old Uncials" (ℵABCD) falsify the Lord's Prayer as given by St. Luke in no less than forty-five words. But so little do they agree among themselves, that they throw themselves into six different combinations in their departures from the Traditional Text; and yet they are never able to agree among themselves as to one single various reading: while only once are more than two of them observed to stand together, and their grand point of union is no less than an omission of the article. Such is their eccentric tendency, that in respect of thirty-two out of the whole forty-five words they bear in turn solitary evidence. (*The Traditional Text of the Holy Gospels Vindicated and Established*. Arranged, completed, and edited by Edward Miller. London: George Bell and Sons, 1896, p. 84.)

Yes indeed, oldest equals worst. For more on this subject, please see pages 130-36 in *The Identity of the New Testament Text IV*.

with the supernatural, those who emphasize reason are generally unfriendly toward the supernatural. [To this day the so-called historic or traditional Protestant denominations have trouble dealing with the supernatural.]

Before Adolf Deissmann published his *Light from the Ancient East* (1910), (being a translation of *Licht vom Osten*, 1908), wherein he demonstrated that Koine Greek was the *lingua franca* in Jesus' day, there even being a published grammar explaining its rules, only classical Greek was taught in the universities. But the NT was written in Koine. Before Deissmann's benchmark work, there were two positions on the NT Greek: 1) it was a debased form of classical Greek, or 2) it was a 'Holy Ghost' Greek, invented for the NT. The second option was held mainly by pietists; the academic world preferred the first, which raised the natural question: if God were going to inspire a NT, why would He not do it in 'decent' Greek? The prevailing idea that Koine was bad Greek predisposed many against the NT.

All of this placed the defenders of an inspired Greek Bible on the defensive, with the very real problem of deciding where best to set up a perimeter they could defend. Given the prevailing ignorance concerning the relevant evidence, their best choice appeared to be an appeal to Divine Providence. God providentially chose the TR, so that was the text to be used (the 'traditional' text).[1] I would say that Divine Providence was indeed at work, because the TR is a good Text, far better than the eclectic one currently in vogue.

To all appearances Satan was winning the day, but he still had a problem: the main Protestant versions (in German, English, Spanish, etc.) were all based on the *Textus Receptus*, as were doctrinal statements and 'prayer books'. Enter F.J.A. Hort, a quintessential 'son of the disobedience'. Hort did not believe in the divine inspiration of the Bible, nor in the divinity of Jesus Christ. Since he embraced the Darwinian theory as soon as it appeared, he presumably did not

---

[1] Please note that I am not criticizing Burgon and others; they did what they could, given the information available to them. They knew that the Hortian theory and resultant Greek text could not be right.

believe in God.[1] His theory of NT textual criticism, published in 1881,[2] was based squarely on the presuppositions that the NT was not inspired, that no special care was afforded it in the early decades, and that in consequence the original wording was lost—lost beyond recovery, at least by objective means. His theory swept the academic world and continues to dominate the discipline to this day.[3]

But just how was it that the Hortian theory was able to take over the Greek departments of the conservative schools in North America? The answer begins with the onslaught of liberal theology upon the Protestant churches of that continent at the beginning of the twentieth century. The great champion of the divine inspiration of Scripture was Benjamin B. Warfield, a Presbyterian. His defense of inspiration is

---

[1] For documentation of all this, and a good deal more besides, in Hort's own words, please see the biography written by his son. A.F. Hort, *Life and Letters of Fenton John Anthony Hort* (2 vols.; London: Macmillan and Co. Ltd., 1896). The son made heavy use of the father's plentiful correspondence, whom he admired. (In those days a two-volume 'Life', as opposed to a one-volume 'Biography', was a posthumous status symbol, albeit of little consequence to the departed.) Many of my readers were taught, as was I, that one must not question/judge someone else's motives. But wait just a minute; where did such an idea come from? It certainly did not come from God, who expects the spiritual person to evaluate everything (1 Corinthians 2:15). Since there are only two spiritual kingdoms in this world (Matthew 6:24, 12:30; Luke 11:23, 16:13), then the idea comes from the other side. By eliminating motive, one also eliminates presupposition, which is something that God would never do, since presupposition governs interpretation (Matthew 22:29, Mark 12:24). Which is why we should always expect a true scholar to state his presuppositions. I have repeatedly stated mine, but here they are again: 1) The Sovereign Creator of the universe exists; 2) He delivered a written revelation to the human race; 3) He has preserved that revelation intact to this day.

[2] B.F. Westcott and F.J.A. Hort, *The New Testament in the Original Greek* (2 Vols.; London: Macmillan and Co., 1881). The second volume explains the theory, and is generally understood to be Hort's work.

[3] For a thorough discussion of that theory, please see chapters 3 and 4 in *Identity IV*. Chapters 3 and 4 in *Identity IV* are little different from what they were in 1977. It has been over thirty-five years, and so far as I know no one has refuted my dismantling of Hort's theory. It has not been for lack of desire. Nowadays one frequently hears the argument that to criticize Hort is to flay a dead horse, since now the ruling paradigm is eclecticism (whether 'reasoned' or 'rigorous'). But eclecticism is based squarely on the same false presuppositions, and is therefore equally wrong.

so good that it is difficult to improve it. Somewhere along the line, however, he decided to go to Germany to study; I believe it was at Tubingen. When he returned, he was thanking God for having raised up Westcott and Hort to restore the text of the New Testament (think about the implication of 'restore'). One of his students, Archibald T. Robertson, a Baptist, followed Warfield's lead. The prestige of those two men was so great that their view swept the theological schools of the continent. I solicit the patience of the reader while I try to diagnose what happened to Warfield in Tubingen.

At Tubingen Warfield found himself among enemies of an inspired Bible. Now he was a champion of divine inspiration, but for an inspired text to have objective authority today, it must have been preserved.[1] Given the prevailing ignorance concerning the relevant evidence at that time, Warfield was simply not able to defend preservation in objective terms (and neither was anyone else—this is crucial to understanding what happened). He was faced with the fact of widespread variation between and among the extant Greek manuscripts. Even worse—far worse—was the presupposition that 'oldest equals best', because the oldest manuscripts are hopelessly at odds among themselves. For example: the two great early codices, Vaticanus and Sinaiticus, differ between themselves well over 3,000 times just in the four Gospels. Well now, they cannot both be right; one or the other **has** to be wrong, quite apart from the places where they are both wrong. So what was poor Warfield to do? Enter Westcott and Hort. Hort claimed that as a result of their work only a thousandth part of the NT text could be considered to be in doubt, and this was joyfully received by the rank and file, since it seemed to provide assurance about the reliability of that text—however, of

---

[1] This has always been a favorite argument with enemies of inspiration; it goes like this: "If God had inspired a text, He would have preserved it (or else why bother inspiring). He did not preserve the NT; therefore He did not inspire it." I confess that I am inclined to agree with that logical connection, except that I am prepared to turn the tables. I believe I can demonstrate that God did in fact preserve the NT Text; therefore He must have inspired it!

course, that claim applied only to the W-H text (probably the worst published NT in existence to this day, so the claim was false).[1] Warfield grasped at this like a drowning man grasps at a straw, thereby doing serious damage to North American Evangelicalism.[2]

Why the Defection Is Continuous

To understand the full impact of the onslaught of liberal theology, one must take account of the milieu. Reason has always been important to the historic or traditional Protestant denominations. In consequence, academic respectability has always been important to their graduate schools of theology. The difficulty resides in the following circumstance: for at least two centuries academia has been dominated by Satan, and so the terms of 'respectability' are dictated by him. Those terms include 'publish or perish', but of course he controls the technical journals. Since he is the father of lies (John 8:44), anyone who wished to tell the whole truth has always had a hard time getting an article published, no matter how good it was. To get an article published one had to toe the party line. 'Taking account of the existing literature' obliges one to waste a great deal of

---

[1] I would say that their text is mistaken with reference to 10% of the words—the Greek NT has roughly 140,000 words, so the W-H text is mistaken with reference to 14,000 of them. I would say that the so-called 'critical' (read 'eclectic') text currently in vogue is 'only' off with reference to some 12,000, an improvement (small though it be). And just by the way, how wise is it to use a NT prepared by a servant (or servants) of Satan? (On the other hand, I claim that God has preserved the original wording to such an extent that we can, and do, know what it is.)

[2] However, I should not be unduly harsh in my criticism of Warfield; no one else knew what to do either. The cruel fact was that the relevant evidence did not exist in usable form at that time. (It follows that any defense of divine preservation at that time had to be based upon faith, faith that God would produce the evidence in His time.) Part of the damage produced by Hort's theory was its disdain for the vast bulk of later manuscripts—they were not worth the bother to collate and study. Since it is precisely those disdained MSS that furnish the necessary evidence, that soporific effect of Hort's theory delayed the availability of the relevant evidence for a century. I remember one day in class (in 1957), the professor filled his lungs and proclaimed with gusto, "Gentlemen, where B and Aleph agree, you have the original." The poor man had obviously never read Herman C. Hoskier's *Codex B and its Allies: A Study and an Indictment* (published in 1914).

time reading the nonsense produced by Satan's servants, all of which was designed to keep the reader away from the truth.

The TRUTH—aye, there's the rub. Consider 2 Thessalonians 2:9-12: "The coming of the *lawless one* is according to the working of Satan, with all power, signs, and lying wonders, 10 and with all unrighteous deception among those who perish, because they did not receive the love of the truth, that they might be saved. 11 And for this reason God will send them strong delusion, that they should believe the lie, 12 that they all may be condemned who did not believe the truth, but had pleasure in unrighteousness" (NKJV). Although verse ten is in the context of the activity of the Antichrist, who will find an easy target in 'those who are wasting themselves' (my translation), it does not follow that no one will be wasting himself before that activity. Obviously, people have been wasting themselves all down through history, and the underlying cause for that 'wasting' has never changed—"they did not receive the love of the truth". (It began in the Garden.)

Please notice carefully what is said here: it is God Himself who sends the strong delusion! And upon whom does He send it? Upon those who do not receive the love of the truth.[1] And what is the purpose of the strong delusion?—the condemnation of those who do not believe the truth. Dear me, this is heavy. Notice that the truth is **central** to anyone's salvation. This raises the necessary question: just what is meant by 'the truth'? In John 14:6 Sovereign Jesus declared Himself to be 'the truth'. Praying to the Father in John 17:17 He said, "Thy Word is truth". Once each in John chapters 14, 15 and 16 He referred to the third person of the Trinity as "the Spirit of the truth". Since the Son is back in Heaven at the Father's right hand, and the Spirit is not very perceptible to most of us, most of the time, and since the Word is the Spirit's sword (Ephesians 6:17), our main

---

[1] Please note that it is not enough to merely 'accept' the truth; it is required that we <u>love</u> the truth. Satan tantalizes us with fame and fortune (on his terms, of course), so to love the truth requires determination.

access to 'the truth' is through God's Word, the Bible. The Bible offers propositional truth, but we need the Holy Spirit to illumine that truth, and to have the Holy Spirit we must be adequately related to Sovereign Jesus.

Now then, for something to be received, it must be offered; one cannot believe in something he has never heard about (Romans 10:14). The use of the verb 'receive' clearly implies an act of volition on the part of those not receiving the truth; that love was offered or made available to them but they did not want it; they wanted to be able to lie and to entertain lies told by others. But the consequences of such a choice are terrible; they turned their back on salvation. I suspect that not many Christians in the so-called 'first world' really believe what Sovereign Jesus said in Matthew 7:14: those who find the way of Life are **few**! And do not forget Revelation 22:15; "whoever loves and practices a lie" is excluded from the heavenly City [any lie, including Hort's].[1] I will here consider the implications for a student entering a graduate school of theology, because of what happens if he becomes a professor, or NT scholar, in his turn.[2]

Most such students presumably come from an evangelical environment, and were doubtless taught that the Bible is God's Word, and therefore inspired. Some may even have been taught verbal, plenary inspiration. However, in most theological schools you cannot get a job as a teacher if you do not agree to use the eclectic Greek text, with all that implies. (Just as you cannot get a teaching job in most uni-

---

[1] Help! "A lie" is rather general, open-ended. What happens if I accepted a lie without realizing that it was one? But the text does not say 'accepts'; it says 'loves' and 'practices'. The implication is that the contrary evidence, to the lie, is available, but has been rejected, or deliberately ignored—the person sold himself to the lie.

[2] At the graduate level, a student has the responsibility to evaluate what is being taught—if it goes contrary to the Text, it should not be accepted. I remember one day in chapel, a visiting scholar was expounding Romans 10:9. He stated that the Greek Text plainly means "Jesus as Lord", but then went on to try to explain why the school didn't believe that. His effort was rather lame; so much so that I determined to delve into the question for myself.

versities unless you at least pretend to believe in evolution.) If the school is at least nominally conservative, they will still say that the Bible is inspired. But if a student brings up the question of the preservation of the text in class, there will be an uncomfortable silence. If it was preserved, no one knows what or where it is. The brainwashing has been so complete that many (most?) seminary graduates do not even know that there is any question about what they were taught. They were taught an eclecticism based on Hort's theory, and for them that is all there is.

But to go back to our student, he finds himself surrounded by professors whose job it is to destroy his faith in an inspired Bible with objective authority. Of course, presumably, very few such professors have ever thought in those terms (so they would object to my statement). They would say that they are just doing their job, doing what they are paid to do, without troubling themselves with the whys and wherefores.[1] But of course the student is not expecting that; he believes that his professors must be men of God, and so he is predisposed to believe them. Besides that predisposition (and it is powerful), what are the tools at their disposal for doing their job? Well, they have ridicule, sarcasm, brainwashing, peer pressure, the 'emperor's new clothes' gambit, and satanic assistance, for starters. (There may also be threats, failing grades, disciplinary actions, foul play, and so on—I write from experience.) Most of the terms above are self-explanatory, but some readers may not be familiar with the ancient myth about the emperor—it boils down to this: you don't want to admit that you can't 'see' it, when everyone else claims to be doing so. But by far the most serious is 'satanic assistance', and here I must needs go into detail.

---

[1] For older, established scholars there is also the matter of pride and vested interest; who wants to admit that he has been wrong all his professional life? Then there is the doctrine of professional ethics, one must respect his colleagues (respect for the colleague trumps respect for the truth). [One must not ask where that doctrine came from.] One other thing: where a school or institution depends on financial help from outside, it will be threatened with the loss of that help, if it does not toe the line, and its very existence may depend on that help.

Returning to 2 Thessalonians 2:10 and the 'love of the truth', as explained above, our main access to 'the truth' is through God's Word, the Bible. Our student may have gone to Sunday school, probably heard sermons with at least some biblical content, and certainly has his own copy of the Bible. In short, he has had, and continues to have, access to 'the truth'. However, the Holy Spirit does 'talk' to us, if we will listen. For example: my father was born in 1906, and in due time went to Moody Bible Institute and Wheaton College. In those days the American Standard Version (ASV) was touted as the best thing since the Garden of Eden; it was 'the rock of biblical integrity', etc. etc. Now my father had the practice of reading through the entire Bible once a year, a practice that he maintained all his life. Due to the hype surrounding the ASV, he got a copy and began to read it. It was hard going from the start, and he soon had to stop—the Holy Spirit simply would not let him go on. He returned to his trusty AV.

I imagine that at least some of my readers will have a question at this point. Am I implying that anyone who embraced the ASV was not listening to the Holy Spirit when he made that decision? The answer is, "Yes". Obviously, the same holds for the Hortian theory, etc. Unfortunately, few students of theology are in the habit of consulting the Holy Spirit, and those who do are marked for persecution. No Establishment can tolerate anyone who listens to the Holy Spirit. Surely, or have you forgotten John 3:8? "The wind blows where it wishes, and you (sg) hear its sound, but you do not know where it comes from or where it goes. So it is with everyone who has been begotten by the Spirit." Notice that the Lord is saying here that it is **we** who are to be unpredictable, like the wind, or the Spirit ("comes" and "goes" are in the present tense). If you are really under the control of the Spirit you will do unexpected things, just like He does.[1] An Establishment is defined by its 'straightjacket',

---

[1] Since Satan is forever muddying the water with excesses and abuses, spiritual discernment is needed.

and the Holy Spirit does not like straightjackets, and vice versa.

In John 8:44 Sovereign Jesus declared that "there is no truth" in Satan, and that he is the father of the lie. Since God cannot lie, Titus 1:2, it being contrary to His essence, any and all lies come from the enemy. So what happens if you embrace a lie? You invite Satan into your mind. And what does he do there? He sets up a stronghold that locks you into that lie; you become blind to the truth on that subject.[1] It is a specific application of the truth expressed in 2 Corinthians 4:4—Satan blinds minds. So what happens to our student? With very few exceptions, he succumbs to the pressure exerted by the tools already mentioned. He accepts the party line, and since it is a lie, Satan goes about blinding him to the truth. If he goes on to become an influential scholar, he will almost certainly come under demonic surveillance (since Satan is not omnipresent).

There is a common misapprehension that trips people up at this point. Since any genuinely regenerated person has the indwelling Holy Spirit, how can Satan or a demon be in that person's mind? There is a fundamental difference between presence and control. Very few Christians have consciously turned over every area of their lives to the control of the Holy Spirit. The Holy Spirit is a gentleman, he will not take over an area against your will (see John 4:23-24). Any areas not under the Spirit's control are open to the enemy's interference, and most especially if you embrace a lie. By embracing a lie you grieve the Holy Spirit; not wise (Ephesians 4:30). You also resist Him; also not wise (Acts 7:51). So why does God not protect you? Because you rejected the love of the truth, and that turned God against you! When God turns against you, what are your chances? Without God's protection, you become Satan's prey (1 Peter 5:8).[2]

---

[1] On that one subject—you will not necessarily be blinded on other subjects, or at least not at first.

[2] Please keep in mind the sequence of cause and effect—it begins with the rejection of the love of the truth. It is not enough to merely 'accept' the truth, one must love it. For those who have embraced a lie, the only

Anyone in rebellion against the Creator is under satanic influence, direct or indirect (in most cases a demon acts as Satan's agent, when something more than the influence of the surrounding culture is required—almost all human cultures have ingredients of satanic provenance; this includes the academic culture). Anyone in rebellion against the Creator will also have strongholds of Satan in his mind. Since Satan is the 'father' of lies (John 8:44), anytime you embrace a lie you invite him into your mind—this applies to any of his sophistries (2 Corinthians 10:5) currently in vogue, such as materialism, humanism, relativism, Marxism, Freudianism, Hortianism, etc.

The selling of the lie is carried on from generation to generation, resulting in a continuous defection. Most professors are 'parrots', simply repeating what they were taught, without ever going back to check the facts. Some older scholars may have become aware of the facts, but because of vested interest they do not mention them to their students; they maintain the party line.

Is there a Way to Stop the Defection?

I believe there is, and it must begin with the TRUTH. To be more precise, it must begin with the love of the truth, which necessitates that the truth be made available. We must promote the love of the truth, and to do that we must also denounce the lie.[1] To promote something, we need vehicles for doing so. To succeed, we must be convincing. Most important, we must do something about the interference in people's minds.

1) Vehicles for promoting the truth:

It is modern technology that comes to our aid here. Blogs are being used to promote anything and everything. We can use them to promote the truth. I have done a fifteen-hour

---

'medicine' is to return to the love of the truth, rejecting the lie. God may require a public renunciation of the lie.

[1] My own denunciation of the Hortian lie has been in print since 1977, and I continue to stand by every bit of it.

lecture series (in Portuguese) on the divine preservation of the NT Text. It was filmed and is available on the net via blog. Websites are being used. Most of my work is available from walkinhiscommandments.com, and even more is available from my own prunch.org. I wish to call special attention to The Center for Study and Preservation of the Majority Text. Their site, cspmt.org, is receiving literally thousands of visits a day, and from dozens of countries around the world. And then there is Twitter, Facebook and so on—the fact is that the technical journals no longer have a stranglehold on any discipline; there are other ways of 'publishing' your ideas. And there has always been word-of-mouth, people telling their friends and acquaintances. I suspect that we may soon see a groundswell of this sort of thing.

The advent of self-publishing represents a real boon to those of us who reject a party line, and do not have the financial means to use an established publishing house. For various reasons it has become increasingly difficult to use a publisher. The contracts place all the onus on the author (including the cost of lawsuits). One must cover the cost of several thousand copies up front, and even so, only if the publisher decides he can make a profit on the book, not to mention an 'acceptable' content (publishers are not charitable institutions). It is the advent of 'print-on-demand' that saves those of us who have no money—copies are produced only as they are ordered. Since a machine does it all, one can order a single copy at the going price, and receive it.

Permit me to cite my own experience. My first book, *The Identity of the New Testament Text*, was published in 1977 by Thomas Nelson Publishers. Each time they wished to do another printing, they graciously allowed me to do some revising. Their final (4th?) printing came out in 1990, so they kept the book in print for at least fifteen years, for which I give them my sincere thanks.[1] It had been out of

---

[1] By then there were well over 10,000 copies is use around the world, quietly making a difference in people's lives. Every now and again I hear from someone, thanking me for the book, including some Greek profes-

print for some years when Wipf and Stock Publishers asked for permission to publish it as an academic reprint. So a revised edition came out in 2003, as *The Identity of the New Testament Text II*. Wipf & Stock also did *Identity III*, in 2012. It was during that interval that I tuned in to Family 35, so *Identity III* was the first edition to present and defend that family. The current *Identity IV*, with further heavy revision, I self-published with Amazon. My other books are also available there—what established publisher would have accepted *The Greek New Testament According to Family 35*?

Self-publishing also permits one to make a book available in electronic form, as I have done with mine. This allows people to download into their notebooks, or whatever, so they don't have to carry a book (or several). This is becoming increasingly important, as more and more people are joining the smart-phone culture. That said, however, we should not despise the good old hard copy; for serious study many still prefer a book (you can make notes in a book). In short, we should use both, electronic and printed.

Especially in cultures where 'who you know' is more important than 'what you know', but also in others, we should promote the 'social' vehicle, the sharing with friends and acquaintances. We can invite people over for a cup of coffee (or tea), spread the word wherever we have contacts.

2) A convincing presentation:

What is the best way to protect a caged lion? Just open the cage! What is the best way to promote the Truth? Just turn it loose! As Sovereign Jesus said in John 8:31-32, "If you abide in my word, you are my disciples indeed. And you shall know the truth, and the truth shall make you free" (NKJV). The truth will make us free from what? In the immediate context (verse 34), it is from sin, but with refer-

---

sors. Such professors are no longer destroying the faith of their students. There is a stirring at the grassroots level, that the Establishment is doing its best to ignore. When obliged to take notice, it is 'pooh-pooh'; but the time is coming, indeed now is, when that will no longer work.

ence to the topic in hand, it is able to free us from Satan's blinding and his lies. The Word is the Holy Spirit's sword, and a sword cuts, whether someone believes it or not. That said, however, what can we do so that people will listen to us?

Bombast and ranting should be avoided. They may appeal to the emotions of those who are already on our side, but they will have a negative effect on those we are trying to reach. The truth is best served by the facts, the evidence. And the evidence should be presented in a straightforward fashion, without undue appeal to emotion. However, emotion must be distinguished from presupposition (as well as from principles of reasoned debate). It is impossible to work without presuppositions; everyone has them. It follows that if someone criticizes me for having presuppositions, while pretending that he has none, that someone is being dishonest and perverse (or perhaps just brainwashed and blinded).

Ever since Burgon, who stated his presuppositions honestly and openly (as any true scholar should), there has been a constant and insistent attack against those presuppositions, and even the stating of them. A psychosis has been created to the extent that even some modern defenders of the majority text have become paranoid on the subject; they have actually reached the point of excluding the supernatural from their model. However, in Luke 11:23 the Sovereign Creator, Jehovah the Son incarnate, declares: "He who is not with Me is against Me, and he who does not gather with Me scatters." Here is a plain statement—there are only two teams in this world; there are only two sides, two kingdoms; there is no neutral ground; there is no true agnosticism.[1] If you are not with Jesus, you are automatically against Him; if you are not gathering with Him, you are automatically scattering. If you do not receive Jesus' affirmations about Scripture, you have rejected them. Neutrality does not exist.

---

[1] Agnosticism is a passive rejection; the agnostic is not accepting the claim.

But how can we reach those who pretend that they have no presuppositions, who refuse, or in any case fail, to declare their presuppositions openly? If those same people criticize us for declaring ours, we may question their basic honesty; but how can we get them to listen? How can you get a blind person to see? How can you get a deaf person to hear? Something must be done about the cause of the condition. The 'cause of the condition' in the area we are discussing is the satanic interference in their thought processes that the Text, 2 Corinthians 4:4, calls 'blinding' (the brainwashing is a consequence of, and an accessory to, that blinding). Just how to address that cause will be treated in the next section. In the meantime, it is necessary to discuss the question of presupposition, but we should attempt to do so with a calm and irenic spirit.[1]

But to return to the matter of presenting the evidence in a convincing fashion, we must keep in mind that brainwashed people are generally ignorant of the evidence. Most professors are 'parrots', simply repeating what they were taught, without ever going back to check the facts. Some older scholars may have become aware of the facts, but because of vested interest they do not mention them to their students; they maintain the party line. For the truth to set people free, the truth must be presented. So I repeat: we must present the evidence in a straightforward manner.

The primary evidence is furnished by the continuous text manuscripts (Greek) of the NT. The evidence furnished by the lectionaries is secondary. The evidence furnished by ancient versions and patristic citations is tertiary. Genuine historical evidence (to the extent that this can be determined) is ancillary. Where the primary evidence is unequivocal, the remaining types should not come into play. For example, at any given point in the four Gospels there will be around 1,700 extant continuous text MSS, representing all

---

[1] I am well aware that it is not easy, which is why I use 'attempt'.

lines of transmission and all locales.[1] Where they all agree, there can be no legitimate doubt as to the original wording.

It should also be evident that a variant in a single MS, of whatever age, is irrelevant—it is a false witness to its family archetype, at that point, nothing more. If a number of MSS share a variant, but do not belong to the same family, then they made the mistake independently and are false witnesses to their respective family archetypes—there is no dependency. Where a group of MSS evidently reflect correctly the archetypal form of their family, then we are dealing with a family (not the individual MSS). Families need to be evaluated just as we evaluate individual MSS. It is possible to assign a credibility quotient to a family, based on objective criteria. But of course, any and all families must first be empirically identified and defined, and such identification depends upon the full collation of MSS.

Although the discipline has (so far) neglected to do its homework (collating MSS), still a massive majority of MSS should be convincing. For example, if a variant enjoys 99% attestation from the primary witnesses, this means that it totally dominates any genealogical 'tree', because it dominated the global transmission of the text. The *INTF Text und Textwert* series, practitioners of the Claremont profile method, H.C. Hoskier, von Soden, Burgon, Scrivener—in short, anyone who has collated any number of MSS—have all demonstrated that the Byzantine bulk of MSS is by no means monolithic. There are any number of streams and rivulets. (Recall that F. Wisse posited thirty-four groups within the Byzantine bulk, with seventy subgroups.) It is clear that there was no 'stuffing the ballot box'; there was no 'papal' decree; there was no recension imposed by ecclesiastical authority. In short, the transmission was predominantly normal.[2]

But to get back to presenting the evidence, we should call attention to the evidence that has been presented down

---

[1] Of course we know that there are many MSS not yet 'extant', not yet identified and catalogued, so the number can only go up.

[2] For a fuller discussion, please see my *Identity IV*, pages 367-69.

through the years: Herman C. Hoskier's *Concerning the Text of the Apocalypse* and *Codex B and its Allies, a Study and an Indictment*; Hermann von Soden's *magnum opus*—in spite of its imperfections, it contains valuable information; S.C.E. Legg's editions of Matthew and Mark; the IGNTP's edition of Luke; Reuben J. Swanson's editions of Matthew through Galatians; Frederik Wisse on Luke; W.F. Wisselink's *Assimilation as a Criterion for the Establishment of the Text*; Tommy Wasserman on Jude; the *Text und Textwert* series from the *INTF*, and even better, their *Editio Critica Maior* series.

Last, but not least, is my own work. My Greek NT is the first to give the archetype of Family 35, and its critical apparatus is the first to offer percentages with the variants, besides including six published editions. The series on f^{35} variants, book by book, gives the detailed result of my collations of representative MSS, usually at least thirty per book. All of this is now freely available on the internet from my site, prunch.org (mostly in English, but also some in Portuguese). The Center for Study and Preservation of the Majority Text (CSPMT) is preparing a critical edition whose apparatus will contain new information about lines of transmission within the Byzantine bulk. We have ways of making evidence available, but how can we get people to look at it? The best, if not the only way, is to use the spiritual authority that Sovereign Jesus has given us.

3) Neutralizing the interference:

On what basis might we neutralize interference? The most fundamental question for human life on this planet is that of authority: who has it, to what degree, and on what terms? As the chief priests said to Jesus, "By what authority are you doing this?" (Luke 20:2). After His death and resurrection Sovereign Jesus said, "All authority in heaven and on earth has been given to me" (Matthew 28:18). So He is perfectly within His rights, clearly competent, to delegate a piece of that authority to us. Consider Luke 10:19: "Take note, I am giving you the authority to trample on snakes and scorpions,[1] and over all the power of the enemy, and nothing at all may harm you." Instead of 'am giving', perhaps 2.5% of the Greek manuscripts, of objectively inferior quality, have 'have given' (as in NIV, NASB, LB, TEV, etc.)—a serious error. Jesus said this perhaps five months before His death and resurrection, addressing the seventy (not just the twelve). The Lord is talking about the future, not the past, a future that includes us!

Consider further John 20:21: Jesus said to them again: "Peace to you! Just as the Father sent me, I also send you." "Just as . . . so also"—Jesus is sending us just like the Father sent Him. So how did They do it? The Father determined and the Son obeyed: "Behold, I have come to do your will, O God" (Hebrews 10:7). And what was that will? To destroy Satan (Hebrews 2:14) and undo his works (1 John 3:8). Since Jesus did indeed defeat Satan (Colossians 2:15, Ephesians 1:20-21, etc.), but then went back to

---

[1] The Lord gives us the authority to "trample snakes and scorpions". Well now, to smash the literal insect, a scorpion, you don't need power from on High, just a slipper (if you are fast, you can do it barefoot). To trample a snake I prefer a boot, but we can kill literal snakes without supernatural help. It becomes obvious that Jesus was referring to something other than reptiles and insects. I understand Mark 16:18 to be referring to the same reality—Jesus declares that certain signs will accompany the believers (the turn of phrase virtually has the effect of commands): they will expel demons, they will speak strange languages, they will remove 'snakes', they will place hands on the sick. ("If they drink . . ." is not a command; it refers to an eventuality.) But what did the Lord Jesus mean by 'snakes'?

In a list of distinct activities Jesus has already referred to demons, so the 'snakes' must be something else. In Matthew 12:34 Jesus called the Pharisees a 'brood of vipers', and in 23:33, 'snakes, brood of vipers'. In John 8:44, after they claimed God as their father, Jesus said, "You are of your father the devil". And 1 John 3:10 makes clear that Satan has many other 'sons' (so also Matthew 13:38-39). In Revelation 20:2 we read: "He seized the dragon, the ancient serpent, who is a slanderer, even Satan, who deceives the whole inhabited earth, and bound him for a thousand years." If Satan is a snake, then his children are also snakes. So then, I take it that our 'snakes' are human beings who have chosen to serve Satan, who have sold themselves to evil. I conclude that the 'snakes' in Luke 10:19 are the same as those in Mark 16:18, but what of the 'scorpions'? Since they also are of the enemy, they may be demons, in which case the term may well include their offspring, the humanoids (for more on this see my article, "In the Days of Noah", available from prunch.org). I am still working on the question of just how the removal is done.

Heaven, what is left for us is the undoing of his works.[1] It seems clear to me that to undo any work we must also undo its consequences (to the extent that that may be possible).

Consider also Ephesians 2:4-6: "But God—being rich in mercy, because of His great love with which He loved us, even when we were dead in our transgressions—made us alive together with Christ (by grace you have been saved) and raised us up together and seated us together in the heavenly realms in Christ Jesus." This is tremendous! Here we have our authority. Christ is now seated at the Father's right, 'far above' the enemy and his hosts. This verse affirms that we who are in Christ are there too! So in Christ we also are far above the enemy and his hosts.[2] Surely, or is that not what is stated in Ephesians 1:16-21?

I really do not stop giving thanks for you, making mention of you in my prayers: that the God of our Lord, Jesus Christ, the Father of glory, may give you the spirit of wisdom and revelation in the real knowledge[3] of Himself, the eyes of your heart having been enlightened, that you may know what is the hope of His[F] calling, and what the riches of the glory of His inheritance in the saints, and what the exceeding greatness of His power into[4] us who are believ-

---

[1] For more on this subject see my article, "Biblical Spiritual Warfare" (available from prunch.org).

[2] We should be consciously operating on that basis, but since few churches teach this, most Christians live in spiritual defeat.

[3] I finally settled on 'real knowledge' as the best way to render επιγνωσις, the heightened form of γνωσις, 'knowledge'. Real knowledge is more than mere intellectual knowledge, or even true theoretical knowledge—it involves experience. The Text goes on to say, "the eyes of your <u>heart</u> having been enlightened". Real knowledge changes your 'heart', who you are.

[4] "Into us"—that is what the Text says. Note that 'believing' is in the present tense. Consider Ephesians 3:20. "Now to Him who is able to do immeasurably more than all we ask or imagine, according to the power that is working in us." Note that "is working" is also in the present tense; having believed yesterday won't hack it, we must believe today. This tremendous power that God pours into us, as we believe, exceeds our powers of imagination. Well now, my personal horizon is limited and defined by my ability to imagine. Anything that I cannot imagine lies outside my horizon, and so obviously I won't ask for it. I sadly confess that I have not yet arrived at a spiritual level where I can unleash this power—I have

ing, according to the demonstration of the extent of His might which He exercised in the Christ when He raised Him[S] from among the dead and seated Him at His[F] right, in the heavenly realms, far above every ruler and authority and power and dominion—even every name that can be named, not only in this age but also in the next.

Now then, "far above every ruler and authority and power and dominion—even every name that can be named, not only in this age but also in the next" must include Satan and his angels. If Christ, seated at the Father's right, is "**far above**" them, and we are in Him, seated at the Father's right, then we too are above all the hosts of the enemy. That is our position and authority for neutralizing interference.

Well and good, but just how are we to go about doing it? Well, at what level should we 'neutralize'? The candidates that suggest themselves are: institutions, teachers, students, church leaders, and lay people. How about working at all levels? Next, what procedures are at our disposal to do the neutralizing? I offer the following: a) forbid any further use of Satan's power, in a specific case; b) claim the undoing of the consequences of the use of that power that there has been (to the extent it may be possible); c) destroy any strongholds of Satan in their minds (including blind spots); d) bind any demons involved and send them to the Abyss, forbidding any further demonic activity; e) take their thoughts captive to the obedience of Christ. In my experience, to be efficient we need to be specific: name the institution; name the person.

But just a minute, I submit for consideration that faith is a basic prerequisite for making use of our position and authority. The theological training I myself received programmed me not to expect supernatural manifestations of

---

yet to make the truth in this verse work for me. But I understand that the truth affirmed here is literal, and I only hope that others will get there before I do (so I can learn from them), if I keep on delaying. The whole point of the exercise (verse 21) is for God to get glory, and to the extent that we do not put His power in us to work we are depriving Him of glory that He could and should have.

power in and through my life and ministry. As a result, I personally find it to be difficult to exercise the kind of faith that the Lord Jesus demands. Consider:

In Matthew 8:5-13 the centurion understood about authority—he gave orders and they were obeyed, promptly and without question.[1] But the Lord Jesus said he had unusually great faith—faith in what? Faith in the Lord's spiritual authority; He could simply give an order and it would happen. Perhaps we should understand this sort of faith as an absolute confidence, without a taint of doubt or fear. In Matthew 21:21 the Lord said, "Assuredly . . . if you have faith and do not doubt" (see Mark 11:23, "does not doubt in his heart") you can (actually "will") shrivel a tree or send a mountain into the sea. See also Hebrews 10:22, "full assurance of faith", 1 Timothy 2:8, "pray . . . without doubting", James 1:6, "ask in faith with no doubting". Mark 5:34 and Matthew 15:28 offer positive examples; while Peter blew it (Matthew 14:31, "why did you doubt?").

If someone gives a commission, they will presumably back it up to the limit of their ability. Since Christ's ability has no limit, His backing has no limit (on His end). In Matthew 28:18 He said, "All authority has been given to me in heaven and on earth." Then comes the commission: "As you go, make disciples . . . teaching them to obey all things that I have commanded you"—the pronoun refers back to the eleven apostles (verse 16). So what commands had Jesus given the Eleven? Among other things, "heal the sick, cleanse the lepers, cast out demons" (in Matthew 10:8 perhaps 94% of the Greek manuscripts do not have "raise the dead"). The Eleven also heard John 20:21. Knowing that we are being backed by the Sovereign of the universe, who has all authority and power, we can and should act with complete confidence.

---

[1] The centurion did not say, "In the authority of Rome . . .", he just said, "Do this; do that." The Lord Jesus did not say, "In the authority of the Father . . .", He just said, "Be clean! Go!" In Luke 10:19 He said, "I give you the authority over all the power of the enemy"—so we have the authority, so it is up to us to speak! Just like Jesus did.

A word of caution is necessary at this point. Consider James 4:7—"Therefore submit to God. Resist the devil and he will flee from you." Note the sequence: we need to verify that we are in submission to God before taking on the devil. Then we should claim our position in Christ at the Father's right hand. Since few Christians have received any remotely adequate level of instruction in the area of biblical spiritual warfare (most have received none), I need to explain the procedures.

a) Forbid any further use of Satan's power:

This procedure is based on Luke 10:19. Sovereign Jesus gives us 'the' authority over all the power of the enemy. Authority controls power, but since we have access to God's limitless power (Ephesians 3:20), we should not give Satan the satisfaction of our using his (and he could easily deceive us into doing things we shouldn't). We should use our authority to forbid the use of Satan's power, with reference to specific situations—in my experience, we must be specific. (I have tried binding Satan once for all until the end of the world, but it doesn't work; presumably because God's plan calls for the enemy's continued activity in this world. We can limit what the enemy does, but not put him completely out of business, or so I deem.) But just how should we go about it?

In the armor described in Ephesians 6 we find "the sword of the Spirit" (verse 17). A sword is a weapon for offense, although it is also used for defense. The Text tells us that this sword is "the ρημα of God"—ρημα, not λογος. It is God's Word <u>spoken</u>, or applied. Really, what good is a sword left in its sheath? However marvelous our Sword may be (Hebrews 4:12), to produce effect it must come out of the scabbard. The Word needs to be spoken, or written—applied in a specific way.

In the Bible we have many examples where people brought the power of God into action by speaking. Our world began with a creative word from God—spoken (Genesis, 1:3, 6, 9, 11, 14, 20, 24, 26; and see Hebrews 11:3). Moses did a lot of speaking. Elijah spoke (1 Kings 17:1, 18:36, 2 Kings

1:10). Elisha spoke (2 Kings 2:14, 21, 24; 4:16, 43; 6:19). Jesus did a great deal of speaking. Ananias spoke (Acts 9:17). Peter spoke (Acts 9:34, 40). Paul spoke (Acts 13:11; 14:3, 10; 16:18; 20:10; 28:8). In short, we need to speak!

b) Claim the undoing of the consequences of the use of that power that there has been:

This procedure is based on 1 John 3:8, allied to Luke 10:19. It should be possible for us to command Satan to use his own power to undo messes he has made, thereby obliging him to acknowledge his defeat (which will not sit well with his pride). The Son of God was manifested for the purpose of "undoing the works of the devil" (1 John 3:8), and it is incumbent upon us to continue His work here in this world (John 20:21). How can you undo a work without undoing its consequences as well? The Father sent the Son to undo Satan's works, and the Lord Jesus Christ is sending us to undo Satan's works. Again, I understand that we must be specific.

c) Destroy any strongholds of Satan in the person's mind:

This procedure is based on 2 Corinthians 10:4 and 1 John 3:8. Since strongholds, and blind spots, in the mind are a work of Satan, and we are here to undo such works, this falls within the area of our competence. It is done by claiming such destruction in so many words, being specific.

d) Bind any demons involved and send them to the Abyss:

This procedure is based on Mark 3:27 and Luke 8:31. "No one can plunder the strong man's goods, invading his house, unless he first binds the strong man—then he may plunder the house" (Mark 3:27). Since the definite article occurs with 'strong man' the first time the phrase occurs, the entity has already been introduced, so the reference is to Satan. Here is a biblical basis for binding Satan, which is now possible because of Christ's victory. If we can bind Satan, evidently we can also bind any of his subordinates.

"And he[1] kept imploring Him that He would not order them to go away into the Abyss" (Luke 8:31).[2] I take it that Jesus did not send them to the Abyss at that time because He had not yet won the victory, and the demons were 'within their rights', under Satan, who was still the god of this world. But the demons were obviously worried! (They knew very well who Jesus was, and what He could do.) I would say that this is one of the 'greater things' (John 14:12) that we may now do—rather, that we should do. As for forbidding any further demonic activity, we have the Lord's example (Mark 9:25), and we are to do what He did (John 14:12).

e) Take their thoughts captive to the obedience of Christ:

This procedure is based on 2 Corinthians 10:5. In the context, the thoughts are of people who are serving Satan (even if unwittingly). (Of course we should always be checking to be sure that we ourselves are operating within 'the mind of Christ', 1 Corinthians 2:15-16.) Now this procedure moves away from simply neutralizing the enemy's interference, since it introduces a positive 'interference', but it is relevant to the issue being discussed here, since it is protection against falling back into the former error. Again we must be specific.

f) Some further texts that may apply: Luke 4:18-21, Psalm 149:5-9, John 14:12.

In Luke 4:18-21 Jesus includes "to set at liberty those who are oppressed" (Isaiah 58:6) as one of the things He was sent to do. Turning to Isaiah 58:6, we find Jehovah stating what kind of 'fast' He would like to see: "To loose the fetters of wickedness [a], to undo the yoke-ropes [b]; to let oppressed ones go free [a], and that you (pl.) break every yoke [b]." As is typical of Hebrew grammar, the two halves are parallel. "To loose the fetters of wickedness" and "to let oppressed ones go free" are parallel. Who placed the "fetters" and who is doing the oppressing? Well, although peo-

---

[1] The boss demon does most of the talking, representing his cohort.

[2] The Text has 'the Abyss', presumably the same one mentioned in Revelation 20:3. The demons knew something that most of us don't.

ple can certainly forge their own bonds through their own wicked lifestyle, I take it that the point here is that wicked beings have placed the fetters on others. "To undo yoke-ropes" and "that ye break every yoke" go together. First we should untie the ropes that bind the yoke to the neck, then we should break the yokes themselves. I gain the clear impression that this text is talking about the activity of Satan's servants, men and angels. Using culture, worldview, legal devices, threats, blackmail, lies, deception and just plain demonizing and witchcraft, they bind individuals, families, ethnic groups, etc., with a variety of fetters and instruments of oppression.

So what does this have to do with our subject? Well, fasting was an important and required component in their worship of God. So this kind of 'fasting' is something that Jehovah overtly wants to see; it is specifically His will. So when we see any work of Satan in someone's life, it is God's will that we undo it. If we know it is God's will, we can proceed with complete confidence. And it is part of our commission (John 20:21).

Notice also Psalms 149:5-9. "Let the saints exult in glory; let them sing for joy in their beds. Let the high praises of God be in their mouth, and a two-edged sword in their hand—to execute vengeance upon the nations and punishments upon the peoples; to bind their kings with chains and their nobles with fetters of iron; to execute upon them the written judgment. This honor is for all His saints." Note that the saints are in their beds, so the activity described in the subsequent verses must take place in the spiritual realm. I assume that the 'kings' and 'nobles' include both men and fallen angels. The activity described is the prerogative of "all His saints"—if you are one of those saints, it is up to you. There are a number of 'written judgments' in the Text: Zechariah 5:2-4, Proverbs 20:10, Isaiah 10:1-2, Romans 1:26-36 and 1 Corinthians 6:9-10, at least.

In John 14:12 the Lord Jesus said: "Most assuredly I say to you, the one believing into me, he too will do the works that I do; in fact he will do greater works than these, because I am going to my Father." "Most assuredly" is actually "amen,

amen"—rendered "verily, verily" in the AV. Only John registers the word as repeated, in the other Gospels it is just "amen". In the contemporary literature we have no example of anyone else using the word in this way. It seems that Jesus coined His own use, and the point seems to be to call attention to an important pronouncement: "Stop and listen!" Often it precedes a formal statement of doctrine or policy, as here.

"The one believing into me, he too will do the works that I do." This is a tremendous statement, and not a little disconcerting. Notice that the Lord said, "will do"; not 'maybe', 'perhaps', 'if you feel like it'; and certainly not 'if the doctrine of your church permits it'! If you believe, you **will do!** The verb 'believe' is in the present tense; if you are believing you will do; it follows that if you are not doing, it is because you are not believing. 2 + 2 = 4. Doing what? "The works that I do." Well, Jesus preached the Gospel, He taught, He cast out demons, He healed all sorts and sizes of sickness and disease, He raised an occasional dead person, and He performed a variety of miracles (water to wine, walk on water, stop a storm instantaneously, transport a boat several miles instantaneously, multiply food, shrivel a tree— and He implied that the disciples should have stopped the storm and multiplied the food, and He stated that they could shrivel a tree [Peter actually took a few steps on water]). So how about us? The preaching and teaching we can handle, but what about the rest? I once heard the president of a certain Christian college affirm that this verse obviously could not mean what it says because it is not happening! Well, in his own experience and in that of his associates I guess it isn't. But many people today cast out demons and heal, and I personally know someone who has raised a dead person. Miracles are also happening. So how about me? And you?

"In fact he will do greater works than these." Well now, if we cast out demons, heal and perform miracles, is that not enough? Jesus wants more, He wants "greater things" than those just mentioned [do not forget what He said in Matthew 7:22-23]. Notice again that He said "will do", not maybe, perhaps, or if your church permits. But what could be 'greater' than miracles? This cannot refer to modern technology because in that event such 'greater things' would not have been available to the believers during the first 1900 years. Note that the key is in the Lord's final statement (in verse 12), "because I am going to my Father". Only if He won could He return to the Father, so He is here declaring His victory before the fact. It is on the basis of that victory that the 'greater things' can be performed. Just what are those 'greater' things? For my answer, see my outline, "Biblical Spiritual Warfare".

In verse 12 the verb 'will do' is singular, both times, so it has to do with the individual. Observe that the Lord did **not** say, "you apostles", "only during the apostolic age", "only until the canon is complete", or whatever. He said, "the one believing", present tense, so this applies to any and all subsequent moments up to our time. To deny the truth contained in this verse is to make the Lord Jesus Christ out to be a liar. Somehow I do not think that is very smart.[1]

The 'Crux' of a 'Lost' Original

Returning to the opening paragraph, is/was the original wording lost? I answer with an emphatic, "**No**". It certainly exists within the Byzantine bulk. To my mind, any time at least 90% of the primary witnesses agree, there can be no reasonable question; it is <u>statistically impossible</u> that a non-original reading could score that high.[2] Any time a reading garners an attestation of at least 80% its probability is high.

---

[1] Also, to affirm that the miraculous gifts ceased when the last shovelful of dirt fell on the Apostle John's grave is an historical falsehood. Christians who lived during the second, third and fourth centuries, whose writings have come down to us, affirm that the gifts were still in use in their day. No 20th or 21st century Christian, <u>who was not there</u>, is competent to contradict them. And please see the footnote at 1 Corinthians 13:12 in my translation, *The Sovereign Creator Has Spoken*. Any 'cessationist' will have a stronghold of Satan in his mind on that subject, because he has embraced a lie. Any doctrine that derives from reaction against excesses and abuses gives victory to Satan. Any argument designed to justify lack of spiritual power cannot be right.

[2] See Appendix C in my *Identity IV*.

But for perhaps 2% of the words in the NT the attestation falls below 80% (a disproportionate number being in the Apocalypse), and at this point we need to shift our attention from MSS to families. Once all MSS have been collated and have been empirically assigned to families, then we can confine our attention to those families from the start (as I have done in the Apocalypse). I have mentioned elsewhere assigning a credibility quotient to each family, based on objective criteria, and this needs to be done. Unfortunately, there is a great deal of 'homework' waiting to be done in this area. So far as I know, only Family 35 has an empirically defined profile (defined by a complete collation of a representative number of the MSS that make up the family), at least to this date.[1]

About the 2% with attestation below 80%, in a heavy majority of the cases the difference can hardly be reflected in a translation. A reader will understand the intended meaning with either variant. But within Family 35 there is very little significant variation, and the archetypal form is demonstrable. For example, of the forty-three family members I have collated for the General Epistles, twenty-eight are identical (perfect) for 2 & 3 John (but not always the same MSS), twenty-two are identical for Jude, five for 2 Peter, four each for James and 1 John, and three for 1 Peter.

For my article, "Copyist Care Quotient" (see prunch.org), I collated fifty-one (now 53) representatives of Family 35 for

---

[1] So far as I know, neither **f¹** nor **f¹³** exists outside of the Gospels, but even there, has anyone ever produced an empirically defined profile for either one? Consider the following statement by Metzger:

> It should be observed that, in accord with the theory that members of f¹ and f¹³ were subject to progressive accommodation to the later Byzantine text, scholars have established the text of these families by adopting readings of family witnesses that differ from the Textus Receptus. Therefore the citation of the siglum f¹ and f¹³ may, in any given instance, signify a minority of manuscripts (or even only one) that belong to the family. (*A Textual Commentary on the Greek New Testament* [companion to UBS³], p. xii.)

Would it be unreasonable to say that such a proceeding is unfair to the reader? Does it not mislead the user of the apparatus? At least as used by the UBS editions, those sigla do not represent empirically defined profiles.

Mark. I analyzed the variants contained in MS 1384 (eapr, XI, Andros)—of the fifty-three MSS I collated, at least forty-four are better than 1384, so it is only a mediocre representative. However, with four exceptions, only a single letter or syllable is involved, and nowhere is the meaning seriously affected. **Someone reading MS 1384 would not be misled as to the intended meaning at any point in the book**. I say this is noteworthy, and it is typical of almost all **f**[35] MSS. Down through the centuries of transmission, anyone with access to an **f**[35] representative could know the intended meaning of the Autograph.[1] Not only that, most lines of transmission within the Byzantine bulk would be reasonably close, good enough for most practical purposes. This is also true of the much maligned *Textus Receptus*; it is certainly good enough for most practical purposes. Down through the centuries of Church history, most people could have had reasonable access to God's written revelation.

Some years ago now, Maurice Robinson did a complete collation of 1,389 MSS that contain the P.A. (John 7:53-8:11),[2] and I had William Pierpont's photocopy of those collations in my possession for two months, spending most of that time studying those collations. As I did so, it became obvious to me that von Soden 'regularized' his data, arbitrarily 'creating' the alleged archetypal form for his first four families, **M**[1,2,3,4] —if they exist at all, they are rather fluid. His **M**[5&6] do exist, having distinct profiles for the purpose of showing that they are different, but they are a bit 'squishy', with enough internal confusion to make the choice of the archetypal form to be arbitrary. In fact, I suspect that they will

---

[1] Since **f**[35] MSS are scattered all over, or all around, the Mediterranean world, such access would have been feasible for most people.

[2] 240 MSS omit the P.A., 64 of which are based on Theophylact's commentary. Fourteen others have lacunae, but are not witnesses for total omission. A few others certainly contain the passage but the microfilm is illegible. So, 1389 + 240 + 14 + 7(?) = about 1650 MSS checked by Robinson. That does not include Lectionaries, of which he also checked a fair number. (These are microfilms held by the *INTF* in Münster. We now know that there are many more extant MSS, and probably even more that are not yet 'extant'.) Unfortunately, so far as I know, Robinson has yet to publish his collations, thus making them available to the public at large.

have to be subdivided. In contrast to the above, his **M⁷** (that I call Family 35) has a solid, unambiguous profile—the archetypal form is demonstrable, empirically determined.

As for the Apocalypse, of the nine groups that Hoskier identified, only his Complutensian (that I call Family 35) is homogenous. Of the others, the main ones all have subdivisions, which will require their own profile.

Given my presuppositions, I consider that I have good reason for declaring the divine preservation of the precise original wording of the complete New Testament Text to this day. That wording is reproduced in my edition of the Greek NT. My presuppositions include: the Sovereign Creator exists; He inspired the biblical Text; He promised to preserve it for a thousand generations (1 Chronicles 16:15); so He must have an active, ongoing interest in that preservation [there have been fewer than 300 generations since Adam, so He has a ways to go!]. If He was preserving the original wording in some line of transmission other than f^{35}, would that transmission be any less careful than what I have demonstrated for f^{35}? I think not. So any line of transmission characterized by internal confusion is disqualified—this includes **all** the other lines of transmission that I have seen so far![1]

On the basis of the evidence so far available I affirm the following:

1. The original wording was never 'lost', and its transmission down through the years was basically normal, being recognized as inspired material from the beginning.

2. That normal process resulted in lines of transmission.

3. To delineate such lines, MSS must be grouped empirically on the basis of a shared mosaic of readings.

4. Such groups or families must be evaluated for independence and credibility.

5. The largest clearly defined group is Family 35.

---

[1] Things like **M⁶** and **M⁵** in John 7:53-8:11 come to mind.

6. Family 35 is demonstrably independent of all other lines of transmission throughout the NT.

7. Family 35 is demonstrably ancient, dating to the 3rd century, at least.[1]

8. Family 35 representatives come from all over the Mediterranean area; the geographical distribution is all but total.[2]

9. Family 35 is not a recension, was not created at some point subsequent to the Autographs.

10. Family 35 is an objectively/empirically defined entity throughout the NT; it has a demonstrable, diagnostic profile from Matthew 1:1 to Revelation 22:21.

11. The archetypal form of Family 35 is demonstrable—it has been demonstrated (see Appendix B in my *Identity IV*).

12. The Original Text is the ultimate archetype; any candidate must also be an archetype—a real, honest to goodness, objectively verifiable archetype—there is only one (so far), Family 35.[3]

13. God's concern for the preservation of the biblical Text is evident: I take it that passages such as 1 Chronicles 16:15, Psalm 119:89, Isaiah 40:8, Matthew 5:18, Luke 16:17 and 21:33, John 10:35, 1 Peter 1:23-25 and Luke 4:4 may reasonably be taken to imply a promise that the Scriptures (to the tittle) will be preserved for man's use (we are to live "by *every* word of God"), and to the end of the world ("for a thousand generations"), but no intimation is given as to just

---

[1] Family 35 readings are attested by early witnesses, but without pattern, and therefore without dependency. But there are many hundreds of such readings. So how did the **f^{35}** archetype come by all those early readings? Did its creator travel around and collect a few readings from Aleph, a few from B, a few from P^{45,66,75}, a few from W and D, etc.? Is not such a suggestion patently ridiculous? The only reasonable conclusion is that the **f^{35}** text is ancient (also independent).

[2] And for some places in Greece, based on their surviving copies, it was all they used.

[3] If you want to be a candidate for the best lawyer in your city, you must be a lawyer, or the best carpenter, or oncologist, or whatever. If there is only one candidate for mayor in your town, who gets elected?

how God proposed to do it. We must deduce the answer from what He has indeed done—we discover that He **did**!

14. This concern is reflected in Family 35; it is characterized by incredibly careful transmission (in contrast to other lines). [I have a perfect copy of the Family 35 archetypal text for most NT books (22); I have copies made from a perfect exemplar (presumed) for another four (4); as I continue to collate MSS I hope to add the last one (Acts), but even for it the archetypal form is demonstrable.]

15. If God was preserving the original wording in some line of transmission other than Family 35, would that line be any less careful? I think not. So any line of transmission characterized by internal confusion is disqualified—this includes **all** the other lines of transmission that I have seen so far.

16. I affirm that God used Family 35 to preserve the precise original wording of the New Testament Text; it is reproduced in my edition of the Greek Text. (And God used mainly the Eastern Orthodox Churches to preserve the NT Text down through the centuries—they have always used a Text that was an adequate representation of the Original, for all practical purposes.)

I claim to have demonstrated the superiority of Family 35 based on <u>size</u> (number of representatives), <u>independence</u>, <u>age</u>, <u>geographical distribution</u>, <u>profile</u> (empirically determined), <u>care</u> (see my "Copyist Care Quotient") and <u>range</u> (all 27 books). I challenge any and all to do the same for any other line of transmission!

APPENDIX A
Chronology of the Life of CHRIST[1]

Based on every verse of the four Gospels[2]

A. **Preamble**.
1. The Lamb slain before the creation—1 Pet. 1:18-20; Rev. 13:8 (Jn. 12:27).
2. The Creator of this world—Heb. 1:10 (see Ps. 102:25 = Jehovah); **Jn. 1:10**; Col. 1:16.
3. Implications—Jehovah the Son, knowing ahead of time what would happen and that He himself would have to pay the terrible ransom price, even so He created our race. Why?
   a. Heb. 12:2—the proposed joy; so great that He endured the cross for it. That joy presumably has to do with the Church; now the Lord Jesus Christ is awaiting His Bride.
   b. Heb. 10:5—the prepared body, forever; now there is a human body at the father's right hand (Acts 7:55-56) [immutability?]. When He accepted the body, He accepted the whole Plan.
   c. Jn. 4:23—the Father seeks; if He is seeking something, then He does not have it, or else He wants more [transcendence?]. The father exposes Himself, waiting for our response; He does not want robots.

4. Anticipated summary—**Jn. 1:1-14.**

---

[1] No one teaches a course on 'Jesusology', just 'Christology'; 'Jesus' relates to His human side, 'Christ' includes His divine side also. It is because He is the God-man that His life gains especial importance.

[2] I am concerned to take the Sacred Text very seriously, because I understand it to have maximum authority. In passing, we may observe that the Truth is not democratic, is not determined by human opinion or vote; the Truth **is**! (It should be obvious as well that the Kingdom of God is not a democracy.) The author is solely responsible for all interpretation herein; he is not tied to any denominational 'package'. (To place any doctrinal package above the Text is a form of idolatry.)

- In the beginning (of this world, or perhaps, of this universe) He already existed. But why the 'word'? Taking the word as the basic unit of verbal communication, and as representing that communication, then we have an important figure. Jehovah the Son in human form becomes the supreme communication between God and our race. Also, since the context is about beginning and creation, 'word' may allude to the act of creation, which was with a spoken word.
- "The Word was **God**"—emphasizes the quality inherent in the noun.[1]
- "Received", not 'accepted'; if you 'accept' something, that something is of inferior quality or offered by someone who is socially inferior. Superior people and things are **received**. If you merely 'accept Jesus', that 'Jesus' can't save you, being lower than you are.
- In the true Text we never encounter 'believe in' (εν in Greek) Jesus or His name; we always encounter 'believe into' (εις in Greek), that involves commitment. People believe 'in' Santa Claus, the Easter bunny, the goodness of man, or whatever, but such belief makes no difference in their lives. Many millions of people affirm that they 'believe in Jesus', but such belief makes no difference in their lives either. You must believe <u>into</u> Jesus, which signifies a change in location—you were on the outside and moved to the inside—it involves commitment and identification; it involves a change in worldview.
5. His human genealogy.

---

[1] The New World Translation (of the JWs) renders "a god". They defend their choice because the noun 'God' occurs without the definite article, and the absence of the article in Greek has the effect of the indefinite article in English—hence, 'a god'. However, another frequent use of the absence of the definite article (in Greek) is to emphasize the quality inherent in the noun—in this case, 'God'. Grammatically, the construction is ambiguous, so those who wish to deny the deity of Christ will naturally translate 'a god'. Since John will himself make perfectly clear that Christ is very God, we take it that he is here emphasizing that inherent quality. A faithful translator will attempt to reflect the meaning intended by the author, so I would say that the New World Translation is not faithful here, since John will repeatedly make clear that Jesus is God. But there is a further consideration. If John had used the definite article we would have an equation (in Greek)—the Word = the God—which would do away with the Trinity. So John could not write 'the God'; he will quote Christ Himself making very clear that the Father and the Son are distinct persons.

a. Through His stepfather, Joseph—**Mt. 1:1-17.**[1]
- The legal right to the throne of David came through Joseph; since this has to do with the covenant people, it begins with Abraham (in contrast to the genealogy through Mary).
- See the curse on Jehoiaquim and Jeconiah—Jer. 36:30; 22:30; in verse 16 the phraseology changes—Jesus could not be a son of Joseph.
- Some 99% of the Greek manuscripts have "Asa" in verse 7 and "Amon" in verse 10; "Asaph" and "Amos", as in the eclectic text (Greek), are gross mistakes.
- The inclusion only of women that represent some violation = grace of God.

b. Through His mother, Mary—**Lk. 3:23-38.**
- Jesus being Son of Man, it begins with Adam; being Son of God, it begins with God.
- In verse 23 the translation "as was supposed" is inadequate, because Jesus was **not** a son of Joseph; in fact the whole verse is generally neither well understood nor well translated. The grammar of the verse is unusual—I would translate it like this: "Now Jesus, beginning *His ministry* at about thirty years of age, being (so it was supposed) a son of Joseph, was really of Heli, of Matthat, of Levi, of Melchi," etc. In other words, Jesus was a grandson of Heli, Mary's father.[2]
- In verse 33 more than 95% of the Greek manuscripts have "of Aram" (see Mt. 1:3) and not "of Admin, of Arni", as in the eclectic text (UBS[4] and N-A[27]); in fact, the exact wording of the eclectic text doesn't occur as such in any ancient Greek manuscript, it is a patchwork quilt.
- Zerubbabel, verse 27—see Haggai 1:1, Zechariah 4:6-10 and Esther 3:8.
- Verse 36—Cainan X Genesis 11:12.[3]

---

[1] This genealogy offers several seeming discrepancies. For my solution, please see "Some related anomalies in Matthew's genealogy of the Christ" in Appendix A of my book, *The Identity of the New Testament Text IV.*

[2] For a more complete discussion, please see "Mary's genealogy—Luke 3:23" in Appendix A of my book, *The Identity of the New Testament Text IV.*

[3] For my solution to this anomaly, please see "Cainan[2]—Luke 3:26 X Genesis 11:12" in Appendix A of my book, *The Identity of the New Testament Text IV.*

B. **Introduction**.
1. John's birth—[**Lk. 1:1-4**].   **5BC**
   - Luke affirms (v. 3) that he had "perfect understanding of all things from Above", $\alpha\nu\omega\theta\varepsilon\nu$ = inspiration.
   - It seems that Luke never saw Jesus personally.
   a. Predicted by the angel Gabriel—**Lk. 1:5-25.**
      - "Your prayer was heard"—presumably a prayer from earlier times; see verse 18.
      - His ministry would be "in the spirit and power of Elijah".
      - Besides being sterile, Elizabeth had passed menopause = a double miracle.
      - Verse 17—"he will go before Him" = the angel affirms that Jesus is Jehovah.
   b. Accomplished—**Lk. 1:57-66.**
      - "His name is to be John!"—the Kingdom of God is not a democracy.
      - The eighth day is the best day of a boy's whole life to undergo minor surgery.
      - The first use that Zacharias made of his voice was to praise God; then the Holy Spirit took over and he began to prophesy.
   c. Zacharias' prophecy—**Lk. 1:67-79.**
      - Verse 70—"prophets . . . since the world began" → Gen. 3:15.
      - Verse 76—Zacharias affirms that Jesus is 'the Lord' and 'the Most High'.
      - Verse 78—99.6% of the Greek manuscripts have "has visited us" instead of "will visit us"—surely, because Jehovah the Son was already in the virgin Mary's womb.
   d. The child grows—**Lk. 1:80.**
2. The birth of Jesus.   **4BC**
   - Taking the chronological information contained in the Massoretic Hebrew Text seriously and literally, it would appear that Jesus was born in the year 4,000 of the world = AM 4000 = 4 BC.
   a. Announced to the virgin Mary—**Lk. 1:26-38.**
      - In 99% of the Greek manuscripts verse 28 ends with: "Blessed are you among women."

- "He will reign over the house of <u>Jacob</u> forever"—
the coming of the Creator to this planet is directly
linked to the covenant with David and the people
of Israel.
- "Let it be to me according to your word"—Mary
agreed, accepted the proposal; it was not something imposed upon her.

b. Mary visits Elizabeth—**Lk. 1:39-45,56.**
- Elizabeth, full of the Holy Spirit, said: "the mother of my Lord"!—Elizabeth gave a prophecy of
confirmation; the point is that Mary was already
pregnant, Jehovah the Son was already in her
womb.
- Those three months were a reinforcement for
Mary; there was a priest in the house with a considerable knowledge of God's Word.
- Mary did <u>not</u> stay to see John's birth (one wonders why).

c. Mary's "Magnificat"—**Lk. 1:46-55.**
- Verse 47—"my Savior"; Mary recognized her
need of salvation.
- Verses 54-55—she links what is happening to the
covenant with Abraham.

d. An angel instructs Joseph—**Mt. 1:18-25.**
- It seems likely that Mary had travelled without
telling her parents what had happened, but upon
returning she had to tell them (three months
pregnant). They being responsible people would
have immediately called Joseph to bring him up
to date; then they waited for his decision.
- "Joseph took to him his wife, but did not know
her <u>until</u> she had brought forth her firstborn
Son."
- Verse 25—99.5% of the Greek manuscripts have
"her firstborn son" and not "a son".)

e. The birth—**Lk. 2:1-7.**
- "She brought forth her firstborn Son, . . . and laid
Him in a manger."
- Quirinius really was the governor, in his 1st term
(his 2nd term is better known).

f. Pastors and angels—**Lk. 2:8-20.**
- The angel said to them: "There is born to you
this day . . . a Savior, who is Christ the Lord."

Verse 8 says it was at night; their 'day' began at 6 p.m.

- Verse 14—99.4% of the Greek manuscripts (1627 x 6) have, "on earth peace, good will toward men!" How could there be a greater proof of God's good will toward our race?! The shepherds spread the word.

g. Circumcision and presentation—**Lk. 2:21-24.**

- See Lev. 12:8—the offering was that of the poor, apparently they were not financially able to offer a lamb; which means that they had not yet received the gifts of the magi.
- The purification was after 40 days—Lev. 12:1-3.

h. Simeon—**Lk. 2:25-35.**

- Verse 27—"the custom of the Law"; see Ex. 34;20, Num. 18:16.
- Verse 33—98.8% of the Greek manuscripts have "Joseph and His mother" and not "His father and mother".

i. Ana—**Lk. 2:36-38.**

- 7 + 84 + 15(?) → Ana would have been over a 100 years old.

j. The magi—**Mt. 2:1-12.**

- The magi: "King of the Jews"; Herod: "the Christ".
- "When they saw the star they rejoiced with exceedingly great joy"—the star reappeared after two years. They had undertaken an expensive and dangerous journey 'in the dark', as it were. Now God confirms that they are on the right road. You can imagine their relief!
- "Coming into the house"—the family probably stayed in the stable only a few days, maybe just that night; Joseph probably started looking for better quarters the next morning, and given the news that the shepherds spread around the town, the people were probably ready to help.
- Because the gifts were three, it is common to suppose that the magi were also three, but the Text doesn't specify that.

k. The flight to Egypt—**Mt. 2:13-15.**

- Joseph got right up, packed and left, immediately. A suspicious man like Herod would certainly have sent a spy to keep an eye on the magi. When they took off in another direction, Herod would have been informed within a very few hours. Had Joseph waited until morning, it would probably have been too late.
- Verse 15, "from Egypt I have called my son"—the quote is from Hosea 11:1, and in that context it refers to Israel, but Jesus was and is God's Son, literally. O.T. prophecies often have a double reference.

I. The massacre—**Mt. 2:16-18.**

- Ramah was a district of Bethlehem; the quote is from Jeremiah 31:15. The birth of the Savior resulted in the massacre of many innocents, and being the fulfilment of prophecy means it was part of the Plan. God's ways may seem strange to us, but He is under no obligation to explain Himself.

3. The return to Natsareth—**Mt. 2:19-23; Lk. 2:39.**

- They probably stayed in Egypt only a few months.
- We know from Luke that Joseph was from Natsareth; his house and business were waiting for him.
- Matthew 2:23—the stated prophecy cannot be found if you spell 'Nazareth' with a 'z'. The seeming difficulty is an artifact of careless transliteration from Hebrew to Greek to English and back to Hebrew.[1]

---

[1] The name of the town in Hebrew is based on the consonants נצר(resh, tsadde, nun), but since Hebrew is read from right to left, for us the order is reversed = n, ts, r. This word root means 'branch'. Greek has the equivalent for 'ps' and 'ks', but not for 'ts', so the transliteration used a ζ (zeta) 'dz', which is the voiced counterpart of 'ts'. But when the Greek was transliterated into English it came out as 'z'! But Hebrew has a 'z', ז(zayin), so in transliterating back into Hebrew people assumed the consonants נזר, replacing the correct tsadde with zayin. This technical information is necessary as background for the solution to the seeming difficulty. Neither 'Nazareth' nor 'Nazarene', spelled with a zayin, is to be found in the Old Testament, but there is a prophetic reference to Messiah as the Branch, netser—Isaiah 11:1—and several to the related word, tsemach—Isaiah 4:2, Jeremiah 23:5, 33:15; Zechariah 3:8, 6:12. So Matthew is quite right—the prophets (plural, being at least three) referred to Christ as the Branch. Since Jesus was a man, He would be the 'Branch-man', from 'Branch-town'. Which brings us to the word 'natsorean'. The familiar 'Nazarene' (Ναζαρηνος) [Natsarene] occurs in Mark 1:24, 14:67, 16:6 and Luke 4:34, but here in Matthew 2:23 and in fourteen other places, including Acts 22:8 where the glorified Jesus calls Himself that, the word is 'Natsorean'

4. The child grows—**Lk. 2:40-52.**
   - Three days in the temple with the doctors of the Law.
   - Jesus did not apologize (He almost reprimanded His mother).
   - "My Father"—Jesus knew who He was (He wasn't discussing carpentry with the doctors of the Law).
   - Verse 43—some 98% of the Greek manuscripts have "Joseph and His mother" and not "His parents".
5. The ministry of John—**Mt. 3:1-12; Mk. 1:1-8; Lk. 3:1-18; Jn. 1:6-8.**
   - In Mk. 1:1 just three Greek manuscripts, all of inferior quality, omit "Son of God", against some 1,700 that have the phrase; for all that the eclectic text places the phrase within brackets so as to cast doubt on its legitimacy—just disregard the brackets [in fact, whenever you encounter brackets enclosing a part of the text in your Bible, just disregard them].
   - Mk. 1:2—96.7% of the Greek manuscripts have "in the prophets" and not "in Isaiah the prophet". Verse 2 cites Malachi 3:1, while verse 3 cites Isaiah 40:3. Most modern versions follow the 3%, creating a seeming discrepancy
   - Evidently John repeated his message many times and would vary the turn of phrase.
   - Mt. 3:10—"already the ax is being laid to the root of the trees"; the Messiah was already present, and He would condemn the Pharisees and Sadducees.
6. The baptism of Jesus—**Mt. 3:13-17; Mk. 1:9-11; Lk. 3:21-22.**   **26AD**
   - Matthew gives John's perspective; Mark and Luke that of Jesus—there was interpretation in the ear, as at Pentecost.
   - Lk. 3:23 → 26 AD.

(Ναζωραιος), which is quite different. (Actually, in Acts 22:8 Jesus introduced Himself to Saul as 'the Natsorean', which Saul would understand as a reference to the Messiah.) I have been given to understand that the Natsareth of Jesus' day had been founded some 100 years before by a Branch family who called it Branch-town; they were very much aware of the prophecies about the Branch and fully expected the Messiah to be born from among them—they called themselves Branch-people (Natsoreans). Of course everyone else thought it was a big joke and tended to look down on them. "Can anything good . . . ?"

- The Trinity is manifested—it was an important confirmation for Jesus.
7. Jesus tested by Satan—**Mt. 4:1-11; Mk. 1:12-13; Lk. 4:1-13.**
    - Matthew gives the correct sequence—Greek words denoting sequence.
    - In more than 99,5% of the Greek manuscripts Lk. 4:4 ends with "but by every Word of God"—the phrase is omitted by the eclectic text.
    - In Mt. 4:10 some 88% of the Greek manuscripts have "get behind Me". In Lk. 4:8 more than 97% of the Greek manuscripts have "Get behind Me, Satan!"
    - Lk. 4:13—"when the devil had ended <u>every temptation</u>"; Jesus was tested in the three areas: "the lust of the flesh, the lust of the eyes and the pride of life" (1 Jn. 2:16).

C. **Jesus begins His ministry, concentrating on Judea**.
1. Jesus returns to John.
    a. The witness of John—**Jn. 1:15-34.**
        - In verse 18 five Greek manuscripts (of objectively inferior quality) have 'an only begotten god', another two (equally inferior) have 'the only begotten god', while some 1,700 have 'the only begotten son'. Clearly God [as God] was never begotten; Jehovah the Son exists from all eternity. The human part of Jesus was begotten, yes; but the divine part, no—as it says in Isaiah 9:6, "unto us a child is born, unto us a Son is given". Note the precision: the <u>Son</u> was "given", not "born".
        1) John answers the Pharisees—**Jn. 1:19-28.**
            - "I am neither the Messiah, nor Elijah, nor 'the prophet' [Dt. 18:15]"; "Who are you?"—"I am 'the voice of one calling out: "Make the LORD's road straight in the wilderness".'"
        2) John identifies the Messiah—**Jn. 1:29-34.**
            - "Behold the Lamb of God, who takes away the sin of the world!" What a tremendous affirmation! The Sacrifice to end all sacrifices was now physically present in the world.
            - "I have seen and testified that this is the Son of God." John fulfilled his office.

b. Jesus calls Andrew, Peter, Philip and Nathaniel—**Jn. 1:35-51.**

- Beginning at 10 a.m. Jesus invested several hours in two future disciples.
- "Rabbi, You are the Son of God! You are the King of Israel!" Wow, that was a real switch—from disdainful doubt in verse 46 to faith and submission in verse 49. What caused the change? A mature fig tree's branches reach to the ground and form a curtain—there is a clear space around the trunk that is cool and private [I have been there]. It was a great place to be alone with God. But for Jesus to see Nathanael there (there were probably hills in between as well) meant that He was supernatural. That statement convinced Nathanael that he was looking at the Messiah, and he immediately declared allegiance.
- The Text says, "<u>the</u> son of Jonah". Since Peter obviously had at least one brother, he was not an only son. Perhaps we should understand that Peter was the firstborn. Perhaps 0.5% of the Greek manuscripts (of objectively inferior quality) read "John" for "Jonah" (as in NIV, NASB, LB, TEV, etc.).
- "Later on you will see the heaven opened and the angels of God ascending and descending upon the Son of the Man." So far as I know, we have no record of when this took place, but no doubt it did. Jesus addressed Nathanael in particular, "He says to <u>him</u>", but used the plural, "ye", about seeing the heaven opened.
- "The Son of the Man" appears to be a phrase coined by the Lord Jesus to refer to Himself; the Text does say "the son of the man", which doesn't make very good sense in English, at first glance, but if "<u>the</u> man" refers to pristine Adam and "<u>the</u> son" to an only pristine descendent, it makes great sense. It seems to indicate a perfect human prototype, like Adam was before the fall—the human side of the God-man.

2. A wedding in Cana; the first "sign"—**Jn. 2:1-11 (12).**

- "On the third day"—Counting from when? 1:19-28 happened on one day; 1:29-34 happened the next (2nd) day; 1:35-42 happened the next (3rd) day;

1:43-51 happened the next (4th) day. So the third day here must count from the last day mentioned (1:43-51), although it could (and in Jewish thought probably did) include it. The wedding started that day, but such weddings often lasted several days (and the wine would run out toward the end, if it did). Jesus and His disciples (four?) probably had about an 80-mile walk, 55 miles up the Jordan valley (relatively smooth and straight) and 25 of rougher terrain. Since they did all their traveling on foot, and were therefore used to it, they could easily make the distance in two days.

- "What is that to you and me, woman?" Jesus was not being disrespectful; this was a normal form of address.
- "Do whatever He may tell you." Mary was evidently in a position to issue orders, which leads me to suspect that she was the mother of the bride, which would also explain why Jesus made a special effort to get there. From verse 12 below, it appears that the whole family was there (and the lack of wine was a family problem).
- "My time has not come yet." I conclude from 1:43 that Jesus was at that wedding on purpose, and probably had an idea of what would happen. Perhaps He was testing His mother's faith, and maybe her determination. However, as He declares, He was not yet ready to really go public—He would do that in Jerusalem, as recorded in 2:13-25. He would start with a bang, right in the Temple!
- "So they filled them to the brim." That was a lot of water! If it was toward the end of the festivity, there would presumably be a great deal of wine left over. Such excellent wine would bring a good price; perhaps Jesus chose this way to give the new couple a financial boost.
- Jesus "revealed His glory". In what sense? As Jehovah the Son He was the Creator of this world. Transforming water into wine was an act of creation. The chemical components that distinguish wine from water had to be created on the spot, and mixed with the water. This "first miraculous sign" was simply tremendous—it revealed Jesus as Creator. However, although presumably all the guests drank of this new

wine, being tipsy they may not have realized what went on. Only the disciples, the servants, and of course Mary, knew what had really happened. Apparently this miracle was not broadcast at that time—like Jesus said, not yet. (Neither Matthew, Mark nor Luke were there, but John, the author of this Gospel, probably was; in which case we have an eyewitness account [John and James were partners with Peter and Andrew; so since Peter and Andrew were invited they probably were too].)

- From verse 12 it appears that Joseph was already dead.

3. The first Passover and purification of temple—**Jn. 2:13-25.**   **27AD**

- The Passover was one (probably the most important) of the three festivals during the year when every God-fearing male had to present himself at the temple in Jerusalem (Deuteronomy 16:16). Often the whole family would go, so perhaps the whole group mentioned in verse 12 went on to Jerusalem. Jesus had just come up from Judea, only to turn around and go back, which gives us some indication of the importance of the wedding in Cana.

- "Stop turning my Father's House into a marketplace!" The impression I get is that it was mainly the animals that He drove, not the people; in the next verse He commands the dove-sellers to remove them, presumably still in the cages. The commerce going on in the Temple was crooked, and was under the direction of the religious leaders. What Jesus did was an affront, a direct challenge to their authority. He got their attention! From this moment on they knew about Jesus! What He did was so unexpected, so outrageous, that the Jews didn't know how to react. Maybe some were just a little afraid He might be the Messiah. (And just maybe a few of them had been there 18 years before and listened to a certain twelve-year-old Boy.)

- The Lord gives an unexpected meaning to "this temple", metaphoric, but this prophecy was literally fulfilled.

- "In three days I will raise it"—since Jesus was referring to His own body, once He was dead how could

He do this? His spirit didn't die, and at the right moment returned to the body and raised it, uniting with it once again (and in so doing He glorified it).

- "So they believed the Scripture, even the word that Jesus had spoken." Note that my rendering, "even the word", has the effect of equating His word with Scripture (there is no O.T. passage that they could be remembering). More precisely, the Lord's statement in verse 19 was repeated as an accusation three years later, as recorded in Matthew 26:61 and 27:40, and Matthew's Gospel had already been circulating as Scripture for decades when John wrote. If this line of reasoning is correct, then John is calling Matthew 'Scripture'! (Of course there was an interval of a number of years (eight) between the resurrection and the publishing of Matthew's Gospel, but perhaps some didn't 'remember' until they saw it written down.)

4. A conversation with Nicodemus—**Jn. 3:1-21.**
   - "So it is with everyone who has been begotten by the Spirit." Notice that the Lord is saying here that it is **we** who are to be unpredictable, like the wind, or the Spirit ("comes" and "goes" are in the present tense). If you are really under the control of the Spirit, you will do unexpected things, just like He does. We all know of types of Christian that are rigid, totally predictable—the Lord Jesus Christ says that such 'Christians' have not been begotten by the Spirit. A word to the wise . . . .
   - "Unless someone is begotten from Above"—the basic meaning of the Greek word here, ανωθεν, is 'from up/above'. A lot of people who say that they have been 'born again' have never been begotten from Above. 'Begotten' refers to the cause; 'born' refers to the result—I take it that the Lord is talking about the cause.
   - In verse 15, less than 2% of the Greek manuscripts, of inferior quality, omit "should not be wasted but" (as in NIV, NASB, LB, TEV, etc.). The phrase is repeated in verse 16, but this is a conversation between two Jews and it is standard Hebrew procedure to repeat things. But why do I render "be wasted" instead of "perish"? Well, what do you think "perish"

means? It can't mean 'to die', because Christians die. It can't mean 'to suffer', because Christians suffer, etc. Although the Greek verb here, απολλυμι, is used in contexts of decay, loss, ruin, destruction, death, I take it that the core idea is 'waste'—the potential of a person or thing is wasted, does not come to fruition. The potential that your life represents, the reason why you exist, can only be realized if you believe into Jesus—otherwise you will be wasted.

- In verse 13, about 1% of the Greek manuscripts, of objectively inferior quality, omit "who is in Heaven" (as in NIV, NASB, LB, TEV, etc.). Presumably those copyists couldn't figure out how Jesus could be on earth and in Heaven at the same time, so they altered the Text. But let's stop and think about what this verse says—Jehovah the Son came down out of Heaven all right, but when did He go up? If "the Angel of Jehovah" in the O.T. was Jehovah the Son, as I believe, then He had been back and forth many times. In John 5:19 Jesus said that He could only do what He saw the Father do—so when and how could Jesus see the Father? Even though Jehovah the Son was in the human body of Jesus Christ, evidently there was some sense in which He was also in Heaven; He existed there. Well, that's what John 1:18 says, "who exists in the bosom of the Father".

- The opposite of 'eternal life' is not 'non-eternal life', it is 'eternal death'. But 'death' does not mean 'cease to exist'—the human spirit, the image of the Creator, is immortal, it exists forever. There are but two destinies for the human being—unending life or unending death. The central idea in 'death' is separation; physical death means the spirit is separated from the body; spiritual death means the spirit is separated from the Creator, forever. The essence of 'life' is to be in communion with the Creator, so we can start enjoying our eternal life right here, right now.

5. John testifies again—**Jn. 3:22-36.**

- "Because there was plenty of water there"—to this day there is plenty of water in the Aijalon valley, some 15-20 miles WNW of Jerusalem (Salem is an ancient name for Jerusalem; see Genesis 14:18 and Hebrews 7:1)—perhaps that is where it was. I take it that Jesus and John were in the same area, at this point.

- "He who comes from Above is above all." "The Father loves the Son and has given all things into His hand." John obviously had a pretty good understanding of who Jesus was.

- There are differing opinions about where the Baptizer's speech ends—the rest would then be a commentary by the author, John. The verbs in the present tense in verse 32 tip the decision in favor of the Baptizer—John would have had to use a past tense. I take it that the Baptizer's speech goes through verse 35, at least. Verse 36 could be an editorial comment by John, but I see no reason in the Text for taking the verse away from the Baptizer. Notice the verb 'will remain'; the only way out is to obey the Son.

- "He who does not obey the Son shall not see life, but the wrath of God abides on him." The Text has "disobeying", not 'disbelieving'. 'Believing into' has to do with commitment, with identification, with relationship. If you enter into a relationship with the Sovereign of the Universe, He is the **Boss**. Either you obey or bad things start to happen to you.

6. John is imprisoned—**(Mt. 14:3-5); (Mk. 6:17-20); Lk. 3:19-20; (Jn. 3:24).**
   - Luke is out of sequence because in his account these two verses constitute an historical aside, and should be placed within parentheses in the Text.
7. Jesus leaves Judea for Galilee—**Mt. 4:12; Jn. 4:1-4.**
   - It was John's imprisonment that motivated His strategic withdrawal into Galilee; a different province with a different governor. If the Pharisees knew that Jesus was doing more than John, then Herod would also know.
   - "He needed to go through Samaria"—He could have gone up the coast and avoided most of the mountains, but He "needed" to go through Samaria. Probably because the Father told Him to—it was harvest time in Sychar.
8. Jesus and the Samaritans—**Jn. 4:5-6.**
   - "It was about 6 p.m." Since John elsewhere always uses Roman time, I assume that he does so here as

well. The Text has "the sixth hour". Many versions put "noon", which reflects Jewish time. But the Text says Jesus was worn out, which agrees better with a full day's walk than with a half day's walk. The distance between Salem and Sychar was probably about 35 miles, as the crow flies, but since the whole distance was over accidented terrain, the walking distance would be a good deal more. They had walked some 50 miles in twelve hours. Like the Text says, He was tired! And He was hot and thirsty. John emphasizes that as a human being He felt the full effects of the day.

   a. The woman—**Jn. 4:7-29.**
      1) "Give Me a drink"—**Jn. 4:7-15.**
- Verse 10, "living water" → "a fountain of water springing up into eternal life", verse 14. That is what the Text says, "into eternal life". Eternal life is a quality of life, more precisely a life in communion with the Father. The picture is not necessarily of a geyser, water spouting up, but there has to be a constant flow. As our capacity increases the flow should also increase. Of course the water must be shared with others, or we become stagnant.

      2) "Go, call your husband"—**Jn. 4:16-26.**
- "You spoke the truth there!" Dear me! Would you say that Jesus was making a special effort not to hurt her feelings? But He knew what He was doing, as verse 29 makes clear. So how about us? Are we prepared to hurt people's feelings?
- "God is Spirit, and those who worship Him must worship in spirit and truth; the Father <u>seeks</u> such to worship Him."[1]

---

[1] The Father "is looking" for those who will worship Him in spirit and truth. It may be that we have here a window on the reason why God created a race such as ours—persons in His image with the capacity to **choose**. God "is looking" for something, which means He does not have it, at least not automatically, nor in sufficient quantity. I take it that He wants to be appreciated for who He is, but to have meaning such appreciation can't come from robots—it has to be voluntary. So He created a type of being with that capacity, but He had to take the risk that such a being would choose <u>not</u> to appreciate Him. Unfortunately, most human beings make the negative choice, and with that

- "The woman: 'I know that Messiah (called Christ) is coming'—Jesus: 'I who speak to you am He'."[1]
  3) "Could this be the Christ?"—**Jn. 4:28-29.**
  b. The disciples—**Jn. 4:27, 31-38.**
  - "My food is to do the will of Him who sent Me, and to finish His work." The Lord was totally committed to the Father's will and game plan; His daily life revolved around it (it was His 'food'). In His excitement at seeing the plan for Sychar unfold He forgot His physical hunger.
  - Verse 36, "fruit into eternal life"—that is what the Text says, "into eternal life". Surely, Jesus is talking about harvesting souls, gathering them into the Kingdom—when someone is born from Above everyone who participated in the process is glad.
  c. The Samaritans—**Jn. 4:30, 39-42.**
  - "We know that this is indeed the Christ, the Savior of the world." All right! They got the message! About 0.5% of the Greek manuscripts, of objectively inferior quality, omit "the Christ" (as in NIV, NASB, LB, TEV, etc.).

D. **Jesus concentrates His ministry in Galilee.**
  1. He arrives in Galilee—**Mk. 1:14-15; Lk. 4:14-15; Jn. 4:43.**
  - "The time is fulfilled, and the Kingdom of God has approached. Repent and believe in the Gospel." John, His herald, is in prison—his ministry and function

---

negative choice come all sorts of negative consequences. Ever since Adam humans are born with an inclination toward sin, so for someone to choose to appreciate God is definitely not automatic, nor even easy. No one can reasonably accuse God of having 'stacked the deck' in His own favor, of 'buying votes'—He seems to have done just the opposite. If a human being, against his natural inclination, chooses to appreciate God, then He receives what He is looking for. "In spirit and truth" presumably means that it can't be faked, can't be forced, can't be merely physical, can't be merely emotional (though both body and emotions can, and often will, be utilized).

[1] As recorded in the four Gospels, this is the first time Jesus declares bluntly that He is the Messiah, and He does it to a woman, and a Samaritan one at that! That woman had had her ups and downs, but was no dummy; that the people of the town listened to her indicates that she had influence. Jesus knew what He was doing.

have ended. So Jesus takes up John's message and continues with it.

2. He is rejected in Nazareth—**Lk. 4:16-30; (Jn. 4:44).**[1]
   - He interrupts the reading of Isa. 61:2 at a comma, because "the day of vengeance" relates to His 2nd coming—'the great parenthesis'.
   - In verse 18 perhaps 1.5% of the Greek manuscripts, of objectively inferior quality, omit "to heal the brokenhearted" (as in NIV, NASB, LB, TEV, etc.).
   - It appears that Jesus antagonized them on purpose. Why? I see two possible answers: to remove any claim to special privilege that they might harbor because of being His home town; to be personally free from possible pressure arising from such a claim. In fact He moved out, choosing Capernaum as His base of operations.
   - "Passing through the middle of them, He went on His way"—now how did that happen? To throw Him down, someone would have to be holding Him, probably a man on each arm, and they had gotten Him there by force, and He was surrounded. Obviously the Lord made use of supernatural power to free Himself from that situation—He had come to this world to die, all right, but not then and not in that way.

3. The nobleman's son (2nd sign in <u>Galilee</u>)—**Jn. 4:45-54.**
   - Just with His word Jesus cured someone in another city.
   - Up to here perhaps one year of His public ministry has passed, a period that the other three Gospels pass over without comment.

4. The ministry in the Capernaum area.
   a. Jesus settles there—**Mt. 4:13-17.**
   b. Peter, Andrew, James & John—**Mt. 4:18-22; Mk. 1:16-20.**
      - "Follow Me and I will make you fishers of men."

---

[1] I believe that the episode recorded in Luke 4:16-30 took place between verses 43 and 45 here (John 4), and verse 44 is an echo of Luke 4:24. From Sychar Jesus went directly to Natsareth, was rejected there, and proceeded to Cana (I suspect that He had a brother-in-law living there). Verse 45 is a summary statement, after the fact. [Of course He was born in Bethlehem, Judea, but I doubt that He is referring to it as 'his own country'.]

c. He expels demons in Capernaum—**Mk. 1:21-28; Lk. 4:31-37.**
  - A man "<u>with</u> an unclean spirit" not "possessed by an unclean spirit" (Mk.).
d. He cures Peter's mother-in-law—**Mk. 1:29-31; Lk. 4:38-39.**
  - "Immediately she arose and served them"—Jesus undid the consequences of the fever.
e. He heals many others—**Mk. 1:32-34; Lk. 4:40-41.**
  - He didn't allow the demons to speak.[1] He would lay hands on the sick (Lk. 4:40), but the demons He expelled with a word (Mt. 8:16). In Lk. 4:41 perhaps 1.5% of the Greek manuscripts, of objectively inferior quality, omit "the Christ" (as in NIV, NASB, LB, TEV, etc.).
f. He retires to pray—**Mk. 1:35-38; Lk. 4:42-43.**
  - Mk. 1:34-35 makes clear that we have a chronological sequence.
5. A tour of Galilee—**Mt. 4:23-25; Mk. 1:39; Lk. 4:44.**[2]
6. A miraculous catch—**Lk. 5:1-11.**
  - The crowd pressed about Him "to hear the word of God"—they were hungry.
  - Presumably some on the beach heard the conversation between Jesus and Peter, so no one went away. I suppose that the 'sermon' occurred right after the catch.
  - Verse 5—Peter was the professional here, and figured he knew better than Jesus (and he was tired),

---

[1] I find this to be curious: the demons kept telling the truth about Jesus, but He evidently didn't want testimony from that quarter. But it seems that the demons felt compelled to identify Him—I wonder why.

[2] Around 4% of the Greek manuscripts read Judea rather than Galilee, possibly influenced by Lectionaries. There is confusion among the 4% such that the prepositional phrase as given in UBS is read by less than 1%. However, Jesus was in Galilee (and continued there), not in Judea, as the context makes clear. In the parallel passage, Mark 1:35-39, all texts agree that Jesus was in Galilee. Thus UBS[3] contradicts itself by reading Judea in Luke 4:44. Bruce Metzger makes clear that the UBS editors did this on purpose when he explains that their reading "is obviously the more difficult, and copyists have corrected it . . . in accord with the parallels in Mt 4.23 and Mk 1.39." Thus the UBS editors introduce a contradiction into their text which is also an error of fact. This error in the eclectic text is reproduced by LB, NIV, NASB, NEB, RSV, etc. NRSV adds insult to injury: "So he continued proclaiming the message in the synagogues of Judea."

but he does obey. However, Jesus had said to let down 'nets' (pl), but Peter let down only one. (Actually, Jesus put 'let down' in the plural, so there was at least one other in the boat, unless it was really His intention that both boats should go out.)

- Verse 11—there would be employees to take care of the fish.

7. The sermon on the mount—**Mt. 5:1-2.**
   - Curiously, only Matthew records this discourse; Lk. 6:17-49 records another occasion.
   a. The beatitudes—Mt. **5:3-10.**
      - Verses 3-10 are in the 3rd person, so are presumably of general application.
   b. "Blessed are you (pl.)"—**Mt. 5:11-12.**
      - From verse 11 on the Lord Jesus utilizes the 2nd person plural—at this point He directs His words specifically to His disciples.
   c. "Salt and light"—**Mt. 5:13-16.**
      - We are to propagate the values of our King. 'Christians' who have caved in to the world's values and life style are like insipid salt—good for nothing except to be thrown out. The implications of this have become increasingly serious in today's world.
      - Nowadays if you stand up for Biblical values you will probably be persecuted, not praised; but the darker the night, the farther a light can be seen.
   d. Christ and the Law—**Mt. 5:17-20.**
      - "Not one iota nor one tittle shall pass away from the Law . . ." The Lord here makes an impressively strong statement about the preservation through time of the precise form of the Sacred Text. Since our only access to the meaning is through the form, any alteration in the form will alter the meaning. One of the most effective ways of annulling a commandment is to corrupt the Text—something Satan understands quite well.
      - The scribes and Pharisees will not go to Heaven.
   e. Reconciliation—**Mt. 5:21-26.**

- To get angry without cause = injustice → God judges injustice.[1] "Numbskull!" = offense → court case. "You absolute idiot!" = an offense against God, denigrating His image[2] → could take you to Hell.
f. Adultery and divorce—**Mt. 5:27-32.**
    - "Fornication" and "adultery" cover distinct semantic areas—the 1st does not include the 2nd.
g. Do not swear—**Mt. 5:33-37.**
    - "Yes", yes, "No", no; whatever is more than these is <u>from the evil one</u>! Do we really believe this? If not, we had better go back to the drawing board.
h. Do not retaliate—**Mt. 5:38-42.**
i. Love your enemies—**Mt. 5:43-48.**
    - In verse 44 more than 99% of the Greek manuscripts have the more complete reading: "Love your enemies, bless those who curse you, do good to those who hate you and pray for those who spitefully use you and persecute you."

---

[1] Less than 2% of the Greek manuscripts, of inferior quality, omit "without cause" (as in NIV, NASB, LB, TEV, etc.). NIV, NASB and LB favor us with a footnote informing us that "some manuscripts" add 'without cause'—by "some" they mean 98% of them!! More serious, the shorter text has the effect of forbidding anger, which would contradict other Scriptures (Ephesians 4:26, Psalm 4:4) and the Lord's own example (Mark 3:5).

[2] **However**, note that the Lord is talking about saying this to a <u>brother</u>. He Himself applied this term to the scribes and Pharisees in chapter 23. Verses 22-24 deal with how we treat 'brothers'. Consider James 4:11-12: "Brothers, do not speak evil of one another. Because the one speaking against a brother and judging his brother speaks against a law and judges a law. So if you judge a law you are not a law-doer but a judge. The Lawgiver and Judge is One, the One who is able to save and to destroy. So who are <u>you</u> (sg) to be judging someone who is different?" I was surprised to find the Greek ετερος here, which usually refers to a different kind. I personally don't enjoy dealing with 'brothers' who are too different; I would rather question whether they are really 'brothers' at all! But James tells me not to do that. Each person is different (background, experiences, personality, training) and we must recognize that God can and will deal differently with different people. He uses one 'law' with me, another 'law' with you, and so on. A law is a set of rules or demands, so when I judge a brother I am questioning the way ('law') that God is working on him. As He is both Lawgiver and Judge, I will have to answer to Him for how I judged my 'brothers'. (For 'different one' the eclectic text currently in vogue has 'neighbor', following some 12% of the Greek manuscripts [as in NIV, TEV, LB, NASB, etc.].)

- Verse 48—"perfect": the Father is the point of reference, we are to be like He is.[1] ["I am not able to sin" VS "I am able not to sin."]
j. Religious ostentation—**Mt. 6:1-8.**
k. A model prayer, and fasting—**Mt. 6:9-18.**
  - In verse 13 the eclectic text omits: "because <u>yours</u> is the kingdom and the power and the glory forever. Amen"—following 1% of the Greek manuscripts, of inferior quality.
l. Treasure, eye and owner—**Mt. 6:19-24.**
  - Of course we have two eyes, but the Text has "eye" in the singular. I take it that the reference is to the way we interpret what we see (which is our real 'eye')—two people, one pure and one vile, observing the same scene will give very different interpretations to it.[2]
m. Do not be anxious—**Mt. 6:25-34.**
  - "Seek first the kingdom <u>of God</u>"—as in 99% of the Greek manuscripts.
n. Do not judge unjustly—**Mt. 7:1-5.**[3]
o. Pearls aren't for pigs—**Mt. 7:6**[4]

---

[1] A standard is a standard; it is not invalidated just because we may feel that it is unattainable. Comparing this passage with texts like Deuteronomy 7:10, "He repays those who hate Him to their face", and Psalm 5:5-6, "You hate all workers of iniquity", I take it that we must distinguish between personal enemies (those who oppose us for personal reasons) and enemies of God and His truth. To be like the Father we also must hate workers of iniquity (because of the consequences to others).

[2] Evil" here has the idea of malignant—aggressively evil. Someone with a malignant mind will give an evil interpretation to <u>everything</u> he sees, and in consequence his being will be filled with unrelenting darkness. Compare Titus 1:15.

[3] Can you have a 'plank' in your eye without knowing it? (The tiniest bit of grit is an unbearable irritant.) When a person does not want to admit or correct his own failures, it is standard defensive procedure to call attention to the failures of others.

[4] This verse may be a chiasmus, ab,ba. But just who are 'the dogs' and 'the pigs'? A pig will sniff the pearl and perhaps think it a stone—it not being edible the pig will ignore it and it will get trampled into the mud. So a 'pig' is someone who is incapable of recognizing or appreciating the 'pearl'—the reaction will be one of total indifference. So don't waste your time. In contrast a 'dog' reacts in an aggressively hostile manner against what is 'holy'. So a 'dog' is presumably someone who is committed to evil and will therefore attack what is holy. In general our media today are controlled by 'dogs'. So don't innocently offer what is holy to a 'dog'—you'll get chewed up! Anyone who has sold out to Satan will almost certainly have a resident demon, and we have the authority to bind such.

p. Ask and do—**Mt. 7:7-12.**
q. The two ways—**Mt. 7:13-14.**
- "Narrow is the gate . . . that leads to life, and there are few who find it."
r. Good and bad trees—**Mt. 7:15-23.**
- It is "he who **does** the will of my Father" who "shall enter the kingdom of heaven."[1]
s. The two foundations—**Mt. 7:24-27.**[2]
8. The people's reaction—**Mt. 7:28-29.**

E. **The hinge: proof, evaluation, rejection, blasphemy, denunciation**.
1. The leper, "as a proof"[3]—**Mt. 8:1-4; Mk. 1:40-45; Lk. 5:12-15 (16).**
- Jesus accepted the worship; an angel will not.
2. A centurion's servant—**Mt. 8:5-13.**
- Although very similar to the account in Luke 7:1-10, close attention to the contexts and details indicates that they are distinct.
3. Peter's mother-in-law, again—**Mt. 8:14-15.**
- It has often been assumed that Matthew's account here is parallel to those in Mark 1:29-31 and Luke 4:38-39, but close attention to the contexts has convinced me that Matthew's account took place some time after that in Mark and Luke. In that event, Jesus healed the woman twice, which means that just

---

[1] The Lord uses 'rotten' and 'evil' (or 'malignant') because He is really talking about people, not trees. The Lord is very clear about the eternal destiny of people who don't produce good fruit. Remember Ephesians 2:8-10—we are not saved by good works, but we are indeed saved for good works; if we don't produce, we aren't saved.

About verse 22, Evidently they did indeed cast out demons and perform mighty works—so if it wasn't by God's power, by whose power was it? Could it be that Satan works with those who think they are serving the Lord but are really 'lawless', to confirm them in their error? When we don't do things God's way we are being 'lawless'.

[2] Here again, we have to do the words. Note that both houses had to face the same circumstances, but the verbs are different. Everyone faces adversity in this life—your foundation determines the outcome. Why do the adverse circumstances 'attack' one house, but only 'beat on' the other? The verb 'attack' implies an intelligence ordering the circumstances.

[3] As a proof about what? This would be the first time in the life of the priest that anyone had done this, because lepers didn't get better. Who but the Messiah could heal leprosy? That they got the point is indicated by the examining council that is described in Luke 5:17.

because God heals you one time, it does not mean
that you will never get sick again.

4. Many others healed—**Mt. 8:16-17.**
5. The paralytic (the <u>evaluation</u>)—**Mt. 9:2-8; Mk. 2:1-12; Lk. 5:17-26.**
   - The 'proof' produced the desired effect.
   - The paralytic didn't ask for forgiveness, he wanted healing—to forgive his sins was a tactical choice.
   - Matthew, a Jew writing to Jews, organizes the subject matter thematically, not sticking to a chronological sequence. Mark, a Jew, but writing to the Roman world, always follows the chronological sequence. Luke, a Greek (apparently) writing for Greeks, also follows the chronological sequence, with a few exceptions. Those three have a lot of material in common but not always in the same order. John appears to have written in order to complement the others, furnishing new material; he also follows the chronological order.
6. Matthew called, makes banquet—**Mt. 9:9-13; Mk. 2:13-17; Lk. 5:27-32.**
7. Fasting, "cloth, wineskins"—**Lk. 5:33-39.**
8. Jesus returns to Jerusalem—(<u>the 2nd Passover</u>) **Jn. 5:1.**
   28AD
9. A paralytic of Bethesda—**Jn. 5:2-15.**
   - Fully 99% of the Greek manuscripts read the familiar 'Bethesda', and this name is attested by the 1st century Copper Scroll from Qumran. The so-called 'critical text' (UBS and N-A) serves up the pitiful 'Bethzatha', following just five Greek manuscripts (as in TEV, RSV, Jer., etc.). The UBS editors have introduced an historical error into their text on the flimsiest of evidence, even going against their favorites, P^{75} and B.
   - About 0.8% of the Greek manuscripts, of objectively inferior quality, omit the last clause of verse 3 and all of verse 4 (as in NIV, NASB, LB, [TEV], etc.). But obviously all those people wouldn't stay there (in discomfort) day in and day out, year in and year out, if nothing was happening. Obviously people got healed (from serious diseases), and verse 7 makes clear that it had to do with the stirring of the water—

so why didn't those manuscripts omit verse 7 as well?[1]

10. Jesus and the Jews—**Jn. 5:16-47.**
    a. The Jews want to kill Jesus—**Jn. 5:16-18.**
    b. Jesus affirms that He is equal with God—**Jn. 5:19-23.**
    c. It is the Son who will judge—**Jn. 5:24-30.**
    d. Four witnesses to Jesus—**Jn. 5:31-40.**
    e. The Jews are accused by Moses—**Jn. 5:41-47.**
       • Jesus places Moses' writings on a level with His own word.
11. Jesus is Lord of the Sabbath—**Mt. 12:1-8; Mk. 2:23-28; Lk. 6:1-5.**
12. Jesus heals on the Sabbath—**Mt. 12:9-13; Mk. 3:1-5; Lk. 6:6-10.**
13. P and H plot to kill (the <u>rejection</u>) —**Mt. 12:14; Mk. 3:6; Lk. 6:11.**
14. Jesus heals by the sea—**Mt. 12:15-21; Mk. 3:7-12.**
15. He chooses the twelve—M**k. 3:13-19; Lk. 6:12-16.**
    • He would entrust the future of the Church to them.
16. The sermon on the plain (not the mount)—**Lk. 6:17-49.**
    • "Came down" here VS "went up" in Mt. 5:1.
    a. Preamble—**Lk. 6:17-19.**
    b. Blessing and woe—**Lk. 6:20-26.**
    c. Love your enemy—**Lk. 6:27-36.**
    d. Don't judge unjustly—**Lk. 6:37-45.**
    e. The two foundations—**Lk. 6:46-49.**
17. A centurion's slave—L**k. 7:1-10.**
18. The son of a widow—**Lk. 7:11-17.**
19. Jesus eulogizes John Baptist—**Mt. 11:2-19; Lk. 7:18-35.**
    • At the end of Mt. 11:19, instead of "her children", just 0.5% of the Greek manuscripts, of inferior quality (objectively so), have "her works" (as in NIV, NASB, LB, TEV, etc.).

---

[1] The UBS editions do us a considerable disservice by following a very small minority of manuscripts and making the angel "of the Lord". Since angels can be good or fallen, it seems most likely to me that the angel involved was fallen. A capricious, occasional healing condemned all those people to added suffering (being at the pool instead of the comfort of home), including the frustration and despair of those who never made it (like the man Jesus healed). A sadistic procedure is just like Satan.

- In Mt. 11:14 the correct rendering is "who is to come".

20. He denounces three cities—**Mt. 11:20-24.**
    - In verses 23-24 Jesus illustrates Mt. 10:14-15—He gives the example.
21. Personal discipleship—**Mt. 11:25-30.**
22. Simon, the Pharisee—**Lk. 7:36-50.**
23. In a house (perhaps His own)—**Mk. 3:20-21.**
24. A demoniac cured, Pharisees <u>blaspheme</u>—**Mt. 12:22-32;**[1] **Mk. 3:22-30.**
25. Jesus <u>denounces</u> the Pharisees—**Mt. 12:33-42.**
26. "Seven others worse"—**Mt. 12:43-45.**

F. **Jesus takes the offensive.**
   - This could be a transitional phase; He uses parables but still tells the disciples to preach the Kingdom as being near.
1. New relationships—**Mt. 12:46-50; Mk. 3:31-35; Lk. 8:19-21.**
2. The parables—**Mt. 13:1-2; Mk. 4:1-2,33-34; Lk. 8:4.**
   - Mt. "On the same day"—Matthew and Mark presumably have the correct order VS Luke.
   a. The sower—**Mt. 13:3-9; Mk. 4:3-9; Lk. 8:5-8.**
   b. Why parables?—**Mt. 13:10-7,34-5; Mk. 4:10-12; Lk. 8:9-10.**
      - So that the people would <u>not</u> understand; Jesus changes direction in His ministry.
      - Items b. and c. presumably come after h. in actual chronological sequence.
   c. "The sower" explained—**Mt. 13:18-23; Mk. 4:13-20; Lk. 8:11-15.**
   d. Wheat and tares—**Mt. 13:24-30,36-43.**
      - "The reapers are the angels" (see 13:49-50).
   e. The lampstand—**Mk. 4;21-25; Lk. 8:16-18.**
   f. Growth and harvest—**Mk. 4:26-29.**
   g. A grain of mustard seed—**Mt. 13:31-32; Mk. 4:30-32.**

---

[1] Although the material in Luke 11:14-32 is very similar to that given in Matthew 12:22-45, it is not identical, and to place it here would be a rather large dislocation. Whereas items 24-26 here happened in Galilee, the events in Luke 11 happened in Judea, about 1.5 years later. It is natural that such a serious subject would be treated in both places, and in a similar sequence.

h. Leaven—**Mt. 13:33.**
i. Further parables—**Mt. 13:44-52.**
   - These 4 parables appear to have been given on another occasion.
3. The scribe—**Mt. 8:18-22.**
   - Although this is similar to Lk. 9:57-62, I believe they were distinct occasions.
4. The tempest—**Mt. 8:23-27; Mk. 4:35-41; Lk. 8:22-25.**
5. The "legion"— **Mt. 8:28-9:1; Mk. 5:1-21; Lk. 8:26-40.**
6. Fasting, "cloth, wineskins"—M**t. 9:14-17; Mk. 2:18-22.**
   - Although <u>very</u> similar to Lk. 5:33-39 [E.7], Matthew's grammar seems to require that verse 18 follow right after verse 17 here. Mark could go in E.7 with Luke, but since the wording in Luke is a bit different and Mark is closer to Matthew, I am placing Mark here. So this becomes the only episode that Mark puts out of sequence (if it doesn't go in E.7), but this is understandable in that the two episodes are virtually identical. Jesus must have used the illustrations of "cloth" and "wineskins" many times.)
7. A hemorrhage and a dead girl—**Mt. 9:18-26; Mk. 5:22-43; Lk. 8:41-56.**
8. Two blind men—**Mt. 9:27-31.**
9. A demoniac healed—**Mt. 9:32-34.**
10. A visit to Natsareth—**Mt. 13:53-58; Mk. 6:1-6**[a]**.**
11. A tour of Galilee—**Mt. 9:35-38; Mk. 6:6**[b]**; Lk. 8:1-3(?).**
12. The Twelve sent out—**Mt. 10:1-5**[a]**; Mk. 6:7,12-13; Lk. 9:1-2,6.**
    a. Commissioned—**Mt. 10:5**[b]**-15; Mk. 6:8-11; Lk. 9:3-5.**
       - In Mt. 10:8 some 94% of the Greek manuscripts do <u>not</u> have "raise the dead".
    b. Prophetic orientation—**Mt. 10:16-42.**
       - Mt. 10:16-42 appears to be medium to long range prophecy.
13. The tour continues—**Mt. 11:1.**
14. Herod and John's death—**Mt. 14:1-12; Mk. 6:14-29; Lk. 9:7-9.**
15. The Twelve return—**Mk. 6:30-31; Lk. 9:10.**

16. Bread for 5.000 men—**Mt. 14:13-21; Mk. 6:32-44; Lk. 9:11-17; Jn. 6:1-14.**
    - This happened near Tiberius—Jn. 6:23.[1]
17. Jesus retires to pray—**Mt. 14:22-23; Mk. 6:45-47; Jn. 6:15.**
    - The disciples embark and go in the direction of Capernaum (Jn. 6:17), but passing by they land at Bethsaida (Mk. 6:45).
18. Jesus walks on water—**Mt. 14:24-33; Mk. 6:47-52; Jn. 6:16-21.**
19. In Genesaret—**Mt. 14:34-36; Mk. 6:53-56.**
    - They cross back over, from Bethsaida to Genesaret—Mk. 6:53 (6:45).
20. Discourse in Capernaum (see verse 59)—**Jn. 6:22-71.**
    a. The people look for Jesus—**Jn. 6:22-25.**
    b. The Bread of Life—**Jn. 6:26-35.**
       - The Bread of Life that came down from Heaven and gives eternal life.
    c. The will of the Father—**Jn. 6:36-51.**
       - In verse 47 about 0.5% of the Greek manuscripts, of objectively inferior quality, omit "into me" (as in NIV, NASB, TEV, etc.). But the object of one's belief is of the essence; it is impossible to live without believing in something, so everyone believes. The reading of the so-called 'critical text' opens the door to universalism—the more so since the Lord is making a formal statement about how to be saved.
    d. Eat flesh, drink blood—**Jn. 6:52-59.**
    e. "You have the words of eternal life"—**Jn. 6:60-71.**
       - Jesus "sifts" His disciples—many turn back.
21. (A secret trip to Jerusalem; the <u>third Passover</u>)—(Deut. 16:16); **(Jn. 6:4, 7:1).**   **29AD**
    - See Mk. 7:1—Pharisees and scribes from Jerusalem.
22. He answers the scribes and Pharisees—**Mt. 15:1-9; Mk. 7:1-13.**
23. That which contaminates—**Mt. 15:10-20; Mk. 7:14-23.**
24. A Canaanite woman—**Mt. 15:21-28; Mk. 7:24-30.**

---

[1] The four accounts surrounding the feeding of the 5000 offer some seeming discrepancies. For my solution, please see "Bethsaida or Tiberius?" in Appendix A of my book, *The Identity of the New Testament Text IV*.

25. In Decapolis—**Mt. 15:29-31; Mk. 7:31-37.**
    - Mark selects one of many cases—in this one, Jesus both touched and spit!
    - Jesus gave him the language as well, if he was born deaf.
26. Bread for 4,000 men—**Mt. 15:32-39; Mk. 8:1-10.**
    - In Mt. 15:39 perhaps 0.5% of the Greek manuscripts, of objectively inferior quality, have "Magadan" instead of "Magdala". The parallel passage in Mk. 8:10 says, "the region of Dalmanutha"—I suppose that Magdala was a town within that region.
27. The "sign of Jonah"—**Mt. 16:1-4; Mk. 8:11-13.**
    - Pharisees and Sadducees were theological/political enemies, but they gang up against Jesus. He calls them 'malignant'—they are aggressively evil.
28. Pharisee 'leaven'—**Mt. 16:5-12; Mk. 8:14-21.**
29. In Bethsaida—**Mk. 8:22-26.**
    - See Mt. 11:21-22; Jesus had already cursed Bethsaida—He went outside the town to heal, and forbid witness in the town. Perhaps 0.5% of the Greek manuscripts, of objectively inferior quality, omit "nor tell anyone in the town".
    - Jesus did a partial cure on purpose.

G. **Jesus ministers on the basis of His impending death** (now openly declared).
   1. Peter's confession—**Mt. 16:13-23; Mk. 8:27-33; Lk. 9:18-22.**
      - Jesus <u>forbids</u> His disciples to say that He is the Christ!—**Mt. 16:20 (Mk. 8:30, Lk. 9:21).**
   2. The price of discipleship—**Mt. 16:24-27; Mk. 8:34-38; Lk. 9:23-26.**
      - Jesus 'tells it like it is'; He is hard on the disciples (1 Cor. 3:11-15).
      - How much does it cost **not** to be a disciple of Christ?
   3. The transfiguration—**Mt. 16:28-17:13; . 9:1-13; Lk. 9:27-36.**
      - The disciples sleep while Jesus prays; they spent the night on the mount (Lk. 9:37).
   4. A demonized boy—**Mt. 17:14-21; Mk. 9:14-29; Lk. 9:37-43**[a].

- "Faithless and perverse generation!" "If you had faith like a mustard seed *has*."
- In Mk. 9:29 just four manuscripts of inferior quality, against 1700, omit "and fasting". Perhaps 0.5% of the manuscripts omit Mt. 17:21.

5. Jesus predicts His death, again—**Mt. 17:22-23; Mk. 9:30-32; Lk. 9:43ᵇ-45.**
   - Lk. and Mk./Mt. may record separate occasions.

6. Money from a fish—**Mt. 17:24-27.**
   - Presumably someone had lost the coin in the sea. The coin, a στατηρ, was the exact amount to pay for two people.

7. Faith and humility—**Mt. 18:1-5; Mk. 9:33-37; Lk. 9:46-48.**

8. If not against us, on our side—M**k. 9:38-41; Lk. 9:49-50.**

9. Offenses bring woe— **Mt. 18:6-9; Mk. 9:42-50.**
   - Some 96% of the Greek manuscripts have verses 44 e 46 (Mk. 9) without question.

10. More about offenses—**Mt. 18:10-20.**

11. Forgive seventy times seven—**Mt. 18:21-35.**

12. His brothers don't believe—**Jn. 7:2-9.**
    - In verse 8 perhaps 3% of the Greek manuscripts, of inferior quality, omit "yet" (as in NASB, TEV, RSV, etc.). The reading of the so-called 'critical' text has the effect of ascribing a falsehood to Jesus, since He did in fact go to the feast (and doubtless knew what He was going to do). Among the 97% are P⁶⁶,⁷⁵ and B—since the UBS editors usually attach the highest value to P⁷⁵ and B, isn't it strange that they reject them in this case?

13. Jesus leaves Galilee—**Mt. 19:1; Mk. 10:1; Jn. 7:10.**
    - Mt. and Mk. pass over the events recorded in Lk. 9:51-16:17 and Jn. 7:11-10:39.

14. He is rejected in Samaria—**Lk. 9:51-56.**

15. What it takes to be a "disciple"—**Lk. 9:57-62.**
    - "No one, having put his hand to the plow and looking back, is fit for the kingdom of God." Although this is similar to Mt. 8:18-22, they appear to be distinct occasions.

16. The feast of Tabernacles—**Jn. 7:11-43.**   **29AD**
    a. Jesus teaches in the temple—**Jn. 7:14-36**.

- Compare verse 17 with Heb. 11:6; "rivers of living water".
    1) Moses against the Jews—**Jn. 7:19-24.**
    2) Public opinion is divided—**Jn. 7:25-36.**
  b. The last day of the feast—**Jn. 7:37-43.**
17. An attempted arrest—**Jn. 7:44-53.**
18. A dirty plot—**Jn. 8:1-11.**
    - Some 85% of the Greek manuscripts have verses 7:53-8:11 without question; the turn of phrase in verse 12 requires their presence; they clearly form part of the original text (it is virtually impossible, statistically, that such an "intrusion" should come to dominate 85% of the transmission).
19. "The Light of the world"—**Jn. 8:12-59.**
    , a. "You will die in your sins"—**Jn. 8:21-29.**
    b. "The Truth will set you free"—**Jn. 8:30-38.**
    c. "You are of your father, the devil"—**Jn. 8:39-51.**
    d. "Before Abraham existed, I AM"—**Jn. 8:52-59.**
20. Blind from birth—**Jn. 9:1-41.**
    a. "Who sinned?"—**Jn. 9:2-5.**
    b. The blind man is cured—**Jn. 9:6-12.**
    c. The Pharisees research—**Jn. 9:13-17.**
    d. Evasive parents—**Jn. 9:18-23.**
    e. Ex-blind man instructs Pharisees—**Jn. 9:24-34.**
    f. Jesus affirms His divinity—**Jn. 9:35-41.**
21. "The good shepherd"—**Jn. 10:1-21.**
    - "I am the door"; "I am the good shepherd"; "No one takes my life from me, I lay it down of myself."
22. The seventy sent out—**Lk. 10:1-16.**
    - Evidently there was an interval between items 22 and 23, but it is difficult to know if any other items should be placed here. The items that follow that only Luke records are not chronologically dependent, so the exact order is not of the essence.
    - "Whoever rejects you, rejects me."
23. The seventy return—**Lk. 10:17-24.**
    - "I saw Satan fall like lightning from heaven." "I **give** you the authority . . ." (as in 97.5% of the Greek manuscripts)—shall we believe Him?
24. The good Samaritan—**Lk. 10:25-37.**
25. Martha and Mary—**Lk. 10:38-42.**
26. A model prayer—**Lk. 11:1-4.**
    - The situation here is different from Mt. 6:9-15.

- Most modern versions, following a mere 1% of the Greek manuscripts, of objectively inferior quality, seriously truncate this prayer by omitting: "Our . . . who is in the heavens . . . . Your will must be done on earth as it is in heaven . . . . but deliver us from the evil one." Some versions, like NIV and NASB, have a footnote saying that "some manuscripts" add this material. How can any honest person use 'some' to refer to 99% (1,600 X 16)? 'The evil one' refers to Satan.

27. The persistent friend—**Lk. 11:5-13.**
28. A demoniac cured, Pharisees blaspheme—**Lk. 11:14-23.**
    - Although the material in Luke 11:14-32 is very similar to that in Matthew 12:22-45, it is not identical, and to place this material there would be too much of a dislocation. I take it that the items E.24-26 happened in Galilee, while the items here (G.28-30) happened in Judea, about a year and a half later. It is to be expected that such an important subject would be taken up more than once—the folks in Judea needed to hear it too.
29. "Seven others worse"—**Lk. 11:24-28.**
30. Jesus denounces the Pharisees—**Lk. 11:29-36.**
31. In a Pharisee's house—**Lk. 11:37-54.**
    - Jesus curses the Pharisees and doctors of the Law = He severed diplomatic relations.
32. Leaven of the Pharisees—**Lk. 12:1-3.**
33. Don't fear people—**Lk. 12:4-12.**
34. Warning against materialism—**Lk. 12:13-21.**
    - He who lays up treasure for himself and is not rich toward God is a "Fool!"
35. The Kingdom mentality—**Lk. 12:22-34.**
    - "Where your treasure is, there your heart will be also."
36. The accounting—**Lk. 12:35-48.**
    - He who knew the Master's will and didn't do it will be beaten with many stripes.
37. Christ divides—**Lk. 12:49-59.**
38. The fig tree—**Lk. 13:1-9.**
    - "Three years"; perhaps Jesus was the vineyard keeper and Israel the vine.
39. A "daughter of Abraham"—**Lk. 13:10-17.**
40. Parables of the Kingdom—**Lk. 13:18-21.**

41. "The narrow gate"—**Lk. 13:22-30.**
- "Strive to enter", "many will not be able"—this word would appear to have been addressed to those who were born within the community of the Faith (whether Israel or the Church).

42. Herod is a "fox"—**Lk. 13:31-33.**

43. The feast of dedication (Monday, Dec. 17, 29)—**Jn. 10:22-23.**
    a. "If you are the Christ, tell us plainly"—**Jn. 10:24-30.**
       - "I and My Father are one."
    b. "We stone you for blasphemy"—**Jn. 10:31-39.**
       - "The Scripture cannot be broken."

44. Jesus laments over Jerusalem—**Lk. 13:34-35.**
- It appears that Jesus left Jerusalem (and the temple) at this point, to return only with the 'triumphal entry', when the prophecy in verse 35 was literally fulfilled. The next item (45) probably happened outside the city, and from there Jesus went to Perea.

45. In a Pharisee's house.—**Lk. 14:1-24**
    a. A man is cured—**Lk. 14:1-6.**
       - Instead of 'son', some 26% of the Greek manuscripts have 'donkey' (as in TR, AV, NKJV). The 74% includes the best line of transmission, which I follow.
    b. "Whoever exalts himself will be humbled"—**Lk. 14:7-11.**
    c. "The great supper"—**Lk. 14:12 -24.**

H. **Jesus ministers (mainly) in Perea.**
   1. Jesus retires to Perea—**(Mt. 19:1); (Mk. 10:1); Jn. 10:40-42.**
   2. Jesus defines "disciple"—**Lk. 14:25-35.**
   - Jesus demands total commitment, the first place without competition—it is a calculated decision.
   3. Response to criticism from Pharisees—**Lk. 15:1-2**
      a. "The lost sheep"—**Lk. 15:3 -7.**
         - One lost VS 99 not lost. It is similar to Mt. 18:12-13, but is different.
      b. "The lost coin"—**Lk. 15:8-10.**
         - "Joy in the presence of the angels"—it must be God Himself who is rejoicing.

c. "The lost son"—**Lk. 15:11-32.**
- There was sincere repentance. Here we can see the Father's heart.
4. "The stupid steward"—**Lk. 16:1-13.**
- Verse 9 is probably sarcasm.
5. Greedy Pharisees—**Lk. 16:14-17.**
- Verse 17 is the key here.
6. Jesus on divorce—**Mt. 19:2-12; Mk. 10:2-12; Lk. 16:18.**
- The Lord Jesus is clear: the Creator's idea is one man and one woman—"the two [not three, four, five, etc.] shall become one flesh".
7. A rich man and Lazarus (another)—**Lk. 16:19-31.**
- I doubt that this is a parable, but one should perhaps not be dogmatic.
- See Mt. 12:40 and Eph. 4:9—Hades is in the center of the earth = hot.
8. Offense and pardon—**Lk. 17:1-4.**
9. "Increase our faith"—**Lk. 17:5-6.**
10. "We are unprofitable servants"—**Lk. 17:7-10.**
11. Ten lepers healed—**Lk. 17:11-19.**

- Perea followed the Jordan river, paralleling a part of Judea, all of Samaria, and a small part of Galilee—in verse 11 it seems that He crossed the river, then went along between Galilee and Samaria.

12. The Day of the Son of the Man—**Lk. 17:20-37.**

- Perhaps 20% of the Greek manuscripts have verse 36: "Two men will be in the field: the one will be taken and the other left"; it appears in the Latin and Syriac traditions, as well as the Lectionaries.[1]
- Jesus declares the historicity of Noah and Lot.

13. "The persistent widow"—**Lk. 18:1-8.**
- "When the Son of man comes, will He really find <u>the</u> faith on the earth?"
14. A Pharisee and a publican—**Lk. 18:9-14.**

- "Everyone who exalts himself will be humbled."

---

[1] I would say that this paragraph deals with the Rapture. In that event, Jesus is addressing those who are left behind, but who had expected to go. I believe that immediately after the Rapture the forces of evil will be unleashed to take complete control. Anyone who is going to refuse the 'mark' had better head for the hills.

15. He blesses children—**Mt. 19:13-15; Mk. 10:13-16; Lk. 18:15-17.**
    - Receive like a little child *receives*.
16. Lazarus (of Bethany) dies—**Jn. 11:1-16.**
    - "This sickness . . . is for the glory of God".
    - In verses 11 and 14 Jesus makes clear that Lazarus had died before He left Perea. Someone in a hurry could cover the distance in one day, but Jesus took several. So I take it that items 17 – 24 took place on the way to Bethany.
17. A rich young ruler—**Mt. 19:16-26; Mk. 10:17-27; Lk. 18:18-27.**
    - Jesus is not denying that He is good. He is challenging the man's opinion about Himself. The man was not recognizing Jesus to be God—if he had, Jesus would not have objected. Perhaps 1% of the Greek manuscripts, of objectively inferior quality, omit "Good" before "teacher" in Mt. 19:16 and have Jesus saying, "Why do you ask me about what is good? There is One who is good" in verse 17 (as in NIV, NASB, LB, TEV, etc.). The minority reading makes Matthew contradict Mark 10:18 and Luke 18:9.
    - It is impossible to serve both God and Mammon.
18. Apostolic reward—**Mt. 19:27-30; Mk. 10:28-31; Lk. 18:28-30.**
19. Parable of the laborers—**Mt. 20:1-16.**
    - The urgency of the harvest is more important than our feelings.
20. Jesus predicts His death (3rd)—**Mt. 20:17-19; Mk. 10:32-34; Lk. 18:31-34.**
21. James' and John's request— **Mt. 20:20-28; Mk. 10:35-45.**
    - James, John and their mother were together; in fact, both of them died for the Gospel—James was the first and John the last, of the Apostles.
22. Bartimaeus—**Mt. 20:29-34; Mk. 10:46-52; Lk. 18:35-43.**

- There were two Jerichos, a short distance apart.[1]

23. Zaccheaus—**Lk. 19:1-10.**
   - "The Son of the Man has come to seek and to save that which was lost." "Whatever I have taken from anyone by false accusation, I restore fourfold"—see Exodus 22:1 and 4.)
   - From verse 5 it appears that Jesus lodged with Zacchaeus that night, and did the climb up to Jerusalem (well over 3,000 vertical feet) the next morning.

24. Parable of the despised king—**Lk. 19:11-27.**
   - It is similar to Mt. 25:14-30, but is different; it may have been spoken while with Zacchaeus.

25. Lazarus is resurrected—**Jn. 11:17-46.**
   - "I am the resurrection and the life"; "If you believe you will see the glory of God".

26. The reaction—**Jn. 11:47-53.**
   - "The Romans will come and take away our place"; Caiaphas prophesies.

27. Jesus retires to Ephraim—**Jn. 11:54**

28. The last Passover is near—**Jn. 11:55-57.**   **30AD**

I. **The last week.**
   1. Mary anoints His feet—**Jn. 12:1-11.**
      a. Saturday, Mar. 30, 30, in Lazarus' house. This can't be the same case registered in Mt. 26:6 and Mk. 14:3 because: the case in John happened on the eve of the triumphal entry (12:12) while the case in Matthew and Mark happened 2 or 3 days after that entry. Mary anointed His feet, in her own house; the other anointed His head, in Simon's house. Only Judas dared to criticize Mary, hostess, friend of Jesus; but the other was severely criticized by several [it was the 2nd time, after all].

   2. The 'triumphal' entry—**Mt. 21:1-11, Mk. 11:1-11, Lk. 19:28-40, Jn. 12:12-19.**
      - Sunday, Mar. 31, 30. Again Matthew records that there were really **two** animals involved [the mother

---

[1] For a more complete discussion of seeming discrepancies in the several accounts, please see "Entering or leaving Jericho?" in Appendix A of my book, *The Identity of the New Testament Text IV.*

was taken along for moral support] but Jesus rode only the colt.[1]

3. He curses the fig tree—**Mt. 21:18-19, Mk. 11:12-14.**

    • Monday, Apr. 01, 30. A fig tree that keeps its leaves may also have some dried fruit—dried figs are edible.

4. Jesus laments Jerusalem (2nd)—**Lk. 19:41-44.**
    • "You did not know the time of your visitation."

5. He purifies the temple (2nd)—**Mt. 21:12-17, Mk. 11:15-19, Lk. 19:45-46.**

6. Certain Greeks seek Jesus—**Jn. 12:20-26.**
    • "If anyone serves Me, him My Father will honor."

7. "Father, glorify Your name"—**Jn. 12:27-36.**
    • "Now the ruler of this world will be cast out [deposed]."

8. His daily routine—**Lk. 19:47-48 (21:37-38).**
    • Lk. 21:37-38 is an historical aside, after the fact.

9. Send a mount into the sea—**Mt. 21:20-22, Mk. 11:20-26.**

    • Tuesday, Apr. 02, 30; it seems that this day included items 9 to 24—a 'full' day. Believe, and receive.

    • Perhaps 4% of the Greek manuscripts omit verse 26 entire, to be followed by NIV, NASB, LB, [TEV], etc. The last three words of verses 25 and 26 are identical (in the Greek Text), giving rise to a common transcriptional error—after writing the first, the copyist's eye returns to the second and he continues, having omitted what was in between. Verse 26 reinforces and emphasizes the need for forgiveness—the reference is to things done against us personally.

10. "The baptism of John"—**Mt. 21:23-27, Mk. 11:27-33, Lk. 20:1-8.**

11. Two sons—**Mt. 21:28-32.**

12. Perverse vinedressers—**Mt. 21:33-46, Mk. 12:1-12, Lk. 20:9-19.**
    • The priests and Pharisees understood that items 11 and 12 were against them.

13. Correct wedding attire—**Mt. 22:1-14.**

---

[1] For a more complete discussion of seeming discrepancies in the several accounts, please see "How many animals?" in Appendix A of my book, *The Identity of the New Testament Text IV.*

- [Participate in the wedding feast of the Lamb only if you are wearing the Groom's righteousness.]
14. Tribute to Caesar?—**Mt. 22:15-22, Mk. 12:13-17, Lk. 20:20-26.**
    - The Herodians, Sadducees and Pharisees all try to trip Jesus up.
15. The Sadducees' question—**Mt. 22:23-33, Mk. 12:18-27, Lk. 20:27-40.**
    - "You are mistaken, not knowing the Scriptures nor the power of God."
16. The greatest commandment—**Mt. 22:34-40, Mk. 12:28-34.**
17. David calls Messiah "Lord"—**Mt. 22:41-46, Mk. 12:35-37, Lk. 20:41-44.**
    - "David himself said by the Holy Spirit"—Jesus affirms the inspiration of Psalm 110, and David's authorship.
    - Defeated, the Pharisees, etc., desist from challenging Jesus.
18. "Beware of the scribes"—**Mk. 12:38-40, Lk. 20:45-47.**
19. The widow's mites—**Mk. 12:41-44, Lk. 21:1-4.**
20. "Woes" for Pharisees—**Mt. 23:1-36.**
    - They are already condemned, but are making it worse. Perhaps 2% of the Greek manuscripts, of inferior quality, omit verse 13 ["widows' houses"] (as in NIV, [NASB], LB, [TEV], etc.). A very small minority, perhaps another 1%, reverse the order of verses 13 and 14 (as in KJV and NKJV).
    - "Serpents, brood of vipers! How can you escape the condemnation of hell?"—Jesus breaks with the Pharisees, etc.
21. He laments Jerusalem (3rd)—**Mt. 23:37-39.**
    - It appears that He never returned to the temple—He declared judgment, "Your house is left to you desolate."
22. The temple will be destroyed—**Mt. 24:1-2, Mk. 13:1-2, Lk. 21:5-6.**
    - This was literally fulfilled in 70 AD.
23. The Olivet discourse—"the end time".
    - Jesus answers the two questions: "When will these things be?" and "What will be the sign of Your com-

ing, and of the end of the age?" The answer to the first question is in Lk. 21:20-24.

a. Preamble—**Mt. 24:3-14, Mk. 13:3-13, Lk. 21:7-19.**
- "Then the end will come"—the question is, which "end": of the world, the millennium, the great tribulation or this Church age?

b. Destruction of Jerusalem—**Lk. 21:20-24.**
- I take it that Jerusalem stopped being "trampled by Gentiles" in 1967.

c. Abomination of desolation—**Mt. 24:15-20, Mk. 13:14-18.**
- See Daniel <u>12:11</u>, 9:27 (11:31).

d. The Great Tribulation—**Mt. 24:21-28, Mk. 13:19-23, Lk. 21:25-26.**
- There has been a great deal of tribulation in this poor world, and continues to be, but the "great tribulation, such as has not been since the beginning of the world until this time, no, nor ever will be", is still coming. The words "saint" and "elect" include the saved of all periods of human history, not just the members of the bride of Christ.

e. Christ's return to earth—**Mt. 24:29-31, Mk. 13:24-27, Lk. 21:27-28.**
- I take it that this event is different and distinct from the rapture of the Church.

f. "The fig tree"—**Mt. 24:32-35, Mk. 13:28-31, Lk. 21:29-33.**
- "Heaven and earth will pass away, but My words will by no means pass away."
- "This generation" could refer to the Israelite race, but it seems to me more probable that it refers to the persons alive on the planet in 1967.

g. <u>Watch!</u>—**Mt. 24:36-44, Mk. 13:32-37, Lk. 21:34-36.**
- It seems to me that these passages require that the rapture of the Church take place before the "abomination of desolation", because from then on the days are literally counted, precisely 1,290 days until Christ's return to earth—so then, there will be no surprise; anyone can know the exact day, counting from the moment that the Anti-

christ takes his seat in the "Holy of Holies". For there to be a <u>surprise</u> factor the rapture must occur before that event, or immediately after—from God's point of view it could be a single package.[1]

- In Lk. 21:36 instead of 'counted worthy', less than 2% of the Greek manuscripts, of objectively inferior quality, have 'be able' (as in NIV, NASB, LB, TEV, etc.). If 'to escape all these things' refers to the Rapture, then only those who are 'counted worthy' will go up. Escape from the events of the Great Tribulation requires a pre-wrath rapture. This verse may suggest a partial rapture—if to be "counted worthy" one must watch and pray, what happens if you don't?

h. The accounting—**Mt. 24:45-51.**
- **Attention**: verse 51 appears to be talking about perdition, really.

i. "The ten virgins"—**Mt. 25:1-13.**
- "Then" = a temporal adverb; it seems to be referring to the time of the rapture. Note that all ten were "virgins", and all had some "oil".

j. "The talents"—**Mt. 25:14-30.**
- Attention again: verse 30 appears to be talking about perdition, really.

k. Sheep and goats—**Mt. 25:31-46.**
- It appears that this text describes the judgment of nations and people at the beginning of the Messianic (Millennial) Kingdom.

24. "After two days is the Passover"—**Mt. 26:1-2.**
- I take it that our Lord's statement here settles the question of the exact day of the crucifixion. It was late Tuesday afternoon, probably about 6:00 p.m.— adding two days takes us to 6:00 p.m. on <u>Thursday</u>, but the proceedings in the upper room began after 6:00 p.m. on that Thursday, which to the Jews was already Friday. Therefore Jesus died on a Friday [not Thursday]. Our Lord's own statements have given rise to some confusion: referring to the time period between His death and resurrection He said—"on the

---

[1] For a more complete discussion, please see "Before or after?" in Appendix A of my book, *The Identity of the New Testament Text IV*.

third day", "after three days" and "three days and three nights". So some have argued that Jesus died on a Thursday, or even a Wednesday. Well, Wednesday won't work because that would make 3 days and 4 nights; but Thursday gives 3 nights and 2 full days, plus a part of a third day; while Friday gives 2 nights and 1 full day, plus a part of a second day. We take it that "3 days and 3 nights" was an idiomatic expression that could refer to three 24 hour days represented by some part of each, but in sequence—in this case: Friday, Saturday and Sunday. See also Lk. 23:54-24:1—Jesus was buried on Friday afternoon, then the women rested during the Sabbath (just one day); then they got up early on the first day of the week.

25. The Sanhedrin conspires—**Mt. 26:3-5, Mk. 14:1-2, Lk. 22:1-2.**
   - Probably Wednesday, Apr. 03, 30; the confrontation the day before impels them to radical action.

26. Someone anoints His head—**Mt. 26:6-13, Mk. 14:3-9.**
   - In Simon's house; see item I.1

27. Judas is contracted— **Mt. 26:14-16, Mk. 14:10-11, Lk. 22:3-6 (Jn. 13:2).**
   - "Then Satan entered Judas."

28. The disbelief of the Jews—**Jn. 12:37-43.**
   - "They loved the praise of men more than the praise of God."
   - In verse 41 John affirms that Isaiah saw Jehovah the Son (Isaiah 6:1).

29. The last word—**Jn. 12:44-50.**
   - Perhaps Thursday, Apr. 04, 30. "He who sees Me, sees Him who sent Me; he who hears Me, hears the Father; he who believes into Me, believes into the Father."

J. **The last night.**
   1. Upper room prepared—**Mt. 26:17-19, Mk. 14:12-16, Lk. 22:7-13.**
      - The proceedings began on Thursday and ended on Friday [Roman time]—by Jewish time it was already Friday from 6:00 p.m. on.
   2. In the upper room—**(Jn. 13:1).**

a. They arrive—**Mt. 26:20, Mk. 14:17, Lk. 22:14.**
b. "I have desired to eat this Passover"—**Lk. 22:15-18.**
   - The "cup" here was not part of "the Lord's supper", it happened before.
c. Traitor identified (1st time)—**Mt. 26:21-25, Mk. 14:18-21, Lk. 22:21-23.**
d. Who is the greatest?—**Lk. 22:24-30.**
   - "You are those who have continued with Me in My trials." "You will sit on thrones judging the twelve tribes of Israel."
e. Foot washing—**Jn. 13:2-20.**
   - In verse 2 less than 0.5% of the Greek manuscripts, of objectively inferior quality, read 'during' supper (as in NIV, NASB, LB, TEV, etc.), rather than 'after', which confuses the account. There was an ordinary meal, and then the Passover ritual itself. The meal was basically over, but they couldn't proceed with the ritual because they were ceremonially unclean—their feet hadn't been washed (they were dirty from the dust of the road). There was water, a basin and a towel, but no slave or servant to do the work. Since the disciples had been arguing over who would be the greatest, none of them wanted to take the servant's place—so the Lord Jesus Himself gave the example. "I have given you an example, that you should do as I have done to you."
f. Traitor identified (2nd time)—**Jn. 13:21-30.**
   - With rare exceptions, John records material that the others don't mention; further, the details here are quite different from the first time, see 2.c.
g. The new commandment—**Jn. 13:31-35.**
   - "Love one another, as I have loved you."
h. Jesus warns Peter (1st time)—**Jn. 13:36-38.**
   - It is hard to know how to intersperse the information given by John with that of the others in an exact chronological order.
i. The Lord's Supper—**Mt. 26:26-29, Mk. 14:22-25, Lk. 22:19-20**, (1 Cor. 11:23-26).
   - In Mt. 26:28 and Mk. 14:24 perhaps 1% of the Greek manuscripts, of objectively inferior quality,

omit 'new' (as in NIV, NASB, LB, TEV, etc.). The original reading, as also in Luke 22:20 and 1 Corinthians 11:25, is <u>new</u> covenant.

- In 1 Cor. 11:23 Paul affirms that he received the details directly from the Lord; in verse 24, 98% of the Greek manuscripts have "My body which is <u>broken</u> for you".

j. The Father's house—**Jn. 14:1-4.**
- "You believe into the Father, and you believe into Me."

k. Thomas' question: "How can we know the way?"—**Jn. 14:5-7.**
- "I am the way, the truth, and the life."

l. Philip's request: "Lord, show us the Father"—**Jn. 14:8-14.**
- "He who has seen Me, has seen the Father."
- "He who <u>believes</u> into Me, the works that I do he <u>will</u> do also; he will do even greater than these, because I go to My Father."

m. The Spirit of Truth—**Jn. 14:15-21.**

n. Thaddeus' question—**Jn. 14:22-26.**
- "The Holy Spirit will teach you all things."

o. "My peace I give you"—**Jn. 14:27-31.**
- "The ruler of this world is coming, and he has <u>nothing</u> in Me."
- In verse 31, "Arise, let us go from here", does not mean that they left immediately; 18:1 makes clear that chapters 15 to 17 also took place in the upper room.

p. The true vine—**Jn. 15:1-8.**
- "He who abides in Me, and I in him, bears much fruit; for without Me you can do nothing."

q. Friends, not slaves—**Jn. 15:9-17.**
- "All things that I heard from My Father I have made known to you."

r. "The world hates you"— **Jn. 15:18-16:4.**

s. Jesus warns Peter (2nd time)—**Lk.22:31-34.**
- The details here are quite different from those in **Jn. 13:36-38.**

t. Buy a sword—**Lk. 22:35-38.**
- Jesus applies Isaiah 53 to Himself.
- In certain circumstances a weapon inspires respect.

u. The work of the Spirit—**Jn. 16:5-15.**
   v. "A little . . . a little"—**Jn. 16:16-22.**
   w. Ask the Father—**Jn. 16:23-28.**
   x. Be of good cheer!—**Jn. 16:29-33.**
   y. Jesus prays—**Jn. 17:1-26.**
      1) For Himself—**Jn. 17:1-5.**
      2) For His disciples—**Jn. 17:6-19.**
      3) For all believers—**Jn. 17:20-26.**
3. They go to the garden—**Mt. 26:30, Mk. 14:26, Lk. 22:39, Jn. 18:1.**
4. Jesus warns Peter (3rd time)—**Mt. 26:31-35.**
   • Since they are no longer in the upper room this warning must be different from those recorded by John and Luke.
5. Jesus warns Peter (4th time)—**Mk. 14:27-31.**
   • Although this warning happened immediately after the 3rd (Mt.), the introduction of a second cockcrow and the phrase, "more vehemently", makes clear that it is different.[1]
6. The agony in Gethsemane.
   a. Takes Peter, James, John—**Mt. 26:36-38, Mk. 14:32-34.**
   b. The first prayer—**Mt. 26:39-41, Mk. 14:35-38, Lk. 22:40-46.**
      • Jesus sweats blood—98.7% of the Greek manuscripts have verses 43-44 (Lk. 22) in their place.
   c. The second prayer—**Mt. 26:42-43, Mk. 14:39-40.**
   d. The third prayer—**Mt. 26:44-46, Mk. 14:41-42.**
7. The betrayal.
   a. The kiss—**Mt. 26:47-50, Mk. 14:43-45, Lk. 22:47-48, Jn. 18:2-3.**
   b. On their backs—**Jn. 18:4-9.**
   c. Peter's sword—**Mt. 26:51-54, Mk. 14:47, Lk. 22:49-51, Jn. 18:10-11.**
   d. The arrest—**Mt. 26:55-56, Mk.14:46,48-50, Lk. 22:52-53, Jn. 18:12.**
8. A naked youth—**Mk. 14:51-52.**
9. Jesus taken to Annas—**Jn. 18:13-14.**
10. Then taken to Caiaphas—**Mt. 26:57, Mk. 14:53, Lk. 22:54, (Jn. 18:24).**

---

[1] For a thorough discussion of the warnings and the denials, please see Appendix H of my book, *The Identity of the New Testament Text IV*.

11. Peter denies (1st--doorkeeper)—**Jn. 18:15-17.**
12. Peter with the servants—**Mt. 26:58, Mk. 14:54, Lk. 22:55, Jn. 18:18.**
13. Caiaphas interrogates Jesus—**Jn. 18:19-23.**
14. Peter denies (2nd--guards)—**Jn. 18:25.**
15. False witnesses—**Mt. 26:59-62, Mk. 14:55-60.**
16. The High priest cheats—**Mt. 26:63-68, Mk. 14:61-65.**
17. Peter denies (3rd--a maid)—**Mt. 26:69-70, Mk. 14:66-68^b, Lk. 22:56-57.**
18. Peter denies (4th--relative)—**Jn. 18:26-27.**
19. Rooster crows first time—**Mk. 14:68^c, Jn. 18:27.**
20. Peter denies (5th--same maid)—**Mk. 14:69-70.**
21. Peter denies (6th--a man)—**Lk. 22:58.**
22. Peter denies (7th--another maid)—**Mt. 26:71-72.**
23. Peter denies (8th--general)—**Mt. 26:73-74, Mk. 14:70-71, Lk. 22:59-60.**
24. Rooster crows 2nd time—**Mt. 26:74, Mk. 14:71, Lk. 22:60.**
25. Jesus stares at Peter—**Lk. 22:61.**
26. Peter weeps—**Mt. 26:75, Mk. 14:72, Lk. 22:62.**
27. Guards abuse Jesus—**Lk. 22:63-65.**
    - No one could go to bed (it was probably 3 or 4 a.m.); while they waited for the dawn the guards kept on mistreating Jesus.

K. **Crucifixion day.**   **(Friday, Apr. 05, 30)**
   1. Sanhedrin tries Jesus—**Mt. 27:1, Mk. 15:1, Lk. 22:66-71.**
      - They "led Him into their council"—this still took place in Caiaphas' house; see Jn. 18:28.
   2. Jesus is taken to Pilate—**Mt. 27:2, Mk. 15:1, Lk. 23:1, Jn. 18:28.**
   3. The 1st accusation—**Lk. 23:2, Jn. 18:29-32.**
   4. Pilate and Jesus (1st time)—**Mt. 27:11, Mk. 15:2, Lk. 23:3, Jn. 18:33-38.**
   5. The 2nd accusation—**Mt. 27:12-14, Mk. 15:3-5, Lk. 23:4-6.**
   6. Jesus is taken to Herod—**Lk. 23:7-12.**
   7. Barabbas or Christ—**Mt. 27:15-21, Mk. 15:6-11, Lk. 23:13-25, Jn. 18:39-40.**
   8. Pilate's wife—**Mt. 27:19.**
   9. "Crucify Him!"—**Mt. 27:22-23, Mk. 15:12-15.**

10. Soldiers mock Jesus—**Mt. 27:27-30, Mk. 15:16-19, Jn. 19:1-3, (Is. 50:6).**
11. "Behold the man!"—**Jn. 19:4-7.**
12. Pilate and Jesus (2nd time)—**Jn. 19:8-11.**
13. "You are not Caesar's friend"—**Jn. 19:12-15.**
14. Pilate washes his hands—**Mt. 27:24-26.**
15. The crucifixion of Jesus—**Mt. 27:31, Mk. 15:20, Jn. 19:16.**
    a. Simon the Cyrenian—**Mt. 27:32, Mk. 15:21, Lk. 23:26.**
    b. "Daughters of Jerusalem"—**Lk. 23:27-31.**
    c. Golgotha; Jesus crucified—**Mt. 27:33-36, Mk. 15:22-25, Lk. 23:33, Jn. 19:17-18.**
       • It appears that Jesus was placed on the cross first, then the other two.
    d. The Accusation—**Mt. 27:37, Mk. 15:26, Lk. 23:38, Jn. 19:19-22.**
       • The board must have been of fair size, because the full Accusation, in three languages, was: "This is Jesus the Natsorean, the king of the Jews." (Unless there were three boards.)
       • "What I have written, I have written!"—Pilate had made a declaration, and would not back down.
    e. Two malefactors—**Mt. 27:38, Mk. 15:27-28, (Lk. 23:32).**
    f. "Father, forgive"—**Lk. 23:34[a].**
       • Lamentably, the eclectic text, despising 99.2% of the Greek manuscripts and clear and strong attestation from the 2nd century, places this precious statement of the Lord Jesus within double brackets, thereby denying that it was written by Luke. Since Luke is the only one who records the statement, one cannot allege assimilation or harmonization in this case. The attitude of the editors is unwarranted and reprehensible.
    g. Soldiers divide clothes—**Mt. 27:35, Mk. 15:24, Lk. 23:34b, Jn. 19:23-24.**
       • Matthew calls David a "prophet"; Psalm 22:18 was literally fulfilled—since the tunic was without seam, they decided not to tear it up, preferring to cast lots.

h. Spectators blaspheme—**Mt. 27:39-44, Mk. 15:29-32, Lk. 23:35-37.**
i. "Behold your mother"—**Jn. 19:25-27.**
   - Joseph being dead, Jesus, the firstborn, passes the responsibility for His mother to John. Jesus was completely lucid and aware, in spite of the terrible suffering.
j. Penitent malefactor—**Lk. 23:39-43.**
   - In verse 42, instead of "to Jesus, 'Please remember me, Lord'", perhaps 3% of the manuscripts have 'Jesus, remember me' (as in NIV, NASB, LB, TEV, etc.), which seriously weakens the man's statement.
   - In verse 43 "Paradise" presumably refers to that half of Hades reserved for the just, which in Lk. 16:22 Jesus Himself called "Abraham's bosom".
k. Dark from 12:00 to 3:00—**Mt. 27:45, Mk. 15:33, Lk. 23:44.**
l. "My God, My God!"—**Mt. 27:46-49, Mk. 15:34-36.**[1]
m. "I thirst"—**Jn. 19:28-29.**
n. Jesus dismisses His spirit—**Mt. 27:50, Mk. 15:37, Lk. 23:46, Jn. 19:30.**
   - "Father, into Your hands I commit My spirit"; "Τετελεσται"!!
   - See John 10:18,"No one takes it from Me, but I lay it down of Myself"—it wasn't the cross that killed Jesus.
o. The veil of the temple is ripped—**Mt. 27:51, Mk. 15:38, Lk. 23:45.**
   - In Lk. 23:45, despising more than 99% of the Greek manuscripts, the eclectic text says that the sun was eclipsed, which is an obvious stupidity.
p. Saints resurrect—**Mt. 27:52-53.**
   - The graves were opened at that point, but the saints only come out after Jesus resurrected.
q. Centurion testifies—**Mt. 27:54, Mk. 15:39, Lk. 23:47.**

---

[1] There is a seeming discrepancy between the two accounts; for my solution please see "Who said what?" in Appendix A of my book, *The Identity of the New Testament Text IV*.

- So what convinced the centurion? It was the shout immediately followed by death; a cross kills by asphyxiation.
r. The crowd laments—**Lk. 23:48.**
s. Women from Galilee—**Mt. 27:55-56, Mk. 15:40-41, Lk. 23:49.**
  - Perhaps we have here the secret of how the public ministry of Jesus was 'financed'.
t. "Not a bone broken"—**Jn. 19:31-37.**
  - The bones of the Passover lamb were not to be broken (Exodus 12:46), and 1 Cor. 5:7 declares Christ to be our Passover lamb.
  - John affirms that he **saw** blood and water coming from Jesus' side, which proves that Jesus really was dead; in order to see that detail John had to be quite close to the cross.
16. Jesus is buried—**Mt. 27:57-61, Mk. 15:42-47, Lk. 23:50-56, Jn. 19:38-42.**
17. The tomb is sealed—**Mt. 27:62-66.**
  - This happened the next day; probably item 18 as well.
18. The traitor's remorse—**Mt. 27:3-10**, (Acts 1:18-19).
  - Presumably he used a tree at the edge of a precipice, the rope (or branch) broke and he fell a sufficient distance so that his abdomen burst open—it was precisely that plot of ground that was bought with the money he returned.
  - Jeremiah?[1]
19. Women buy spices—**Mk. 16:1, (Lk. 23:56).**
  - Probably on Saturday, after 6:00 p.m., which by Jewish reckoning would no longer be the Sabbath. If Lk. 23:56 records a different action, it would be before 6:00 p.m. on Friday.

L. Resurrection Day.[2]   (Sunday, Apr. 07, 30)

---

[1] Matthew ascribes a prophecy to Jeremiah that doesn't seem to be there; for my solution please see "Jeremiah?" in Appendix A of my book, *The Identity of the New Testament Text IV*.

[2] For a more complete harmonization of the events recorded for this day, please see "Harmonizing the accounts of the Resurrection" in Appendix A of my book, *The Identity of the New Testament Text IV*.

1. (Jesus rises from the dead!!—the firstfruits.)
2. Women go to the tomb—**Mt. 28:1, Mk. 16:2-3, Lk. 24:1, Jn. 20:1.**
   - Bright and early Magdalene (Mt., Mk., Lk., Jn.), Mary (Mt., Mk., Lk.), Salome (Mk.), Joanna and others (Lk.) get together and head for the tomb.
3. An angel removes the stone—**Mt. 28:2-4.**
   - The angel removed the stone so the resurrection could be verified; Jesus was already on the outside. The angel neutralized the guards.
4. Women arrive at the spot—**Mk. 16:4, Lk. 24:2, Jn. 20:1.**
   - They see the stone to one side and the guards on the ground; the angel was no longer visible—it was still fairly dark.
5. Magdalene runs to Peter—**Jn. 20:2.**
   - If the angel had been visible, she would not have thought the body stolen; "we don't know" makes clear that she was with the others.
6. Women enter the tomb—**Mt. 28:5-7, Mk. 16:5-7, Lk. 24:3-8.**
   - They took their time—a cemetery, kind of dark, "dead" guards on the ground [impetuous Magdalene had left]. The first angel declares the resurrection, but since they doubt, a second angel also appears, with brightness.
7. Women take off running—**Mt. 28:8, Mk. 16:8.**
   - They said nothing to the guards, nor to anyone they met on the road, until they reached the disciples.
8. Guards take off—**Mt. 28:11-15.**
9. Peter and John come, see and go—**(Lk. 24:12), Jn. 20:3-10.**
   - They saw no one, neither guards nor women nor angels [invisible]; the linen cloths were lying there like they were still around a body, that is what John "saw and believed".
   - Lk. 24:12 is an historical aside, not in chronological order.
10. Then Magdalene arrives—**Jn. 20:11-13.**
    - She is still dominated by the idea that the body had been stolen.

11. Jesus appears to Magdalene (1<u>st</u>)—**Mk. 16:9, Jn. 20:14-17.**
12. Jesus appears to the women (2nd)—**Mt. 28:9-10.**
13. Women inform the eleven—**Lk. 24:9-11.**
14. Magdalene informs the eleven—**Mk. 16:10-11, Jn. 20:18.**
15. Saints appear in Jerusalem—**Mt. 27:53.**
    - It is hard to know the exact sequence of items 15,16 and 17.
16. Jesus appears to Peter (3rd or 4th)—**(Lk. 24:34) (1 Cor. 15:5).**
17. On the road to Emmaus (3rd or 4th)—**Mk. 16:12, Lk. 24:13-32.**
18. The two return to Jerusalem—**Mk. 16:13, Lk. 24:33-35.**
19. Jesus appears to the eleven (5th)—**Mk. 16:14-18, Lk. 24:36-49, Jn. 20:19-23.**
    - It seems that Mk. 16:15-18 forms part of this episode; but Lk. 24:44-49 may have been said on another occasion. Thus it appears that the "Great Commission" according to Mark and John were proffered on Resurrection Day.
20. Thomas arrives later—**Jn. 20:24-25.**

M. **Epilogue.**
1. Eight days later (Thomas present)—**Jn. 20:26-29.**
2. By the sea of Galilee—**Jn. 21:1-23.**
3. On a mount, in Galilee—**Mt. 28:16-20.**
    - It is hard to know the exact order of items 3, 4 and 5.
4. Jesus appears to over 500—(1 Cor. 15:6).
5. Jesus appears to James—(1 Cor. 15:7).
6. The ascension, from Mount Olivet—**Mk. 16:19, Lk. 24:50-51**, Acts 1:4-11.
7. Jesus sends the Holy Spirit—**(Jn. 16:7)** Acts 2:1-4.
8. The Lord works with the disciples—**Mk. 16:20.**
9. Jesus appears to Stephen—Acts 7:55-56.
10. Jesus comes back to earth to deal with Paul—(Acts 26:13-18, 1 Cor. 15:8).
11. Jesus appears to Ananias—Acts 9:10-11.
12. Appears to Paul several times—Acts 22:17-21, 23:11.
13. Appears to John on Patmos—Rev. 1:9-13, etc.
14. (Acts 1:3, 10:41 and 13:31 suggest other appearances.)

APPENDIX B
THE SOVREIGNTY OF GOD
COVERS EVERYTHING
(Ephesians 1:11, Isaiah 45:9b-10)

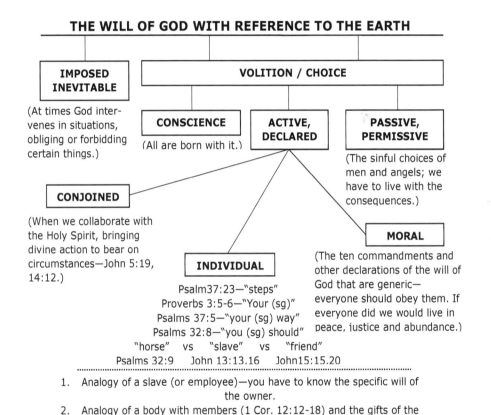

THE WILL OF GOD WITH REFERENCE TO THE EARTH

IMPOSED INEVITABLE

(At times God intervenes in situations, obliging or forbidding certain things.)

VOLITION / CHOICE

CONSCIENCE
(All are born with it.)

ACTIVE, DECLARED

PASSIVE, PERMISSIVE
(The sinful choices of men and angels; we have to live with the consequences.)

CONJOINED

(When we collaborate with the Holy Spirit, bringing divine action to bear on circumstances—John 5:19, 14:12.)

MORAL

INDIVIDUAL

Psalm37:23—"steps"
Proverbs 3:5-6—"Your (sg)"
Psalms 37:5—"your (sg) way"
Psalms 32:8—"you (sg) should"
"horse" vs "slave" vs "friend"
Psalms 32:9   John 13:13.16   John15:15.20

(The ten commandments and other declarations of the will of God that are generic—everyone should obey them. If everyone did we would live in peace, justice and abundance.)

1. Analogy of a slave (or employee)—you have to know the specific will of the owner.
2. Analogy of a body with members (1 Cor. 12:12-18) and the gifts of the Spirit (1 Cor. 12:7-11, 27-28)—the functions are specific and different.
3. Be guided by the Spirit (Rom. 8:14; Gal. 5:16,18,25; Eph. 5:18)

HOW TO DISCERN THE INDIVIDUAL WILL?
? (Cicumstances, counsel, Bible, common sense, what you want?) **?**
See Ps. 37:4 → Isa. 58:13-14; Jer. 17:5,9; Ps. 106:15.

1. The witness of the Holy Spirit in our spirit (Col. 3:13; Philip. 4:6-7; Isa. 26:3)
2. This is only for disciples/slaves—you cannot play games with God (James 1:2-8)
3. Oswald Chambers—"the checks of the Spirit"
4. Wait for God [when He puts you in the dark], do not devise your own 'light' (Is. 50:10-11).
5. Intimacy → sensitivity (Psalm 32:8)

APPENDIX C
REDEMPTIVE MINISTRY

The Purpose

1. A total commitment to the Lord Jesus Christ and His Kingdom;
2. An informed and sincere respect for the full authority of the Biblical Text;
3. A disposition to make visible use of the power of God (take John 14:12 seriously);
4. To impose the victory of Christ, undoing the works of Satan;
5. To make disciples and not just win souls.

How to Achieve it?

1. By doing evangelism that disciples;
2. Learn by doing;
3. By giving people space to grow and work;
4. Provide the necessary instruction;
5. Emphasize missions;
6. Encourage intercession (not least, for the country and the world);
7. Through the warmth of house groups and the enthusiasm of a joint weekly meeting.

Other books by the Author:

The Greek New Testament, According to Family 35 (second edition)
The only significant line of transmission, both ancient and independent, that has a demonstrable archetypal form in all 27 books; plus a totally new critical apparatus that gives a percentage of manuscript attestation to the variant readings, and that includes six competing published editions

The Sovereign Creator Has Spoken, Objective Authority for Living (second edition)
New Testament Translation with Commentary (over 4,000 footnotes)

The Identity of the New Testament Text, IV
The theoretical explanation for The Greek New Testament

A Framework for Discourse Analysis II

Coming soon:

God Has Preserved His Text! The Divine Preservation of the NT

Assorted Biblical Topics—Clarifications, Difficulties, 'Discrepancies', Poison

Internet sites with further works by the author:

www.walkinhicommandments.com
www.prunch.org

Made in the USA
Columbia, SC
02 November 2022

70332562R00226